DISCOVER WORDPERFECT SUITE 8

GENERAL SUITE

To:	Select:	Then:
Start an application	Start→Programs→Corel WordPerfect Suite 8	Select the application.
Save file	File→Save or click 🖫	Type name, select destination folder, and click Save.
Open file	File→Open or click 📂	Select folder and file and click Open.
Close file	File→Close or click ✕ for the document	Save any modified files, if necessary.
Print file	Choose File→Print	Select options and click Print.

WORDPERFECT

WordPerfect Toolbar

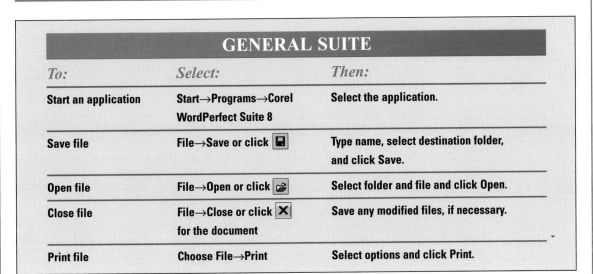

New Blank Document · Save · Cut · Paste · Redo · Draw Picture · Draw Object · Highlight · Bullets · Table · QuickCreate · Zoom · PerfectExpert

Open · Print · Copy · Undo · QuickFormat · Clipart · Text Box · Numbers · Columns · Spell Check · Change View

Text (Standard) Property Bar

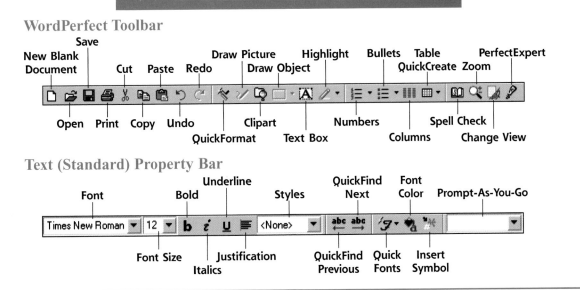

Font · Bold · Underline · Styles · QuickFind Next · Font Color · Prompt-As-You-Go

Times New Roman ▼ 12 ▼ b i U ≡ <None> ▼

Font Size · Italics · Justification · QuickFind Previous · Quick Fonts · Insert Symbol

PRESENTATIONS

Presentations Toolbar

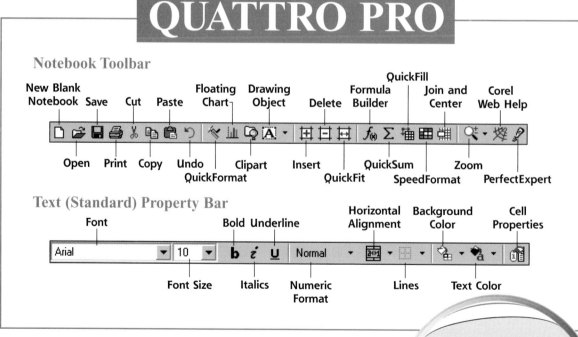

New Blank Show, Save, Cut, Paste, Redo, Play Show, Selection Tool, Chart, Bitmap, Closed Object Tools, Zoom, PerfectExpert

Open, Print, Copy, Undo, Slide Appearance, Clipart, Organizational Chart, Text Object Tools, Line Object Tools, Corel Web Help

Standard Property Bar

Master Gallery, Slide Transition, Speed, Display Sequence, QuickKeys, Custom Audiences, Show on the Go

Blinds | Original Slide Show

Select Layout, Direction, Sound, Speaker Notes, Skip, Play Slide Show, Internet Publisher

QUATTRO PRO

Notebook Toolbar

New Blank Notebook, Save, Cut, Paste, Floating Chart, Drawing Object, Delete, Formula Builder, QuickFill, Join and Center, Corel Web Help

Open, Print, Copy, Undo, QuickFormat, Clipart, Insert, QuickFit, QuickSum, QuickSum, SpeedFormat, Zoom, PerfectExpert

Text (Standard) Property Bar

Font, Bold, Underline, Horizontal Alignment, Background Color, Cell Properties

Arial | 10 | b | i | U | Normal

Font Size, Italics, Numeric Format, Lines, Text Color

DISCOVERY CENTRAL

DISCOVER
WORDPERFECT® SUITE 8

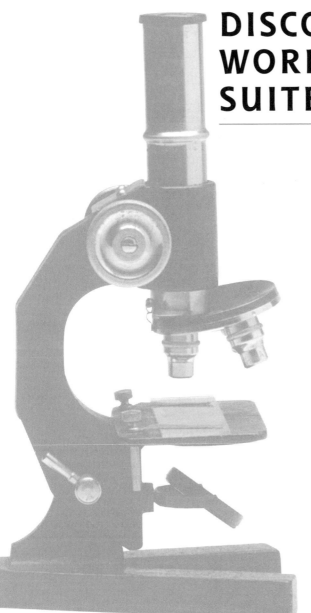

DISCOVER WORDPERFECT® SUITE 8

BY DENISE VEGA

IDG BOOKS WORLDWIDE, INC.

AN INTERNATIONAL
DATA GROUP COMPANY

FOSTER CITY, CA • CHICAGO, IL •
INDIANAPOLIS, IN • SOUTHLAKE, TX

Discover WordPerfect® Suite 8

Published by
IDG Books Worldwide, Inc.
An International Data Group Company
919 E. Hillsdale Blvd., Suite 400
Foster City, CA 94404

http://www.idgbooks.com (IDG Books World Wide Web site)

Library of Congress Catalog Card No.: 97-72190

ISBN: 0-7645-3086-0

Printed in the United States of America

10 9 8 7 6 5 4 3 2 1

1E/RY/QX/ZX/FC

Distributed in the United States by IDG Books Worldwide, Inc.

Distributed by Macmillan Canada for Canada; by Contemporanea de Ediciones for Venezuela; by Distribuidora Cuspide for Argentina; by CITEC for Brazil; by Ediciones ZETA S.C.R. Ltda. for Peru; by Editorial Limusa SA for Mexico; by Transworld Publishers Limited in the United Kingdom and Europe; by Academic Bookshop for Egypt; by Levant Distributors S.A.R.L. for Lebanon; by Al Jassim for Saudi Arabia; by Simron Pty. Ltd. for South Africa; by Pustak Mahal for India; by The Computer Bookshop for India; by Toppan Company Ltd. for Japan; by Addison Wesley Publishing Company for Korea; by Longman Singapore Publishers Ltd. for Singapore, Malaysia, Thailand, and Indonesia; by Unalis Corporation for Taiwan; by WS Computer Publishing Company, Inc. for the Philippines; by WoodsLane Pty. Ltd. for Australia; by WoodsLane Enterprises Ltd. for New Zealand. Authorized Sales Agent: Anthony Rudkin Associates for the Middle East and North Africa.

For general information on IDG Books Worldwide's books in the U.S., please call our Consumer Customer Service department at 800-762-2974. For reseller information, including discounts and premium sales, please call our Reseller Customer Service department at 800-434-3422.

For information on where to purchase IDG Books Worldwide's books outside the U.S., please contact our International Sales department at 415-655-3023 or fax 415-655-3299.

For information on foreign language translations, please contact our Foreign & Subsidiary Rights department at 415-655-3021 or fax 415-655-3281.

For sales inquiries and special prices for bulk quantities, please contact our Sales department at 415-655-3200 or write to the address above.

For information on using IDG Books Worldwide's books in the classroom or for ordering examination copies, please contact our Educational Sales department at 800-434-2086 or fax 817-251-8174.

For press review copies, author interviews, or other publicity information, please contact our Public Relations department at 415-655-3000 or fax 415-655-3299.

For authorization to photocopy items for corporate, personal, or educational use, please contact Copyright Clearance Center, 222 Rosewood Drive, Danvers, MA 01923, or fax 508-750-4470.

is a trademark under exclusive license to
IDG Books Worldwide, Inc., from
International Data Group, Inc.

ABOUT IDG BOOKS WORLDWIDE

Welcome to the world of IDG Books Worldwide.

IDG Books Worldwide, Inc., is a subsidiary of International Data Group, the world's largest publisher of computer-related information and the leading global provider of information services on information technology. IDG was founded more than 25 years ago and now employs more than 8,500 people worldwide. IDG publishes more than 275 computer publications in over 75 countries (see listing below). More than 60 million people read one or more IDG publications each month.

Launched in 1990, IDG Books Worldwide is today the #1 publisher of best-selling computer books in the United States. We are proud to have received eight awards from the Computer Press Association in recognition of editorial excellence and three from *Computer Currents'* First Annual Readers' Choice Awards. Our best-selling *...For Dummies*® series has more than 30 million copies in print with translations in 30 languages. IDG Books Worldwide, through a joint venture with IDG's Hi-Tech Beijing, became the first U.S. publisher to publish a computer book in the People's Republic of China. In record time, IDG Books Worldwide has become the first choice for millions of readers around the world who want to learn how to better manage their businesses.

Our mission is simple: Every one of our books is designed to bring extra value and skill-building instructions to the reader. Our books are written by experts who understand and care about our readers. The knowledge base of our editorial staff comes from years of experience in publishing, education, and journalism — experience we use to produce books for the '90s. In short, we care about books, so we attract the best people. We devote special attention to details such as audience, interior design, use of icons, and illustrations. And because we use an efficient process of authoring, editing, and desktop publishing our books electronically, we can spend more time ensuring superior content and spend less time on the technicalities of making books.

You can count on our commitment to deliver high-quality books at competitive prices on topics you want to read about. At IDG Books Worldwide, we continue in the IDG tradition of delivering quality for more than 25 years. You'll find no better book on a subject than one from IDG Books Worldwide.

John Kilcullen
CEO
IDG Books Worldwide, Inc.

Eighth Annual
Computer Press
Awards ≥1992

Ninth Annual
Computer Press
Awards ≥1993

Tenth Annual
Computer Press
Awards ≥1994

Eleventh Annual
Computer Press
Awards ≥1995

Welcome to the Discover Series

Do you want to discover the best and most efficient ways to use your computer and learn about technology? Books in the Discover series teach you the essentials of technology with a friendly, confident approach. You'll find a Discover book on almost any subject — from the Internet to intranets, from Web design and programming to the business programs that make your life easier.

We've provided valuable, real-world examples that help you relate to topics faster. Discover books begin by introducing you to the main features of programs, so you start by doing something *immediately*. The focus is to teach you how to perform tasks that are useful and meaningful in your day-to-day work. You might create a document or graphic, explore your computer, surf the Web, or write a program. Whatever the task, you learn the most commonly used features, and focus on the best tips and techniques for doing your work. You'll get results quickly, and discover the best ways to use software and technology in your everyday life.

You may find the following elements and features in this book:

Discovery Central: This tearout card is a handy quick reference to important tasks or ideas covered in the book.

Quick Tour: The Quick Tour gets you started working with the book right away.

Real-Life Vignettes: Throughout the book you'll see one-page scenarios illustrating a real-life application of a topic covered.

Goals: Each chapter opens with a list of goals you can achieve by reading the chapter.

Side Trips: These asides include additional information about alternative or advanced ways to approach the topic covered.

Bonuses: Timesaving tips and more advanced techniques are covered in each chapter.

Discovery Center: This guide illustrates key procedures covered throughout the book.

Visual Index: You'll find real-world documents in the Visual Index, with page numbers pointing you to where you should turn to achieve the effects shown.

Throughout the book, you'll also notice some special icons and formatting:

A Feature Focus icon highlights new features in the software's latest release, and points out significant differences between it and the previous version.

Web Paths refer you to Web sites that provide additional information about the topic.

Tips offer timesaving shortcuts, expert advice, quick techniques, or brief reminders.

The X-Ref icon refers you to other chapters or sections for more information.

Pull Quotes emphasize important ideas that are covered in the chapter.

Notes provide additional information or highlight special points of interest about a topic.

The Caution icon alerts you to potential problems you should watch out for.

The Discover series delivers interesting, insightful, and inspiring information about technology to help you learn faster and retain more. So the next time you want to find answers to your technology questions, reach for a Discover book. We hope the entertaining, easy-to-read style puts you at ease and makes learning fun.

Credits

ACQUISITIONS EDITOR
Ellen Camm

SENIOR DEVELOPMENT EDITOR
Susan Pines

ASSOCIATE DEVELOPMENT EDITOR
Kerrie Klein

TECHNICAL EDITOR
Dick Kahane

EDITORIAL ASSISTANT
Timothy J. Borek

PROJECT COORDINATOR
Katy German

GRAPHICS AND
PRODUCTION SPECIALISTS
Ritchie Durdin
Stephanie Hollier
Jude Levinson
Ed Penslien
Christopher Pimentel
Dina Quan

PROOFREADER
David Wise

INDEXER
Richard Evans

BOOK DESIGN
Seventeenth Street Studios
Phyllis Beaty
Kurt Krames

About the Author

Denise Vega received her Masters in Education from Harvard University, specializing in interactive technologies. She started out as a software trainer and works mainly as a freelance writer now, occasionally training select clients on computers and software. Among the books and manuals Vega has written or contributed to are *GroupWise Essentials*, *WordPerfect for Windows 7 Essentials* (levels I and II), *WordPerfect 101* and *WordPerfect 201 for the Law Office*, and *Discover Office 97*. Her computer-related articles have appeared in a number of publications, including *WordPerfect for Windows Magazine* and the *Corel WordPerfect Suite Expert* newsletters. She is also a regular contributing editor to *WordPerfect for the Law Office* magazine. Vega is a certified movie fanatic and enjoys camping, fishing, and other mountain activities. She lives with her husband and two children in Denver and is currently working on a children's novel.

TO MY HUSBAND, MATT, ALWAYS

FOREWORD

When I was 16, I cut the lawn of a college professor who lived in my neighborhood. I knew that it stretched the professor's budget to pay me a few dollars a week; he was supporting a growing family that would eventually include 12 children, and on a minimal stipend from the university. The only reason he hired me was because none of his children was old enough to run the lawnmower.

By 1989, Alan Ashton, the aforementioned college professor, was one of the wealthiest men in the United States, joint owner with one of his former graduate students of WordPerfect Corporation, makers of the industry-leading WordPerfect word-processing software. Depending on the numbers one chose to believe, WordPerfect held anywhere from 75 percent to 90 percent of the DOS word-processing market.

But the computer industry is nothing if not volatile. Unable to compete in the DOS applications market, Microsoft Corporation rewrote the rules, released Windows 3.0, and the world began to change. And WordPerfect stumbled, not realizing how pervasive Windows would become, betting that DOS would continue to reign strong, if not supreme.

Dr. Ashton was no marketing genius — all he wanted to do was make software and spread the wealth by providing jobs. But the new rules required marketing savvy, something WordPerfect didn't have much of, and soon WordPerfect was on the defensive. By the mid-'90s, WordPerfect had lost most of its ground. Hoping to save WordPerfect, Dr. Ashton and his partner sold the company to Novell, and for a while things looked brighter. Novell/WordPerfect released the first version of WordPerfect for Windows that could go head-to-head with Microsoft Word, and then released the PerfectOffice, the first software suite that could compete with Microsoft Office. Then Novell put the WordPerfect division up for sale. Whether they made much of an effort to market the software while they had it remains a bone of contention among observers.

It looked for a while that WordPerfect was doomed to become what one pundit had predicted as the new decade dawned, "the WordStar of the Nineties." Not a few observers opined that WordPerfect was as good as dead, requiring only a stake through the heart and burying at the crossroads, a service soon to be provided by the juggernaut of Mr. Gates and Company.

Corel Corporation picked up WordPerfect for a tiny fraction of what Novell paid for it, on the theory that giving Microsoft an effective monopoly in business applications was tantamount to accepting tyranny. Corel smoothed off a few rough edges, released WordPerfect 7 within a few months of acquiring the software...

And the product exploded. In the final four months of 1996, the Corel WordPerfect Suite took first place in retail suite sales, ending the popular perception that Microsoft business applications are runaway favorites.

No, it's not like "the old days" when WordPerfect 5.1 reigned virtually unchallenged and the question was always, "Is it compatible with WordPerfect?" But Corel has shown what most of us have felt all along — that when it comes to the business of buckling down and creating documents, and now integrating the capabilities of different software applications in a suite while giving the user maximum control over both the document and the software, nobody beats WordPerfect. Pardon me if my region of origin shows through in this example, but you can compare Microsoft Office to a racehorse — a fine animal, well bred, highly specialized, but that runs one kind of race, and if you want the race run, you'll do it his way or not at all. The WordPerfect Suite, by contrast, is the quarter horse — a strong, flexible worker that will do whatever you ask, a horse that keeps working long after the racehorse has collapsed from exhaustion, and most especially, a horse that will do it *your* way.

As the former caretaker of Alan Ashton's lawn, I'm glad to see the success of the "second coming" of his brainchild, WordPerfect, now with the added muscle of the rest of the suite. As you get into the intricacies of WordPerfect Suite 8, you'll see why it's been such a success in so short a time.

This book by Denise Vega is a great tool to get you started in your WordPerfect Suite 8 discovery. Have fun!

Terry Bruning
A veteran of WordPerfect Corporation and Novell, Inc., Terry Bruning is Editor-in-Chief of *WordPerfect for Windows Magazine,* published by IVY Communications of Orem, Utah.

PREFACE

'm glad there's someone besides myself who's interested in a little adventure. Yes, I said *adventure*. "What does a computer book have to do with adventure?" you ask. Quite a bit, actually. This book is about *discovery* — which is always an adventure — and in this particular case, about discovering the key features in Corel WordPerfect Suite 8 that will help you perform many of your daily tasks faster and more efficiently. And what's an adventure without a little fun, excitement, and danger? Throughout this book you'll play with cool features like pictures and colors (fun), work with Web pages and browse the Web (excitement), and explore some more advanced features (danger — okay, so maybe a better word is *challenge*, but *danger* is so much more thrilling, don't you think?).

Is This the Book for You?

f this is your first experience with the WordPerfect Suite, I wrote this book for you. Or, if you've had some experience with the suite but don't feel entirely comfortable with it, this book is for you, too. *Discover WordPerfect Suite 8* shows you the basics of each program included in what the media and others sometimes call the "standard suite" but what is called "Corel WordPerfect Suite 8" on the packaging. An occasional advanced feature is thrown in to keep you on your toes. My goal is to make sure you can quickly begin working, without bogging you down with a lot of technical terminology and features you may not need right away. I hope I've provided enough pointers to more advanced features so that you will explore them at your leisure.

What's in This Book?

've divided *Discover WordPerfect Suite 8* into five parts and divided each part into chapters to keep it organized. Here's how it goes:

Part One: Exploring the Suite

The first part covers an overview of the suite, describes how to access programs, and reviews features and elements that are common to all the applications.

Part Two: Creating Documents with WordPerfect

Part Two gets you started in the word processing application, creating documents ranging from letters to résumés to flyers.

Part Three: Creating Slide Shows with Presentations

Part Three is for those who need to create slide shows. You can also use Presentations to create drawings that you can use in other applications.

Part Four: Creating Notebooks with Quattro Pro

Part Four gets you into serious number crunching as you work with notebooks and worksheets in Quattro Pro.

Part Five: Using Internet and Customization Tools

Part Five takes you on a special journey where you learn how to browse the World Wide Web with Netscape Navigator, create Web pages with Internet Publisher, and customize the suite to suit the way you work.

Following Part Five, you'll find some extra goodies, including a troubleshooting appendix to help you solve common problems and two other appendixes that introduce you to extra features and shortcuts.

A Few Points to Note

Here are a few points to keep in mind as you read the book. *Online chapter on CorelCENTRAL and Netscape Communicator:* Your WordPerfect Suite 8 shipped with a voucher or coupon that allows you to obtain CorelCENTRAL and Netscape Communicator when they become available from Corel and Netscape. CorelCENTRAL is a personal information manager (PIM) that helps you maintain your schedule, keep track of your daily tasks, and track contacts, addresses, and much more. It works in concert with Netscape Communicator to help you control your information both on and off the Internet so that you can send and receive e-mail and access the Internet (and your company intranet, if it has one) without a lot of fuss. Note that Netscape Communicator will contain Netscape Navigator 4.0, the browser tool. In Chapter 16, I cover Netscape Navigator 3.0, it's predecessor, because the suite ships with this version.

In addition, these dual tools support workgroups, including group tasks and projects, group scheduling, and online conferencing and discussion — you can actually hold meetings right on your computer! If you use your voucher to obtain CorelCENTRAL and Netscape Communicator, visit `http://www.idgbooks.com` where we will have a chapter for you to download. Just search the site for *Discover WordPerfect Suite 8* and follow the bonus content link.

Button info: Throughout this book, I introduce new tools and buttons. When you use a button for the first time, you'll see its icon to the left of the step or text referencing it. After that, I'll refer to the button by its name in the step or text. I've included tables with descriptions for most of the buttons so you can always refer back to the tables.

The great mouse caper: Being left-handed, I'm sensitive to the needs of the ten percent of us who have the mouse on the other side of the keyboard and may switch the buttons to accommodate our fingers. To this end, I refer to the "right" mouse button as the secondary button throughout the book, and I'll write secondary-click instead of right-click. For you right-handers, this would be the right mouse button, and for us lefties who've swapped the buttons, it'll be the left mouse button. For trackballers, laptoppers, and miscellaneous others, apply this information to your own device.

Web addresses: Although the Web site addresses cited in this book were current at the time of publication, they — like so many things on the World Wide Web — are subject to change with little or no notice.

As the title of this book indicates, I hope to take you on a trip of discovery, where you learn to make the most of the WordPerfect Suite in your work and play.

Acknowledgments

All you have to do is take a look at the credits to know that no book is an island and that this was truly a collaborative effort. I owe a huge debt of thanks to the many people who came along on this adventure with me. First, a big thank you to Sue Pines, my development editor, and Kerrie Klein (who not only did a stellar development edit on several chapters in the book but doubled as copy editor extraordinaire). Their attention to detail, their encouragement, and their humor made the process a joy. And big kudos to Dick Kahane, the technical editor, who's eagle eye and thoughtful suggestions improved the book immensely.

I'd also like to thank Ellen Camm, my acquisitions editor, whose willingness to go the extra mile knew no bounds. Thanks, Ellen, for your enthusiasm and belief in the project — you made it all worthwhile. And thanks also to Andy Cummings, who took the hand off and headed down the field with hardly a pause. Thanks for your continued commitment.

Huge thanks and appreciation to Katy German and the production folks — Stephanie Hollier, Jude Levinson, Ed Penslien, Christopher Pimentel, and Dina Quan — who managed to make order out of chaos. The result is beautiful and I thank you.

Finally, I'd like to thank the folks at home because without them, I wouldn't have had the time or stamina to finish this book. Thanks to my immediate family (Matt, Zachary, and Jesse) and my extended family (Mom, Dad, Bill, Betty, John, Michelle, Wayne, Jordan, Baby Sam, Cheryl, James, and Rebecca). Once again you let me hole up for weeks on end, fingers to the keyboard, providing encouragement and support all the while. I love you.

CONTENTS AT A GLANCE

TABLE OF CONTENTS

PART FIVE—USING INTERNET AND CUSTOMIZATION TOOLS, 00

16 USING NETSCAPE NAVIGATOR, 315

QUICK TOUR

The WordPerfect Suite provides you with all the tools you need to work successfully in your home or office. To help get you off on the right foot, take a quick look at the main applications so they will be more familiar to you when you begin working with them.

Checking Out the Desktop Applications Director

If you performed a standard installation of WordPerfect Suite, the setup program placed the Desktop Application Director (DAD) on the Windows taskbar. DAD is a handy little tool that gives you quick-click access to all the applications. You learn more about DAD in Chapter 1, but take a quick peek at it here. Look at the bottom of the screen, on the right side of the Windows taskbar. You'll see DAD there (see Figure 1). You can access any of the applications by clicking its associated button on DAD.

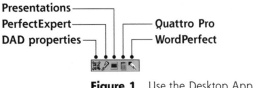

Presentations
PerfectExpert — Quattro Pro
DAD properties — WordPerfect

Figure 1 Use the Desktop Applications Director to access your applications.

 X-REF Get the full story on DAD in Chapter 1.

Starting and Exploring WordPerfect

You'll probably do more work in WordPerfect than any other application. It's the word-processing workhorse in the suite. Here you create letters, memos, resumes, flyers, and so on. Any document you can think of, you can create it in WordPerfect.

To take a peek at WordPerfect, follow these steps:

1. Click the WordPerfect 8 icon on DAD or click `Start` →
    `Corel WordPerfect Suite 8` → `Corel WordPerfect 8`. You'll see a blank
    document in WordPerfect (see Figure 2).

2. See that blinking vertical line? That's called the *insertion point* and tells
    you where text will appear if you start typing. Go ahead and type a few
    words. See how the insertion point moves along, leading the way?

3. Look at the top of the screen. You'll see the *title bar* which tells you the
    application you're working in and the name of the document if it has
    a name. If it doesn't, WordPerfect just numbers it. You'll also see the
    menu bar below the title bar. It has the words *File, Edit, View,* and other
    names. The menu bar contains all the features available to you. Below
    that is the WordPerfect 8 toolbar and the Standard property bar,
    providing the tools you need just a click away.

4. Choose `File` on the menu bar, and then choose `Exit`. This closes
    WordPerfect so you can continue your tour. Because you have text in the
    document, WordPerfect will ask you if you want to save the document
    before it closes up shop. Normally you would — and you'll learn about
    that in Chapter 2. However, because this is just practice, click No. You're
    back at the Windows desktop.

X-REF Get the full scoop on WordPerfect in Part Two.

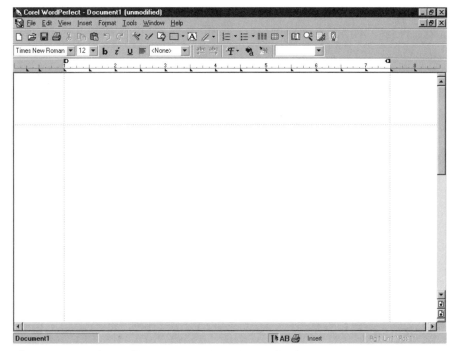

Figure 2 Create your literary masterpieces in WordPerfect.

Starting and Exploring Presentations

Presentations is normally considered a tool for those who put on big presentations for employees or others. However, you can use Presentations to create a slide show for personal use. Imagine the look on your friend's face if he or she receives an electronic greeting card in the form of your slide show. Or perhaps someone is celebrating a big anniversary — why not put a retrospective of their marriage (or other event) in a slide show as part of the entertainment at a party? You can use Presentations for business or pleasure, using its vast array of features to create just the right show for your intended audience.

To take a peek at Presentations, follow these steps:

1. Click the Presentations 8 icon on DAD or click **Start** →
   Corel WordPerfect Suite 8 → **Corel Presentations 8** . You'll see the New dialog
   box appear.

2. Choose the Work On tab, select Welcome! from the list, and click Open.
   Presentations opens the Welcome slide show that ships with the
   application, giving you a taste of a real slide show (see Figure 3). Notice
   that Presentations shares similar elements with WordPerfect — it also
   has a title bar, menu bar, toolbar, and property bar.

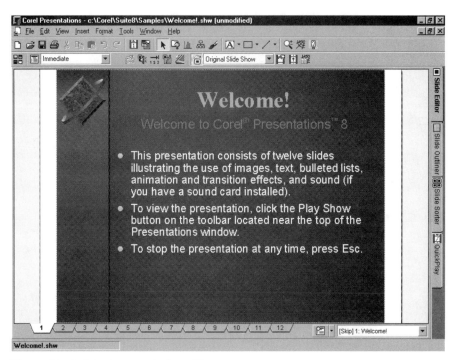

Figure 3 A slide show ready for editing.

3. Select the QuickPlay tab on the right side of the screen to see the show as it would appear during an actual presentation. If you see a message about DirectDraw, just click Continue. The slide show is set to play automatically .

4. To return to the Presentations window before completing the show or whrn the slide show is complete, press Esc.

5. Choose File on the menu bar and then choose Exit . Because you didn't make any changes to the Welcome slide show, you shouldn't see any messages about saving the show. If you do see a message, click No.

 Part Three clues you in on Presentations.

Starting and Exploring Quattro Pro

I f you have to deal with budgets at home or at the office, or need to keep track of sales for your business, Quattro Pro is the application to do it. This is your number-crunching buddy, with all the tools you need to enter and format data and calculate it automatically.

To take a peek at Quattro Pro, follow these steps:

1. Click the Quattro Pro 8 icon on DAD or click `Start` →
   `Corel WordPerfect Suite 8` → `Corel Quattro Pro 8`. Quattro Pro opens a new
   blank notebook. Notice how the elements are similar to those of the
   other applications in Figure 4.

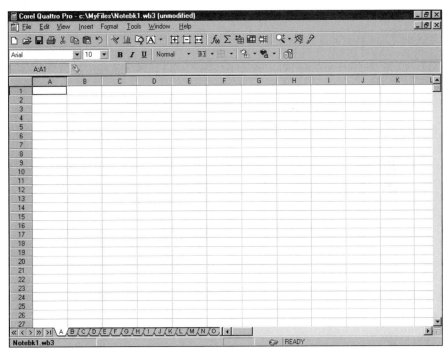

Figure 4 Use Quattro Pro to work wonders with your financial data.

2. Use the arrow keys to move from box to box. (These boxes are called *cells.*)

3. Type some text and press Enter. It aligns to the left. Type some numbers
   and press Enter. They align to the right. Quattro Pro recognizes the
   content and formats it accordingly.

4. Choose `File` on the menu bar and then choose `Exit`. Because you added
   a few things to the notebook, Quattro Pro will ask if you want to save it.
   Since this is just practice, click No.

X-REF Get the dirt on Quattro Pro in Part Four.

Now that you've successfully completed your whirlwind tour of the suite,
you're ready to begin your adventure in earnest. First, make sure you've packed
the necessary supplies — coffee cup (with an unlimited supply of steaming coffee
nearby), candy bars, and portable stereo. Got them? Good. Let's go!

EXPLORING THE SUITE

THIS PART CONTAINS THE FOLLOWING CHAPTERS

CHAPTER **1** CHECKING OUT THE SUITE

CHAPTER **2** WORKING WITH COMMON TOOLS

This part introduces the WordPerfect Suite, showing you how to start the applications and helping you understand their different elements. You also learn how to use elements that are common to the core applications, so that you can use these elements between programs.

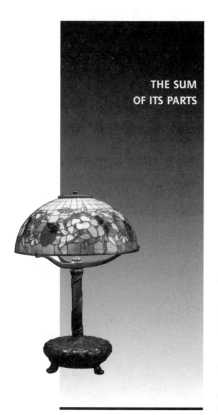

I f you're not too familiar with WordPerfect Suite, you're probably wondering what all the fuss is about. Isn't it just a group of programs? Sure, they come all bundled together and it's cheaper than all of the components separately, but beyond that, what?

Well, it's true that WordPerfect Suite is composed of several different programs, each of which is a tour de force in its own right. But the programs combine to form a whole that's much greater than the sum of the parts. For example, while some productivity suites are like a country jug band, you'll find that WordPerfect Suite is like the London Philharmonic. As you learned in grade school, it's great to be successful on your own, but it's equally important to work and play well with others. And when it comes to skills such as sharing and communicating, WordPerfect Suite scores an easy A.

One mark of a truly integrated suite is the ability of the components to speak each other's language. When you want to paste a spreadsheet table into a word processing document, what will happen? Before WordPerfect Suite, not much happened, and whatever it was probably looked scary. But the different teammates in WordPerfect Suite understand each other. When you paste a Quattro Pro table into a WordPerfect document, it's still the same table you expect it to be. The formulas work just like they used to, and you can still click a few buttons and have a professional-looking chart or graph. No surprises here.

And don't forget about the Net. Whether your interest is the Internet or a corporate intranet, this suite will help you take your ideas from your imagination to the world with Internet Publisher, a fully functional Web publishing program. What starts off as a WordPerfect document or a Presentations slide can be accessible to the world in minutes.

Throughout this book, you learn the best ways to harness the power of the WordPerfect Suite components, both as individual programs and as a team. You also meet people who have already made WordPerfect Suite a successful part of their business and private lives. Later on you meet Sara, who uses the suite as an integral part in relocating executives to the New York City area. Sara found that as much as the separate programs can do, together they can accomplish even more.

Then you meet Brian, a self-proclaimed pack rat who has harnessed the power of Quattro Pro to calculate his ever-growing net worth. What started as a hobby for him might one day be a lucrative source of income. You also take a look back at the WordPerfect that existed long before anyone heard of a software suite. Quite a bit has changed since then, but much is still the same — WordPerfect is still a state-of-the-art word processor that is as powerful as you need it to be.

By the end of the book, you'll understand what a discriminating brand WordPerfect is. Dozens of productivity applications exist, but only a handful have the WordPerfect name. It's time to find out why.

CHECKING OUT THE SUITE

The WordPerfect Suite is a collection of world-class, tightly integrated applications that can help you get your work done quickly and efficiently. Using these tools, you can create, publish, and distribute documents, presentations, and spreadsheets with minimal pain and a lot of gain. Because of the tight integration, it's easy to use information between applications (such as when you move or copy text). Additionally, you can *link* information so that it will update automatically in one application when changed in another.

Getting Familiar with the Suite

The WordPerfect Suite is like a party kit for a birthday bash. Inside the kit, you have just about everything you need to put on a good party. Plates, cups, and silverware are like the core applications in the suite — WordPerfect, Presentations, and Quattro Pro. The streamers, party hats, and other party favors are like the other fun, useful stuff that comes with the suite, such as Photo House, which you can check out in Appendix A.

WordPerfect is a word processing program for text-intensive documents; Presentations is a program to create slide show presentations; and Quattro Pro is a spreadsheet program for financial information. You'll also find an option called Corel New Project on the Corel WordPerfect Suite 8 menu. This option allows you to create specific document types — such as a budget, a book report, or a slide show that teaches a skill — using the PerfectExpert.

 For more on the PerfectExpert, see Chapter 2.

The WordPerfect Suite also ships with Netscape Navigator, one of the most popular Web browsers on the market. And if you decide you want to do more with the Web and with information management, consider upgrading to Netscape Communicator and CorelCENTRAL using the voucher provided in your suite package. CorelCENTRAL is your "information station," allowing you to maintain a calendar, schedule, and contact list in one place. You can then use this information in any Corel application. Netscape Communicator allows you to expand your Internet capabilities in concert with CorelCENTRAL. You can send and receive e-mail and perform workgroup tasks and conferencing. This last is like having an online meeting, where everyone can "listen" and provide input in real time.

 For more on using Netscape Navigator, refer to Chapter 16.

 If you decide to upgrade to Netscape Communicator and CorelCENTRAL, check out `http://www.idgbooks.com` **for a chapter written just for you. Perform a search for** *Discover WordPerfect Suite 8* **and click the bonus content link. Download the chapter to learn more about these applications.**

You'll find everything that comes with the WordPerfect Suite shown on the taskbar. Click Start and select Corel WordPerfect Suite 8. Figure 1-1 shows the menu selection for the WordPerfect Suite and the Desktop Applications Director (DAD).

Starting an Application

To start any core application, click Start→Corel WordPerfect 8 Suite from the Windows taskbar and then select the desired application. It will open on top of any other application currently running. You can also click the application button on the Desktop Applications Director. For more on these buttons, see "Using the Desktop Applications Director" later in this chapter.

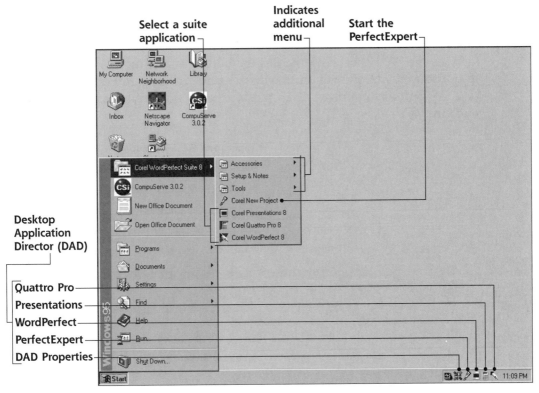

Figure 1-1 Corel WordPerfect Suite menus.

Understanding Common Window Elements

Each application shares a similar structure for accessing features and selecting options. When you start an application, you see several similar elements on the screen (see Figure 1-2), such as the title bar, menu bar, and toolbar. Table 1-1 provides a brief description of common elements. In addition to similar elements in the main window, you will encounter *dialog boxes* when you use menus and certain toolbar buttons. First you look at common window elements and then move into menus, toolbars, and dialog boxes.

Each application window actually contains two windows: the application window and the document window. The document window is your first point of contact with an application and provides many of the tools you need to get your work done. Think of it as a desktop where you write or draw (if you're the artistic type) and grab for a pen, eraser, file, or other tool.

By default, each application will maximize the document window so that it fills the screen. But if you look at the title bar and menu bar, you'll see that each has a Minimize, Restore, and Close button on the right side (an underscore, two boxes, and an *X* respectively). The buttons on the title bar control the application itself. This means, for example, that if you click the Close (*X*) button on the title bar, you are closing the entire application. If you click the Close (*X*) button on the menu bar, you are closing the current document; the application will remain open.

To see the difference, click the Restore button on the menu bar (two boxes). The document window will shrink in size and the Restore button becomes a Maximize button (one box). Click the Maximize button to increase the document window to full size.

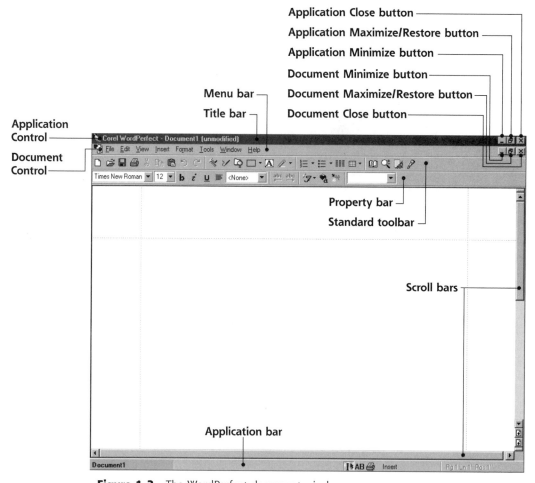

Figure 1-2 The WordPerfect document window.

TABLE 1-1 Common Window Elements

Element	Description
APPLICATION CONTROL	Displays the control menu for the application.

TABLE 1-1 Common Window Elements

Element	Description
DOCUMENT CONTROL	Displays the control menu for the document.
TITLE BAR	Indicates the application followed by a file indicator (for example, *Document 1*).
APPLICATION MINIMIZE BUTTON	Minimizes the application on the Windows taskbar.
APPLICATION MAXIMIZE BUTTON	Displays the application full screen.
DOCUMENT MINIMIZE BUTTON	Minimizes the document window within the application window.
DOCUMENT MAXIMIZE BUTTON	Displays the document window full within the application window.
APPLICATION CLOSE BUTTON	Closes the application.
DOCUMENT CLOSE BUTTON	Closes the document.
MENU BAR	Lists the available features for the application.
TOOLBAR	Contains buttons that allow one-click access to many of the features on the menu.
PROPERTY BAR	Contains additional buttons, usually related to formatting. Property bars are context-sensitive and change according to the task you are performing.
SCROLL BARS	Allow quick vertical and horizontal scrolling through a file. Click the arrow buttons or drag the scroll box along the bar to display other parts of the file.
APPLICATION BAR	Displays all open files and information about the active file.

USING MENUS AND TOOLBARS

You use menus to access a particular feature. To use a menu, simply click on the feature name (for example, File) and select one of the options from the menu that appears. To hide a menu without making a selection, click the feature name again.

To use a toolbar button, click the button for the feature you wish to use. If a button contains an arrow next to it, multiple options are available, and the icon you see on the button shows you the current option. If you click the button itself, you activate the option indicated on the button by the current icon. If you click the arrow on the button, you see a list of options. Figure 1-3 shows an example of the Numbering button. It contains an arrow indicating that if you click it, you will have selections from which to choose.

When you click a toolbar button, the action may occur immediately or the application will display a dialog box so you can make additional selections. You will learn more about toolbars when you explore each application in upcoming chapters.

To see a brief description of a button's function, point to the button. The description (called a *QuickTip*) pops up in a box attached to the pointer (refer again to Figure 1-3).

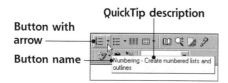

Figure 1-3 Display a QuickTip.

USING DIALOG BOXES

When you select a menu option or click a toolbar button, you will often see a dialog box, where you can make additional selections (see Figure 1-4). Table 1-2 describes the most common dialog box elements, many of which you can see in Figure 1-4.

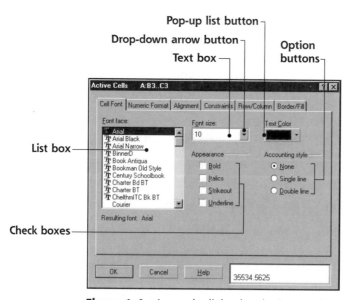

Figure 1-4 A sample dialog box in Quattro Pro.

TABLE 1-2 Dialog Box Elements

Element	What You Do with It
LIST BOX	Select an item from the list, using the vertical scroll bar to see additional items.
TEXT BOX	Type information directly into this box.
DROP-DOWN ARROW	Click to display additional options.
POP-UP LIST	Click and hold the button to display the list/palette and select an option.
OPTION BUTTON	You can select only one from the group.
CHECK BOX	You can select any or all in the group.

In some dialog boxes, you may also see other elements, such as *pop-down menus*, which allow you to select a menu item when you click an option button, and *spin arrows* or *counter buttons* that allow you to select an increment for a particular setting. Generally, these increments increase or decrease the current measurement by $1/10$.

Exiting an Application

When you finish with an application like WordPerfect or Quattro Pro, you exit it. You exit all programs the same way and can use any of the following methods:

* Choose File → Exit .
* Click the Close *(X)* button on the right side of the title bar.
* Click the application icon on the left side of the title bar (upper left corner of the screen) to display the control menu. Then choose Close.

If the application prompts you to save the file, choose Yes to save it or No to exit without saving.

Using the Desktop Applications Director

The *Desktop Applications Director*, or DAD, is where you go when you need something. If you're like me and often ran to Mom or Dad for extra cash, the keys to the car, or permission to jump in a lake, you'll agree this is aptly named. DAD is an inconspicuous toolbar that sits in the Task tray of the Windows taskbar (refer back to Figure 1-1). You can access your WordPerfect Suite programs quickly and easily using DAD.

Everything you need is a click away. The Desktop Applications Director contains buttons for the core applications, plus a few other fun treats. To start an application, just click its associated button.

Displaying and Hiding DAD

When you install the WordPerfect Suite using the standard installation option, Corel sets up to display DAD automatically when you start Windows. However, if you don't want to display DAD for a particular session, you can easily exit it.

To exit DAD, right-click DAD Properties (the four arrows) or any of the other WordPerfect Suite 8 application icons in the Windows taskbar's Task tray to display the QuickMenu. Then select Exit DAD. To display DAD again, choose Start→Corel WordPerfect Suite 8→Accessories→Corel Desktop Applications Director.

Customizing DAD

By default, Corel sets up DAD to display the core applications. You can easily add applications or remove others if you find you won't need them. For example, if you will often use the Address Book, you can add it to the taskbar.

To add an application to or remove one from DAD, follow these steps:

1. On the Windows desktop, click the DAD Properties button or secondary-click any button on DAD and choose Properties. You get the dialog box shown in Figure 1-5.

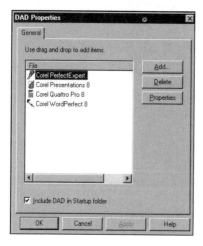

Figure 1-5 Change DAD settings in the DAD Properties dialog box.

2. On the General tab, click Add, locate and select the file you wish to add, and click Open. Repeat this step for all programs you wish to add. To remove a program, select it and click Delete.

3. Click OK to add or remove the program(s) on DAD.

FEATURE FOCUS You can also drag an item from your desktop to the File list in the DAD Properties dialog box to add it.

Exploring Corel Accessories, Setup & Notes, and Tools

As I mentioned previously, the WordPerfect Suite ships with a number of accessories and tools, contained under the Corel WordPerfect Suite 8 main menu on the Windows taskbar. Some are smaller applications (such as the Address Book), and others are useful references and tools. Following is a description of each accessory or tool. If you don't see one or more of those listed here on your Accessories menu, it may be that you didn't install it during Setup.

Accessories

To use an accessory, choose Start→Corel WordPerfect Suite 8→Accessories and select the desired accessory.

Corel Address Book works like an electronic Rolodex, maintaining a list of people and organizations for easy access. You can also use the information in the Address Book in documents. For more information, see "Working with the Address Book" later in this chapter.

Corel Desktop Applications Director is the friendly tool that you've already met. It provides quick access to all your WordPerfect Suite programs.

Setup & Notes

To access setup and additional information, choose Start→Corel WordPerfect Suite 8→Setup & Notes. Following is a brief description of each option.

Corel Approved Partners Help provides a worldwide list of the names, addresses, and telephone numbers of authorized trainers and training centers for WordPerfect products as well as *service bureaus*. A service bureau is a company that can take the slides in your Presentations file and convert it to overhead transparencies, slides, or photographs.

Corel Remove Program provides a quick way for you to remove all or part of the WordPerfect Suite from your computer.

Corel WordPerfect Suite 8 Setup allows you to add or remove suite applications or components. Make sure you have the Setup disk in your CD-ROM drive before selecting this option.

Distribute Envoy 7 Viewer guides you through the steps of creating an Envoy viewer to give to people that need to view Envoy documents but don't have Envoy on their systems.

Reference Center is your complete set of online manuals for each application that ships with WordPerfect Suite 8. Use this when online help isn't enough.

X-REF **For more information on the Reference Center, see Chapter 2.**

Release Notes provides a text file that you can view. It provides information that didn't make it into the Reference Center or online help.

Technical Support Help opens the Corel WordPerfect Technical Support help window, which explains how you can access assistance from a variety of sources.

Tools

To use a tool, choose Start→Corel WordPerfect Suite 8→Tools. Choose the following options.

Corel PerfectScript lets you record macros that automate the process of opening suite applications and performing specific tasks. The PerfectScript macro language is available in the core applications — WordPerfect, Presentations, and Quattro Pro.

X-REF **For more on recording and playing macros, see Chapter 8.**

Corel Settings Editor allows you to change settings in the Windows 95/NT Registry for installed Corel applications. Be careful! This is for advanced users who have a solid understanding of the Registry.

Data Modeling Desktop allows you to create Quattro Pro reports by dragging and dropping rows and columns from spreadsheets.

Database Desktop allows you to work with tables in databases such as Paradox.

Database Engine 4.0 helps you configure ODBC (Microsoft's Open Database Connectivity), which is a way for databases and other programs to share information. This is a feature for advanced users and programmers.

Envoy 7 Viewer provides the means for viewing electronic documents created in Envoy 7. This includes the Reference Center that ships with the WordPerfect Suite.

QuickFinder Manager 8 lets you create fast searches to speed up the task of locating files and folders. This is different from QuickFinder (available on DAD), which lets you search for specific folders and files in addition to working with fast searches (see next entry).

QuickFinder Searcher runs the QuickFinder, which allows you to enter criteria to locate a particular file or folder. From the QuickFinder dialog box, you can access the QuickFinder Manager. You explore QuickFinder in the Bonus section in Chapter 2.

Working with the Address Book

Your Rolodex sits on your desk, cards worn and tattered, names and addresses changed, erased, and scratched out until they're nearly illegible. The *D*'s are out of order, and you can't find your dentist's number. Is it under *D* for "Dentist" or "Doctor," or *F* for "Franklin"? Ah, finally, there it is, under *T* for "Teeth."

If you were using the Address Book, you could have searched and found the name in seconds. The Address Book stores names, addresses, phone numbers, e-mail addresses, and other information. Because the Address Book is fully integrated, you can use its information to create form letters, mailing labels, and envelopes in WordPerfect. You see how to do that in Chapter 8. For now, set up the Address Book for its first use.

Adding an Entry to the Address Book

You can work with either an individual or an organization in the Address Book. When you're starting out, you'll want to add yourself to the Address Book, in addition to your other contacts. It's a good idea to add yourself and even your colleagues because WordPerfect can access and use personal information stored in the Address Book in templates.

To add an entry to the Address Book, follow these steps.

1. Click **Start** → **Corel WordPerfect Suite 8** → **Corel Address Book 8** . The Address Book opens, showing two tabs — My Addresses and Frequent Contacts (see Figure 1-6).

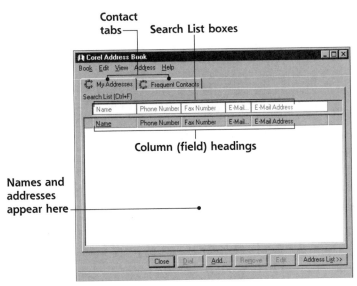

Figure 1-6 Use the Address Book for organizing and maintaining your contacts.

2. Click Add at the bottom of the dialog box to display the New Entry dialog box. You can also choose Edit → Add Name .

3. Select Person or Organization and choose OK to display the Properties for New Entry dialog box (see Figure 1-7).

4. Fill in each piece of information, pressing Tab to get to the next field box, or Shift+Tab to return to the previous field box.

5. To add another entry, click New. Then click Yes to save the changes before continuing.

6. Choose OK when you're finished. The entry is added to the Address list in alphabetical order by first name. A small icon next to an entry indicates an organization.

To edit an existing entry, select it in the list and click Edit. Make the necessary changes and click OK. To delete an entry, select it in the list and click Delete. Click Yes to confirm the deletion.

TIP To access the Address Book from WordPerfect, choose Tools→Address Book.

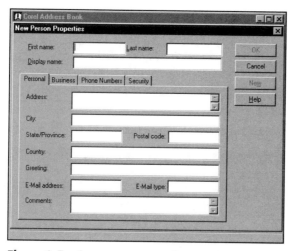

Figure 1-7 Create a new entry for a person.

Sorting Entries

If you want to display your addresses in an order other than by first name (which is the first column or *field*), you can do so. Most often, you will probably want to sort your addresses by last name.

Here's how to sort:

1. Choose **Edit** → **Column** → **Sort** to display the Column Sort dialog box (see Figure 1-8).

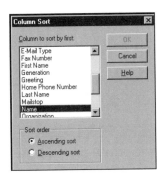

Figure 1-8 Sort addresses in the Column Sort dialog box.

2. Select the field by which to sort.

3. Choose Ascending sort or Descending sort and then choose OK. An underline beneath a column heading indicates the field by which you are sorting. If the heading for the sorted column isn't displayed, you won't see an underlined heading.

TIP To view the entries with the last name first, you can choose View→ Name Format→Last, First. However, keep in mind that if you use the Name field in a WordPerfect document, it will display with the last name first. To avoid this, you must use the First Name and Last Name fields separately in WordPerfect. Read more about this in Chapter 8.

Searching for Addresses

Once your Address Book starts to fill up, you may find it more difficult to locate addresses. The fastest way to search for an entry is to type information into one of the Search List boxes. These boxes appear between Search List (Ctrl+F) and the column headings. (Refer back to Figure 1-6.) The boxes contain dimmed column heading names.

Follow these steps to search for an address:

1. With the Address Book open, click in one of the Search List boxes, such as Name.

TIP You can also press Ctrl+F and click OK to position the insertion point in the Name box. Press Tab to move to the next box or Shift+Tab to move to the previous box.

2. Type the text you wish to locate (for example, **Kathleen Smith**). The Address Book scrolls down to display the first entry matching this criterion.

BONUS

Filtering Your Addresses

Although the Address Book lets you scroll through addresses or search for a particular address, it has an additional feature that's very useful — filtering. Just like its name, filtering allows you to filter out or hide those items that don't match particular criteria. For example, if you only want to see people who live in Idaho, you can create a filter that will do this. When you create a filter, the Address Book lists only those entries that match your criteria and you can scroll or search through this resulting filtered list.

Understanding Logical Statements

When you set up a filter, you use what's often referred to as a *logical statement*. You'll tell the Address Book something like "Show me those folks who live in Idaho" or "Show me the people who have a zip code greater than 60050." This statement consists of four parts: the field, the operator, the criteria, and the condition.

The *field* is the actual field containing the criteria (for example, the state field or the zip code field). The *operator* allows you to indicate how the Address Book treats the criteria for the field. Table 1-3 describes the operators. The *criteria* is the information by which you wish to filter. This could be "Idaho" or "60050."

The *condition* can be And, Or, or End. *And* tells the Address Book that it should filter entries that meet *both* the first and second criteria. *Or* tells the Address Book to filter those entries that meet *either* of the criteria. *End* tells the Address Book that this is the last filter.

If you were going to filter by my first example, your filtering statement would look like this: State/Province = Idaho End. If you wanted to filter by my second example, your statement would look like this: Zip Code > 60050 End.

Filtering statements are *case-sensitive*, which means if you type "id" for the state abbreviation and all your Idaho entries use "ID," the Address Book will come up empty when you use the filter.

TABLE 1-3 Filtering Operators

Operator	Description
=	Equal to.
!	Not equal to.
>	Greater than.
>=	Greater than or equal to.
<	Less than.
<=	Less than or equal to.`
[ ]	Contains. Has the criteria somewhere in the selected field.

Working with Filters

Once you're familiar with the structure of a logical statement, you're ready to set up a filter that will force the Address Book to display only certain entries. Here's how you do it:

1. With the Address Book open and your entries displayed, choose View → Define Filter to display the Building a Filter dialog box (see Figure 1-9).

2. Click the field arrow button and select the field by which you wish to filter. All fields in your Address Book appear in this drop-down list.

3. Click the operator button and choose an operator from the pop-up list. For example, if you want to include entries that have a zip code greater than 60050, choose >.

4. Type the criteria in the text box. Using the zip code example, you would type **60050**.

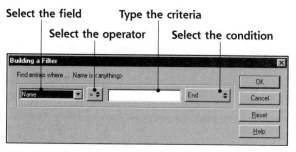

Select the field **Type the criteria**

Select the operator **Select the condition**

Figure 1-9 Set up your logical filter statement.

5. If you want to have an additional criteria — also known as a *compound filter* — click the condition button and choose And or Or and complete the second row. See Figure 1-10 for an example of a compound filter.

TIP If you need additional rows, click the condition button and select Insert Row. If you want to start over, click Reset.

6. When you're finished building your filter, click OK.

Plain statement

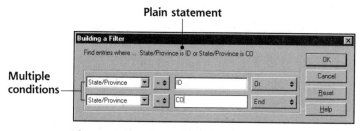

Multiple conditions

Figure 1-10 Set multiple conditions for a compound filter.

The Address Book enables the filter and displays entries that meet the criteria you specified. To see all entries again, choose View→Filtering Enabled to remove the check mark.

Summary

For your first foray into the WordPerfect Suite, you reviewed the core applications — WordPerfect, Presentations, and Quattro Pro — as well as a few of the bonus applications. You learned how to start and exit the programs through the Start menu as well as through the Desktop Applications Director (DAD). You got a taste of how the applications work using menus, toolbars, and dialog boxes, and you worked with DAD and the Address Book. In the next chapter, you'll see how similar the core applications are and how easily you can use one of them after using another.

CHAPTER TWO

WORKING WITH COMMON TOOLS

IN THIS CHAPTER YOU LEARN THESE KEY SKILLS

One of the beauties of the WordPerfect Suite is that the applications within it share some common elements and features. In Chapter 1, you saw that all the applications use menus, dialog boxes, and toolbars to access features and select options. Here you find that the applications also share other features. Though WordPerfect, Presentations, and Quattro Pro are different tools for different tasks, they all can perform similar functions, such as having the capability to switch between multiple windows, spell check, and edit with *QuickMenus* (small menus that pop up when you secondary-click).

Working within the suite is similar to driving different vehicles. If you can drive a car, you can probably maneuver a boat. Even though a boat performs different functions and has different features, it has enough similarities to your car that you can get started with it with minimal instruction. In this chapter, you look at the editing features that the applications have in common.

Starting a New Project

In Chapter 1, I mentioned that you could use the PerfectExpert to help you perform specific tasks. This tool is a fabulous time saver and one of the best things about the WordPerfect Suite. The PerfectExpert leads you through a wide range of tasks, from helping you decide if you should buy or lease a car, to designing a newsletter or creating a marketing slide show. The PerfectExpert asks questions and provides options and instructions for designing the type of document, report, or slide show you need.

To use the PerfectExpert, use one of the following methods:

* If you have an application open, choose `File` → `New`.

* If you don't have an application open, click the PerfectExpert button on the DAD toolbar or choose `Start` → `Corel WordPerfect Suite 8` → `Corel New Project`.

You'll see the PerfectExpert or New dialog box (see Figure 2-1), depending on the method you used. However, the dialog boxes are identical, and the steps for using them the same.

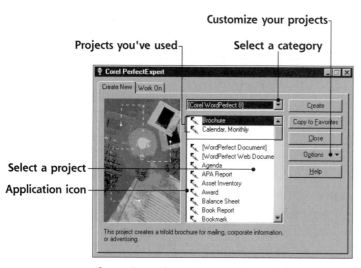

Figure 2-1 Create a new project using the PerfectExpert.

Once you have the PerfectExpert or New dialog box displayed, take a look at a few things. First, notice that if you select an application as your category (as is the case in Figure 2-1), you'll see any projects you've used in that application above the projects list. Next, you'll see the application icon next to a project, showing you which application you'll use to complete the project. Depending on the category you select, you may see multiple application icons.

To start a project, follow these steps:

1. Click the category down arrow and choose a category for your project from the drop-down list. Or, to see all projects for a particular application, choose the application. For example, if you want to create a newsletter, choose the Publish category. If you want to see a list of all WordPerfect projects, choose Corel WordPerfect 8.

2. In the list of projects that displays, either double-click the project or select it and click Create. The associated application launches with any helping tools you'll need to continue on your way. This may include the PerfectExpert panel, a dialog box, or other tool to help you complete the project.

3. Follow the instructions or select from the dialog boxes that display. (For information on working in the different applications, see Parts Two, Three, and Four.)

 X-REF For more on the PerfectExpert panel, see "Using the PerfectExpert as a Helper" later in this chapter.

 CAUTION If the project you selected requires personal information and you have not completed this in your Address Book, you will be prompted to do so. Just follow the instructions and refer back to Chapter 1 if you need help in the Address Book.

 TIP You can add, move, copy, or remove projects using the Options feature in the PerfectExpert or New dialog box. See online help for more information.

Working with Files

You explored the similarities in menus, dialog boxes, and toolbars in Chapter 1. You also saw that you start and exit WordPerfect, Presentations, and Quattro Pro the same way. Here you'll see that you open, save, and close files identically, too. Keep in mind that Presentations works slightly different when you first start it, and I'll address that briefly here and in more detail in Part Three. However, before we actually start opening and saving files, take a look at a *file management dialog box*.

Using File Management Dialog Boxes

A file management dialog box is any dialog box that allows you to deal with files — that is, a WordPerfect document, Presentations slide show, or Quattro Pro notebook (spreadsheet). This could be the Open, Save, or Insert File dialog boxes, or any of the many other dialog boxes that allow you to insert or work with files and filenames.

If you've used the Windows Explorer, many parts of this file management dialog box will be familiar to you. If you haven't, I highly recommend you explore the Explorer (hee, hee), and take a look at a book or two on Windows so you feel comfortable with file management dialog boxes. However, I will quickly point out some of the features that are unique to the file management dialog boxes in the Corel applications, and you'll see why you can easily do most, if not all, of your file management without leaving your application (see Figure 2-2).

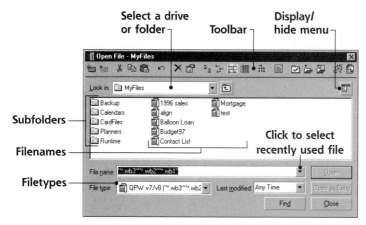

Figure 2-2 The Open File dialog box in Quattro Pro.

As you can in the Windows Explorer, you can move, copy, and delete files, as well as change how files display in the window. The toolbar provides quick access to many of these options and makes it easy to manage your files (see Table 2-1). In addition, you can view the contents of a selected file using Preview, which is especially helpful if you're not sure whether you've selected the correct file and want to take a peek at it before you open it.

When you use Preview, it defaults to the Page View, which shows you a thumbnail version of your file in a separate window. To see the detail of the file, click the Menu button to turn on the menu. Next, choose View→Preview and then choose Page View.

X-REF To learn how to locate files in a file management dialog box, check out the Bonus section at the end of this chapter.

TABLE 2-1 File Management Toolbar

Button	Name	Description
	MAP NETWORK DRIVE	Connect to and display the contents of a network drive.
	DISCONNECT NETWORK DRIVE	Disconnect and hide the contents of a network drive.
	CUT	Remove the selected item.

Button	Name	Description
	COPY	Make a copy of the selected item.
	PASTE	Paste the cut or copied item.
	UNDO	Undo last action.
	DELETE	Remove the selected folder or file from disk.
	PROPERTIES	Display the Properties dialog box for the selected item.
	LARGE ICONS	Display folder and filenames beneath a large icon. Same as choosing View→Large Icons.
	SMALL ICONS	Display folders and filenames to the right of a small icon. This button introduces a vertical scroll bar when the window can't display all files at once. Same as choosing View→Small Icons.
	LIST	Display folders and filenames to the right of a small icon with a horizontal scroll bar when the window can't display all files at once. Same as choosing View→ List.
	DETAILS	Display folders and filenames to the right of an icon while including the file size, type, and the date and time it was created or last revised. Same as choosing View→ Details.
	TREE VIEW	Provide a separate window so folders appear in the left pane and folder contents in the right pane. Same as choosing View→Tree View.
	PREVIEW	Display and hide the preview window to display the contents of the selected file.
	FAVORITES	Go to/from the Favorites folder.
	ADD LOCATION	Add the current folder to Favorites.
	ADD ITEM	Add the current item to Favorites.
	COREL INTERNET	Go to Corel's home page on the World Wide Web.
	QUICKFINDER SEARCH RESULTS	Go to/from the QuickFinder Search Results window.
	MENU	Turn the menu on/off to access additional features.

 X-REF To learn more about the Favorites list, see Chapter 18.

TIP If you want to move, copy, or delete several files simultaneously, you can select them. To select files in sequence, press and hold the Shift key, then click the first and last files in the sequence. To select files out of sequence, press and hold the Ctrl key, then click each file you want to select.

Opening an Existing Document

In each of the subsequent sections, you learn how to create and work with WordPerfect documents, Presentations slide shows, and Quattro Pro notebooks. Once you've created and saved files, you can open them and work on them again. Depending on your system, you may or may not have existing files on your hard drive, and if you have a brand new system, you may not have any existing files. However, because the steps for opening files are the same for each application, I want to cover them here so I don't have to repeat them for each application; thus saving room to talk about more important stuff.

 To open an existing document, make sure that the application is open and running. Click the Open button on the Standard toolbar or choose File→Open. The application displays the Open File dialog box (refer back to Figure 2-2 for an example in Quattro Pro). Depending on the application, you may see only a limited number of files. WordPerfect defaults to list all files in a folder, Presentations lists only slide shows (indicated by the SHW extension), and Quattro Pro lists only Quattro Pro notebooks (indicated by the WB3 extension).

To open a file, double-click the folder containing the file you wish to open, then double-click the filename you want to open. The file opens in the application and you can begin working on it.

As I mentioned earlier, Presentations works a bit different than WordPerfect and Quattro Pro if it isn't open before you open an existing show. When you start WordPerfect or Quattro Pro, these applications open a blank document (WordPerfect) or notebook (Quattro Pro). When you start Presentations, you see the New dialog box that asks you if you want to create a new show or drawing or open an existing show. This is the dialog box I discussed in "Starting a New Project" at the beginning of this chapter. You learn more about using this Presentations dialog box in Chapter 9.

TIP You can open as many as nine files in any application. All three main applications — WordPerfect, Presentations, and Quattro Pro — recognize and can automatically convert other formats. For example, WordPerfect can convert and open a Word document (including most Word for the Macintosh formats), Presentations can open a PowerPoint presentation, and Quattro Pro can open Excel and Lotus files.

Opening a Recently Used File

If you're like me, you probably have file folders, books, or manuals you use frequently in close proximity to your desk. If you have to fill in a timesheet every week or complete a status report, you don't store them in a file cabinet across the room. Perhaps they are in a hot file directly on your desk or in a file drawer or on a shelf within arm's length. Wherever their location, they are where you can get to them quickly and with minimal effort. The WordPerfect Suite applications offer this same convenience by placing the last ten files you used on the File menu.

To open a recently used file in any application, click File. At the bottom of the menu, just above the Exit command, you'll see a list of the most recently used files. The application always displays the last file you worked with first, then the others in descending chronological order. Click the desired filename or press the corresponding number to open it.

If you don't see any filenames at the bottom of the File menu, this means you either haven't worked on and saved documents yet, or that this option has been turned off (in Quattro Pro, it's always available — you can't turn it off and on).

To display recently used files in WordPerfect and Presentations, choose Tools→Settings to display the Settings dialog box:

* In WordPerfect, double-click the Environment icon and select the Interface tab. Under Menus, choose Display last open documents on the File menu. Click OK and then click Close.

* In Presentations, double-click the Display icon. Under Items to display on menus, choose Last doucments opened. Click OK and then click Close.

Moving Between Open Files

If you want to work with two files at the same time, you can quickly move between them using two different methods. For example, perhaps you have text you want to copy from one WordPerfect document to the other, or you want to compare numbers in one Quattro Pro notebook to another. You can switch between files, as well as display them in multiple windows so you can see each file at the same time. This last option is similar to the option on new televisions that let you tune into the fourth game of the World Series on the big screen while viewing one or more other programs on smaller screens.

With the application open and running, open the first file you wish to work with using one of the methods described previously in "Opening an Existing Document." Open any additional files using one of the same methods. To switch to another document, click the document or filename on the Application bar or choose Window and select the file to which you want to switch. The Window menu displays all open documents at the bottom, just as the File menu displays the most recently used files. The number next to the filename corresponds to the window the document resides in.

FEATURE FOCUS The Application bar provides quick access to open documents. You can also cut and copy between documents using the Application bar. See Chapter 3 for more information.

Sharing Information

One of the beauties of the integrated suite is that you can use information from one application in another. For example, if you create an outline in WordPerfect, you can use it as the basis for a slide show in Presentations (see Chapter 9). Or you can use a Quattro Pro spreadsheet in a report you're working on in WordPerfect. The applications work seamlessly together to help you get your work done quickly and efficiently.

In additon to exporting files into other applications, you can easily cut, copy, and paste between applications. Chapter 3 describes how to perform these tasks between applications.

Cascading and Tiling Windows

If you need to move and copy information between files, or need to do line-by-line comparisons, you can arrange your display to see more than one window at a time. The WordPerfect Suite applications provide two display options for displaying multiple files:

* *Cascade* displays the file windows so that they overlap. Each title bar is visible so you can easily click it, which makes a file active and moves it to the front.

* *Tile* displays the file windows so you can see them next to each other. Depending on the application and your selection, the files will either display side-by-side or above and below each other.

To cascade your files after you've opened them, choose Window→Cascade. Your files will arrange in a staggered fashion on your screen (see Figure 2-3). To move between the windows, click the title bar for the window. This makes it the active document and brings it to the front, ready for your scrutiny.

To tile your files after you've opened them, choose Window→Tile Top to Bottom to display windows stacked on top of each other horizontally (see Figure 2-4) or choose Window→Tile Side by Side to display windows side by side vertically.

Title bars   Active window

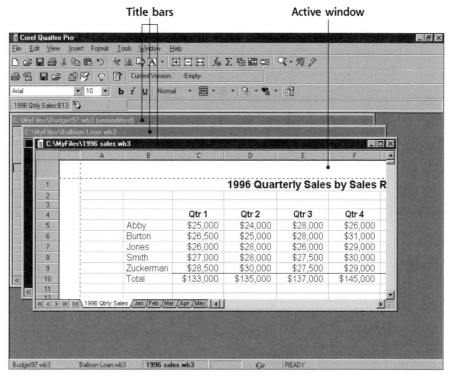

Figure 2-3 Cascaded windows in Quattro Pro.

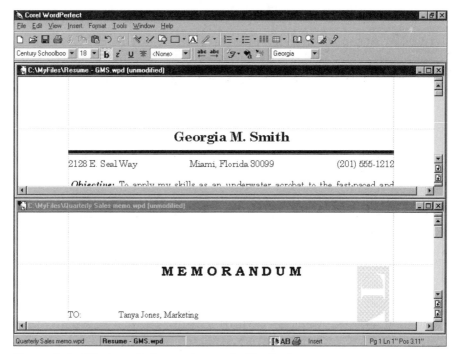

Figure 2-4 Windows tiled top to bottom in WordPerfect.

Saving and Closing a File

Once you make changes to a WordPerfect document, Presentations show, or Quattro Pro notebook (which are known generally as *files*), you will want to save it so that you have a permanent copy of it for future use. You also will want to close the document if you no longer need to work on it, to free up memory.

SAVING A FILE

Once you create and work on a file, you will want to keep a permanent copy on disk. Saving is one of the most important actions you'll take on your file. And once you save it with a name, click the Save button on the toolbar periodically as you continue to work on it to ensure that your changes don't get lost in the event of a power outage or other unpredictable event. Though some applications provide automatic backup of your documents, saving guarantees that you've saved up to the point of your last change. For more on backup options, see Chapter 18.

To save a file in any application, follow these steps.

1. Click the Save button (shown at left) or choose File → Save to display the Save As dialog box, which is very similar to the Open File dialog box you saw in Figure 2-2.

2. In the Name text box, type a name for the file. You can use up to 255 characters, including spaces. See the Caution after the steps for important file naming information.

3. Select a folder in which to store the file.

4. Click Save. The application saves the file to the designated folder.

The following characters are not allowed in a filename, because the system has reserved them for other uses: / \ > < * ? " | : ;

CLOSING A FILE

Once you're finished working with a file, it's a good idea to close it to conserve system resources. If you need to use it again, you can always reopen it. To close a file in any application, click the Close button or the Document Control button on the menu bar. You can also choose File→Close. Note that if you have not saved the file since you last made changes to it, the application will prompt you to save. Click Yes to save or No to close without saving.

TIP Save a step by saving and closing at the same time. Just click the Close button or the Document Control button on the menu bar and then choose Yes when prompted to save the file.

Using QuickMenus and QuickCorrect

So far you've seen that the WordPerfect Suite of applications makes things pretty simple for you with menus, click-on toolbars, and features like recently used files on the File menu. But for those of you who want even more comfort and convenience, the core applications provide some "quick" features to speed up formatting and typing.

Using QuickMenus

QuickMenus are available in all applications to speed up the formatting of specific elements. In WordPerfect, these elements may be paragraphs, tables, or graphic images. In Presentations, they may be slides or slide text, and in Quattro Pro, they might be cells, columns or rows, or entire worksheets. Whatever the element, if you need to format it quickly, you can use a QuickMenu.

To use a QuickMenu, point to the element you want to format (a paragraph, bullet point on a slide, or a cell in Quattro Pro), then secondary-click. The application displays the corresponding QuickMenu, and you can select the desired option. Depending on your selection, the application may immediately perform an action or open a related dialog box so that you can set additional options. You will explore many of the QuickMenus as you work with the applications in the book.

Using QuickCorrect

I've been typing for years, even before I typed a 144-page horribly contrived novel when I was 14. But even after all this time, I still type "teh" for "the" and "form" for "from," or "odn't" for "don't." If you share any of the same typing habits, you can cure them by using QuickCorrect. This wonderful, time-saving feature automatically corrects all your common typing errors, as well as speeds up the entry of frequently used abbreviations. For example, if you do type "teh," QuickCorrect automatically changes it to "the" when you press the space bar. Or, if you often use the phrase "for your information," you can include a QuickCorrect entry that will change "fyi" to "for your information" automatically. Magic? No, but almost.

Note that you wouldn't want to use QuickCorrect for my second example (form and from) because both of these are valid words. You'll have to count on Grammatik or your own keen eye in this case.

QuickCorrect comes with a number of predefined entries, including changing "teh" to "the" and "alot" to "a lot." The list that follows highlights the features that make QuickCorrect an invaluable typing tool. It can help you fix common typos such as "teh" to "the" and mixed capitalization corrections, such as changing "mONDAY" to "Monday" (yes, we all leave the Caps Lock on occasionally, don't we?).

When you use QuickCorrect, you'll notice that it differs somewhat in WordPerfect. That's because word processing is very text-intensive, and WordPerfect provides extra tools in QuickCorrect to help you with your text. The QuickCorrect dialog box in WordPerfect will look quite a bit different than the sample in Figure 2-5 because WordPerfect provides additional options on multiple tabs. Some of these extras include the following:

* QuickLines to insert single and double graphic lines (see Chapter 6 for more on this)

* SmartQuotes to convert straight quotes (") to the more attractive curly quotation marks (" ")

* QuickOrdinals to replace ordered numbers such as 1st and 2nd with superscript characters to indicate ordinal numbers like 1st and 2nd

* QuickLines to insert graphic lines

Adding Your Own QuickCorrect Entry

If you have your own peculiar typing errors, you can add these to your QuickCorrect list so they will be "corrected as you go." And one of the best things about QuickCorrect is that it is a *shared* feature, which means that entries you add in one application show up and are used in all applications. So, if you add an entry in Presentations, QuickCorrect will use the entry in WordPerfect and Quattro Pro. Pretty cool, huh?

To add your own entry in any application, follow these steps:

1. Choose Tools → Quick Correct or press Ctrl+Shift+F1. The application displays the QuickCorrect dialog box (see Figure 2-5). The entries are listed in alphabetical order, with single characters and symbols listed first. Scroll through the entries to see what already exists. Note that in WordPerfect, the QuickCorrect feature is part of an entire QuickCorrect dialog box because there are several tabs you can use to customize QuickCorrect options in WordPerfect. The dialog box in Figure 2-5 is from Presentations.

Create new entries here

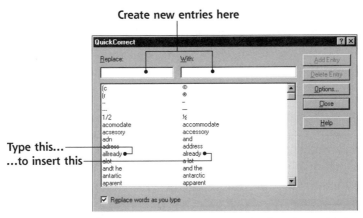

Figure 2-5 Correct typos on-the-fly using QuickCorrect.

Type this...
...to insert this

2. In the Replace text box, type your misspelled word or the abbreviation you want to use.

3. In the With text box, type the word spelled correctly or the entire phrase the abbreviation represents.

4. Click Add Entry. QuickCorrect places the entry in the list, in alphabetical order.

5. Repeat Steps 2 through 4 for all entries you want to add, then click Close.

You can delete an entry you don't need by selecting it in the QuickCorrect dialog box and clicking Delete Entry. To turn QuickCorrect off altogether, select Tools→QuickCorrect or press Ctrl+Shift+F1 to display the QuickCorrect dialog box. Then choose Replace words as you type at the bottom of the dialog box to remove the check mark.

QuickCorrect is on by default in all applications. If you decide you want to turn it off, choose Tools→QuickCorrect and clear the Replace words as you type check box. Note that turning off QuickCorrect in one application doesn't turn it off in the other applications.

As I mentioned, you can use QuickCorrect to expand abbreviations such as *fyi* and *asap*. However, if your work calls for text that requires formatting, or the abbreviations are less common than those I just mentioned, consider using the QuickWords feature, which I cover in the Bonus section at the end of Chapter 3.

Using Writing Tools

In addition to the amazing QuickCorrect, the WordPerfect Suite also offers a trio of invaluable tools to assist in your writing. Spell Check helps you correct misspelled words. Grammatik examines sentence structure, difficulty, and word usage to help you become grammatically correct. The third member of the trio, the Thesaurus, helps you find just the right word when you can't think of it. And because these three tools reside in the same dialog box, it's easy to switch between them to perform the desired task.

Using the Spell Check

When you run a spell check on a WordPerfect document, Presentations show, or Quattro Pro notebook, the Spell Check utility checks every word against an existing word list. If Spell Check comes up without a match, it displays the word as a possible misspelling and usually offers correct spelling suggestions. I say usually because sometimes the Spell Check can't come up with anything close to your word. In those cases, you can either accept the word as correct and add it to the word list, or skip it.

To spell check a file, follow these steps:

1. Open the file you want to check in the associated application. In Presentations, make sure that you have selected the text box containing the text you want to check or use Outliner view to check the entire slide show.

For information on the Outliner view in Presentations, see Chapter 9.

2. Choose ⬛ Tools → ⬛ Spell Check . The application displays the Spell Checker tab in the dialog box (see Figure 2-6) and then begins checking the WordPerfect document, Presentations slide, or selected Quattro Pro cells.

TIP **You can also press Ctrl+F1 to access the Spell Checker tab in the dialog box. In WordPerfect, you can click the Spell Check button on the toolbar, and in Presentations, you can click the Spell Check button on the Outliner property bar.**

When Spell Check locates a possible misspelled word, it selects the word in the document and inserts it in the Not found text box. You then need to decide what to do with it.

3. If the word is spelled incorrectly, you have two options: select the correct spelling from the Replacements list and choose Replace, or if the correct spelling is not in the Replacements list, click in the Replace with text box

and correct the text. If the word is spelled correctly (perhaps it's a proper name the dictionary doesn't recognize), use one of these options:

* Click Skip Once to skip over this occurrence of the word but stop at a future occurrence.

* Click Skip Always to skip over all occurrences of the word from this point forward.

* Click Add to add the word to a user word list so Spell Check won't catch it in the future for this document.

Unrecognized word

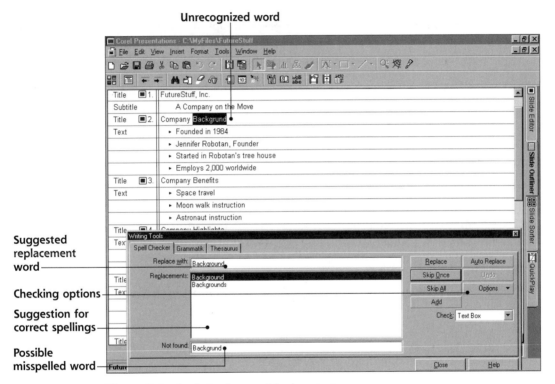

Figure 2-6 Spell check your slide show text.

4. When Spell Checker is finished, it displays a message telling you it's done and asking if you want to close the entire dialog box. Click Yes to close the dialog box or No to close the message box and still use the features in the dialog box.

Because of the text-intensive nature of WordPerfect documents, this application also comes with the Spell-As-You-Go feature, which checks your spelling as you type. If WordPerfect can't match a potential misspelling with a word in the dictionary, it marks the word with a squiggly red line. When you see this mark, you can correct the word immediately. Just secondary-click the word to display the QuickMenu and select the desired spelling option.

If you don't want to use Spell-As-You-Go, you can turn it off by choosing Tools→Proofread→Off in WordPerfect.

The Prompt-As-You-Go box on the WordPerfect Standard property bar allows you to select from a list of possible spellings or grammar options as you type. See Figure 4-1 in Chapter 4 to identify this box.

Using the Thesaurus

If you've used a printed thesaurus to help you come up with synonyms for your writing, you'll be familiar with the concept of an online thesaurus. The WordPerfect Suite Thesaurus provides a list of synonyms and antonyms for the root of your word and will insert the replacement and make any necessary grammatical corrections to make it match the original word. You can use the thesaurus to replace an existing word, or you can look up a word from scratch and display synonyms for it.

The Thesaurus is not available in Corel Quattro Pro.

To use the Thesaurus, follow these steps:

1. With the file open in WordPerfect or Presentations, position the insertion point in the word you want to replace with a synonym.

2. Choose Tools → Thesaurus or press Alt+F1. The application displays the Thesaurus tab in the dialog box (see Figure 2-7). The Thesaurus displays your word in the Replace with text box and lists synonyms for it in the lower box. Notice that your word appears directly above the list box.

3. Select the word in the list that you would like to use and then click Replace.

TIP   If you want to see synonyms for a word in the synonym list, select the word and then click Look Up or double-click the word. The synonyms for the word will appear in the next column with the word displaying directly above the list box.

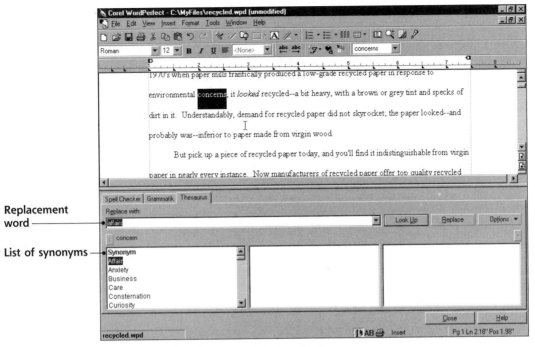

Replacement word

List of synonyms

Figure 2-7 The Thesaurus tab in WordPerfect.

Using Grammatik

Not sure when to use "who" or "whom"? Do "which" and "that" trip you up? Leave it to Grammatik to solve most, if not all, of your grammar problems. Whereas the Spell Checker has a dictionary of words it uses for comparison, Grammatik has a list of predefined grammar rules that it uses as the standard by which it checks your words, phrases, and sentences. Before using Grammatik, make sure that you have the text box selected or are using Outliner view in Presentations or have your document open in WordPerfect.

To use Grammatik in WordPerfect or Presentations, follow these steps:

1. Choose **Tools** → **Grammatik** or press Alt+Shift+F1. The application displays the Grammatik tab in the dialog box (see Figure 2-8). Grammatik selects the potential discrepancy in your text and then displays possible corrections, a sample of how the corrected text would read, and a description of the problem. At the bottom you'll see the type of check Grammatik is performing.

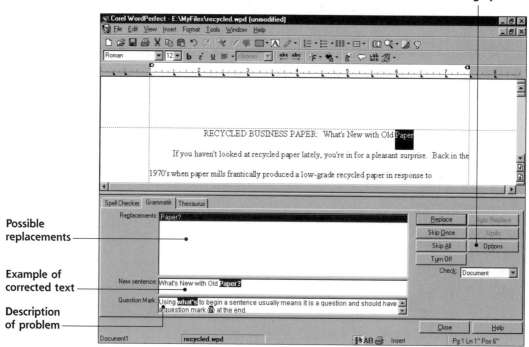

Checking options

Possible replacements

Example of corrected text

Description of problem

Figure 2-8   Check your grammar with Grammatik.

2. Review the information for the error and do one of the following:

* Click Replace to accept the selected replacement and replace your text with it. If there is more than one replacement option, select each one to see how it will affect your text before determining which works best.

* Click Skip Once to skip over this occurrence of the word or phrase but stop at a future occurrence.

* Click Skip Always to skip over all occurrences of the word or phrase from this point forward.

* Click Turn Off to ignore any words or phrases from this point forward that violate the current grammatical rule.

3. When you're finished with Grammatik, choose Close.

TIP   Depending on the type of document you're writing, you can select from a variety of checking styles. On the Grammatik tab, click Options and then choose Checking Styles. Choose the desired style from the list and click Select.

Inserting Symbols

If you need to insert special symbols into your WordPerfect document, Quattro Pro notebook, or Presentations slide show, you can use the Symbols feature. Symbols include such things as a copyright symbol (©) or a section symbol (§) if you're a legal eagle. You can also insert a variety of iconic images (smiley faces, hands, and other small pictures).

To select a symbol in WordPerfect and Presentations, follow these steps:

1. Position the insertion point in the location for the symbol and click the Insert Symbol button on the property bar or choose **Insert** → **Symbol**. The application displays the WordPerfect Characters dialog box showing iconic characters (see Figure 2-9). This character set has the most interesting options. However, you can click the Character set button and select a different character set from the pop-up list. For example, the Typographic list contains such symbols as copyright, registered trademark, section symbol, and paragraph mark.

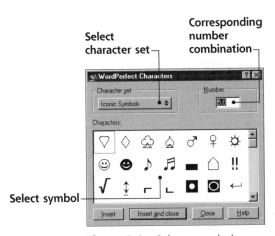

Figure 2-9 Select a symbol.

2. In the Characters box, choose the character you want to use and then click Insert to insert the character; keep the WordPerfect Characters dialog box open to insert additional characters. Otherwise, click Insert and close.

To insert a symbol in Quattro Pro, double-click the cell that will contain the symbol and position the insertion point. Click the Character button on the Standard property bar (the second button from the right) and select the desired character. To see a list of different characters, select a different font. For example, to use one of the iconic symbols in Figure 2-9, choose the WP Iconic SymbolsA font. When you click the Character button, these symbols will display.

Using Help

I f you are familiar with other Windows applications, you've probably used the Help system in one or more of them. The WordPerfect Suite uses the same type of Help system — Help Topics, Ask the PerfectExpert, PerfectExpert, and Corel Web Site and the Reference Center. I'll look at each of these and when you might use them. Note that each application may have slight differences because of its unique nature.

Understanding Help Windows

Most of the Help options will eventually lead you to a Help window (see Figure 2-10), where you will find descriptive text and step-by-step instructions to perform a variety of tasks. Let's review the elements of a Help window so you know what to do when you display one through any of the Help features. Words underlined with a dashed line in a Help window indicate *pop-up* terms; click the word to display a brief definition and click again (anywhere in the Help window) to make the definition vanish. Use Table 2-2 to assist you in learning the other elements.

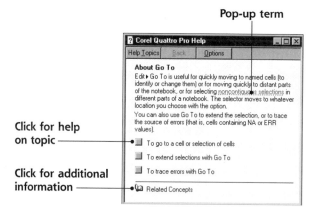

Figure 2-10 A sample Help window.

TABLE 2-2 Help Window Elements

This Button/Icon	Displays
HELP TOPICS	The Help Topics dialog box.
BACK	The previous Help window.
OPTIONS	A pop-up menu with a variety of Help window options, such as creating an annotation to mark the topic with your own notes, copying Help window text to a document, and printing the topic.

TIP To get help about an element in an application, press Shift+F1 so your mouse pointer displays with a question mark. Then click the element to display a Help window about the element.

Using the Contents Tab

The Contents tab is like the table of contents for a book, giving you jumping off point for your help needs. With your application of choice open and running, choose Help→Help Topics to display the Help Topics dialog box. If this is the first time you've used help in this application, you will see a message telling you the application is preparing the Help file for first use. The application you are using appears in the title bar. Select the Contents tab, if it isn't already displayed. A *book* icon indicates topic headings. A *question mark* icon indicates that you will display a Help screen with information and step-by-step instructions for the topic.

Using the Index

The Index tab works much like an index you find at the back of a textbook or other nonfiction book. It displays a list of topics in alphabetical order, with subtopics listed beneath main topics. However, instead of page number references, the Index allows you to select a topic and display instructions on how to use it.

To use the Index, follow these steps:

1. With your application of choice open and running, display the Help Topics dialog box by choosing **Help** → **Help Topics** , and then choose the Index tab.

2. In the first box, type the first few characters of the topic for which you're looking. Help jumps to the first word beginning with those characters in the second box.

3. Use the vertical scroll bar in the second box to locate the desired topic and then select it and click Display. You can also double-click the topic.

Using Find

Unlike the Index, the Find tab enables you to locate topics without having to know how they begin. When you use Find, Help searches all words in the Help database, pulling up a wider array of options.

To use Find, follow these steps:

1. With your application of choice open and running, display the Help Topics dialog box by choosing **Help** → **Help Topics** , and then choose the

Find tab. If this is the first time you've used Help in this application, Help displays the Find Setup Wizard with three options. To make things easier, you'll use Minimize database size. You can explore the other options by choosing Rebuild on the Find tab.

2. Select Minimize database in the first Find Setup Wizard dialog box and then choose Next.

3. Choose Finish to have Help create the word list and then display the Find tab in the Help Topics dialog box.

4. In the box denoted by a 1, type the first few characters of the topic you're looking for. Help displays information in box 2 and box 3. Box 2 contains any matching words found in the Help database, and box 3 lists the actual topic titles containing the words you typed in the first box.

5. If you want to narrow your search, select a word or phrase in box 2, then see what topics display in box 3.

6. When you see your topic in box 3, select it and then click Display. You can also double-click the topic.

 TIP   **If a dialog box contains a Question Mark button on the title bar, you can get *context-sensitive help* on topics within the dialog box. Just click this button and click the topic you want to learn about. The topic becomes a pop-up term, and the application will display a brief description of it. If there is no Question Mark button, press Shift+F1, and then click the topic.**

Asking the PerfectExpert

So, you've looked at locating topics using the Index and Find tabs and how to get more hands-on assistance from Help. But what if you're not sure what to call a topic. What if your question is "How do I make my paper go longways?" or "How do I add a slide?"

Enter the PerfectExpert, which — depending on what type of help you need — can either answer a question or act as a helper within your document. Here you look at how it answers your questions, and in the next section, you'll see the PerfectExpert as a helping hand.

To ask the PerfectExpert a question, follow these steps:

1. With your application of choice open and running, display the Help Topics dialog box by choosing `Help` → `Ask the PerfectExpert` . If the Help Topics dialog box is already displayed, choose the Ask the PerfectExpert

tab. Help may take a few seconds to load this feature.

2. In the What do you want to know? box, type your word, phrase, or question and then click Search. The PerfectExpert displays the possible topics in the lower box.

3. Select the desired topic and choose Display. You can also double-click the topic.

Using the PerfectExpert as a Helper

If you've ever watched a cooking or home improvement show on television, you probably noticed that the host leads you step by step through a particular task, showing you how much of this, where to nail that, and so on. The PerfectExpert operates in a similar fashion, providing guidance or options along the way.

  To use the PerfectExpert in any application, click the PerfectExpert button on the Standard toolbar or select Help→PerfectExpert. The PerfectExpert panel appears on the left side of the screen, providing a list of common tasks you may want to perform. Figure 2-11 shows the PerfectExpert panel in Presentations. Select the task and follow the instructions or complete the dialog box as PerfectExpert helps you through the task.

Here are some tips for using the PerfectExpert panel:

* If you get several layers deep into the PerfectExpert and want to return to the main panel, click the Home icon at the top of the panel.

* To move the panel, point to the outside frame until you see the Move pointer (four-headed arrow) and then click and drag the panel to a new location.

* To close the PerfectExpert, click the PerfectExpert button on the toolbar again or click the X in the upper-right corner of the panel. Note that if you don't close the PerfectExpert, it will remain on. If you close the application and then start it again, the PerfectExpert panel will display.

Using the Corel Web Site

If you want to connect directly to Corel's Web site and get help, you can use Help to do so. This option takes you directly to the opening Web page for the application you are currently using. With your application of choice open and running, display the Help Topics dialog box by choosing Help→Help Corel Web Site.

You must have your Web browser installed and properly configured to use this feature. For more information, see Chapter 16.

Home ─┐ ┌─ Close

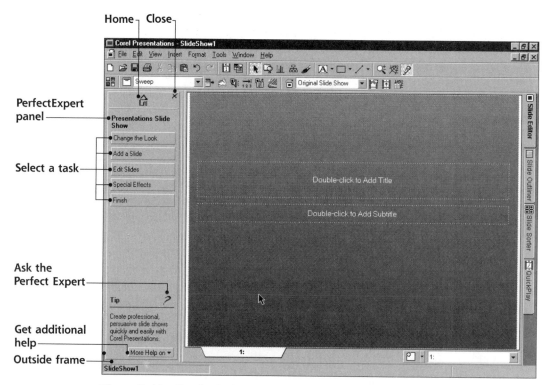

PerfectExpert panel ──

Select a task ──

Ask the Perfect Expert ──

Get additional help ──

Outside frame ──

Figure 2-11 Use the PerfectExpert to assist you in any application.

Your browser should launch automatically and begin connecting you to the Corel Web site. Depending on which application you are using, Netscape or your browser will go to the appropriate page. For example, if you select this option in Quattro Pro, your browser will take you directly to the Quattro Pro document on the Corel Web site.

 X-REF For more on browsing Web documents, see Chapter 16.

 WEB PATH For more on Corel's products, visit `http://www.corel.com`.

Using the Reference Center

When you received the WordPerfect Suite and opened the box, did you say, "Hey, wait a minute! Where's the rest of the manuals?" No, they didn't forget them. You've got the manuals, all of them — on your CD.

It's called the *Reference Center,* and it contains comprehensive manuals for each of the suite applications. The Reference Center manuals are literally online manuals, complete with graphics and lots of descriptions, just like their paper counterparts. But the biggest advantages of the online manuals are that they don't take up valuable shelf space, they're searchable, and you can tag specific sections with bookmarks for easy reference.

Opening the Reference Center

You can open the Reference Center from the Windows desktop or from within any application. Before using either of these methods to open the Reference Center, make sure the WordPerfect Suite CD is in your CD-ROM drive.

To open the Reference Center from an application, make sure that the CD is in your CD-ROM drive and follow these steps:

1. Choose `Help` → `Help Topics`, and then choose the Contents tab. Double-click View Manuals and then double-click Go to the Reference Center. Corel opens the Corel Reference Center in Envoy (see Figure 2-12).

TIP **If you don't have an application open, just click Start→Corel WordPerfect Suite 8→Setup & Notes→Reference Center.**

Figure 2-12 Using Corel's electronic manuals for additional help.

2. Click the manual for the desired application. The Reference Center displays the first page of the manual in the Envoy Viewer, which has elements that are identical for each manual.

3. Select one of the following options:

   * *Getting Around* provides a brief overview of how to use the online manual and move around in it.

   * *Contents* provides a table of contents with hyperlinked topics. Click any topic to move directly to it in the manual.

   * *Index* provides buttons for the letters A-Z. Click on an alphabetic button to see the index section beginning with that letter. Note the page number and use the Go to feature to jump to the page by choosing `Edit` → `Go To Page`.

The Reference Center for the application you selected opens in Envoy, an application for electronic documents. If you've never worked with Envoy or another electronic document application (such as Acrobat), I suggest you choose Getting Around. This page gives you a quick overview of how to use some of the navigation buttons on the Envoy toolbar to help you get around your document. These buttons include getting to particular pages and using the Find feature to locate text within the document.

And if you can't bear not having real paper pages to thumb through, you can print part or all of an online manual. Just follow these steps:

1. If you don't want to print the entire manual, note which pages you do want to print or select the sections you'd like to print.

 2. Click the Print button or choose `File` → `Print` to display the Print dialog box.

3. Under Print range, indicate the page range you'd like to print or choose Selection if you selected a block of text and click OK.

BONUS

Locating Files

You've started WordPerfect and already have a lot of documents on your hard drive. (I'm assuming that you upgraded, switched from another word processing application to WordPerfect, or have already read Chapter 3.) Now say that you need to find a document you created last week that you named Joe's Letter (or was it Joe's Confirmation Letter?). Or you know the file made a reference to "Barbara's Barbecue Boutique" but you can't remember the filename. How do you find it using this shaky information? You can use the QuickFinder feature to locate the file without leaving your application.

In the first instance, you're locating by *filename;* in the second instance, you're locating by *content.* If you can only remember part of the filename, you can use *wildcards.* Wildcards are characters that stand in for other characters, and you use them to help narrow your search. Use the following tips to locate files using QuickFinder.

★ If you know the entire filename but can't remember the folder that contains it, type the name in the File name text box.

★ If you know the starting characters for the name, type the characters followed by an asterisk in the File name text box. For example, to look for Joe's letter, type **Joe***. The application will find all files that begin with the letters *joe.*

* If you know the filename is a certain number of characters long, you can use a question mark to stand in for those characters that you're not sure about in the File name text box. For example, to look for a document that may be either Stanley or Stimley, type **St??ley**. The application will find all files that begin with *st,* have two letters following, and end in *ley.*

* If you only remember a word or phrase from the file, type this word or phrase in the File name text box.

To locate a file using the Open File dialog box, follow these steps:

1. Click the Open button in any application or choose [File] → [Open] to display the Open File dialog box you saw earlier.

2. In the File name text box, type the filename you're looking for or use wildcards. If you want to locate a file by its contents, type the word or phrase to search for in the File name text box.

3. If you want to limit the search to a particular time frame, click the Last modified arrow button and select a restriction from the list. Note that if you select a restriction, you won't have to go to Step 4. The application will automatically begin the find process when you release the mouse button.

4. If you're not sure which folder contains the file, click the Look in down-arrow button and select a drive, or select My Computer in the drop-down list.

5. Click Find. The application locates all the files that match your criteria and displays the list in the QuickFinder Search Results window (see Figure 2-13). You can then do whatever you want with the results from the QuickFinder Search Results window, including previewing, opening, moving, and deleting. Note that if QuickFinder doesn't find a match, the QuickFinder Search Results window will come up empty.

6. To return to the previous dialog box, click Back or click the QuickFinder Search Results button on the toolbar. Note that your criteria will still be in effect.

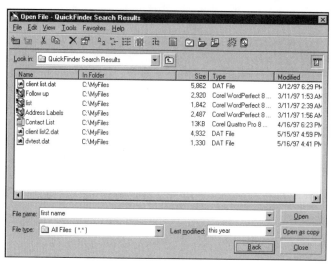

Figure 2-13   The results of a Find in WordPerfect.

The fastest way to return your file management dialog box to its state before you performed the search is to close the dialog box and reopen it. You can also reset all criteria in the File name, File type, and Last modified text boxes, and then position the insertion point in the File name text box and press Enter.

Summary

You covered a lot of ground in this chapter, from working with files and file management dialog boxes to exploring the Help feature in detail. In between, you learned how to use QuickMenus, worked with QuickCorrect to speed up typing and text entry, and explored the writing tools — Spell Check, Thesaurus, and Grammatik — that will help polish your prose. Next, I take you into the world of word processing, using the oh-so versatile and powerful WordPerfect.

CREATING DOCUMENTS WITH WORDPERFECT

THIS PART CONTAINS THE FOLLOWING CHAPTERS

This part teaches you the most common skills you'll need to create just about any type of document. Much of what you learn here you'll use repeatedly in various documents, as well as in other applications. If you've used other word processing applications, you'll be familiar with some of these features and methods; that will give you the confidence to explore some of the unknown stuff. If you're brand new to word processing, know that this part will help you feel comfortable and secure in your skills when you're finished.

So you're here to learn WordPerfect. This part discusses all of the tools that will help you learn the world's best word-processing program, including the WordPerfect diskettes, the keyboard template, and perhaps most importantly, your data diskette.

Now wait just a minute. Keyboard template? Data diskette? What about the traditional WordPerfect tools — menus, buttons, and toolbars?

Well, tradition is a sticky concept. In the computer industry, where time is measured in nanoseconds and accomplishments are labeled in cycles per second, tradition is often defined as anything that happens a second time. And not so long ago, keyboard templates and data diskettes were the traditional tools of any WordPerfect user.

When WordPerfect appeared for the original IBM PC, technical advancements now taken for granted did not exist. One of these is the hard disk drive. Fortunately, WordPerfect was a much smaller program then, and the application fit on a few diskettes. Every time you started WordPerfect, you loaded it from the WordPerfect diskettes into the computer's RAM. But with less than a megabyte of RAM, the PC couldn't remember all of WordPerfect's instructions. As a result, when you tried to do something "extravagant," such as print your document, you often got a message such as "Insert WordPerfect Diskette B into Drive A and press Enter."

The lack of a hard disk drive also made it necessary have a special data disk. This is where you stored all of the documents that you created with WordPerfect and other programs. Because many computers had only one floppy drive, when you wanted to save your document, you had to replace a WordPerfect diskette with your data diskette before you could save your work. As you can imagine, computer security was quite different then. When your computer was turned off, you didn't have to worry about the information it contained, because it contained practically none. Information lived on diskettes.

Older versions of WordPerfect also survived without menus, buttons, and toolbars. Instead, the program relied mostly on the function keys that run along the top and left side of most keyboards. When used alone, with the Ctrl key, or with the Alt key, the function keys could be used for dozens of tasks. The trouble was, no one could remember the different key combinations. As a result, old versions of WordPerfect came with a cardboard template that fit over the function keys.

WordPerfect templates were a valuable commodity; without one, it was very difficult to get much work done. In fact, wherever multiple computers were present, the templates were so highly sought after that they began to disappear rapidly from keyboards. Many college computer labs, tired of ordering more and more templates, made students trade their student IDs for the templates as the students entered the lab.

In addition to making computing much easier, the invention of hard disks and graphical interfaces did much more. They stopped a generation of students from becoming hardened criminals.

CREATING A LETTER

Welcome to the wonderful world of word processing (how's that for alliteration?). You are about to experience the most versatile, powerful, and useful word processing tool on the market today — Corel WordPerfect 8. From time-saving features to ease of use, you'll be delighted with the documents that you can create with WordPerfect. Using this single program, you can create everything from a basic letter to your Aunt Georgette to an eye-catching, professional newsletter for your small business. Ready? Let's go!

Understanding the WordPerfect Window

When you start WordPerfect for the first time, you'll notice a plethora of elements in the window. You first saw a WordPerfect document window in Chapter 1 and were introduced to some of the elements it shares with the other applications. However, several things about it are unique to WordPerfect. Let's look at a document window again more closely.

Start WordPerfect by clicking the WordPerfect button on DAD or clicking Start→Corel WordPerfect Suite 8→Corel WordPerfect. WordPerfect opens, displaying a blank document window so you can begin working immediately (see Figure 3-1).

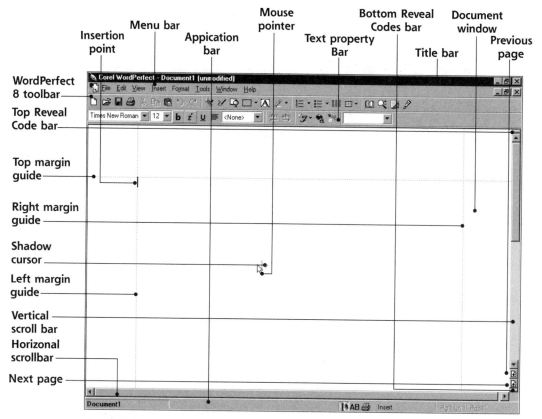

Figure 3-1 Begin a new document in WordPerfect.

The title bar, menu bar, and toolbar are all common among the suite applications. However, some of the other window elements are unique to WordPerfect. Explore these elements, starting at the top of the window and moving down.

✳ The *title bar* contains not only the application name but also the document name and its status if it is unmodified — that is, if you haven't made any changes since you started the new document or opened an existing document. Once you start typing, the word "unmodified" disappears, indicating that you have made changes to the current document. WordPerfect numbers unsaved documents consecutively up to nine, because you can have up to nine documents open at once.

✳ The *WordPerfect 8 toolbar* provides quick-click access to frequently used editing and formatting features. This is sometimes referred to as the *Standard toolbar*. See Table 3-1 for a description of the buttons.

✳ The *Text property bar* allows quick-click access to frequently used formatting features that aren't available on the preceding toolbar. Here you can change the look of text, justification, and so on.

- The *document window* is the white area below the Text property bar. This is where you strut your stuff, typing your text and formatting it.

- The *insertion point* is the vertical black line that blinks in the document window. This marks your place in the text and indicates where text will appear if you begin typing.

- The *shadow cursor* is the colored insertion point that follows the mouse pointer around. It indicates where you are at any given time and helps you position the insertion point more precisely.

- The *mouse pointer* lets you position the insertion point in another location with a single click. If you've turned the shadow cursor off, the mouse pointer will look like a large capital *I* in the document window (which is why it is sometimes called the "I-beam").

- The *margin guidelines* indicate your top, bottom, left, and right margins. Your text will appear within these guidelines, showing you how much white space surrounds it. You can adjust any margin using the guidelines, and you can also hide the guidelines.

- The *vertical* and *horizontal scroll bars* allow you to view different areas of your page without moving the insertion point.

- The *page buttons* allow you to move to the top of the previous or next page quickly, without moving the insertion point.

- The *Reveal Codes bars* allow you to display/hide the Reveal Codes window by clicking and dragging.

X-REF   **You learn more about Reveal Codes in Chapter 4.**

- The *Application bar* displays information about the current document, all other open documents, and the location of the insertion point. It also provides buttons for other features.

FEATURE FOCUS   **Property bars are context-sensitive in WordPerfect 8. This means that the bar will change depending on what you're doing at any given time, providing features you would use for a particular task.**

TABLE 3-1 WordPerfect 8 Toolbar

Button	Name	Description
	NEW BLANK DOCUMENT	Open a new blank document window.
	OPEN	Open an existing document.
	SAVE	Save the current document.
	PRINT	Print the current document.
	CUT	Remove selected text and place it on the Clipboard.
	COPY	Copy selected text.
	PASTE	Paste the contents of the Clipboard.
	UNDO	Reverse the last edit.
	REDO	Return to the state before you used the last Undo.
	QUICKFORMAT	Apply an existing format to other text.
	DRAW PICTURE	Draw a picture.
	CLIPART	Insert an image from the Scrapbook.
	DRAW OBJECT	Create shapes or lines.
	TEXT BOX	Create a text box.
	HIGHLIGHT	Toggle the highlighter on or off.
	NUMBERING	Create a numbered list.
	BULLETS	Create a bulleted list.
	COLUMNS	Create a newspaper column.
	TABLE QUICKCREATE	Create a table.
	SPELL CHECK	Start the spell checker.
	ZOOM	Switch between Page and Full Page view.
	CHANGE VIEW	Switch between Page and Web view.
	PERFECTEXPERT	Display the PerfectExpert panel on the left side of the screen.

See Figure 3-2 and Table 3-2 for specifics about the Application bar areas. You will use and understand each of these areas more fully as you continue with each chapter.

TIP If you use a 14-inch monitor, you may not be able to see all the buttons on the toolbar at once.

The Application bar provides easy access to open documents, specific document features, and the insertion point location. Figure 3-2 shows each element in the Application bar, and Table 3-2 describes these elements in more detail.

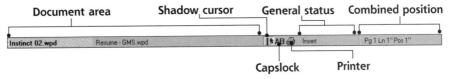

Figure 3-2   Access open documents and features quickly on the Application bar.

TABLE 3-2   WordPerfect Application Bar

Area/Button	Description
DOCUMENT	Indicates the names of your open documents. Click a document # name to use it. Point to a document to see its complete path.
SHADOW CURSOR	Toggles between showing and hiding the shadow cursor.
CAPS LOCK	Turns Caps Lock on and off.
PRINTER	Opens the Print to dialog box. Point to this button to see your current printer.
GENERAL STATUS	Indicates your status at any given time. You will see Insert or Typeover mode here, the current style name, the current column number or table cell, and so on.
COMBINED POSITION	Shows the current page number and the line and position of the insertion point. Click once to display the Go To dialog box.

 TIP If you don't think you'll use the information on the Application bar very much, you can hide it. Just secondary-click the Application bar and then choose Hide Application Bar from the QuickMenu.

A Doc with a View

By default, WordPerfect displays your document in *Page view*, which shows your document close to how it will look when you print it. This includes the fonts, graphics, headers, footers, and other elements you use in your document. If you don't want to be bothered with these extras until your document is near completion, you can use Draft view. Just choose View→Draft or press Ctrl+F5. Draft view will hide page numbers, headers, footers, and a few other elements and will also speed up scrolling a bit. When you're ready to see everything again, choose View→Page or press Alt+F5. You learn about features such as graphics and headers and footers in later chapters and see how some features display differently depending on the view you use.

X-REF For information on customizing toolbars, property bars, and the Application bar, see Chapter 18.

Now that you're a little more comfortable with these WordPerfect window elements, you can start writing. This chapter takes you through the steps of creating a letter to help you learn some basic typing and editing techniques in WordPerfect.

 Table 3-2 shows the default Application bar areas. If you or someone else has customized your Application bar, your areas may not match those in Figure 3-1 or Table 3-2.

X-REF For a complete description of the buttons on the Text property bar, see Chapter 4.

Working with Text

Obviously, one of the main purposes of a word processor is to *process words*, or deal with text. If you're new to word processing, you should know that WordPerfect uses what's called *word wrap* to help control your lines of text. Rather than pressing Enter to move to the next line, you just keep typing. When WordPerfect reaches the right margin, it will automatically move to the next line. You only press Enter to end a paragraph. However, before you begin typing, you learn how to insert an automatic date, because the current date is a crucial element of any business letter.

Inserting the Current Date

Most business letters begin with the current date, followed by the recipient's name and address, then the salutation and body of the letter. WordPerfect contains a Date Text feature that automatically inserts the current date at the insertion point location. This feature saves time and effort by inserting the date correctly. You don't have to worry about checking your calendar or misspelling the month. Keep in mind that the date is based on your computer's clock. If your computer clock is wrong, your automatic date will be, too.

To insert the current date, position the insertion point for the location of the date and press Ctrl+D. WordPerfect inserts the current date using the default date format, which is the month and day, followed by the year.

Selecting a Date Format

If you prefer to have your dates display in a different format, you can select a date format. For example, if you'd rather your date looked like *11/14/97* or *14 November 1997*, you can make the change before or after you've inserted the date text.

To change the date format, follow these steps:

1. Position the insertion point in the location for the date or delete the existing date.

2. Choose ⬛ **Insert** ⬛ → ⬛ **Date/Time** ⬛ to display the Date/Time dialog box (see Figure 3-3). Format types displayed in the Date/Time formats list show an example of how your date will look if you select that type.

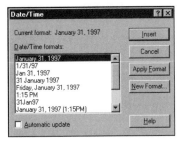

Figure 3-3   Select a new date/time format.

3. In the Date/Time formats list, select the desired format and then click Insert.

TIP   If you select Automatic update in the Date/Time dialog box or press Ctrl+Shift+D at the document window, the date will change so that it always reflects the current date. Use this feature with caution; if you need proof of a date on a document, don't use this feature.

Entering Text

You can type text for the body of your letter just as you would in another word processing program (if you've used one) or on a typewriter — by pressing the keys on your keyboard, using the spacebar to separate words. The main difference from a typewriter is that you only press Enter when you want to end a paragraph, not a line.

To begin, just start typing. If you make a mistake, use the keys described here to correct any mistakes:

* Press the backspace arrow to remove the previous character (the one to the left of the insertion point).

* Press Delete to remove the next character (the one to the right of the insertion point).

Inserting and Replacing Text

If you don't catch a mistake, or if you change your mind about text after you've typed several lines, you can easily make changes without backspacing over everything you've already done. You can insert new text between words or replace existing text with new words. You can also select and delete portions you don't need.

INSERTING NEW TEXT

After rereading the first paragraph of a letter to a consultant you're hiring, you realize that you left out a crucial sentence regarding project deadlines. It's easy to position the insertion point and add the sentence with no one the wiser. Just make sure that you don't see "Typeover" in the General Status area of the Application bar (bottom right side of window). If you do, press Insert. Click in the location for the text you want to insert. This is called *positioning the insertion point*. Then just type the text, including end punctuation and spaces where necessary.

FEATURE FOCUS You can also position the insertion point in an empty part of the document using the shadow cursor. Just point to the empty location for the text and click. WordPerfect inserts the necessary hard returns, tabs, and other codes to position the insertion point properly.

REPLACING TEXT

Oops. The street address for your recipient uses "Street" when it should say "Road." You can replace the text using Typeover. Simply press Insert so that you see "Typeover" in the Insert area of the Application bar (bottom right corner of window). Click to the left of the first character you want to replace and then type your new text. WordPerfect will replace the existing characters with the new ones you're typing.

If the existing word is shorter than the replacement word, you may find yourself typing over text you didn't want to replace. Just keep an eye on your typing and press Insert when you replace the last existing character. WordPerfect then inserts the remaining characters you type, pushing existing characters out of the way. You'll need to delete any extra characters that remain after you replace your text.

To ensure that you only replace the text you want to replace, make sure you are in Insert mode. Next, select the text and type the replacement text. For information on selection techniques, see "Selecting Text" in the next section.

For some quick ways to move around a WordPerfect document, see Table B-3 in Appendix B.

Remember to save your documents frequently. Refer back to Chapter 2 if you need to refresh your memory on how to save a file in an application.

Editing Your Text

It's a rare document that works the first time it falls out of your head and onto the document screen. Inevitably, you'll need to make some serious changes, including moving and copying text from one place to another. You've already seen how to insert and replace text; now you learn how to move, copy, and delete text in your document.

Selecting Text

One of the best things about most applications today is the capability to select blocks of text or data and do something with the blocks. On the screen, selected text appears inverse to your document text. That is, the text will be white on a black background. Once you select text, you can do any number of things with it, as you will see in this and subsequent chapters.

If you've never done it before, selecting text may feel awkward at first, and you may end up selecting too much or too little. Hang in there. With a little practice, you'll be selecting like a pro.

SELECTING WITH THE MOUSE

Once you are used to the mouse, it's the fastest way to select text. Just position the pointer before the first character you want to select. Next, press and hold the primary mouse button, then drag the mouse across until you can see that you've selected the text you want. To select multiple lines of text, drag down or up. When you've selected the text, release the mouse button.

 TIP **If you accidentally release the mouse button before you select all your text or you selected too much text, you can pick up where you left off. Press and hold Shift, and then point to the end of the current selection (where you left off). Click and drag until you've completed the selection, release Shift, and then release the mouse button.**

Table 3-3 describes quick methods for selecting specific text elements. Note that when you select a sentence, WordPerfect includes its punctuation; when you select a paragraph, WordPerfect includes the punctuation and the hard return following the paragraph, if there is one.

TABLE 3-3 WordPerfect Selection Techniques

To Select	Do This
SINGLE WORD	Double-click the word.
SINGLE SENTENCE	Triple-click the sentence or choose Edit→Select→ Sentence.
SINGLE PARAGRAPH	Quadruple-click the paragraph or choose Edit→Select→ Paragragh.
SINGLE PAGE	Choose Edit→Select→Page.
ENTIRE DOCUMENT	Press Ctrl+A or choose Edit→Select→All.

 TIP **If you select a single word, then drag your mouse left or right, WordPerfect will select the text word by word, rather than character by character, as happens when you simply click and drag over text.**

SELECTING WITH THE KEYBOARD

If you haven't broken in those mouse fingers, and your clicking and dragging isn't quite what it could be, relief is in sight. You can also use the keyboard to select text, with some fast ways to select large blocks. Just position the insertion point before the first character you'd like to select and press F8. Now use the arrow keys to select your text.

TIP   When Select mode is on, you can use it in combination with the document navigation keys in Table B-3 in Appendix B to select larger portions of text. You can also press Enter to select to the next paragraph or type any character to select to the next occurrence of that character. You can also display the word "Select" on the Application bar.

Changing the Case of Text

I've occasionally left Caps Lock on, then looked up in horror to see half of my paragraph GLARING AT ME IN UPPERCASE LETTERS.

With the Convert Case feature, you can quickly change the case of letters:

1. Select the text you want to convert.

2. Choose Edit → Convert Case .

3. Select lowercase, UPPERCASE, or Initial Capitals.

Note that the lowercase option converts all selected text to lowercase except "I" and its variations ("I'd," "I'll," and so on). And if you've selected an entire sentence, line, or paragraph with the first character capitalized, WordPerfect will keep it capitalized.

TIP   Press Ctrl+K to switch selected text between uppercase and lowercase.

Moving, Copying, and Deleting Text

If you've ever rearranged the stuff on your desk, you know that feeling when things are just right. Thankfully, WordPerfect lets you rearrange your text, just as you would move your files from one spot to another or place your Rolodex closer to your phone. Once you decide you need to move or copy text, it's easy to do so. You can also move and copy between documents.

MOVING AND COPYING WITH THE WINDOWS CLIPBOARD

The most common method for moving text — especially large blocks — is using the *Windows Clipboard*, which is a temporary holding place for text you move or copy. Once text is on the Clipboard, you can paste it any place in a document.

However, once you cut or copy new text, the new text replaces the existing text on the Clipboard.

Here's how you cut or copy text using the Clipboard:

1. Select the text to move or copy, using one of the selection techniques described previously.

2. Click the Cut button or press Ctrl+X to move the text, or click the Copy button or press Ctrl+C to copy the text. WordPerfect places the text on the Clipboard.

3. Position the insertion point in the location for the moved or copied text and click the Paste button or press Ctrl+V. WordPerfect inserts the text in the new location, leaving a copy of the text on the Clipboard. If you want, you could position the insertion point in a different location and paste the same text again.

 TIP   You can also choose Edit→Cut, Edit→Copy, and Edit→Paste.

To move or copy text between documents, use the techniques described in Chapter 2 for moving between files within an application, before cutting, copying, or pasting.

MOVING AND COPYING USING DRAG AND DROP

If you don't need to have cut or copied text on the Clipboard and you don't need to move or copy the text very far from its place of origin, try using drag and drop. This means that after you select text, you can drag it to another location, bypassing the Cut and Copy commands altogether. Keep in mind that though this method can be faster, it doesn't place a copy of the text on the Clipboard, so you can't paste it over and over in a document.

To move or copy using drag and drop, follow these steps:

1. Select the text to move or copy, using one of the selection techniques described previously.

 2. Point to the selection, and then click and drag toward its new location. As you drag, you'll see the move pointer and a dotted insertion point following you.

 3. When the dotted insertion point is in the new location, release the mouse button. To copy the text, press and hold Ctrl before releasing the mouse button so you see the copy pointer. Then release the mouse button.

TIP If your destination is not immediately visible, that's okay. Just keep dragging past the top or bottom of the window, and WordPerfect will scroll the document automatically to display additional text.

FEATURE FOCUS You can click and drag between open documents. Select the text you wish to move or copy, then drag so that it covers the document name on the Application bar and continue pressing the mouse button. When WordPerfect displays the target document, position the pointer in the location for the new text and release the mouse button. To copy the text, press and hold Ctrl before releasing the mouse button.

DELETING TEXT

If rearranging your desk includes tossing a few unnecessary items into the garbage, you have the equivalent in WordPerfect when you delete text. And, like your garbage can, you can still retrieve deleted text (up to the last three deletions) before the night folks haul it off permanently. (You learn more about this in the next section.)

To delete text, select it and press Delete. Wow, that was pretty difficult, wasn't it? Seriously, the fact that it's so easy to delete text makes the next section a must-have. Let's see how you can resurrect deleted text or undo an editing mistake you made.

Undoing Your Mistakes

As I mentioned in the previous section, deleting text is very easy in WordPerfect. No warning; no flag waving; just the press of a button and it disappears. Luckily, if you delete text and decide you really didn't want to get rid of it, you can use the Undelete feature to restore it. Additionally, WordPerfect has an Undo feature, which "undoes" the last edit you made. This could be a deletion, or it could be a paste, a cut, or another editing or formatting task.

The difference between Undelete and Undo is simple: *Undelete* restores deleted text in the insertion point location. *Undo* returns your document to its previous state before the most recent action. Got it? Okay, let's see how these two help save you from yourself.

Using Undelete

So you selected a whole slew of paragraphs and wanted to move them. Instead, you deleted them. Bummer. But wait, you can bring them back. No, it's not some weird seance thing; it's the Undelete feature. Undelete stores the last three deletions you made, allowing you to restore them at the current insertion point location.

To use Undelete, follow these steps:

1. Position the insertion point in the location you want to restore the deleted text. Note that you can restore the deleted text *anywhere*, not just in the location where you deleted it.

2. Press Ctrl+Shift+Z. WordPerfect displays the Undelete box and inserts the most recent deletion at the insertion point location. Notice that the deleted text is selected. This is to call your attention to it and to allow you to make a selection in the Undelete box.

 TIP **Click and drag the Undelete title bar to move the dialog box if you can't see the text behind it.**

3. Click Restore to insert the selected text into your document, or Next or Previous to display another deletion.

 TIP **Many folks — myself included — use Undelete for cut and copy. It's nice to get a preview of your text before you actually paste the text in, and Undelete allows you to do this before you restore your deletion.**

Using Undo

The previous feature — Undelete — allows you to restore text you've deleted in any location. But if you need more powerful "Oops" insurance, check out Undo and Redo. As I mentioned before, Undo reverses the last action you performed, whether it's a deletion, a paste, a drag-and-drop move, or a sentence you typed that you no longer need.

To use Undo, click the Undo button or choose Edit→Undo. You can also press Ctrl+Z. WordPerfect automatically reverses the last action you performed. For example, if the last thing you did was select text and cut it, WordPerfect returns the text to the document. If you typed four words and then used Undo, the words disappear.

 You can't undo every action. For example, you can't undo a save or undo sending a document to the printer. Generally speaking, you can use undo for any editing and formatting actions you perform.

Using Redo

Some people say it's a *woman's* prerogative to change her mind but I say it's *anyone's* prerogative — especially when it comes to creating documents. So if you just used Undo to remove those four words you typed, you can use Redo to bring them back.

To use Redo, click the Redo button or choose Edit→Redo. You can also press Ctrl+Shift+R. WordPerfect undoes your undo.

As you work on documents, you should save often. If you haven't saved the document yet, do so using the steps you learned in Chapter 2. Once you've saved it on disk, remember to click the Save button on the toolbar periodically to save your work with any changes you've made since the last save.

Printing Your Document

Once you've perfected the text in your document — especially if it's a letter — you'll want to print it out and distribute it or send it to the appropriate recipients — or just admire the great job you did on paper. You can also create and print an envelope from an open document that contains an address.

 TIP Before printing any document, you should run the Spell Checker. If you need help doing this, refer to Chapter 2.

Printing a Document

WordPerfect provides a wealth of printing options, including printing a single page, printing multiple copies of a document, and printing two-sided documents (automatically if your printer supports this option or manually if it does not).

To print a document, follow these steps:

1. With the document you wish to print open, click the Print button on either the WordPerfect 8 toolbar or the Applications bar, or choose **File** → **Print** to display the Print to dialog box (see Figure 3-4). You choose your printing options here. Notice the name of your printer and its port appear in the dialog box title bar.

Your selected printer and port

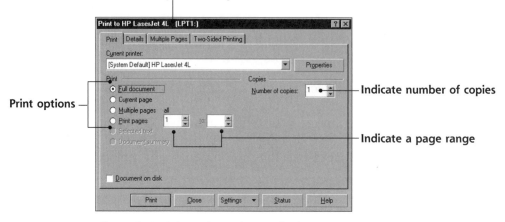

Print options

Indicate number of copies

Indicate a page range

Figure 3-4 Select print options and print a document.

2. Under Print, choose what you'd like to print: Full document, Current page, Multiple pages, or Print pages. If you've selected text before opening the Print to dialog box, WordPerfect makes the Selected text option active. For information on printing multiple pages, see the information that follows these steps.

3. If you selected Print pages, type the range of pages in the associated text boxes, indicating the starting page in the first text box and the ending page in the to text box.

4. Indicate the number of copies to print in the Number of copies text box.

5. Click Print. WordPerfect sends the pages you specify to your printer, printing multiple copies if you indicated more than one under Copies.

If you want to pick and choose the pages you print because you've only made corrections to a few of them, use the Multiple Pages tab in the Print to dialog box and the examples here to do so:

* Type **7-** to print page 7 through the end of the document.
* Type **-7** to print the first page through page 7.
* Type **2 4 7** to print pages 2, 4, and 7.
* Type **6-8, 10** to print pages 6 through 8 inclusively, and page 10.
* Type **iii** to print roman numeral page iii.

Printing an Envelope

You just finished printing your beautiful letter and now you'd like something to put it in. No problem. With WordPerfect's Envelope feature, you can print an envelope in a matter of seconds. The default size for the envelope feature is a standard #10 envelope. However, you can select a different size, if necessary.

To print an envelope from an existing document, follow these steps:

1. With the document containing the address open, choose **Format** → **Envelope**. WordPerfect locates and selects the address in your document, and then displays the Envelope dialog box (see Figure 3-5). Notice that your recipient's address appears in the Mailing addresses box.

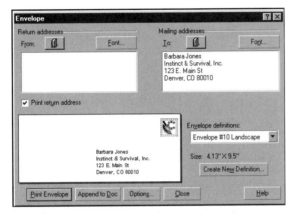

Figure 3-5 Print an envelope using your document address.

2. If you want to include a return address, type it into the Return addresses box, pressing Enter to end each line. If you will use an envelope preprinted with your return address, choose Print return address to clear the check box.

TIP If you've added entries to your Address Book, you can click the Address Book button to open your Address Book and select an addresses to use as the return address. For more on the Address Book, see Chapter 1.

3. You can change the fonts for the Return and Mailing address if desired as well as pick a different envelope size. Note that the post office prefers all caps, no punctuation, and a *sans serif* font such as Arial for accurate address scanning.

4. To send the envelope directly to the printer, click Print Envelope, or to place it at the end of your document to print later, click Append to Doc. Depending on your printer and its attachments, WordPerfect may prompt you to insert an envelope.

X-REF For more information on Fonts, see Chapter 4.

TIP When you're finished using a document, it's a good idea to close it if you don't need it open. If you need to refresh your memory on closing files, refer to Chapter 2.

BONUS

Inserting Repetitive Text

Have you ever had a situation where you needed to insert the same text over and over? Perhaps you must refer to a company name throughout a document or need to refer to the title of a manual. You could copy the text, then paste it throughout the document, but this assumes you can paste it where you want it all at one time before you replace the text with something else on the Windows Clipboard.

If it's a common phrase that you don't mind WordPerfect changing automatically, use QuickCorrect to insert it (see Chapter 2). If it's a phrase you may only use in a few documents, and one that you want more control over, use the QuickWords feature. QuickWords lets you name a block of text using a shorter name and then insert it wherever you need it. QuickWords can include text, graphics, lines, and any formatting you may need.

Creating a QuickWord Entry

As I mentioned, a QuickWord allows you to enter frequently used or complicated text (such as medical or scientific terms) using a shortcut or abbreviated version of the text. A good use of a QuickWord would be a letter closing, which would contain the closing phrase — "Sincerely," or "Best regards," — several blank lines for the signature, and the name typed out. Depending on the letter style you're using, the closing may be against the left margin or indented toward the center of the page.

To create a QuickWord entry, follow these steps:

1. Type the longer version of the text you wish to insert using a QuickWord, and then select it. If the text already exists in your document, just select it. For example, if you want "meb" to insert "Martin, Enderlyn, and

Bates, Inc.," type **Martin, Enderlyn, and Bates, Inc.** and select it. If the text already exists in the document, select it there rather than typing it again.

2. Click the QuickWords button on the Selected Text property bar or choose **Tools** → **QuickWords** to display the QuickWords tab in the QuickCorrect dialog box (see Figure 3-6). WordPerfect provides a few default QuickWords for your use; these are indicated with a backslash before the word. You can delete these if you don't think you'll use them.

Type QuickWord for selected text

Figure 3-6 Create shortcuts for repetitive text using QuickWords.

Default and exisiting QuickWords

Preview of selected QuickWord

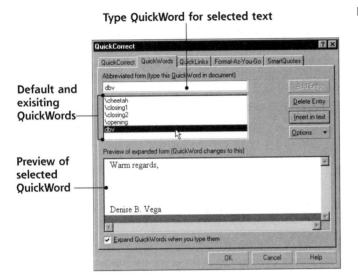

3. In the Abbreviated form (type this QuickWord in document) text box, type the short form you want to use for the selected text. Choose something that is short, yet accurately reflects the longer text it will insert. Do *not* use a real word! If you do, WordPerfect will expand it automatically when you press the spacebar, even when you want to use the word as is.

4. If you want the text to insert without any existing formatting, click Options, and then select Expand as Plain text from the pop-down menu.

5. Click Add Entry. WordPerfect adds the QuickWord to the list and returns to the document window.

QuickWord names are case sensitive. This means that each of the following is a different QuickWord: "meb," "Meb," "MEB," "MeB," and so on.

Using a QuickWord

Once you've created a QuickWord, it is stored and available for all new documents you create with the default *template*, which is a special file that holds a lot of default formatting in addition to QuickWords. You can access the QuickWord whenever you need it.

To insert a QuickWord, position the insertion point in the location for the text. Type the QuickWord name (for example, **meb** or **fyi**), and then press the spacebar. WordPerfect replaces the name with the full text stored in the QuickWord. If punctuation will follow your full text, and you don't want the extra space, type the QuickWord and then press Ctrl+Shift+A. WordPerfect replaces the name and you aren't left with a space after the text.

TIP   If you absolutely can't remember your QuickWord name, you can choose Tools→QuickWords and select the QuickWord name in the list box. Click Insert in text.

Summary

In this chapter, you began your journey through WordPerfect and word processing by learning about the WordPerfect window. You also learned how to insert the current date, enter and edit text, and print a document. Further, you learned how to change the case of text and fix your boo-boos using Undelete and Undo. Next, you'll get into document makeovers — formatting text and other fancy stuff.

CHANGING THE LOOK OF A RÉSUMÉ

IN THIS CHAPTER YOU LEARN THESE KEY SKILLS

FORMATTING TEXT   PAGE   76

FORMATTING PARAGRAPHS   PAGE   80

FINDING AND REPLACING TEXT   PAGE   83

USING STYLES   PAGE   86

4

Have you ever looked at a document and asked how someone made the heading bigger than the rest of the document? Or wondered how to make text stand out with bold and italics? In this chapter, you explore several formatting techniques by creating your own résumé. You can use these techniques in any document, but it helps to see how they can affect a document with which you are familiar. Note that throughout the chapter I refer to *codes*. These are invisible items WordPerfect places in your document to mark formatting and other elements. For more information on codes, see the Bonus section, "Checking under the Hood with Reveal Codes," later in this chapter.

For many of these techniques, you will use the Text property bar, which is the default property bar in WordPerfect and works a bit differently than the toolbar (see Figure 4-1). Notice that you have several drop-down lists. Also, these buttons will change to reflect current settings. For example, if you select text and click the Bold button, the button will appear depressed whenever the insertion point is inside the bold text. This tells you that the Bold feature is active. Other buttons will reflect the setting for the text at the current insertion point location. For example, if you change your justification to Center, the Justification button will show the Center icon for that text when you place the insertion point in the centered text. If you change text color, the Text Color button will reflect the color for the current text. Because the button icon can change, I don't use a picture of the buttons next to steps referring to them.

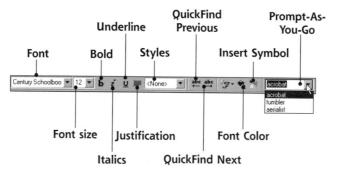

Figure 4-1 Format text using the Text property bar.

NOTE As I mentioned in Chapter 1, the Prompt-As-You-Go box provides writing assistance on the fly, indicating possible spelling and grammar problems, as well as offering synonyms, depending on where the insertion point is located in your text. In Figure 4-1, the Prompt-As-You-Go is acting as a thesaurus, providing alternatives to the word in which the insertion point is located — acrobat.

Remember that property bars are context-sensitive, and if you select text in the document, WordPerfect displays the Selected Text property bar with different buttons that provide options unique to selected text. These options include such things as creating a QuickWord (as you saw in the Bonus section in Chapter 3) and creating a hyperlink. For more on hyperlinks, see Chapter 17.

Formatting Text

This chapter focuses on learning basic formatting techniques to improve the appearance and readability of a document. Though you're using a résumé as an example, you'll concentrate on formatting the text, and not the do's and don'ts of résumé layout, and so on. You can find out more about designing a résumé in a number of books available on the subject, including *Résumés For Dummies* from IDG Books Worldwide, Inc.

Remember, if you format text and then decide you don't like the result, you can also use the Undo feature. Refer back to Chapter 3 if you need a refresher on Undo.

Justifying Text

You can design your résumé any number of ways. One of the first things you'll need to decide when you begin is where you will place your personal information, such as your name, address, and phone number. You can align it in several ways (see Figure 4-2).

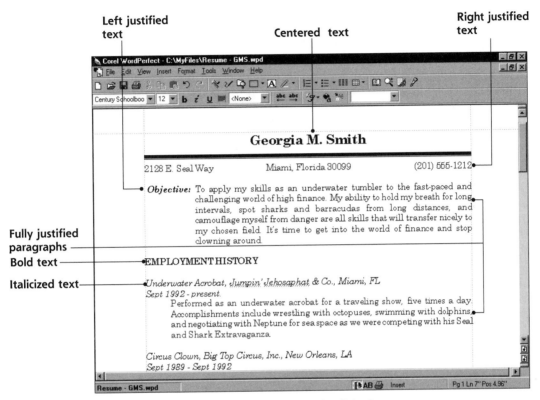

Figure 4-2 Examples of justified, bold, and italicized text.

Here's how to justify text:

1. Type the text you want to justify and then select it.

X-REF **For a refresher on selecting text, see "Selecting Text" in Chapter 3.**

2. Click the Justification button on the Text property bar to display the pop-down list, then select the desired justification. WordPerfect justifies the text, keeping it selected so that you can perform additional formats on it, if you want.

3. Click after the last character in the last line to position the insertion point and deselect the text. Then press Enter.

If the justification is still in effect, change it back by clicking the Justification button on the Text property bar and selecting a different justification as desired.

> **TIP** You can also choose Format→Justification and select the desired justification or the shortcut keys for any of them. You can turn justification off and on throughout your documents to get the look you want.

If you want to format a single line, position the insertion point before the first character in the line and press Shift+F7 to center it or Alt+F7 to align it flush right. Note that when you right-justify a single line using this shortcut, WordPerfect refers to it as flush right. You can also find these features by choosing Format→Line.

Working with Fonts

A *font* is the appearance of characters — whether the lines making them up are curved or straight, thick or thin, fancy or standard. A *font size* controls the height and width of a character within a *font family*. You know, that crazy family that lives around the corner. Okay, so there probably isn't a *font family* in your neighborhood, but there are several living in your system. See Figure 4-3 for some font examples.

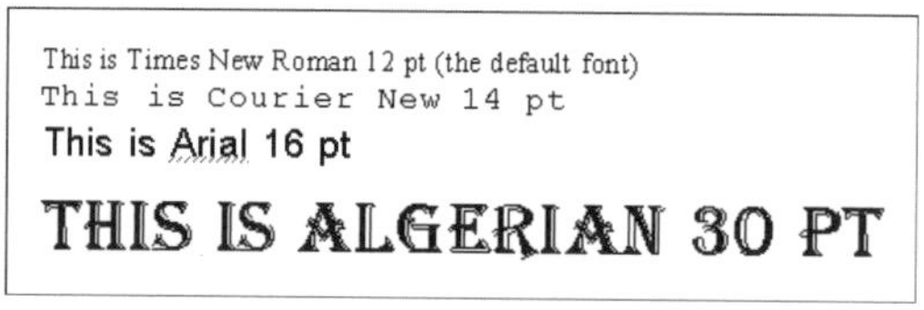

```
This is Times New Roman 12 pt (the default font)
This is Courier New 14 pt
This is Arial 16 pt
THIS IS ALGERIAN 30 PT
```

Figure 4-3 A sampling of fonts.

WordPerfect provides two main methods for applying a font to your document — the Text property bar and the Font dialog box. If you only want to change the font face, size, or color, you can use the property bar. If you want to get a little fancier, like using small caps or superscript, you need to use the Font dialog box.

Adding Fonts with the Property Bar

The font you choose can help convey your message in a document. In a résumé, for example, you wouldn't want to pick a script-type font because it would be difficult to read and is usually used for invitations and announcements, not professional presentations.

In WordPerfect, you can quickly change fonts and font sizes in your document using the property bar. If you select text first, choosing another font will only change the selected text. If you position the insertion point before a character, the font you choose will affect all text (new or existing) from that point on, or until WordPerfect encounters another font change.

TIP A good design rule of thumb: avoid using too many different fonts and sizes in a single document. Most design books say to limit it to two, three at the most, because any more often makes the document confusing to read and messy.

To change the font and font size, select the text you want to format, or if you want the font to affect all text from the insertion point forward, position the insertion point in the location for the font to begin affecting text. Click the Font and Font Size down-arrow buttons on the Property Bar to display the list of available fonts and sizes, and then select the desired font.

FEATURE FOCUS When you point to a font in the list, WordPerfect displays a sample to the right of the list.

TIP To format selected text with a font and font size you've used previously, click the QuickFonts button on the property bar and select the desired font.

Adding Text Enhancements

Changing fonts can really make an impact on your document, but you may also want to emphasize particular words or phrases to call attention to them. For example, you will probably want to call attention to your name, and possibly the rest of your personal information, using **bold**. You may also want to indicate subtopics, such as the location and duration of a job, in *italics*. Refer back to Figure 4-2 for examples of bold and italicized text.

To add a text enhancement to existing text, select the text and choose one of the following text enhancements. Notice that the button depresses to indicate it is in use.

* To bold text, click the Bold button or press Ctrl+B.
* To italicize text, click the Italics button or press Ctrl+I.
* To underline text, click the Underline button or press Ctrl+U.

Formatting Paragraphs

In addition to using justification to make paragraphs stand out, you can also use indents and paragraph margin adjustments to indicate a change of topic. For example, in a résumé, you may want to indent each job description beneath its heading to set it apart. You can have three types of left indents: first line indent, standard indent, and a hanging indent (sometimes known as an *outdent*). You also can create a double indent, which indents both the left and right sides of the paragraph. Figure 4-4 provides a visual description of each of these types. Now you explore the various ways you can make your paragraphs work for you by using indents.

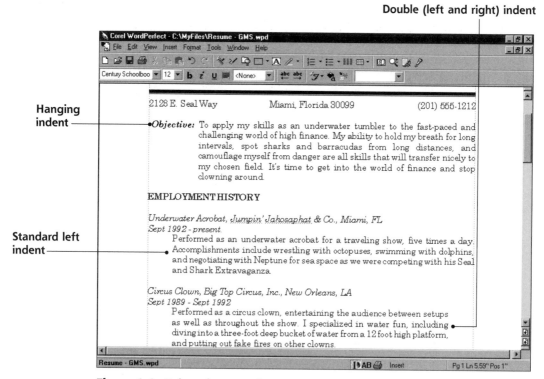

Figure 4-4 Indented paragraphs.

Setting Indents and Paragraph Spacing

Many books and newsletters use a first line indent and spacing between paragraphs to help the flow of the text. For example, they may indent the first line the equivalent of three or four characters and have a space equal to one and one-half lines between each paragraph. Using the Paragraph Format feature, you can set the first line indent and indicate the amount of spacing you want between paragraphs when you press Enter. This can save you from pressing Tab before each paragraph and pressing Enter two or three times to create the spacing you want. This formatting is great for letters, résumés, newsletters, and other documents.

INDENTING PARAGRAPHS USING KEYSTROKES

You can quickly indent paragraphs using keystrokes. Position the insertion point before the first character in the paragraph you wish to indent, then use one of the methods in Table 4-1. This indenting follows the current tab stops.

X-REF For more on tabs and tab sets, check out Chapter 6.

TABLE 4-1 Indent Shortcuts

To Insert	Do This
LEFT INDENT	Press F7 or choose Format→Paragaph→Indent
HANGING INDENT	Press Ctrl+F7 or choose Format→Paragaph→Hanging Indent
DOUBLE INDENT	Press Ctrl+Shift+F7 or choose Format→Paragaph→Double Indent

INDENTING PARAGRAPHS USING THE RULER

Expert mousers can use the Ruler to click and drag your way to indented paragraphs. If you're not an expert mouser, or you are but don't like the idea of trying to maneuver a teeny tiny triangle across a ruler, skip this section altogether. However, if you like a dexterity challenge, read on.

First, choose View→Ruler to display the Ruler (see Figure 4-5).

First Line Indent marker   Left Indent marker   Right Indent marker

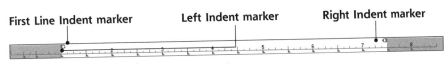

Figure 4-5 Format paragraphs on the Ruler.

With the text selected or the insertion point positioned where you want the indents to begin, click and drag the appropriate marker to the desired indent location on the Ruler. To create a hanging indent, click and drag the Left Indent marker (the small, bottom triangle) to the right. Next, click and drag the First Line Indent marker (the small, top triangle) to the left where you want the first line to hang.

FORMATTING CUSTOM PARAGRAPHS AND SPACING

If you want more control over when and how your paragraphs format, you can use the Format Paragraph dialog box. Here you can set specific indents, set paragraph margins, and set spacing between paragraphs. For example, if you can hark back to your school report days, you may remember that if you had a quotation longer than two lines, you were supposed to place it in a separate paragraph and indent it from the left and right without quotation marks. This is an excellent way to set off a phrase on your résumé, such as the following:

Complete list of references, publication credits, and project awards available upon request.

To set paragraph formatting, follow these steps:

1. Position the insertion point anywhere in the paragraph to format, or select existing paragraphs you wish to format.

2. Choose Format → Paragraph → Format to display the Paragraph Format dialog box.

3. Set your options according to the following and then click OK:

   * Use First line indent to indent the first line of all paragraphs. The default is one-half inch, though many documents use .25" or .3".

   * Use Spacing between paragraphs to add space between each paragraph without having to press Enter.

   * Use Paragraph adjustments to set left and right paragraph margin adjustments.

TIP To create a hanging indent, type a negative number in the First line indent text box in the Format Paragraph dialog box.

SIDE TRIP

SQUEEZING INTO A SIZE 5

Remember when your teacher said your essay on blue whales should be three pages long, and yours was barely two so you wrote REALLY BIG? And now that you're an adult and could write three pages, many "experts" say you should try to limit your résumé to one page, even though a single page can't do justice to your stellar list of achievements. What's a student or job hunter to do? Use WordPerfect's Make It Fit feature, that's what:

1. With the document you need to adjust open, choose Format → Make It Fit to display the Make It Fit dialog box.

(continued)

2. In the Desired number of pages text box, type your page maximum, and under Items to adjust, indicate which items WordPerfect can fiddle with when performing the big squeeze or expansion. If you can't or don't want to change the font size, make sure that this check box is not selected.

3. Click Make It Fit. WordPerfect makes several passes through the document, making adjustments to the formatting to make it fit your page restriction.

This feature can be a real lifesaver when you find, for example, that you have typed a long letter, and the signature block is in solitary splendor on the last page! Note that if you don't like the end result, you can use Undo to return the document to its original state.

Finding and Replacing Text

4

You've just created a document and printed it out. You review the text and realize that you need to revise some text several pages into your document. You open the document in WordPerfect and start scrolling through the document page by page, looking for text, right? This might be easy for a one-page résumé, but for longer documents, it can get pretty tedious. With the Find and Replace Text feature, you can quickly locate a word or phrase and make any changes you need to make. Additionally, if you used the word "boss" and have decided, instead, to use "supervisor," you can have WordPerfect replace every instance of "boss" with "supervisor."

Finding Text

You can use the Find and Replace Text feature to locate a word, phrase, or even a specific code in your document. The text you ask WordPerfect to search for is sometimes referred to as the *search string*. The feature locates the first instance of the search string, and you can instruct WordPerfect to look for the next instance if the first one is not what you want. Also, WordPerfect defaults to locate the exact text in your search string, so if you're looking for "project," WordPerfect will find "project" as well as "projects," "projection," and "projecting." However, you can force WordPerfect to look only for the whole word.

To locate text using the Find and Replace Text feature, follow these steps:

1. With the document you want to search open in WordPerfect, position the insertion point at the top of the document. (Just press Ctrl+Home, and you'll be there!)

2. Choose [Edit] → [Find and Replace], or press Ctrl+F. WordPerfect displays the Find and Replace Text dialog box (see Figure 4-6), with the insertion point blinking in the Find text box. Notice that this dialog box contains its own menu bar from which you can select a variety of search options. You'll learn about many of these in a moment.

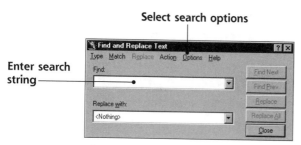

Select search options

Enter search string

Figure 4-6 Locate and replace text quickly using Find and Replace Text.

3. In the Find text box, type the text you want to locate. If you suspect that there may be more than one occurrence of the text, try to enter as much as possible to make the search string unique.

4. Choose [Match] on the Find and Replace Text menu bar and indicate any options you wish to use. Refer to Table 4-2 for assistance.

5. Click Find Next. WordPerfect stops at the first occurrence of your search string. By default, WordPerfect selects the search string in your document, leaving the Find and Replace Text dialog box. You can move between the document and the Find and Replace Text dialog box if needed.

6. If this is the occurrence for which you were looking, click Close to close the Find and Replace Text dialog box and begin working in your document. Otherwise, click Find Next until you locate the desired occurrence.

7. When WordPerfect displays the Not Found message box, click OK and then Close. This message tells you that WordPerfect has reached the end of the document and that there are no more occurrences of the search string.

TABLE 4-2 Match Options in Find

Option	Description
WHOLE WORD	Locates search text as a whole word. For example, if you use this option to locate "remain," WordPerfect will find "remain" but not "remaining" or "remainder."

Option	Description
CASE	Locates search text only if it uses the same case. If you use this option to locate "Manager," WordPerfect will skip "manager" in lowercase. This option is turned off by default.
FONT	Locates a specific font, either by itself or in conjunction with your search text. For example, if you use this option to locate "office" using the New Century Schoolbook font, WordPerfect will skip "office" when it's formatted with Times New Roman.
CODES	Locates specific codes, either by themselves or in conjunction with your search string. For example, you could search for "Awards and Certifications" when it is centered in the document by inserting a Center code before the search text.

TIP You can return to previous occurrences of your search string by clicking Find Prev in the Find and Replace Text dialog box.

Replacing Text

You probably noticed that the Find and Replace Text dialog box contained a Replace with text box in addition to the Find text box. Use this box when you want to replace the search text with different text. For example, if you misspelled a company name throughout your résumé, you can easily fix it by replacing the misspelled name with the correct name. WordPerfect provides two types of replacements, both of which you'll learn how to use in a moment:

* *Automatic replacement* means WordPerfect replaces every occurrence of the search string with the contents of the Replace with text box.

* *Confirming a replacement* means WordPerfect stops at each occurrence and waits for you to decide if you will replace it with the contents of the Replace with text box or not. This is helpful when you're not sure you want to replace every instance.

To replace text, follow these steps:

1. With the document open, choose Edit → Find and Replace or press Ctrl+F to display the Find and Replace Text dialog box.

2. If the insertion point isn't at the top of the document and you want to begin there, choose Options → Begin Find at Top of Document on the Find and Replace Text menu bar.

3. In the Find text box, type the text you want to locate and set any options using Match.

4. In the Replace with text box, type the replacement text. If you want to set any options for the replace text, choose Replace on the Find and Replace Text menu bar and make your selections.

5. Click Find Next. WordPerfect stops at the first occurrence of the search string. Choose one of the following for your next action:

   ✴ Find Next skips this occurrence and locates the next one.

   ✴ Find Prev returns to the previous occurrence.

   ✴ Replace replaces this occurrence and locates the next one.

   ✴ Replace All replaces this occurrence and all future occurrences in the document.

6. When you reach the end of the document, click Close to close the Find and Replace Text dialog box.

 TIP **You can Undo a series of replacements if you change your mind.**

Using Styles

S tyles allow you to apply several formats to text at once. For example, you will want the headings for your résumé — Employment History, Education, References — to share a common look. Perhaps you want them all to be Times New Roman 14 point bold with a hanging indent. You can give this group of formats a style name, then use the name to format each heading. It's like recording your favorite show on your VCR every week. You indicate the program number (style name), then tell the VCR to tape a show on Channel 7 at 9 p.m. every Thursday (the formatting). The VCR automatically records when you turn it on. You can use this program number over and over to record the same program (format similar headings.)

And the biggest advantage to styles? If you change your mind about the look of your headings, you need only change the formatting in the style. All headings formatted with the style change automatically.

WordPerfect provides three types of styles— paragraph, character, and document. The third — document — works like an open code; it formats all text following the code until WordPerfect encounters another open style code that changes the formatting or a regular formatting code. Because you will use paragraph and character styles more frequently, I explore these in detail here.

Understanding Style Chaining

Most styles have a style name, description, and the formatting codes you want to use when formatting text with the style. There is also another element, referred to as *chaining*, that allows you to start one style automatically after another has ended. This is very useful if you will use your styles as you type your text. The Enter key controls style chaining, and when you chain styles, you'll actually chain the Enter key. After you've turned on a style and typed the text you wish to be formatted by it, pressing Enter will cause the style to chain to another style (or to the same style), or it will act as a normal hard return, depending on the option you select.

With the Styles feature, you can chain the Enter key to the following elements:

* *<None>*. This style breaks the chain. Enter will perform as it normally does, turning off the style and positioning the insertion point on the next line.

* *<Same Style>*. This style effectively repeats the style formatting for the very next paragraph (paragraph style) or word(s) (character style).

* Any style in your style list. All styles listed in the drop-down menu. See "Editing a Style Using the Styles Editor" later in the chapter for details on accessing the dialog box that controls chaining

Creating and Using Styles

A *paragraph style* allows you to automatically format a paragraph, which Corel WordPerfect identifies by the hard return at the end of text. This style is best for headings or full paragraphs that need a similar look — for example, if you want all quoted material longer than three lines indented and italicized.

A *character style* allows you to format text contained *within* paragraphs. For example, perhaps you refer to several company names throughout your document and want each one to be bold and italicized. Because the company names will appear within sentences and don't stand by themselves as separate paragraphs, you will need to format them with character styles.

WordPerfect provides two types of paragraph and character styles — *paired* and *paired-auto*. A paired style works like a paired code and turns on and off around the paragraph or text it formats. To edit a paired style, you must use the Styles Editor dialog box. A paired-auto style works exactly like a paired style except that you can edit the style right in the document. The disadvantage of paired-auto styles is that you can't include such things as graphics, graphic lines, and certain other elements. To use these in your style, you must use the paired style type and create it using the Styles Editor.

CREATING A STYLE WITH QUICKSTYLE

As I mentioned previously, you create paragraph styles for headings and para-graphs that you want to maintain a consistent appearance. Let's look at the fastest way to create a style— using QuickStyle. With QuickStyle, you can create a style from existing formats, and WordPerfect automatically assigns it the paired-auto type. QuickStyle "copies" existing formatting into a style that you name, saving it so you can use it again and again.

To create a style using QuickStyle, follow these steps:

1. Format the text using the formatting you'd like in the style, if you haven't already done so. For paragraphs, you can include justification, paragraph margins, paragraph borders, and other paragraph formatting.

QuickStyle won't pick up indents, tabs, line alignment, and other single code formats. To indent, use the **Format Paragraph** dialog box, and to align, use justification, *not* **Shift+F7** or **Alt+F7**.

2. Position the insertion point anywhere in the formatted text and click the down arrow on the Styles button on the Text property bar. Then choose QuickStyle from the bottom of the list. WordPerfect displays the QuickStyle dialog box (see Figure 4-7).

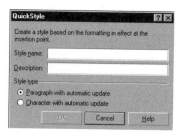

Figure 4-7 Create a style from existing formats.

3. In the Style name text box, type a name for the style. Keep this name short but indicative of its purpose. For example, you may call it "Résumé Head."

4. In the Description text box, type a description for the style. The description appears at the bottom of the Styles List dialog box when you select the style in the list. You may want to include specific formatting information, such as the font, size, any character enhancements, and so on.

5. Under Style type, indicate the style type: Paragraph with automatic update or Character with automatic update.

6. Click OK. WordPerfect adds the style to the list where it is available for use. It also removes the formatting codes for the text you used for the QuickStyle and replaces them with the style code you created.

TIP **If you want to add graphics or other elements to a style, create it using QuickStyle, and then edit it to include the other elements. See "Editing a Style Using the Styles Editor" later in the chapter for more information.**

USING A STYLE

Once you've created your style, you can use it on new or existing paragraphs. Follow these steps to apply your styles to paragraphs.

To format an existing paragraph, place the insertion point anywhere within the paragraph. Next, click the Styles down-arrow button on the Text property bar, then select the style from the list. To format existing text using a character style, select the text, click the Styles down-arrow button on the Selected Text property bar, and select the style from the list.

If you want to use a style for text you haven't typed yet, select the style from the Styles list, type the text, then select the style again to turn it off.

You can also access your styles by choosing format→Styles or pressing Alt+F8 to display the Styles List dialog box. Next, select the style in the Name list box and click Apply.

Editing a Style

At the beginning of the section on styles, I mentioned that one of the best things about styles is that it makes it easy for you to change the formatting of text. If text is formatted by the Résumé Head style, and you decide you'd rather use Arial Narrow instead of Arial, just make the change in the style. All headings will the use Arial Narrow.

EDITING A PAIRED-AUTO STYLE

Earlier I mentioned that the difference between a paragraph or character paired style and a paired-auto style is that you can edit the paired-auto style right in the document.

Here's how:

1. Position the insertion point in the text formatted with the paired-auto style you want to edit.

2. Make the desired changes, selecting new fonts, colors, indenting, or other settings. WordPerfect changes the style to reflect these changes. If you edit the style in the Styles Editor, you'll see new or changed codes to reflect the changes you made here.

EDITING A STYLE USING THE STYLES EDITOR

If the style you want to edit isn't a paired-auto style, or you need to add elements that QuickStyle didn't pick up, you can use the Styles Editor dialog box. This is also helpful to see what is happening "behind the scenes."

1. Choose **Format** → **Styles** or press Alt+F8 to display the Styles List dialog box. In addition to any styles you've created — which WordPerfect refers to as *user styles* — WordPerfect lists *system* styles. System styles ship with WordPerfect and provide formatting for common tasks, such as headings for a table of contents.

2. Select the style you want to edit and click Edit to display the Styles Editor dialog box (see Figure 4-8). This is where you can change the name or description, as well as add, remove, or change the formatting codes for a style.

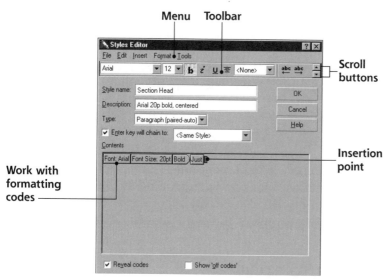

Figure 4-8 Add or change style elements in the Styles Editor dialog box.

3. Change the name and description if desired.

4. Click in the Contents box to position the insertion point. Here you use the Styles Editor menu to insert formatting codes. If your style will format something like a résumé heading, you will use the Format menu option frequently.

5. Use the Styles Editor menu and toolbar to select the formatting you want to include in the style. For example, if you want to include Arial 14 point with small caps bold, use the Font, Size, and Bold buttons on the Styles Editor toolbar. If you want to insert a horizontal line or a picture, choose

`Insert` → `Graphics` and then make your selections. WordPerfect inserts the codes for your selections into the Contents box.

TIP Use the scroll buttons to display additional buttons for the toolbar.

6. After you finish inserting the codes, click OK. Your style name appears in the list, and WordPerfect selects it automatically.

FEATURE FOCUS The toolbar in the Styles Editor dialog box provides easy access to the most common formatting features.

X-REF You delete codes just as you do in the Reveal Codes window. For more information, see the Bonus section, "Checking under the Hood with Reveal Codes," at the end of this chapter.

You can also insert text and other codes — such as hard returns, tabs, and indents — into a style. Use the Insert menu in the Styles Editor dialog box or shortcut keys to insert the codes. And note that you can Undo your changes by choosing Edit→Undo on the Styles Editor menu.

TIP To quickly edit a specific style, locate the style in Reveal Codes and double-click it. See the Bonus section for more on Reveal Codes.

Deleting a Style

Sometimes, if you use styles from one document in another document, styles appear in the styles list that you don't need. You can easily remove these styles from the list. Deleting styles only affects the list in the current document and will not affect the style in other documents. For more information on using styles in other documents, see "Stylish Documents" below.

When you choose to delete a style, WordPerfect provides two options:

* *Including formatting codes* will remove the style and the formatting codes associated with the style.

* *Leave formatting codes in document* will remove the style but leave the formatting codes so they will continue to format the text.

To delete a style, follow these steps:

1. With the document containing the style open, choose Format → Styles or press Alt+F8 to display the Styles List dialog box.

2. In the Name list box, select the style you want to delete. Click Options and select Delete from the pop-down menu. Alternatively, you can press Delete. WordPerfect displays the Delete Style dialog box.

3. Under Options, select the desired delete option and then click OK.

 You can't delete system styles, only user styles (those you've created).

SIDE TRIP

STYLISH DOCUMENTS

Your styles aren't limited to the document in which you create them; you can use them in any document. Just remember the name of the document containing the styles, and you're on your way.

1. Open the document in which you want to use the styles and choose Format → Styles or press Alt+F8 to display the Styles List dialog box.

2. Click Options and then select Retrieve from the pop-down menu to display the Retrieve Styles From dialog box, which looks similar to the Save Styles As dialog box.

3. In the Filename text box, type the name of document containing the styles. If you aren't sure of the name, click the Folder button next to the Filename text box to locate and select the file.

4. Indicate the styles you want to retrieve under Style type and click OK. If there are duplicate style names, WordPerfect asks if you want to overwrite the current styles. Click Yes or No. WordPerfect adds the retrieved styles to the current list. You can now use the styles in your document.

If you want to save a list of your styles in a separate file for use in other documents, you can do so. See online help for more information.

BONUS

Checking under the Hood with Reveal Codes

Every time you format text — whether centering a line or bolding your name — WordPerfect inserts invisible codes into the document, marking the text with the formatting. If you find you aren't having problems formatting and working with text, you may never need to work with the underlying codes. However, if things just aren't doing what you think they should, you may want to use the Reveal Codes feature. Aptly named, this feature "reveals the codes" affecting your document so you can see exactly what's going on. Let's check under the hood of your document to see how these work.

Displaying the Reveal Codes Window

When you want to see what codes are affecting your document, you can display the Reveal Codes window. You can display this window along with your document to see how changes you make in the Reveal Codes window affect the way the text looks. To display the Reveal Codes window, use one of these methods:

✳ Choose View → Reveal Codes .

✳ Press Alt+F3.

✳ Point to one of the Reveal Codes bars on the vertical scroll bar until you see the double-headed black sizing arrow. Next, click so that you see a thick black horizontal line and drag up or down to the desired size.

 X-REF Refer back to Figure 3-1 in Chapter 3 to locate the Reveal Codes bars on the vertical scroll bar.

WordPerfect displays the Reveal Codes window (see Figure 4-9). If you used one of the first two options to display the window, WordPerfect defaults to using only 25 percent of the entire window for the Reveal Codes window, leaving the remaining portion for your document. If you used the third option, your Reveal Codes window size depends on where you dragged the Reveal Codes bar.

In the Reveal Codes window, the insertion point appears as a small red rectangle, and codes appear in gray boxes. Notice that in the Reveal Codes window, the text itself is not formatted; you see only the codes that are affecting the text.

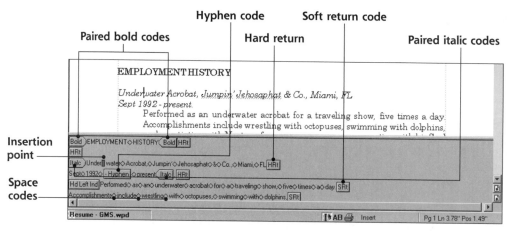

Figure 4-9 Use Reveal Codes to check formatting.

Working with Codes

Formatting codes act as single characters in the Reveal Codes window, and you can move around in the Reveal Codes window just as you move around text. WordPerfect uses two types of codes to format your text:

* *Paired codes* contain both an "on" and "off" code, and everything between the on and off codes is formatted. The bold, italic, and underline formats use paired codes to format text. Notice that paired codes appear to point in toward the text they format. If you delete one of the paired codes, both are removed.

* *Open codes* are single codes that affect all text that follow them until they encounter another like code. For example, if you change the line spacing to double at the top of your document, WordPerfect keeps it at double until or unless it encounters another line spacing code with a different measurement.

You move the insertion point around the Reveal Codes window just as you do the document window. You can then delete or move codes just as you would text. Keep in mind, however, that you can't move or undelete paired codes because WordPerfect has no way of knowing what text to surround the codes with.

Hide the Reveal Codes window using one of the same methods you did to display it.

TIP   You can easily edit nearly all of your formatting of codes by double-clicking the code in the Reveal Codes window. When you double-click a code that's associated with a dialog box, the dialog box opens so you can make changes.

Summary

This chapter dove into a lot of serious formatting stuff. You learned to change the look of characters using fonts and sizes and character enhancements such as bold, italics, and underline. You adjusted paragraphs using indents and paragraph spacing, and you used justification to align text. You explored locating text with Find and Replace and formatting it with styles. Next, you'll delve into some design features that add flair to your documents.

CHAPTER FIVE

WORKING WITH LONGER DOCUMENTS

IN THIS CHAPTER YOU LEARN THESE KEY SKILLS

CHANGING LINE SPACING   PAGE 98

USING AUTOMATIC PARAGRAPH NUMBERS
   AND BULLETS   PAGE 99

CREATING AN OUTLINE   PAGE 100

USING FOOTNOTES   PAGE 101

USING PAGE NUMBERS   PAGE 104

WORKING WITH HEADERS AND FOOTERS   PAGE 106

5

Open a nonfiction book or examine a report and you'll find many elements designed to assist readers in navigating the material. Increased line spacing makes the text more readable, and tables of contents and page numbers help you locate specific topics. Footnotes provide references to text in the document's body, and headers and footers help keep track of chapters or sections so that you know where you are. These features make the book or report more organized and help the reader follow the text in a logical manner.

In this chapter you explore these elements and more, learning about each as you create your own longer document, whether it is a report, employee manual, instruction manual, or textbook.

Changing Line Spacing

I f you've ever looked across a narrow median at the cars speeding in the opposite direction, you may have wished the roads had a bit more space between them. When creating documents, think of the lines of text as the roads and the white space between them as the medians. You can easily increase the white space by using line spacing. This can make the text more readable, especially if the document has a lot of text without illustrations to break it up. By default, WordPerfect uses single line spacing, adjusting the line *height* so that the lines will have standard spacing between them no matter what font and font size you choose.

WordPerfect uses an open code to format line spacing for a document. This means that if you position the insertion point at the top of the document and set line spacing, the spacing affects the text to the end of the document, *unless* you insert another line spacing code later in the document.

To set line spacing, follow these steps:

1. Position the insertion point in the location where you want to begin the new line spacing. Or, if you only want part of the document to use new line spacing, select the text to which it will be applied.

2. Choose Format → Line → Spacing to display the Line Spacing dialog box (see Figure 5-1). Here you can indicate the precise spacing you need.

Figure 5-1   Set precise line spacing.

3. In the Spacing text box, type the spacing you want to use. For example, type **2** for double spacing or **1.5** for one and one-half spacing. You can also use the spin boxes to select a spacing. Note that the spin boxes increase or decrease the spacing in one-tenth increments, using the standard line space as the base measurement.

4. Click OK. WordPerfect changes the line spacing from the insertion point forward.

TIP   If you think you'll change line spacing frequently, consider adding the Line Spacing button to the Text property bar. See Chapter 18 for more information on customization techniques.

Using Automatic Paragraph Numbers and Bullets

If you are creating an instruction manual or another type of document that requires leading your reader through steps, you can have WordPerfect number the steps for you. When you do this, WordPerfect automatically renumbers your steps if you add or remove a step between two steps. This way, you never have to worry about incorrect numbering. It also can create automatic bullets.

Creating Numbered Paragraphs

With the QuickBullets option set to on, you can create numbered paragraphs without much effort. WordPerfect is set to recognize the beginning of a numbered list and will continue the numbering after you begin it.

To create numbered paragraphs, follow these steps:

1. Position the insertion point in the location for the numbered list or paragraphs.

2. Type 1., press Tab, and then type the text for the line or paragraph.

3. Press Enter. WordPerfect automatically inserts "2." followed by a tab. Notice that the Text property bar changes to the Outline property bar because the Outline property bar can assist you in working with your list.

 X-REF **For more on the Outline property bar, see "Creating an Outline" later in this chapter.**

4. Type the text and press Enter for the next numbered paragraph. If you press Enter and realize you don't need the number, press Backspace to remove it.

To insert a new line or paragraph between two existing paragraphs, position the insertion point at the end of the paragraph you wish the new one to follow and press Enter. WordPerfect inserts a new number. Type the text for the new number.

 If WordPerfect doesn't automatically number your paragraphs, this means the QuickBullets feature isn't on. Choose Tools→QuickCorrect and then choose the Format-As-You-Go tab. In the Format-As-You-Go choices list, select QuickBullets and click OK.

To add numbers to existing paragraphs, select all the paragraphs, click the Numbering button arrow on the WordPerfect 8 toolbar, and select the desired numbering style.

Creating a Bulleted List

 WordPerfect also provides fast ways to create bulleted lists. If you have a series of lines or paragraphs that don't make up sequential steps but merely provide a list of similar points, you may want to use bullets to set them off. If you're creating a new list, position the insertion point, click the Bullets button arrow on the WordPerfect 8 toolbar, select a bullet type, and away you go. If you're adding bullets to an existing list, select the list and then apply a bullet style to it.

You can also use QuickBullets to insert a bullet type. WordPerfect provides several predefined bullets that you can access simply by typing a particular character. Position the insertion point where you want the bulleted list to begin and then use the table that follows to create the bullet you want. Just type the character and press Tab or Indent (F6) to watch WordPerfect convert the character to the associated bullet.

Type This Character	To Use This Bullet
* or o (lowercase *o*)	•
O (uppercase *O*)	●
>	▶
^	◆
+	★
-	—

Creating an Outline

Outlines are great ways to organize your thoughts, and you can use them to lay out the structure of a speech you don't want to read verbatim, to set up a meeting agenda, and more.

With WordPerfect's Outline feature, rearranging, adding, and deleting topics is a snap:

1. Position the insertion point in the location for the first item in your outline.

2. Choose | **Insert** | → | **Outline/Bullets & Numbering** | to display the Numbers tab in the Bullets and Numbering dialog box (see Figure 5-2). Depending on whether you've used automatic numbering previously, the numbering types may not always be in the same position on the Numbers tab.

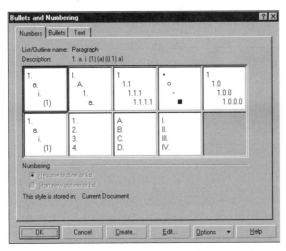

Figure 5-2   Select a numbering, bullet, or outline style.

3. On the Numbers tab, select the outline numbering type (I., A., 1., a.) and click OK. WordPerfect inserts the first number for the outline and displays the Outline property bar.

4. Type the text for the first level and press Enter. Use the following information to work with your outline.

✳ To go to the next level (A, for example), press Tab or click the Next Level button on the Outline property bar.

✳ To go to the previous level, press Shift+Tab or click the Previous Level button on the Outline property bar.

✳ To move a single level (for example, item I.A.), position the insertion point in the line and click the Up button on the Outline property bar to move it up or click the Down button on the Outline property bar to move it down. The *level* remains the same but the number will change.

Using Footnotes

Remember those extensive reports you wrote in school, footnotes and all? Guess what? Even if you're not in school, you may still need to use footnotes. For example, suppose you're writing a report on the use of employee benefits and need to refer readers to their employee manuals. You could use a footnote to indicate the section and page they should refer to in their manual. Footnotes provide additional information without interrupting the flow of the document.

WordPerfect lets you create both footnotes — which appear at the bottom of pages — and endnotes — which appear at the end of a document. Because footnotes are more common, I focus on them here. With the Footnote feature in WordPerfect, you not only have automatic numbering of footnotes, you also don't have to calculate the amount of white space you'll need at the bottom of each page. WordPerfect does that for you.

Creating a Footnote

You already saw how WordPerfect automatically numbers your paragraphs. It automatically numbers footnotes the same way. So, if you delete, insert, or move a footnote, all footnote numbers — both in the document and in the footnotes themselves — update automatically. WordPerfect also formats the footnote number as superscript, which is the standard format. By default, the footnote text appears at the bottom of the page containing the footnote number, below a two-inch separator line.

To insert a footnote in your document, follow these steps:

1. Position the insertion point in the location for the footnote number in your document text. This may include typing text leading up to the footnote number. In the example in Figure 5-3, you would place the insertion point after the period following *recycling stream*.

2. Choose **Insert** → **Footnote/Endnote** to display the Footnote/Endnote dialog box and click Create. WordPerfect inserts the footnote number in the document and displays the Footnote property bar before positioning the insertion point at the bottom of the page (see Figure 5-3).

3. Type the text for the footnote and then click the Close button on the Footnote property bar. WordPerfect returns to the document, positioning the insertion point directly after the footnote number.

If you're using Draft view, WordPerfect displays a Footnote window rather than taking you to the footnote area at the bottom of the page. Follow Step 3 in the preceding list and then choose View→Page to see your footnotes when you return to the document window. Refer to Chapter 3 for more on Draft view.

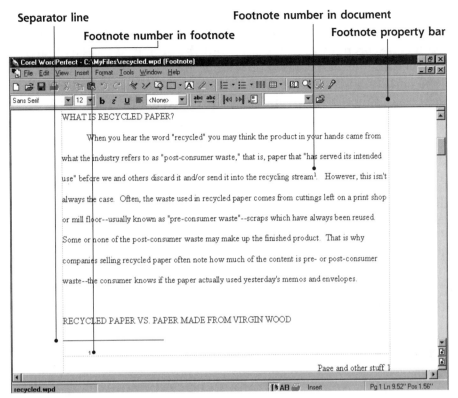

Separator line

Footnote number in footnote

Footnote number in document

Footnote property bar

Figure 5-3 Create a footnote in your document.

You can also use symbols instead of numbers to indicate footnotes. Position the insertion point at the top of the document, choose Insert→Footnote/Endnote, click Options, and choose Advanced from the drop-down menu. In the Advanced Footnote Options dialog box, click the Method down-arrow button and select Characters from the drop-down list. Enter the character in the Characters text box to position the insertion point and type the desired character or press Ctrl+W to insert the desired symbol. After you're finished, click OK to accept the setting and close the Footnote Options dialog box. If you have existing footnotes, they change to reflect your selection.

X-REF **Refer to Chapter 2 for more information on using WordPerfect Characters.**

Editing a Footnote

Just like everything else in your document, you're allowed to goof up a footnote or change your mind about what you want it to say. To modify the contents of your footnote, make sure that you're using Page view. Then display the footnote at the bottom of the page and click in the footnote area. Make the desired changes and click back in the document text to hide the Footnote property bar and return to your document.

TIP If you have a lot of footnotes and can't locate the one you wish to edit, you can search for it. Make sure that the option to search elements such as footnotes is on. Choose Edit→Find and Replace. Choose Options on the menu and make sure Include Headers, Footers, etc. in Find is checked. Proceed with your search, as described in Chapter 4.

Deleting a Footnote

If you no longer need a footnote, it's easy to delete. Just delete the associated footnote number in the document. WordPerfect removes the number in the document text and the footnote at the bottom of the page, renumbering all existing footnotes. You can use Undo or Undelete to bring the footnote back if you change your mind.

Using Page Numbers

When you create a document that's longer than one page, more than likely you're going to want to number the pages consecutively so you and your reader can keep track of their order. WordPerfect has a powerful numbering feature that allows you to add page numbers with or without accompanying text (for example, "page 2" or "- 2 -") and in six different locations on the page.

WordPerfect provides a sample of *facing pages* to show you how your position selection will look with actual pages. What are facing pages? You're reading them right now. With the book open before you, you should see an even-numbered page on the left and an odd-numbered page on the right. If you were to close this book, these two pages would actually face each other. Hence, *facing pages*. Usually when you're creating a book or manual that you will bind, you use alternating outside numbering (as this book does) so the numbers are easier to read and locate.

Note that if you have a title page or other introductory pages and you want numbering to start at 1 on the first page of actual body text, you'll need to adjust the page number *value*, which you'll learn how to do in the following steps.

To add page numbers to a document, follow these steps:

1. Position the insertion point on the page where you want numbering to start. Because of WordPerfect's Auto Code Placement, WordPerfect places the page numbering code at the top of the current page, no matter where you position the insertion point on the page.

2. Choose Format → Page → Numbering to display the Select Page Numbering Format dialog box (see Figure 5-4). Here you can select the appearance of the actual page number and where it will appear on the page.

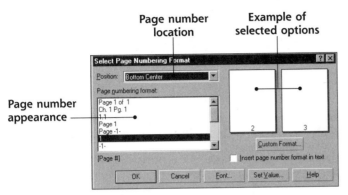

Page number location

Example of selected options

Page number appearance

Figure 5-4 Set page numbering.

3. Click the Position down-arrow button and select the desired position from the drop-down list.

4. In the Page numbering format list, select the way you'd like your page number to look on the page. You can choose to display the page number by itself or include text with the number. Notice that you can also select a Roman numeral to number your pages. This is good for introductory and other similar pages but be sure to change the formatting to regular Arabic numbers (1, 2, 3) for the body of the document.

5. If you want numbering to start with a different number, click Set Value to display the Values dialog box (see Figure 5-5). The current page number appears in the Set page number text box. So, for example, if you're on the first page of your body text in a document with a title page, the page number will indicate "2."

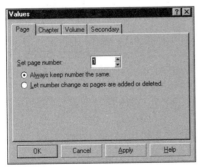

Figure 5-5 Indicate a starting page number.

6. In the Set page number text box, type the starting number for the page and click OK.

7. When you're finished, click OK to close the Select Page Numbering Format dialog box. WordPerfect numbers the pages consecutively, starting with the current page.

 TIP To see the page numbers, you must use Page view (View→Page) or print the document.

Working with Headers and Footers

Open just about any big manual or nonfiction book and you'll see that it's divided into chapters or sections. These chapters or sections are often identified at the top or bottom of the page. These identifications are called *headers* if they run across the top of the page and *footers* if they run across the bottom of the page. Headers and footers help keep a document organized and provide additional identification when a reader is locating a particular topic.

You can include just about anything in a header or footer — text, graphic lines, your company logo, and page numbers. Headers and footers provide many more alternatives when you want to do more than indicate a page number.

Adding a Header or Footer

Headers and footers are identical except for the fact that one appears across the tops of pages (header) and the other appears across the bottoms of pages (footer). You create each in a similar manner. WordPerfect lets you create two headers (Header A and Header B) and two footers (Footer A and Footer B). This gives you the flexibility to use Header or Footer A for odd pages and Header or Footer B for even pages, for example. And because WordPerfect uses codes, you can actually add an unlimited number of headers or footers to the document. Once WordPerfect encounters a new code, the formatting in that code takes effect from that point forward.

To add a header or footer to your document, follow these steps:

1. Position the insertion point anywhere on the page where you want the header or footer to begin appearing.

2. Choose `Insert` → `Header/Footer` to display the Header/Footer dialog box. You work with headers or footers here.

3. Under Select, choose the header or footer you want to create and click Create. WordPerfect places the insertion point within the header or footer guidelines, which are indicated by the dotted box below the top

margin (headers) and above the bottom margin (footers). In addition, WordPerfect displays the Header or Footer property bar (see Figure 5-6). Notice that in Page view, you can still see the text of your document in the document area.

As with footnotes, WordPerfect displays the Header or Footer window if you're using Draft view. Once you've created the header or footer and returned to the document window, choose View→Page to see your header or footer.

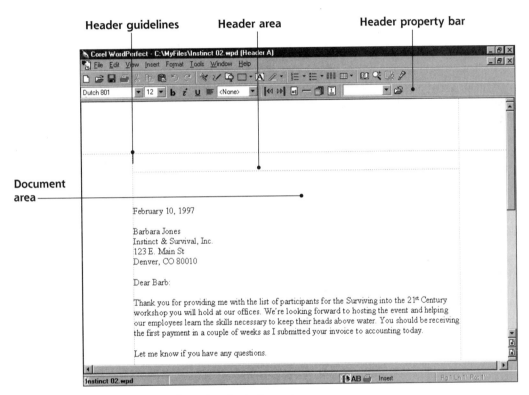

Figure 5-6   Creating a header in Page view.

4. Type any text for your header or footer.

5. To add a page number, click the Page Numbering button on the Header or Footer property bar and then choose the desired page number option from the pop-down menu.

6. To add a horizontal line, position the insertion point in the location for the line and click the Horizontal Line button on the Header or Footer property bar.

X-REF For more on horizontal lines, see Chapter 6.

 7. If you want the header to appear on just the odd or even pages of the document, click the Header/Footer Placement button on the Header or Footer property bar to display the Pages dialog box, choose Odd pages or Even pages, and click OK. Otherwise, the header or footer will appear on every page.

 8. To change the distance between the header and footer contents and the document text, click the Header/Footer Distance button on the Header or Footer property bar, specify a measurement for the distance, and click OK. You can also click and drag the lower header or upper footer guideline.

 9. After you're finished creating your header or footer, click the Close button on the Header or Footer property bar or click anywhere in the document area.

Editing a Header or Footer

Once you've returned to the document window and viewed or printed your pages, you may find that you need to make a change to your header or footer.

To edit a header or footer, follow these steps:

1. In Page view, display a page containing the header or footer you want to edit.

2. Click in the Header or Footer area and make the necessary changes.

3. Click Close on the property bar or click in the document area to return to the document.

 TIP With the Header or Footer property bar displayed, you can easily edit other headers and footers in the current document. Click the Header/Footer Previous button or click the Header/Footer Next button on the Header or Footer property bar to display the previous or next header or footer and make your changes.

HIDING HEADERS

At times you don't want headers or footers to print. Perhaps you have a chart or illustration that takes up an entire page, and the header or footer would confuse the reader. You can *suppress* a header, footer, page number, or other elements for the current page. Here's how.

1. Position the insertion point on the page where you don't want the header, footer, or page number to appear and choose | Format | → | Page | → | Suppress | to display the Suppress dialog box.

2. Under Suppress on current page, select all the elements you want to hide on the page and click OK. WordPerfect inserts a suppress code and won't show or print the header, footer, page number, or other element you suppressed for the current page only.

To stop a header or footer from printing on consecutive pages, follow these steps:

1. Position the insertion point on the page where you don't want the header, footer, or page number to appear from that point forward.

2. Choose | Insert | → | Header/Footer | to display the Header/Footer dialog box.

3. Click Discontinue. WordPerfect turns off the header or footer from this point forward.

BONUS

Creating a Table of Contents

For big documents, such as an employee handbook or a lengthy budget report, you may need a table of contents to help readers locate information quickly and easily. If you look at the table of contents in this book, you'll see that the chapters contain *levels* for the topics or headings beneath them. Sublevel headings are indented below the main level headings to show the structure and flow of a chapter.

Creating a table of contents requires three steps. First, you *define* the table of contents page. This page will contain the actual table of contents, and you need to tell WordPerfect how to set it up. Second, you *mark* each heading in your document that you want included in the table of contents. Third, you *generate* the table of contents, so WordPerfect can gather all your headings along with their associated page numbers and create the table of contents.

Defining a Table of Contents Page

As just mentioned, your first step is defining a table of contents page. Because the table of contents page will take up one or more pages in your document, you want to make sure that your body text begins numbering at 1 after the table of contents page.

To define your table of contents page, follow these steps:

1. Create a new page for the table of contents and format it as desired.

2. Position the insertion point on the page where you want the table of contents to appear and choose ⟦Tools⟧ → ⟦Reference⟧ → ⟦Table of Contents⟧. WordPerfect displays the Table of Contents toolbar.

3. Click Define on the Table of Contents toolbar to display the Define Table of Contents dialog box (see Figure 5-7).

Indicate number of levels

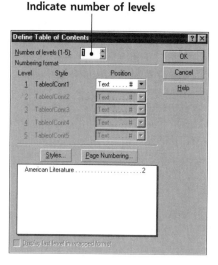

Figure 5-7 Define your table of contents.

4. In the Number of levels text box, type the number of levels you want to use. If you aren't sure how many levels your document uses, type 5. WordPerfect will only use the number of levels actually indicated in your document, so overstating them won't affect your table of contents.

5. Click OK. WordPerfect inserts a definition code at the insertion point location and displays the message `<Table of contents will generate here>`. WordPerfect replaces this message with the actual table of contents when you generate the document.

To change the way your table of contents displays, you can edit the Level styles in the Define Table of Contents dialog box. Note that the changes you make to the Level styles will affect the look of tables of contents you create in any future documents.

Marking Text for the Table of Contents

The second step in creating your table of contents is marking all headings and subheadings that you want to show up in the table of contents. If you created the document, you should have a good idea of which headings and subheadings you want to include and more than likely they are formatted (hopefully with styles!) using the techniques you learned in Chapters 3 and 4.

To mark text for the table of contents, select the heading text you want to include and then click the appropriate Mark button on the Table of Contents toolbar. For example, Mark 1 for a Level 1 heading, Mark 2 for a Level 2 heading, and so on.

X-REF Refer to "Editing a Style" in Chapter 4 for more information on changing these styles.

Generating a Document

Once you've marked your headings and subheadings, you can generate the document to gather the page numbers and place them on the table of contents page. To generate a document, click Generate on the Table of Contents toolbar or select Tools→Reference→Generate. WordPerfect displays the Generate dialog box. Click OK. WordPerfect displays its progress, taking you to the table of contents page when the process is complete

SIDE TRIP

SMART MARKING

For huge time savings when marking text, use the Heading system styles. For example, position the insertion point in the heading you want to mark as Level 1, then click the Style down-arrow button on the Standard property bar and choose Heading 1. This formats the heading and marks it as Level 1 (Mark 1). Heading 2 marks the heading as Level 2 (Mark 2), Heading 3 marks the heading as Level 3 (Mark 3), and so on. If you don't like the way these styles format your headings, edit them to suit your needs. The changes you make to the Heading styles will only affect the current document. The Heading styles remain untouched for other documents.

Because you may have made changes to a document that affect pagination, always generate marked documents before printing them so that the table of contents reflects accurate page numbers.

Summary

n this chapter, you pulled together some major tools for organizing and ordering a long document. You learned how to change line spacing, created automatic paragraph numbering, and used footnotes. You also added page numbers, headers, and footers and learned how to create an outline, as well as how to provide a document "map" with the Table of Contents feature. All this without breaking a sweat (I hope). Next you're going to take a break from serious documents such as reports or manuals and cut loose by creating a flyer, complete with lines, graphics, columns, and more. Onward!

CREATING A FLYER

U p to this point, you've explored many WordPerfect features by using basic business documents as examples — letters, resumes, and long documents such as reports or manuals. In this chapter, you get to let loose a little, to be creative, and to check out some features that set WordPerfect apart in terms of desktop publishing. True, if your work requires heavy desktop publishing, you're better off using one of the excellent programs designed for that purpose. But if you require the occasional flyer, newsletter, or brochure, you can create a professional-looking, visually exciting document in WordPerfect.

In this chapter, you get to sink your teeth into such features as TextArt, which lets you create fancy titles and headings, add flair to your flyer with graphic lines and images, and set up columns to organize text and information. In this chapter, I use a flyer as an example, but you can use these features in a variety of document types.

Setting New Margins

A s you probably know, the white space surrounding text in a printed document is called a *margin*. In WordPerfect, you can change the top, bottom, left, and right margins to increase or decrease that white space.

Note that codes for left and right margins will take effect at the line containing the insertion point. Top and bottom margin codes will be placed at the top of the current page (the page containing the insertion point).

In Page view, the margin guidelines appear as colored lines that fence in your text. You can easily adjust the margin settings by adjusting these guidelines (see Figure 6-1). Note that the bottom margin is not shown in Figure 6-1, but in a document on screen, you could display it by scrolling down.

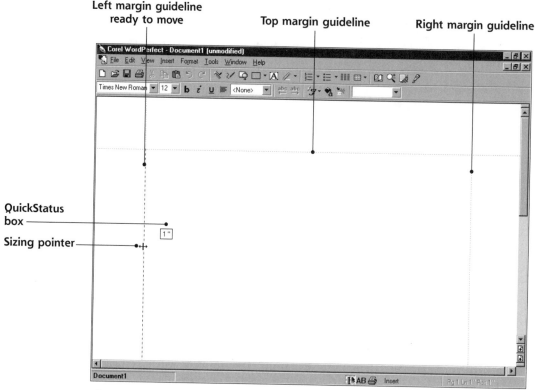

Figure 6-1 Set margins using margin guidelines.

To adjust margins using the guidelines, point to the guideline you want to adjust (left, right, top, or bottom) until you see the pointer change to a sizing pointer (black, double-headed arrows). Refer to Figure 6-1 to see the sizing pointer. Then click and hold the mouse button and drag the guideline to the new setting, using the floating QuickStatus box, which shows you the current measurement for this margin.

 If you don't see the guidelines in one of the Page views, they've been turned off. Choose View→Guidelines. Under Display guidelines for, select Margins and click OK.

TIP You can also set precise margins. Choose Format→Margins to display the Page Margins tab in the Page Setup dialog box, enter your measurements, and click OK.

FEATURE FOCUS On the Page Margins tab in the Page Setup dialog box, you can type a measurement in the Left text box and then choose Make all margins equal to insert this same measurement in all remaining boxes.

Using TextArt

*T*extArt is a mini-application that's integrated into WordPerfect for creating headings, banners, logos, and more. TextArt can twist and bend characters to produce a variety of effects, making your headings and banners fun and eye-catching.

Say you've set up the margins for your flyer and are ready to create the attention-grabbing heading that will make your readers sit up and read the entire flyer. Here's how you do it:

TIP You can select existing text for your heading before choosing the TextArt option. When you do, the selected text appears in the Type here text box.

1. Position the insertion point in the location for the TextArt. For example, for your flyer, you'd position it at the top of the document.

2. Choose Insert → Graphics → TextArt . WordPerfect inserts a graphic box in your document containing the word *text*. Then the Corel TextArt 8.0 dialog box displays (see Figure 6-2).

3. On the General tab, type the text for your heading in the Type here text box. Notice that the TextArt graphic box in the document changes to reflect changes you make in the TextArt 8.0 dialog box.

4. Choose a Font and Font style and then choose a shape in the Shapes box. Click the More button to display a palette of all shapes and select from those.

5. Set Justification, Text, and any Pattern, Outline, Shadow, and Rotation options in the 2D Options tab. Check the graphic box in your document to see the effect each has on your heading.

6. For 3D options, choose the 3D check box and set options on the 3D tab. Note that you must have installed 3D options using a Custom installation for these to be available. When you're finished, click Close.

TextArt graphic box

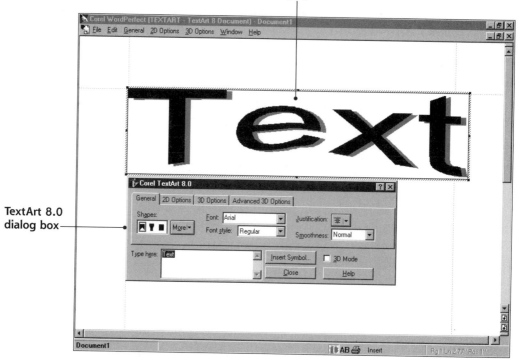

TextArt 8.0
dialog box

Figure 6-2 Create fancy headings and logos with TextArt.

TIP To edit your TextArt heading, double-click the graphic box containing the TextArt. WordPerfect displays the TextArt 8.0 dialog box where you can make your changes. To adjust its size, see "Moving and Sizing a Graphic" later in this chapter.

Using Newspaper Columns

When you open a newspaper or read a newsletter, most of the text appears in columns. You read down the first column, then jump up to the next column to continue reading. Columns make text easier to read because the eye doesn't have to roam far afield to take in the entire line of text. Columns are great for newsletters and even flyers that will contain significant amounts of text. WordPerfect's Columns feature enables you to set up columns for your text. When you type your text and reach the bottom of the first column, WordPerfect automatically wraps the text to the top of the next column.

Creating Newspaper Columns

When you set up columns, WordPerfect inserts a Column On code, which tells it to set all the subsequent text in columns until it reaches a Column Off code. This flexibility means that you can have TextArt, headings, graphics, and other elements sprinkled throughout your document that aren't confined to your columns. If you want a horizontal line to stretch across the entire page through columns of text, simply turn columns off, insert the line, and turn columns on again. (Later in the chapter, you will learn about inserting horizontal lines.) You can also select existing text and place it in columns.

To create newspaper columns for text, follow these steps:

1. With your flyer or other document open, position the insertion point where you want columns to begin and click the Columns button on the WordPerfect toolbar. Select the desired number of columns (you can have up to five). You should see the insertion point inside the first column, as indicated by the column guidelines and the status bar showing that the insertion point is currently in Column 1 (see Figure 6-3). Also, if you have the Ruler displayed, you will see the columns indicated there, with their widths clearly marked.

TIP

To turn the Ruler on, choose View→Ruler.

2. Type the text in the column. The text will wrap within the column margins. When the text reaches the bottom of the first column, it snakes up to the next column and continues.

If you don't see the guidelines (which appear as dotted lines), make sure that you're using Page view (View→Page). If you still don't see the guidelines, select View→Guidelines. Under Display Guidelines for, select Columns and click OK.

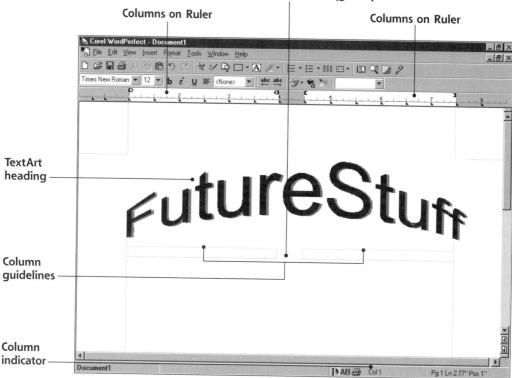

Space between columns (gutter)

Columns on Ruler

Columns on Ruler

TextArt heading

Column guidelines

Column indicator

Figure 6-3 Use newspaper columns for a tidy look.

SIDE TRIP

COLUMN CAPERS

To set columns with precise measurements, click the Columns button on the WordPerfect toolbar and choose Format, or choose Format→Columns to display the Columns dialog box. Type the number of columns, select any other options in the dialog box, and click OK.

Here's a column tip: Say that you have a new topic and you want it to start at the top of the next column but WordPerfect hasn't wrapped the text to the next column yet. To force a new column before WordPerfect automatically wraps your text, press Ctrl+Enter, or click the Columns button on the WordPerfect toolbar and choose New Column.

Adjusting Column Width

When you first create columns, WordPerfect sets the columns with equal widths. However, once you enter text into columns, you may decide you want one column to be wider than the others for effect. Adjusting the width of columns is easy using the guidelines or the Column Markers on the Ruler. And when you use the column guidelines, it's nearly identical to adjusting margins using the margin guidelines.

To adjust a column width, point to the column guideline for the column you wish to adjust until you see the pointer change to a sizing pointer (black, double-headed). Then click and drag the guideline to the new setting, using the QuickStatus box to guide you.

SIDE TRIP

COLUMNS RULE!

As with margins, you can adjust column widths if you have the Ruler displayed. To display the Ruler, choose View→Ruler. To adjust the columns, click and drag the desired column indicator on the Ruler to the desired location. To adjust columns without affecting the white space between them, click and drag the gray area separating two column indicators. Refer to the accompanying figure for guidance.

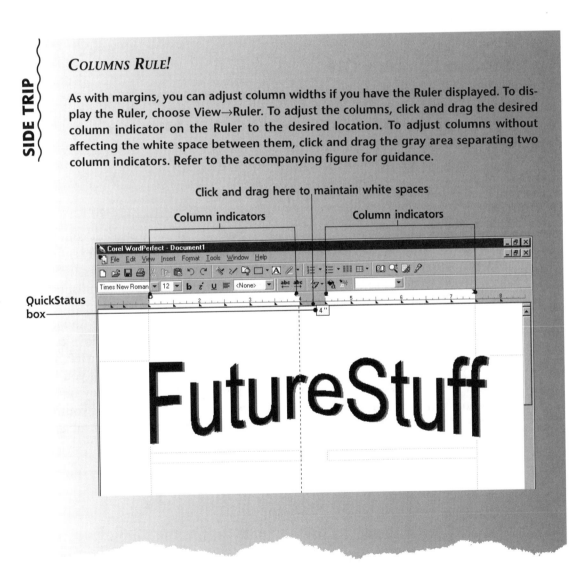

Click and drag here to maintain white spaces

Column indicators

Column indicators

QuickStatus box

Adjusting Columns and White Space

If you want to adjust your column widths while maintaining the amount of white space between them, you can use the sizing pointer between columns. Point to the white space between the columns so that the pointer changes to a sizing pointer (two vertical lines with a black arrow attached to each). Next, click and drag to the new setting, using the QuickStatus box to guide you. WordPerfect adjusts the text to account for the new column width(s), leaving the white space width intact.

TIP To surround columns with a border or to insert a vertical line between columns, position the insertion point in any of the columns, click the Columns button, and select Format. Click Border/Fill, select the border style or vertical line in the Available Border Styles box, and click OK.

Turning Columns Off

Once you've completed your columns, you can turn them off and continue with standard body text. First, position the insertion point where you'd like to turn off the columns. Then click the Columns button on the WordPerfect toolbar and select Discontinue.

Using Tabular Columns

When you have information that is best set up in short, neat columns, you can set tabs to create these columns. If you have longer text that you want to set up in columns, consider using the Tables feature, which I cover in detail in Chapter 7. Here you look at setting up a short list using tabs, similar to the example in Figure 6-4.

Remember in Chapters 4 and 5 when I made references to *tab stops* and their relationship to indenting and outlines? WordPerfect's default is to have a tab stop every one-half inch. This means that if the insertion point is at the left margin and you press Tab, WordPerfect stops a half an inch to the right. If you type text and press Tab, WordPerfect stops at the next tab stop, which may or may not be one-half inch from your text. It depends on how many tab stops your text overlaps. If you have the Ruler displayed, you can see exactly which tab stops WordPerfect is using as you press Tab.

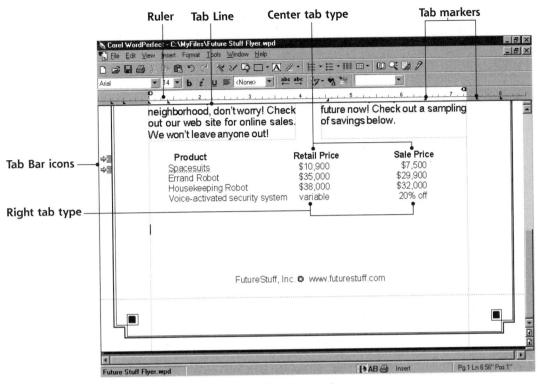

Figure 6-4 Set up information in tabular columns.

Setting Tabs on the Ruler

If you want to create a list of products and their prices on your flyer, or a list of employees, their departments, and their extensions, you can use tabular columns. The following example has short entries for each column, which is the best use of tabs. You can use the Ruler to set tabs quickly and easily.

 TIP If the Ruler is not displayed, choose View→Ruler.

Setting new tabs involves three steps: clearing the current tab settings, selecting a tab type, and setting the tab on the ruler. WordPerfect provides a number of different tab types, all of which are described in Table 6-1. The Left tab type is the most common, and WordPerfect uses it as the default.

To set new tabs, follow these steps:

1. Position the insertion point in the location for the tabular columns.

2. Secondary-click the Tab Line or one of the tab markers and choose Clear All Tabs from the QuickMenu. WordPerfect removes all tabs from the Ruler, giving you a clean slate with which to work.

CAUTION If you click *above* the Tab Line, WordPerfect displays the QuickMenu for the Ruler, not for tabs.

3. Secondary-click the Tab Line and choose the desired tab type from the QuickMenu, referring to Table 6-1 for assistance. You can see examples of some types in Figure 6-4.

4. Click the Tab Line below the measurement on the Ruler to insert a tab marker.

TABLE 6-1 Tab Types

Type	Tab Marker	Description
LEFT		Align the text against the left of the tab stop. Similar to text aligned against a left margin.
CENTER		Center the text. Similar to centering between left and right margins.
RIGHT		Align the text against the right of the tab stop. Similar to flush right against the right margin.
DECIMAL		Align text containing a decimal point on the decimal point.
...LEFT		Align the text against the left of the tab stop with dot leaders leading up to it.
...CENTER		Center the text with dot leaders leading up to it.
...RIGHT		Align text against the right of the tabular column with dot leaders leading up to it.
...DECIMAL		Align text on the decimal point with dot leaders leading up to it.

Once you've set your tabs, press Tab to position the insertion point at the tab stop and type your text. Depending on the type of tab you've selected, WordPerfect will format the text accordingly.

TIP You can also set precise tab measurements using the Tab Set dialog box. Just secondary-click the Tab Line or a tab marker on the Ruler and choose Tab Set. Enter your measurements and select your options, clicking Set after each one. After you're finished, click OK.

Returning to the Default Tab Setting

A Tab Set is an open code and affects all text from the location of the code forward. What if you want to have some normal text — complete with indents and regular tabs — after your tabular columns, and you want the text to follow the default tab settings? No problem; just insert a tab code for the default settings, following these steps:

X-REF Refer back to Chapters 4 and 5 for more information on open codes.

1. Position the insertion point in the location for the default tab setting.

2. With the Ruler displayed, secondary-click the Tab Line or a tab marker and choose Default Tab Settings from the QuickMenu. Alternatively, you can choose `Format` → `Line` → `Tab Set` to display the Tab Set dialog box, click Default, and then click OK.

Moving and Deleting Tab Stops

Once you set your tabs and start typing your column text, you may see that text is too close together or is overlapping other columns because of the tab types you've selected. You can easily adjust the tab stops to improve the look of your columns. Position the insertion point and use the following methods:

* To move a tab, click and drag the tab marker to a new location on the Ruler.

* To delete a tab, click and drag the tab marker completely off the Ruler.

* To change a tab type, secondary-click the tab you want to change, select the new type, and click the existing tab marker.

SIDE TRIP

TAB TIPS

Beginning with WordPerfect 7, WordPerfect inserts a Tab Bar icon in the left margin area every time you create new tab settings, effectively marking the spot for a new Tab Set code. (Refer back to Figure 6-4 to see what the Tab Bar icon looks like.) When you click the Tab Bar icon, WordPerfect positions the insertion point at the beginning of the tabular columns and displays the Tab Bar, enabling you to adjust the tabs for the current tabular columns only, which can speed up your tab setting.

To use the Tab Bar, use the horizontal scroll bar to display the left margin area so you can see the Tab Bar icon. Next, click the Tab Bar icon associated with the tabular columns you want to change. WordPerfect displays the Tab Bar, and you can add, move, and delete tab stops just as you do on the Ruler.

TIP To select multiple tab markers on the Ruler or Tab Bar, press and hold Shift, then click and drag over the markers, while still pressing Shift. WordPerfect covers the selections in gray. You can then move or delete them as desired.

Using Graphic Lines

Remember the vertical line you could add between two columns, earlier in this chapter? Well, you can do more — so much more — with vertical and horizontal lines. Lines separate different areas of your flyer or document, highlighting or calling attention to specific information. You may have inserted a line into a header or footer in Chapter 5 to separate the header or footer text from the body text. In this section, you learn how to create and customize your lines so they're just right.

Inserting a Horizontal Line

Although vertical lines are good for column separation, you will find that you use horizontal lines more frequently to separate sections and add flair to your documents. Because of this, I concentrate on horizontal lines here. WordPerfect provides a couple of ways to insert horizontal lines, and I have you take a look at both.

INSERTING A LINE USING QUICKLINES

If you just want a simple single or double line running between the left and right margins, use QuickLines. First, position the insertion point in the location for the line. Then use one of these methods:

- ✳ For a single line, type ---- (four hyphens) and press Enter.
- ✳ For a double line, type ==== (four equals signs) and press Enter.

WordPerfect inserts a standard single or double line. If no line appeared, your QuickLines option may be turned off. To turn it on, choose Tools→ QuickCorrect and then select the Format-As-You-Go tab. In the QuickCorrect Format-As-You-Go choices list, select QuickLines and click OK to return to the document window. Try the method again.

TIP You can also choose Insert→Shape→Horizontal Line or press Ctrl+F11 to insert a default single line. You can change a line once you've inserted it. See "Modifying a Line" later in this section to do so.

INSERTING CUSTOM LINES

If you want something a little fancier than a single or double line, WordPerfect provides a wealth of predefined line styles from which to choose. You can create colored lines, change line thickness and lengths, and indicate the position of the line on the page. When you insert a horizontal line, WordPerfect places it on the *baseline* by default. This means the line runs along the invisible line that traces the bottom of all your characters in any given line.

TIP You can also just insert a standard line using one of the techniques I described earlier, and then edit it by double-clicking the line.

To insert a custom line, follow these steps:

1. Position the insertion point in the location for the line.

2. Choose **Insert** → **Shape** → **Custom Line** to display the Create Graphics Line dialog box (see Figure 6-5).

Sample line

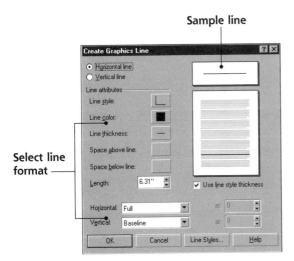

Select line format

Figure 6-5 Create your own line.

3. Make your selections in the dialog box for a custom line. At the top of the dialog box, select either Horizontal or Vertical. WordPerfect changes the dialog box display slightly to accommodate your selection.

4. Under Line attributes, select a Line style, Line color, and Line thickness. Use Space above line and Space below line to indicate how much space you want to leave between the line and the text surrounding it. Finally, indicate the Length for the line. Note that the default is to run the line the full length between the left and right margins. Check the sample line to see how your selections affect your line.

5. At the bottom of the dialog box, set horizontal and vertical positions. Note that if you don't select a specific length, your horizontal position will set to Full automatically. You can still change the position, but you won't see any change in the line unless the length changes. If you want the line to start at a specific measurement from the left edge of the page, select Set, and type the measurement in the at text box.

6. After you're finished with your selections, click OK. WordPerfect inserts your beautiful line at the insertion point location.

Modifying a Line

Once you've inserted a standard or custom line, you may see that it doesn't quite work with the text around it. Maybe it's too thick, too long, or not long enough. Or maybe you want to move it up or down slightly. Depending on the changes you want to make, you can use the mouse or open the Custom Line dialog box to do some fine-tuning.

If you only need to move a line or adjust its length or thickness, click the line once to select it. You should see *sizing handles* appear on the line (see Figure 6-6). You use these handles to make your adjustments. Note that thin lines won't have the thickness handle.

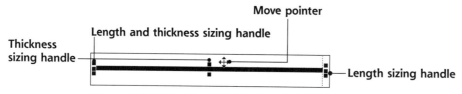

Figure 6-6 Edit a horizontal line.

✳ To move the line, point to the line to display the move pointer, and then click and drag the line to its new location.

✳ To increase or decrease line length, make sure you've selected the line, and then click and drag one of the sizing handles on either end of the line. Make sure the pointer is a horizontal double arrow. Dragging in toward the center of the line decreases the length; dragging out toward the left or right of your page increases the length.

✳ To increase or decrease line thickness, make sure you've selected the line, and then click and drag one of the top or bottom sizing handles. Make sure the pointer is a vertical double arrow. Dragging in toward the center of the line decreases the width; dragging out toward the top or bottom of your page increases the length.

✳ To change both the length and the width at the same time, use a corner sizing handle (pointer becomes a diagonal double arrow).

If you want to change something other than location, length, or t'ckness, double-click the line to display the Edit Graphics Line dialog box. Make your changes and click OK.

Using Graphic Images

Graphic lines are great for separating sections in a flyer or other document, but if you really want to add pizzazz, nothing beats a picture. The WordPerfect suite ships with *thousands* of public domain images and clipart, which means that you can use them freely without violating copyrights. When you installed the WordPerfect Suite, you may have opted not to have all the images copied to your hard drive, taking up valuable disk space. That's okay. With WordPerfect's new Scrapbook feature, you can access images off your hard drive and the CD-ROM. Let's play with pictures!

Inserting an Image

When you insert an image, WordPerfect places the image in a *graphic box*, complete with four sides. These four sides may be invisible, but the box is still there, helping you control the image it contains. By default, WordPerfect wraps any text surrounding the graphic box around it, so the box doesn't cover your text.

To insert an image, first position the insertion point in the location for the graphic image and click the Clipart button on the WordPerfect toolbar. You can also choose Insert→Graphics→Clipart. WordPerfect displays the Scrapbook, where you can display and select the image you want to use (see Figure 6-7). The Clipart tab displays folders and clipart that were copied to your hard drive during a Typical installation. The CD Clipart accesses the CD-ROM where thousands of images and photos are stored. Select the Clipart or CD Clipart tab. Double-click a folder to see its contents.

To return to the previous folder, click the Up One Level button. When you've located the image you want to use, simply click and drag it directly into your document. WordPerfect inserts a copy of the image, leaving the original intact.

When you've finished inserting images, close the Scrapbook by clicking the Close button (*X*) on the title bar.

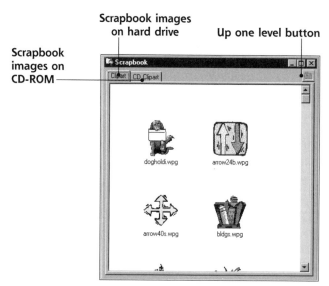

Figure 6-7 Choose your clipart image in the Scrapbook.

SCRAPBOOK SECRETS

The Scrapbook is a great way to insert graphics into any WordPerfect document, Presentations slide show, and Quattro Pro spreadsheet. Here are a few tips for getting the most out of this handy feature.

✳ To change how Scrapbook icons appear, secondary-click the background (not one of the images or folders), choose View from the QuickMenu, and select the desired view. Most of these match the way you can display files in the Windows Explorer or any file management dialog box. Selecting Details will display keywords to the right of each image to help identify it.

✳ To get more information about an image, secondary-click the image and select Properties from the QuickMenu.

✳ To use one of the folders on the CD Clipart tab as your default folder, secondary-click the folder, and select Set as Default from the QuickMenu.

✳ To resize the Scrapbook window, click and drag an edge or corner.

FEATURE FOCUS When you use the Clipart button on the toolbar or choose Insert→Graphics→Clipart, WordPerfect and the other applications display the Scrapbook, where you can quickly add graphics to your document.

TIP To insert an image that is not part of the Scrapbook, choose Insert→Graphics→File and locate and insert the desired image.

FEATURE FOCUS When you insert an image, WordPerfect displays the Graphic property bar. See Table 6-2 for an explanation of these handy little buttons.

TABLE 6-2 Graphic Property Bar Tools

Button	Name	Description
Graphics	GRAPHICS MENU	Display a list of feature options.
	PREVIOUS BOX	Select the previous graphics box in the document.
	NEXT BOX	Select the next graphics box in the document.
	BORDER STYLE	Select a border for the box.
	BOX FILL	Select a fill color or style for the box background.
	CAPTION	Add a caption to an image.
	FLIP LEFT/ RIGHT	Flip the image left to right or right to left within the graphic box.
	FLIP TOP/ BOTTOM	Flips the image top to bottom or bottom to top within the graphic box.
	IMAGE TOOLS	Display the Image Tools palette.
	OBJECT(S) FORWARD ONE	Move a layered object one layer up.

(continued)

TABLE 6-2 Graphic Property Bar Tools (*continued*)

Button	Name	Description
	OBJECT(S) BACK ONE	Move a layered object one layer down.
	WRAP	Indicate how text wraps around an image or animage box.
	HYPERLINK CREATE	Set the image as a hyperlink.

X-REF For information on layered objects, see Chapter 10.

Moving and Sizing a Graphic

You've inserted your beautiful image of a sailboat to advertise your sailboat rental business on a flyer. But wait, the boat is HUGE, taking up a fourth of the page and hogging all the attention. Because a graphic image should *enhance* your text, you don't want it to be too large, nor do you want it to be in a place where it detracts from your message. Here you learn how to move and resize a graphic quickly. If you feel a sense of deja vu, that's because moving and sizing a graphic is nearly identical to moving a line or changing its length and thickness.

First select the graphic, then use one of the following methods:

* To move a selected image, point inside the graphic box until you see the move pointer (four-headed black arrow), then click and drag the box to the next location.

* To delete a selected image, press Delete.

* To resize a selected image, use one of the following techniques:

  * Click and drag a corner sizing handle to adjust the height and width proportionally at the same time.

  * Click and drag a height (top or bottom) sizing handle to increase or decrease the image height.

  * Click and drag a width (left or right) sizing handle to increase or decrease the image width.

 Note that using a width or height sizing handle may distort your image. If this isn't what you want, use a corner sizing handle.

SIZING UP YOUR GRAPHICS

If you want a little more control over the exact height and width of an image, secondary-click the image and choose Size from the QuickMenu to display the Box Size dialog box. Next, under Width and Height, select one of the following options and click OK. The most common method is to set the width to a specific measurement and then set the Height to Maintain proportions, so the image isn't distorted by the change in width.

* *Set* enables you to set a specific measurement.

* *Full* sets the image to span the width or height of the page between the left and right (width) or top and bottom (height) margins.

* *Maintain proportions* adjusts the box to ensure that the image doesn't distort.

To draw a picture, click the Draw Picture button on the WordPerfect toolbar. WordPerfect launches Presentations and inserts a drawing box into your document. You can add objects and create pictures to your heart's content. Refer to "Working with Objects" in Chapter 10 for more information on the Drawing toolbar that displays.

BONUS

Using Advanced Graphics Options

Using the features in this chapter, you've got a good feel for some cool stuff such as graphic lines and images. But if you really want to get into high gear with graphic images, check out this Bonus section. Here I show you how to flip an image inside its graphic box, resize an image within its graphic box (not just resize the box), and contour text around a box (so it ain't so boxy). If you're ready for some serious fun, dig in!

Mirroring a Graphic Image

You've found a great picture of a running cheetah that perfectly conveys the fast, sleek feeling your paragraph is trying to evoke as you describe the new running shoes you're selling. But the cheetah is facing the wrong way. With WordPerfect's Mirror Image feature, this isn't a problem at all. Watch.

With the document containing the image open, select the graphic you want to flip and use one of the following options:

* Click the Flip Left/Right button on the Graphics property bar to flip the image on its vertical axis — that is, from left-facing to right-facing or vice versa.

* Click the Flip Top/Bottom button on the Graphics property bar to flip the image on its horizontal axis — that is, right-side up to upside down or vice versa.

Contouring Text

As I mentioned before, text defaults to wrap around any graphic box you insert into your document. And that's great. It looks pretty good. But if your image doesn't need captions, wouldn't it look even better if the text wrapped around the *image* instead of around the *graphic box*? If you're not sure what I mean, take a look at Figure 6-8.

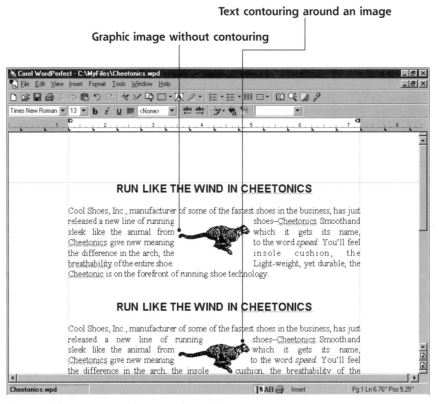

Figure 6-8 Text wrapping around graphics.

Twirl and Zoom

In addition to flipping an image inside its box, you can also rotate the image to give it a different feel or to create a sense of movement. With your image selected, click the Image Tools button on the Graphics property bar to display the Image Tools palette. Next, click Rotate on the Image Tools palette to display the rotation handles inside the image. Click and drag any handle in the direction you want to rotate the image. When you're finished, click Rotate on the Image Tools palette to remove the rotation handles.

If your image rotates left when you're dragging right, that's because it remembers the original position of the image. If you flipped this image, WordPerfect remembers that it used to face the other way and rotates accordingly. This can be confusing, so rotate with care!

Once you rotate an image, parts of it may disappear because of the confines of the graphics box. If you want to see the entire image, you'll need to decrease the image size within the graphic box. Display the Image Tools palette, click the Zoom tool, and select the second option (two arrows). This places a scroll bar on your image. Click and drag the scroll box up to decrease the image within the box until you get the desired effect. Close the Image Tools palette when you're finished.

If you want your text to wrap like the example in Figure 6-8, select the graphic you want to contour, click the Wrap button, and select the desired wrapping/contouring option from the pop-up menu.

TIP To return the graphic image to its original settings, click the Image Tools button and click Reset Attributes. Though this is similar to Undo, note that this returns all settings — not just the most recent one — to the original settings.

Summary

In this chapter, you journeyed through some serious desktop publishing features — changing margins, using TextArt to create headings, and working with newspaper and tabular columns. You also worked with graphic lines and graphic images, learning how to move and resize them using the mouse. Next, you'll look at how to use one of WordPerfect's most powerful and useful features: tables.

WORKING WITH TABLES

One of the most powerful and useful tools in WordPerfect is the Tables feature. Because tables are one of my top three favorite and most-used features, I believe they deserve an entire chapter. And when you see what tables can do, you'll think so, too. Tables are one of the best ways to organize your information, enabling you to set up neat rows and columns by adding and removing border lines and formatting text as you would in a document (see Figure 7-1). Tables have a number of advantages over tabs, not the least of which is the ability to enter and manage large blocks of text within a column and row. WordPerfect wraps the text, keeping everything nice and neat. You'll see how this works later in the chapter.

Creating a Table

In Chapter 6, you learned how to set up columns using the Tab feature. As I mentioned, tabs are good for short text that you want to line up quickly and easily. However, if you need a little bit more from your columns, your best bet is to use the Tables feature.

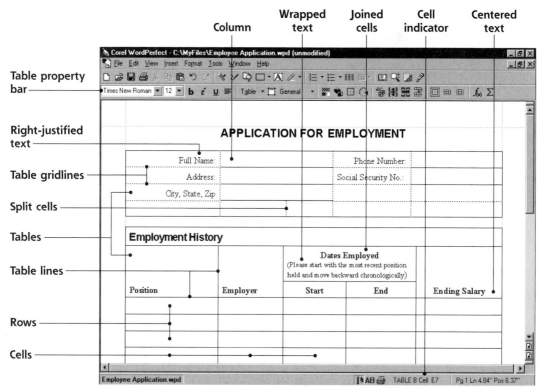

Figure 7-1 An example of a table.

Understanding Tables

If you've used a spreadsheet application, such as Quattro Pro, you'll have a
basic understanding of table structure. Tables are made up of columns and rows.
WordPerfect refers to columns using letters (A, B, C, D, and so on) and to rows
using numbers (1, 2, 3, 4, and so forth). The intersection of a column and row is
called a *cell,* and WordPerfect references the cell with a combination of the letter
and number. For example, column A, row 1 is cell A1, and column D, row 5 is
cell D5. When the insertion point is located within a table cell, the cell reference
displays on the Application bar (refer back to Figure 7-1).

The example in Figure 7-1 also shows *joined cells*. These cells were once separate cells but have been joined to create a single cell to suit the contents. You can
also split a cell into multiple cells to further organize your information. Joining
and splitting cells are just two of many features that make Tables a powerful
organizational tool.

CALLING ALL CELL ADDRESSES

You can display row and column indicators to help you identify your rows and columns. With the insertion point anywhere inside the table, click the Table menu button on the Tables property bar and choose Row/Col Indicators. If you have the Formula toolbar displayed, you can click the Row/Column Indicator button (next to Close).

Row indicators appear down the left side of the screen and column indicators appear across the top of the document window. The letter and number buttons that appear depressed indicate the insertion point location.

Creating a New Table

Before you create a table, try to determine how many columns and rows you're going to need. Although you can easily add or remove either later, starting out with a table that is close to what you really want is great. Consider sketching your table to see how the cells will contain your information. For example, if you're creating a fill-in-the-blank application that users complete at their computers, you'll want to determine what information to include (applicant name, address, phone, Social Security number, job history, and so on) and how much space to allot to each piece of information. Obviously, any open-ended questions will require a great deal of blank space, whereas short entries such as the applicant's phone number will require a finite number of characters.

To create your table, position the insertion point in the location for table. Click and hold the Table QuickCreate button on the WordPerfect toolbar and then select the number of columns and rows from the grid that displays by dragging the mouse. When you release the mouse button, WordPerfect inserts a table at the insertion point location, using the selection you indicated, and displays the Table property bar whenever the insertion point is located inside a table.

FEATURE
FOCUS   The Table property bar is context-sensitive and changes depending on whether you've selected cells.

WordPerfect uses a single line border around all cells by default. For more on changing the line appearance or removing lines and borders altogether, see "Adding Table Lines and Fill" later in this chapter.

TIP If you have a "slippery mouse" and don't trust it to select the correct number of rows and columns from the grid, choose Insert→Table or press Ctrl+F12 to display the Create Table dialog box. Under Table size, type the number of columns in the Columns text box, type the number of rows in the Rows text box, and click OK.

Entering Information in a Table

Once you have created your table, you can enter any text or numbers. To enter text, make sure the insertion point is in the appropriate cell and type the text, letting it wrap within the cell margins if necessary. The row height will adjust to accommodate all text. For example, if you are creating a form such as Application for Employment in Figure 7-1, you would type **Full Name** in cell A1.

TIP To fill in information quickly, you can use the QuickFill feature, which is identical to QuickFill in Quattro Pro. See "Using QuickFill" in Chapter 12.

To position the insertion point in the next cell, press Tab. To position it in the previous cell, press Shift+Tab. Refer to Table B-6 in Appendix B for additional tips on moving around a table using the keyboard. Note that if the insertion point is in the last cell in a table and you press Tab, WordPerfect adds a new row to the bottom of the table. For more on inserting and removing rows and columns, see "Changing Table Structure" in this chapter.

TIP If your table is quite large or you have more than one table (as Figure 7-1 does), you can use the Go To feature to move to a particular cell. Position the insertion point in the table and then select Edit→Go To or press Ctrl+G to display the Go To dialog box. Select Table, indicate the table name, enter the cell in the Cell/Range text box, and click OK.

Changing Table Structure

Say you have your text in the cells and it looks okay — except the width of column C is really too narrow for the information cell C4 contains, and cell A2 is too wide to contain only the person's middle initial. And what about the stuff you forgot? You don't have any rows or columns left into which you can insert it. Not to worry. If you need to prop up a wobbly table with a book under one leg or insert a leaf to accommodate an unexpected guest, you can do so quickly. WordPerfect lets you add and remove columns and rows, join and split cells, and increase the width of columns to ensure that there's room for Uncle Stan and his belly.

Using the Table Property Bar

Before you begin making changes to the table, review the buttons on the Table property bar in Table 7-1. These buttons are available when you have no cells selected. Remember that the property bar will change when you select cells. You see this later in the chapter.

TABLE 7-1 Table Property Bar

Button	Name	Description
Table ▼	Table	Select table options from a drop-down menu.
	Vertical Alignment	Set the placement of cell contents top to bottom.
General ▼	Numeric	Format numbers in cells.
	Cell Fill	Change the fill style of the cell background.
	Foreground Fill Color	Change the color of the cell background.
	Change Outside Line	Change the style for lines surrounding the cell or selected cells.
	Rotate Cell	Rotate the cell contents by 90 degrees, moving counterclockwise.
	QuickJoin	Join selected cells with a single click.
	QuickSplit Row	Split selected cells into rows with a single click.
	QuickSplit Column	Split selected cells into columns with a single click.
	Insert Row	Insert new row(s) automatically.
	Select Table	Select the entire table.
	Select Table Row	Select the current row.
	Select Table Column	Select the current column.
$f_\times$	Formula Toolbar	Display the formula toolbar.
Σ	QuickSum	Total a row or column.

Selecting Cells

Just as you can select text before you move or format it, you can also select cells, rows, and columns before performing some action on them. Perhaps you want the first two rows to appear bold, or you want to change the column widths of columns B, C, and D. Selecting them first saves time and effort. The key to selecting is the selection arrow, which is a white arrow that appears when you point to the edge of a cell (see Figure 7-2).

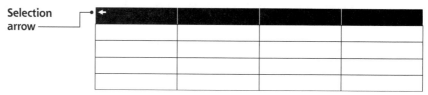

Selection arrow

Figure 7-2 Select multiple cells with the selection arrow.

Use Table 7-2 to select different elements of the table. You use these techniques throughout the rest of this chapter.

TABLE 7-2 Table Selection Techniques

To Select	Do This
A single cell	Point to the *left* edge of the cell to display the selection arrow and then click once.
Multiple cells	Point to the *left* edge of the first cell to display the selection arrow and then click and drag over all cells you want to select.
Entire row	Point to the *left* edge of any cell in the row to display the selection arrow and then double-click; or, position the insertion point in the row and click the Select Table Row button.
Entire column	Point to the top edge of any cell in the column to display the selection arrow and then double-click; or, position the insertion point in the column and click the Select Table Column button.
Entire table	Point to the left or top edge of any cell in the table to display the selection arrow and then triple-click; or, position the insertion point in any cell in the table and click the Select Table button.

When you select cells, the Table property bar changes and becomes the Table Cell Selected property bar or the Table Everything Selected property-bar, reflecting options for selected cells.

Adjusting Column Widths

You may find that although your text wraps within cells, you've typed a great deal of text, and it looks strange because the columns aren't wide enough. Or perhaps you only have a middle initial in a cell that's two inches wide. The following sections explain how to easily adjust column widths.

ADJUSTING INDIVIDUAL COLUMNS

To quickly adjust a column width, point to the right border of the column you want to adjust until you see the sizing pointer (a black, double-headed arrow). Then click and drag in the appropriate direction to increase or decrease the width.

EQUALIZING AND FITTING COLUMNS

WordPerfect lets you format single and multiple columns so that they are either all the same width or are the width of the widest entry in a column. For example, if you have a narrow middle column that contains the name *Jennifer A. Smith*, her name may wrap because of the width of the column. To make sure that Jennifer's name stays on one line, you can size the column to fit the text it contains. Note that you can use either of these column features, but not both; one will always override the other.

To use either of these column formatting features, you must first select the column(s) you want to format (See "Selecting Cells" earlier in this chapter for more information.) Then choose one of the following:

* To make all selected columns the same width, click the Equalize Columns button on the Table Cell Selected or Table Everything Selected property bar. You can also click the Table menu button on the property bar and choose Equal Column Widths from the drop-down menu.

WIDE LOAD

To increase or decrease column width using the keyboard, position the insertion point in the column you want to adjust. Press Ctrl+< (the key with the less than symbol and comma on it) to decrease the width, or press Ctrl+> (the key with the greater than symbol and period on it) to increase the width. If you are using a table in a form and are looking at an existing hard copy form to guide its design, you may want to use precise measurements for each column so that your text flows accordingly. You can measure the columns on your hard copy and then use those measurements for the table column in WordPerfect.

To enter exact measurements for a column, select the column(s) to adjust, click the Table menu button on the Table property bar, and select Format from the drop-down menu. WordPerfect displays the Properties for Table Format dialog box. Then choose the Column tab to display the options for table columns and type the measurement in the Width text box under Column width. Click OK.

7

✳ To adjust the width automatically so that it is as wide as the widest entry, click the Size to Fit button on the property bar. Or, click the Table menu button on the property bar and choose Size Column to Fit from the drop-down menu.

Inserting Rows and Columns

After you've created your table and added information, you may find that you need additional rows or columns. You can quickly insert rows using the keyboard. If you want to insert columns, you use the menu. Here's how.

INSERTING ROWS

To insert rows into a table, follow these steps:

1. Position the insertion point in the location for the new row. For example, if you want a new row above or below row 4, position the insertion point in row 4.

2. Use one of the following shortcut key combinations to perform the desired task:

   ✳ To insert a row above the current row, press Alt+Insert or click the Insert Row button on the Table property bar.

   ✳ To insert a row below the current row, press Alt+Shift+Insert.

If you select rows before pressing these keys, you can insert multiple rows at once.

TIP **If the insertion point is located in the last cell of the table, press Tab to add a new row to the bottom of the table.**

INSERTING COLUMNS

If you need more than one new row, or you need to insert columns, you can use the Insert Columns/Rows dialog box.

1. Position the insertion point in the location for the new rows or columns. For example, if you want a new column next to column B, position the insertion point in column B.

2. Click the Table menu button on the Table property bar and choose Insert. WordPerfect displays the Insert Columns/Rows dialog box (see Figure 7-3).

Figure 7-3 Insert columns and rows.

3. If you're inserting columns, you can select the Keep column width the same check box to make sure that all columns remain the same widths.

4. Click OK. WordPerfect inserts the columns or rows, adjusting the table as necessary.

Joining and Splitting Cells

Many times you'll find that your vision of your fill-in-the-blank form or the table you are using for other information doesn't fit into the predefined cell widths of your columns. For example, if you'd like the address cell to span the cells for city, state, and zip (similar to the example in Figure 7-1), you can join two or more cells. Conversely, if you need to divide a single cell into multiple cells, you can do that, too.

JOINING CELLS

Using the fill-in-the-blank application example, you may want row 3 to be one cell so it can contain the complete address of an applicant. Or you may want to have a single cell act as a heading for the cells below it. In either case, you'll want to join the cells and make them one. To join cells, click the QuickJoin button to turn on the QuickJoin tool. When you position the pointer in the table, you'll see two facing arrows attached to the pointer. In your table, select the cells you want to join. WordPerfect joins them automatically. Click the QuickJoin Cells button to turn off the QuickJoin tool.

 TIP You can also select the cells first, click the Table menu button on the Table property bar, select Join from the drop-down menu, and then select Cells.

Note that WordPerfect uses the first cell you select for the cell reference. For example, if you joined cells B2 and C2, the joined cells become cell B2, and C2 no longer exists.

SPLITTING CELLS

If you want to create a series of cells below a single cell, you can split the cell or cells into rows or columns.

To split cells into rows, follow these steps:

1. Click the QuickSplit Row button to turn on the QuickSplit Row tool. When you position the pointer in the table, it becomes a box that has top and bottom arrows with a dashed line to guide the split (see Figure 7-4).

Figure 7-4   Split a cell row to further divide your information.

2. In your table, position the dashed line where you want to split the cell and then click the mouse button. WordPerfect splits the cell automatically.

3. Continue clicking all cells you want to split.

4. Click the QuickSplit Row button to turn off the QuickSplit Row tool.

To split cells into columns, follow these steps:

1. Click the QuickSplit Column button to turn on the QuickSplit Column tool. When you position the pointer in the table, it becomes a box that has left and right arrows with a dashed line to guide the split (see Figure 7-5). Use the QuickStatus box to help divide the cell into appropriate sections.

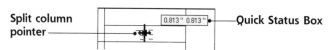

Figure 7-5   Split a cell column with the QuickSplit Column button.

2. In your table, position the dashed line where you want to split the cell and then click the mouse button. WordPerfect splits the cell automatically.

3. Continue clicking all cells you wish to split.

4. Click the QuickSplit Column button to turn off the QuickSplit Column tool.

The QuickJoin, QuickSplit Row, and QuickSplit Column buttons on the Table property bar allow you to join and split with a single click.

If clicking to split isn't your cup of tea, or if you want to split multiple rows or columns at one time, you can use the Split Cell dialog box. Just follow these steps:

1. In your table, position the insertion point in the cell you want to split, or if you want to split multiple cells, select them.

2. Click the Table menu button on the Table property bar, choose `Split` → `Cell` from the drop-down menu. WordPerfect displays the Split Cell dialog box and assumes that you want to split the current cell(s) into two columns.

3. Under Split, choose either Columns or Rows and indicate the number to split into in the associated text box. Note that if you have multiple cells selected, *each cell* will split into the number indicated.

4. Click OK.

Moving and Copying Rows and Columns

Your table is fabulous, with all your text exactly where you want it, right? Right — except maybe the row containing the phone number and Social Security number should be farther up. Or maybe you want to switch the order of two columns. WordPerfect lets you move or copy entire columns and rows, keeping their contents intact.

Here's how to move or copy entire columns and rows:

1. Select the row(s) or column(s) you want to move.

2. Click the Cut or Copy button on the WordPerfect 8 toolbar, or secondary-click the selection and choose Cut or Copy from the QuickMenu. WordPerfect displays the Table Cut/Copy dialog box (see Figure 7-6).

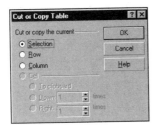

Figure 7-6 The Cut or Copy Table dialog box.

3. Under Cut or copy the current, choose Row or Column and then click OK. If you want to move or copy the *contents* of the selected row(s) or column(s), choose Selection. WordPerfect removes the entire row or column from the table, or just the contents if you chose Selection.

4. Position the insertion point in the new location for the rows, columns, or contents. For example, if you want the row to insert before (above) row 2, position the insertion point in row 2. If you want the column to insert before (to the left of) column C, position the insertion point in column C.

5. Click the Paste button on the Tables toolbar; or, right-click the destination row or column and choose Paste from the QuickMenu.

Deleting Rows and Columns

Like everything else you put in a document, you can take out rows and columns in a table, or just the text within them. The latter is nice if you've decided that you want to scrap the contents of several cells and start over. You don't have to remove the cells; you can just delete their contents.

To delete rows or columns, follow these steps:

1. Select the row(s) or column(s) you want to delete.

2. Press Delete or click the Table menu button on the Table property bar and choose Delete from the drop-down menu. WordPerfect displays the Delete dialog box.

3. Under Delete, select the element you want to delete — Columns, Rows, Cell contents only, or Formulas only. For more on formulas, see the Bonus section at the end of this chapter.

4. Click OK. WordPerfect will remove rows, columns, or cell contents, depending on your selection.

Formatting Tables

Once you have your information typed in the table, and your columns and rows are the way you want them, it's time to do a little formatting to spruce it up. You can format your table the way you formatted your documents, changing fonts, adding character enhancements, and justifying text within cells. If you use numbers in your table, you can select from a variety of number formats to display those numerals in just the right way.

If you joined the cells in row 1 because they contain a heading for the table, you can format that heading with fonts and justification. This makes it stand out and provides an appealing look. When you're formatting text in a table, you have two choices: You can format *all* the text contained in a cell or group of cells, or format individual words or phrases *within* a cell. To format text in a cell or range of cells, select the entire cell or cells. To format text *within* a cell, select the text itself. Then format the text as you did in "Formatting Text" in Chapter 4, using such tools as fonts, bold, italics, justification, and text colors.

Adding Table Lines and Fill

When it's your turn to host the big holiday dinner, you may include an attractive centerpiece or runner to add a little pizzazz to the meal. You can do the same with your tables in WordPerfect. Using borders, lines, and fill, you can set an attractive table that would even impress Martha Stewart. Here is a description of each of these elements:

* *Borders* are the lines around the perimeter of a table. They format the table separately from the lines and work as a single unit.
* *Lines* are the interior lines between the cells or outside lines around a table. WordPerfect treats each line as a separate unit.
* *Fill* enables you to shade parts of cells with varying shades of gray, a pattern, or color.

By default, WordPerfect uses a single line to surround each cell and create the grid that you see when you create a table for the first time. However, if you want to make more of a statement with your table, you can change the lines and add shading behind the text in your table. Use care when adding lines and fill; you don't want the appearance of a table to overshadow the importance of its contents.

Note that the property bar and your line and fill buttons are different, depending on whether you've selected a few cells or the entire table.

To change lines and fill, follow these steps.

1. Select the cells that have the lines you want to change.

2. Click the appropriate line button on the property bar and choose the desired line format, using Tables 7-3 and 7-4 as guides.

Tables 7-3 and 7-4 describe only those buttons that deal with lines and fill on the Table Cell Selected and Table Everything Selected property bars. Use the Cell Fill and Foreground Fill Color buttons to add color or patterns to cell backgrounds.

NIFTY NUMBERS

You can format table numbers to contain a comma and decimal point followed by two zeroes (1,200.00). Or, if you'd like, have the number convert to a percentage, complete with a percentage symbol (%).

To format numbers, select the cells containing the numbers you want to format. Next, click the Numeric button on the Table property bar and select the desired format from the pop-down list.

Format the cells before entering numbers so that WordPerfect can do a great deal of the work. For example, if you want your numbers to appear with commas and decimal points and you format them using the Numeric Format feature, you can type 2075 in the cell. When you move to the next cell, WordPerfect automatically changes it to 2,075.00.

TABLE 7-3 Line and Fill Buttons on the Table Cell Selected Property Bar

Button	Name	Description
	Left Line	Select a line style for the left line of selected cells.
	Right Line	Select a line style for the right line of selected cells.
	Top Line	Select a line style for the top line of selected cells.
	Bottom Line	Select a line style for the bottom line of selected cells.
	Inside Lines	Select a line style for the inside lines of selected cells.
	Outside Lines	Select a line style for the outside lines of selected cells.
	Fill	Select a fill for selected cells.

TABLE 7-4 Line and Fill Buttons on the Table Everything Selected Property Bar

Button	Name	Description
	Change Table Border	Select a line style for the border surrounding the table.
	Default Line Style Alternating Fill	Select a line style for all inside lines in the table. Select an alternating method for the fill you've selected. Note that you must select a fill style before you can use the Alternating Fill option.

BORDERS AND LINES TO GO

WordPerfect ships with a number of predefined border/line/fill styles. Using the SpeedFormat feature, you can apply any of these to your table for instant pizzazz. Keep in mind that many of these styles contain a border that will appear on top of any existing lines. This means the lines surrounding the table may not appear as you intended.

1. Secondary-click anywhere in the table and choose SpeedFormat from the QuickMenu. WordPerfect displays the Table SpeedFormat dialog box.

2. Under Available styles, select the type of formatting you want to apply. Check the sample table to see how it looks.

3. To make sure that you don't overlap existing table lines, choose the Clear current table format before applying check box. Then click Apply. WordPerfect formats your table using the selected style.

Note that if you add and remove rows and columns after applying a style, you may need to make some changes to your lines and fill to ensure that the table remains formatted correctly.

TIP To format lines and fill simultaneously, select the cells. Click the Table button on the Table property bar and choose Borders/Fill from the drop-down menu. Make your line and fill selections and then click OK.

BONUS

Using Calculations in a Table

If you have a short sales report or budget projections you want to include in a document, you can put the data in a WordPerfect table and use the calculation features to add, subtract, multiply, and divide. And WordPerfect provides a wealth of functions to perform more advanced calculations for amortized loans, for example. Calculating in WordPerfect tables is easy, and if you don't do a great deal of work in Quattro Pro, you may find you can do your number crunching right here.

Summing Numbers

Probably the most common calculation you will perform is adding up a column or row. You can select the cells you want to include in your sum or let WordPerfect sum an entire column. Your table should include all the numbers you want to sum, plus empty cells at the bottom or right where the totals will appear.

To sum a row or column, position the insertion point in the cell to contain the total and click the QuickSum button on the Table property bar. If you can't see the QuickSum button on the Table property bar, click the Table button and select Formula Toolbar. Click QuickSum on the Formula toolbar.

TIP **If you can't see all the buttons on a toolbar or property bar, move the bar so that it appears as a floating palette, or display multiple rows. For more information, see Chapter 18.**

When you sum cells in a table, WordPerfect inserts a formula into the total cells. If you click in a cell containing a total, you will see the formula display on the Application bar and in the Formula Edit Box on the Formula toolbar. For example, if you used QuickSum to total cells A1 through A4, cell A5 will contain the formula +SUM(A1:A4). The colon indicates that the formula is summing cells A1 through A4 *inclusively*.

If you position the insertion point in a cell that could potentially sum a column *or* a row, QuickSum will sum the column.

If you have a column containing subtotals, you may have empty cells to mark each subtotal. If so, when you place the insertion point in an empty cell, WordPerfect totals only until it reaches the next empty cell. This means that the total in the cell will show a *subtotal*. To get a grand total of all subtotals, you need to create your own formula. For information on this, see "Creating a Formula" next.

If your cells contain numbers as headings, such as the last three years (1994, 1995, 1996), WordPerfect will include these years in a total at the bottom of a column. To ensure that this doesn't happen, you can format the cells so WordPerfect ignores them. See "WordPerfect Problems" in Appendix C for more information.

Creating a Formula

QuickSum is great for adding up entire columns or rows, but if you have subtotals in your table and need grand totals, or if you need to perform subtraction, multiplication, or division, you'll need to create a formula.

X-REF For detailed information and explanations of formulas and functions, see Chapter 13.

WordPerfect uses the Formula toolbar to create and perform calculations. You can type formulas into the Formula Edit Box on the Formula toolbar, which is similar to using the input line in Quattro Pro. To display the Table Formula feature bar, position the insertion point in the table and use one of the following methods:

* Click the Formula Toolbar button on the Table property bar.
* Right-click the table and choose Formula Toolbar from the QuickMenu.
* Click the Table menu button on the Table property bar and choose Formula Toolbar.

Any of these methods will display the Formula toolbar at the top of the document window under the property bar (see Figure 7-7).

For example, if you want to multiply the contents of cell B2 by the contents of cell D4, your formula would look like this: =B2*D4.

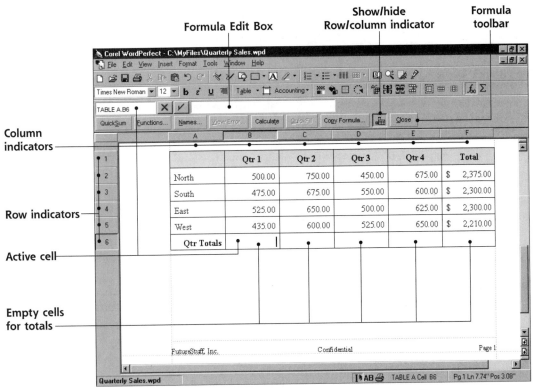

Figure 7-7 Perform calculations in tables with the Formula toolbar.

X-REF If you think you may use WordPerfect rather than Quattro Pro for calculations, review "Working with Operators" in Chapter 13 to understand calculation and operator precedence.

You create a formula similar to creating one in Quattro Pro, only you click in the Formula Edit Box on the Formula toolbar in WordPerfect. WordPerfect displays the words "Formula edit mode is on" to the right of the box and inserts the cell reference in the box at the left end of the Table Formula feature bar. Refer to "Entering Formulas" in Chapter 13 for details on entering a formula and inserting it into a cell.

Calculating Your Table

If you change the numbers in your table, WordPerfect will not automatically update your calculations. To update the table, choose Calculate on the Formula toolbar or right-click anywhere in the table and choose Calculate from the QuickMenu. You can also set WordPerfect to update your formulas automatically when you make changes to your numbers. Click the Table button on the Table property bar and choose Calculate from the drop-down menu. WordPerfect displays the Calculate dialog box (see Figure 7-8).

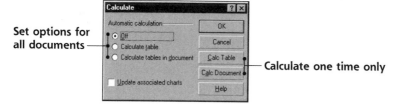

Figure 7-8 Set automatic calculation options.

Under Automatic calculation mode, choose Calculate tables in document and click OK. WordPerfect calculates all tables in your document and updates changes automatically from now on. When you make a change to a number in your table, WordPerfect updates the formulas after you move the insertion point out of the cell. This setting for Automatic calculation stays in effect for all documents until you change it.

 TIP If you have information in a Quattro Pro spreadsheet that you'd like to use in a WordPerfect document, you can import the spreadsheet as a WordPerfect table. Check online help.

Summary

Here you learned about one of WordPerfect's most valuable features — Tables. You learned how to create and format a table by doing such tasks as inserting and removing columns and rows, formatting table contents, and improving table appearance. Next up, the final chapter in your WordPerfect adventure. There you'll learn how to use the Merge feature to create form letters and create a macro to let WordPerfect perform a task.

CHAPTER EIGHT

AUTOMATING WITH MERGES AND MACROS

IN THIS CHAPTER YOU LEARN THESE KEY SKILLS

When you get a sweepstakes letter or solicitation letter, you'll notice a few things about it. First, if you compare it to your neighbor's letter, you'll see that the body of the letter is nearly identical. Second, you'll notice that those who created the letter personalized it by including your name and address. These two parts — the identical body of the letter and the personalized areas — are the key to *merging*, which enables you to personalize a form letter before sending it to dozens of people. In this chapter, you learn how merging can make your life easier when creating form letters, envelopes, or address labels. You also learn how to use the Macros feature for repetitive tasks.

Understanding Merge Concepts

A merged document uses two types of files to complete its task. The *form file* contains the standard body text that all letters will contain. The *data source* contains the variable information that allows you to personalize each document with a name, address, or any other information. The data source can be your Address Book or a data file you create separately. In this chapter, you learn how to merge with both types of data sources.

X-REF For more information on the Address Book, see Chapter 1.

When you create your form document, you insert codes in the places where you want the variable information to appear. When you merge the form file with the data file, WordPerfect replaces the codes in the form file with the personalized information in the data file, creating a new document containing the final output.

Creating the Data File

As I mentioned previously, the data file contains the information that you use to personalize your form letters. The data file can contain names, addresses, phone numbers, and more. Creating the data file first is a good idea so that you have a sense of your information before setting up your form documents.

Understanding Data Files

Depending on what information your data file contains, you can use it to create form letters, mailing labels, phone lists, and more. A data file consists of three elements:

* A *field* is a single piece of information related to a particular person or organization.

* A *record* is all related fields for a person or organization taken as a whole. When you merge the data file with a form file, WordPerfect creates a new form document for each record, keeping all form documents within the same WordPerfect document.

* A *field name* helps identify the information in a field and appears at the top of the data file or in the first row of the table if you set up your data file in a table.

 NOTE Refer to Figure 8-3 to understand these elements. Note that Figure 8-3 places records in a table and that the page size has been changed to help display the information more clearly in each cell.

Creating Your Data File

Before you actually start creating your data file, you should think about how you will use the information it will contain. You have a lot of flexibility when you set up your records and fields in WordPerfect. You can have the first and last name as one field, or break it up into two fields. What's the difference? Well, if you ever want to refer to the person by his or her first name, you can't do it unless the first and last names are in separate fields. A good rule of thumb is to break up your information into the smallest pieces possible to provide the greatest flexibility.

To create your data file, follow these steps:

1. At a new document window in WordPerfect, choose Tools → Merge or press Shift+F9. WordPerfect displays the Merge dialog box.

2. Click Create Data to display the Create Data File dialog box (see Figure 8-1). This is where you enter your field names to help identify the information you will put in your data file.

3. If you want to see your records displayed in a table, choose Format records in a table at the bottom of the dialog box.

If you have an existing document open, WordPerfect displays the Create Merge File dialog box, asking if you want to use the file in the active window or in a new document window. Choose New document window and then click OK.

Figure 8-1 Set up your field names in the Create Data File dialog box.

4. In the Name a field text box, type the first field name and press Enter or click Add. For example, if your data file will contain names, addresses, and phone numbers, type **First Name** or **FName.** WordPerfect inserts what you've typed into the Fields used in merge list box and clears the Name a field text box, making it ready for the next field name. Repeat for each field name you want to add.

TIP

To change the order of the field names, select the field name to change and use the Move Up and Move Down buttons.

5. After you're finished creating your field names, click OK. WordPerfect sets up your data file in the document window and displays the Quick Data Entry dialog box (see Figure 8-2). If you chose to set up your data

file in a table, your field names will appear in the first row of the table in your document. Notice that your field names appear as the headings in this dialog box.

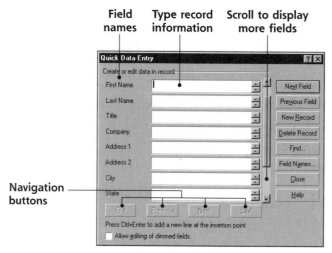

Figure 8-2 Enter record information in the Quick Data Entry dialog box.

6. In the first field text box, type the information for your first record and then press Tab to position the insertion point in the next field text box. For example, if the first field text box is "First Name," type **Robert** or **Marilyn** in the text box. Repeat for all fields for the current record.

7. After you enter the information for the last field for the record, press Enter or click New Record. WordPerfect records this information in the document and displays a new Quick Data Entry dialog box for the next record.

8. Complete the information for this record. When you're finished, click Close. WordPerfect displays a message asking if you want to save the changes to disk.

9. Click Yes to display the Save File dialog box.

10. Type a name for the data file, then locate and display the folder in which you want to store it. WordPerfect automatically adds a DAT extension to the file to designate it as a data file.

11. Click Save. WordPerfect saves the data file and displays the Merge toolbar (see Figure 8-3). Using the Merge toolbar, you can add or edit records, go to your form file (if it exists), and merge the data file with a form file. Note that the Merge toolbar will contain different buttons, depending on whether or not you've placed your data in a table.

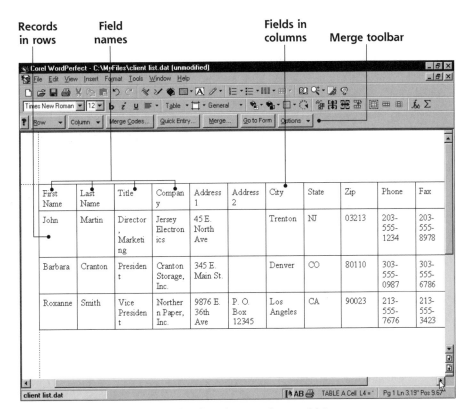

Figure 8-3 A data file in WordPerfect (formatted as a table).

Working with Records

If you placed your data in a table, each cell contains a single field, and each row contains a record. If you didn't place your data in a table, each field ends in an ENDFIELD code, and each record ends in an ENDRECORD code (see Figure 8-4).

After you create your data file, you may notice that it contains some errors, or you may realize you forgot a few records. You can make your changes right in the document, or use the Quick Data Entry dialog box.

EDITING RECORDS IN THE DOCUMENT WINDOW

If you notice a typographical error or other minor problem in a record, you can just position the insertion point in the location of the error and fix it like you do text in any WordPerfect document, whether the data is in a table or not.

X-REF For information on working with information in tables, see Chapter 7.

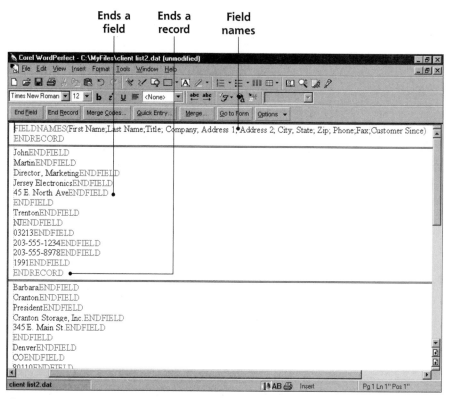

Figure 8-4 Work with records in the default format.

If you didn't place your data in a table and it looks similar to the data in Figure 8-4, here are some tips for making sure things stay the way they need to be. If you accidentally delete an ENDFIELD code, you can undo the deletion or position the insertion point at the end of the field and click End Field on the Merge bar.

If you accidentally delete an ENDRECORD code, you can undo the deletion or position the insertion point at the end of the field and click End Record on the Merge bar.

If you want to edit a record in an open data file and are nervous about working directly in your document, click Quick Entry on the Merge toolbar to display the Quick Data Entry dialog box. Use the First, Previous, Next, and Last buttons at the bottom of the dialog box to display the desired record, then make your changes. You can also click Find to search for a record based on its field contents. This Find option works similar to the Find and Replace Text feature in WordPerfect. See Chapter 4 for more information.

TIP Position the insertion point in the record you want to edit before you click Quick Entry on the Merge toolbar to display the information for that record.

ADDING NEW RECORDS

If you want to add new records to your data file, all you need to do is display the Quick Data Entry dialog box and you're on your way. You can also modify existing records in this dialog box if you're nervous about working in the data file itself. To add a new record to an open data file, click Quick Entry on the Merge toolbar to display the Quick Data Entry dialog box. If you aren't at a blank record in the Quick Data Entry dialog box, click New Record and then type the information for the record. Click Close and save the changes to disk using the same filename.

SIDE TRIP

I NEED MORE FIELDS!

Besides adding new records, you may find that you haven't included information about each record that you'd like to have. For example, maybe you're compiling a list of employees and want to have their Social Security numbers as part of their records. To add new fields, follow these steps:

1. With the data file open, click Quick Entry on the Merge toolbar and then click Field Names.

2. In the Field Names list, select the location for the new field. For example, if you want the Social Security number to be the last field in the list, select the last field in the Field Names list. WordPerfect inserts the selected field in the Field name text box.

3. Double-click the field in the Field name text box to select it, then type a name for the new field.

4. Click Add to place the name after the selected field in the Field Names list or click Add Before to place the name before the selected field.

5. After you're finished, click OK to return to the Quick Entry dialog box. Enter information for the new fields for each record, using navigation buttons at the bottom to display records before or after the current record.

Creating a Form File

The form file contains the text that will be the same for all your recipients and the field codes that coincide with the fields in your data file or the Address Book. You can start from scratch or use an existing document as the basis of your form document, replacing text with field codes where you want to personalize the document.

Associating an Existing Data File

The easiest way to create a form file is to associate it with an existing data file. When you associate a new form file with an existing data file, WordPerfect automatically lists the field names from the data file so you can quickly insert them into your form file. To create a form file without having the data file open, see "Reuse, Recycle for Merge" in this chapter.

To associate an open data file with a form file, click Go to Form on the Merge toolbar. WordPerfect displays the Associate dialog box telling you that no associated file exists. Click Create. WordPerfect opens a new document window and displays the Merge toolbar for a form file. Notice that it contains some buttons that are different from those on the Merge toolbar for the data file, such as Insert Field, Date, and Keyboard, all of which are tools for automating your merge. Format the document and type any standard text that will remain the same for all documents.

Inserting Field Codes

Once you've created your form file, you can insert field codes from either a data file or the Address Book. Remember, the field codes stand in for the information that WordPerfect will take from either the data file or Address Book to personalize each letter.

To insert field codes, follow these steps:

1. With the form file open, position the insertion point in the location for the first field. For example, if this is a letter, position the insertion point after the space following "Dear."

2. Click Insert Field on the Merge toolbar to display the Insert Field Name or Number dialog box (see Figure 8-5). Because you associated this file with a data file, you'll see a list of the field names here.

Position insertion point for field   Select a field to insert

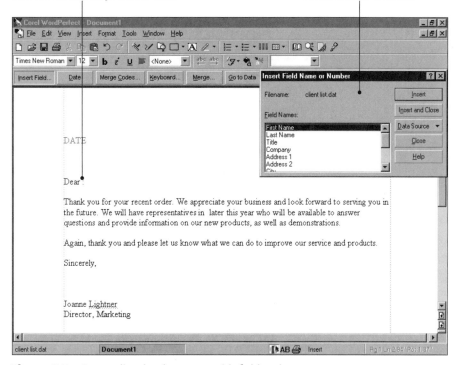

Figure 8-5   Personalize the document with field codes.

3. In the Field Names list in the Insert Field Name or Number dialog box, select the field you want to insert, and click Insert. Alternatively, you can double-click the field in the Field Names list. Continue inserting field codes, making sure you include any spaces or punctuation around the fields so that the text will appear correctly upon merging.

4. When you've inserted the last field in your form file, click Close to close the Insert Field Name or Number dialog box. Your document should contain field codes, as in Figure 8-6.

5. Save your form file as you would any other file. WordPerfect automatically adds an FRM extension to the file to designate it as a form file.

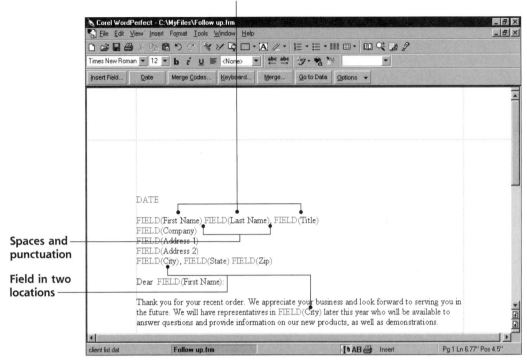

Spaces and punctuation

Field in two locations

Figure 8-6 A sample form file containing body text and field codes.

Associating a Form File with the Address Book

If you decide you also need to merge a form file with your Address Book, or if you have a new form file you want to associate with the Address Book, you can change or add an association at any time. Once you select the Address Book, you need to change any fields in the form file that don't match the fields in the Address Book.

SIDE TRIP

REUSE, RECYCLE FOR MERGE

If you have a letter or other document that contains the bulk of boilerplate information you want to use for a form file, converting it is easy. Just open the document and choose Tools → Merge click and click Create Document in the Merge dialog box. In the Create Merge File dialog box, click OK to use the file in active window option (it's the default). In the Associate a Data File dialog box, associate the form file with an existing data file and click OK. Replace the existing information (such as name and address for a letter) with the appropriate field codes. Choose File → Save As and save the document. When you give it a new name, WordPerfect automatically saves it with an FRM extension. If you just use Save, WordPerfect will replace the old file with the form file and won't use an FRM extension to identify it.

To associate a form file with the Address Book, follow these steps:

1. With the form file open, click Insert Field on the Merge toolbar to display the Insert Field Name or Number dialog box.

2. Click Data Source and select one of your address lists (for example, Frequent Contacts or My Addresses) from the pop-down list. WordPerfect displays the fields associated with the address list in the Insert Field Name or Number dialog box.

If there is no listing for Frequent Contacts or My Addresses, you haven't entered any addresses in your Address Book. See Chapter 1.

3. Insert or replace the fields using the steps in "Inserting Field Codes" earlier in this chapter.

TIP **You can also use a different data source for an existing form file by clicking Data Source and selecting Data File from the pop-down list. You then can select the desired data file. Just remember that the field names in your form file must match those in your data file for the merge to work.**

Merging Documents

Now that you have created the form and data files, you can merge them to create personalized documents. WordPerfect places all the merged records into a single document, separating records with a hard page break.

Merging Standard Documents

If you have a basic form and data file, you can quickly merge them using these steps:

1. With the form file open in WordPerfect, click Merge on the Merge toolbar to display the Perform Merge dialog box (see Figure 8-7). Here you can indicate different form or data files to merge with, as well as where you want the final output to go. Notice that because you started with the form file open, WordPerfect assumes you want to merge with the Current Document. You should see the associated data source in the Data source text box.

2. Make sure that you have the correct form and data files selected and click Merge. WordPerfect merges the form and data files in a new document window.

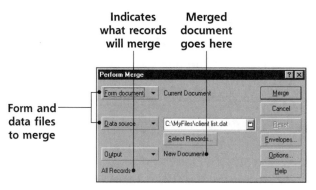

Indicates what records will merge

Merged document goes here

Form and data files to merge

Figure 8-7 Merge your form and data documents.

You can now scroll through the document to check for problems. Note that WordPerfect is set to close up any blank fields so you don't notice them. For example, if some of your recipients don't have company names, you won't see a blank line where the company name would appear for these folks.

Also, WordPerfect separates the document for each new record by a hard page break. This is true even if your form document is longer than a single page. WordPerfect makes sure each record has its own document, which means you actually have several individual documents in a single file. Once you've checked your document, you can print it.

TIP Unless you will use the merged document over and over again, there's really no need to take up disk space by saving it to a file. If you need the merged document again, just re-merge the form and data files.

Merging to Envelopes

If you want to print envelopes to accompany your form letters, you can merge your data file to an envelope form file as you're merging the letters to a new document.

To merge envelopes, follow these steps:

1. With the form file open in WordPerfect, click Merge on the Merge toolbar to display the Perform Merge dialog box.

2. Make sure that you have an associated data source in the Data source text box and click Envelopes to display the Envelope dialog box. You may remember this dialog box from Chapter 3. The only difference here is that this dialog box has a button for inserting field codes into the Mailing address box.

3. Click in the Mailing address box to position the insertion point and click Field at the bottom of the dialog box to display the Insert Field Name or

Number dialog box. You insert fields in the Mailing addresses box just as you inserted them in your form file.

TIP **If you can't see the contents of the Mailing addresses box, click and drag the Insert Field Name or Number dialog box title bar to move the dialog box.**

4. In the Field names list, double-click the field you want to insert, or single-click it and click the Insert and Close button. Repeat this for each field you want to insert. Make sure that you add spaces and punctuation between fields where necessary. To position the insertion point on the next line in the Mailing address box, press Enter.

5. After you're finished, click OK, and then click Merge to perform the merge. WordPerfect merges the envelopes after merging the letters and places them at the end of your letters in the document window. Then you can print them.

The Envelope feature remains set until you exit WordPerfect. If you don't want to print envelopes but need to perform other merges, you can reset the merge. Click Merge on the Merge toolbar, click Reset, and click OK. This also resets any output options you've selected or record selection options. You're all clear now.

X-REF **For more on record selection, see the Bonus at the end of this chapter.**

TIP **You can also merge address labels, create lists, and make many other documents using the Merge feature. See online help for more information.**

Working with Macros

If you worked through Chapters 2 and 3, you saw how features like QuickCorrect and QuickWords can speed up the process of inserting repetitive text. However, you may find yourself needing to perform specific *actions* over and over as opposed to inserting repetitive text. In that case, you can turn to the Macros feature for help. A *macro* is a mini-program of sorts. It lets you record actions — whether they be menu selections, text insertions and formatting, or creating a table — that you can play back any time you need to perform the action. It's sort of like a tape player, where you speak into the microphone and record your voice. Then you can play the recording of your voice later.

WordPerfect lets you store your macros on disk or with a particular template. Disk macros are available for playback at any time; template macros are only available when you're using a particular template. In this section, I focus on creating a macro that's available at all times.

Recording a Macro

The easiest way to create a macro is to record the keystrokes and commands you want to play back. For example, if you want to include the filename in a footer on the last page of every document, you can create a macro to do this. Depending on what your macro does, you will either have an existing document open or will start at a new document window.

To record a macro, follow these steps:

1. Open a document that will be affected by the steps you will record or start at a new document window.

2. Choose Tools → Macro → Record or press Ctrl+F10 to display the Macro Record dialog box. You name your macro here. Notice that WordPerfect automatically provides the WCM macro extension and is ready to store it in the default macros folder (usually \Corel\Suite8\Macros\WPWin).

3. In the File name text box, type a name for your macro and press Enter or click Record. WordPerfect returns to the document window and displays the Macro bar, waiting for you to perform the actions it will record (see Figure 8-8). Notice that the pointer becomes a circle with an X through it in the document window. This indicates an action you can't record. For example, you can't record selecting text with the mouse. To record a selection, you need to select using the keyboard.

 X-REF **For more on selecting with the keyboard, see Chapter 4.**

4. Perform the actions you want to record. WordPerfect will record any text you type, keystrokes you press, or commands you select. For example, if you were going to insert the filename on the last page of a document, your first action would be to press Ctrl+End to position the insertion point at the end of the last page of the document. Your next action would be to create the footer and then insert and format the filename in the footer.

5. After you're finished typing, pressing keys, and choosing commands, click the Stop button on the Macro feature bar or choose Tools → Macro → Record to stop recording. WordPerfect saves the actions you've performed and returns to the document window. Any actions you recorded were also performed in the current document window.

6. If you have a document open that you want to save after performing your recorded actions, save it now. Otherwise, close the document without saving.

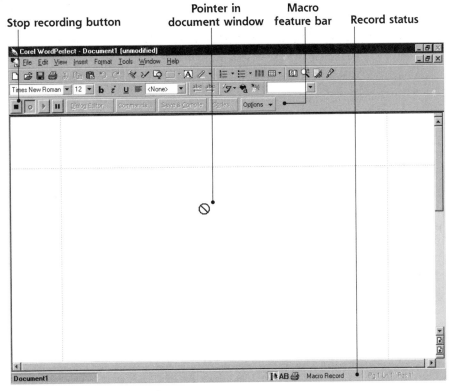

Figure 8-8   Record actions for a macro.

Playing a Macro

Once you've recorded a macro, you can play it back any time. WordPerfect stores your macros in the default Macros folder, so that's where it looks first when you use the Play feature. To play a macro, start at a new document window or open the document in which you want to use the macro. Choose Tools → Macro → Play or press Alt+F9 to display the Play Macro dialog box. Notice that WordPerfect automatically displays only the macro files in the Macros folder, designated by the WCM or WPM extension. Select the macro you want to play in the list and then click Play. Alternatively, you can double-click the macro filename in the list. WordPerfect performs the actions you recorded in the order you recorded them.

TIP Once you play a macro, WordPerfect lists its name on the Macro menu so you can play it again more quickly. WordPerfect stores the last four macros you've played, with the most recently played macro listed first. To use a macro you've used recently, choose Tools→Macro, then select the macro you want to play from the list at the bottom of the menu.

X-REF For information on adding a macro to the toolbar, see Chapter 18.

Editing a Macro

After you play a macro, you may realize it didn't work as you expected or that you left out a particular action. You can record the entire macro again, or if you're not afraid of a challenge, you can edit the macro itself. For more on editing macros, select Help→Help Topics and select the Index tab. Type macro: edit and then click Display. Note that while editing, you can also record actions and insert the associated commands using the Record button on the Macro toolbar.

CAUTION Because the macro online help takes up significant disk space, Corel doesn't install it during a Typical Installation. If you get an error when you try to access macro help online, you'll need to install it. See "WordPerfect Problems" in Appendix C for more on this.

BONUS

Selective Merging

In this chapter you learn how to merge all the records in a data file with a particular form file. However, what if you only want to send the letter to those people living in Portland or Louisiana? You can do this using the Specify conditions option.

To merge using specific criteria, follow these steps:

1. Open the form file that you want to merge and click Merge on the Merge toolbar. WordPerfect displays the Perform Merge dialog box.

2. Make sure that you have a data source selected and then click Select Records under the Data source text box to display the Select Records dialog box.

3. Under Selection method, choose Specify conditions, if it isn't selected by default (see Figure 8-9). Notice that there are three *Field* columns. The first one is the main condition. If WordPerfect finds two or more records meeting the main condition, it will use conditions in the second Field column to break the tie. Conditions in the third Field column break any tie in the second column.

Figure 8-9 Pick and choose your records by specifying conditions.

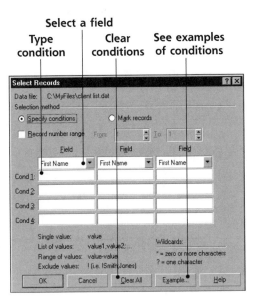

4. Use the drop-down list button under Field and select the field containing the information for which you want to set conditions. For example, if you only want to merge records from Portland, choose City from the Field drop-down list.

5. In the Cond 1 text box, type the criteria this field should meet. For example, if you want to merge records from Portland, type **Portland** in this text box. Use Table 8-1 for other examples of how to enter criteria. For more examples, click Example in the Select Records dialog box.

6. If you have more than one condition, type additional conditions in the Cond 2, Cond 3, and Cond 4 text boxes. Note that all conditions must relate to the field you've selected for this column (for example, "City").

7. When you're finished setting conditions, click OK and then click Merge in the Perform Merge dialog box to merge the files. WordPerfect merges only those records meeting the specified criteria.

 If your merge comes up empty, return to the Select Records dialog box and make sure that you entered your criteria correctly.

PICK AND CHOOSE

If you only have a few documents to merge, or if you don't have a specific criteria you can give to WordPerfect to merge certain records, you can use the Select Records feature to select each record you want to include. Follow these steps:

1. With the form file, click Merge on the Merge toolbar. WordPerfect displays the Perform Merge dialog box.

2. Make sure that you have a data source selected and then click Select Records under the Data source text box.

3. Under Selection method, choose Mark records. WordPerfect changes the dialog box to reflect your selection. Notice that WordPerfect uses the first field in the data file to list your records in the Record list box and that your records are listed in the order they appear in your data file.

4. In the Record list box, click the check box next to each record you want to include in the merge. Click OK and then click Merge in the Perform Merge dialog box to merge the files. WordPerfect merges only those records you selected in the Record list box.

TABLE 8-1 Merge Condition Examples

If you type this	WordPerfect will merge
Portland	All records containing "Portland" in the selected field.
!Oregon	All records except those containing "Oregon" in the selected field.
<70000	All records that are less than 70000 in the selected field.
>=600	All records that are greater than or equal to 600 in the selected field.
B*	All records beginning with the letter B in the selected field.
Smith;Jones	All records containing "Smith" *or* "Jones" in the selected field.

Summary

A utomation to the max! That's what you did in this chapter on merging and macros. You learned how to create a data file containing field names and information. Next, you learned how to create a form file and insert field codes as placeholders for information from the data file. Then you merged the form file with either the data file or the Address Book. Finally, you automated with macros, learning how to record and play back actions. Here you say good-bye to WordPerfect and move into slide shows with Presentations.

8

PART THREE

CREATING SLIDE SHOWS WITH PRESENTATIONS

THIS PART CONTAINS THE FOLLOWING CHAPTERS

This part teaches you everything you need to know to create an attractive, attention-grabbing slide show. Your slide show may be an anniversary "slide show" greeting card, celebrating 25 years of marriage at your party. Or it may be an overview of your department's progress presented to the bigwigs at your company. Presentations gives you all the tools you need to create stunning slides and put them together into a smooth, no-snooze slide show. Look out, Hollywood, here you come!

Sara Franklin doesn't remember the first signs of the computer revolution. For her, it wasn't an overnight invasion. Her experience with computers has been one of many quiet discoveries, each of which has made her life simpler and more efficient. "By nature, I'm an explorer," she says. Whether it's a country, a book, or the inner workings of her computer doesn't matter. "I'm not happy until I know something inside and out. I constantly want to learn more."

Going the extra mile has helped Sara not only live an exciting life, it has also helped her career. Sara is a "relocation specialist" in the New York City area. Local companies are constantly searching for executives, and often the right person for the job is from another city. Sara's company works as a liaison between local businesses and local realtors to simplify the relocation process for new executives.

"Moving to a new city can be an awful experience," Sara says. "My job is to make it great, and that's where Presentations comes in." Sara uses Presentations to create slide shows for prospective clients, tailored to their individual tastes. "The realty industry in New York is well represented," Sara explains, "but it caters to those who already live in or near the city."

Presentations enables Sara to bring the New York area to her distant customers. "Generally, I create a four-slide show for each property," she says. "The first slide, of course, is a full-color photo of the house. Until they see the property, no other infor-

mation matters. Second is a bulleted list of the essential information, such as number of bedrooms, number of bathrooms, and total square footage. Third is a paragraph that goes into detail about the special features of the home, such as its age, condition of the floors, restoration progress, and so on." Presentations' ability to format text quickly and easily is a real help on the second and third slides, and because she's not creating a newspaper ad, she can spell out words and elaborate on important details.

The final slide is the greatest help to out-of-towners. "I have several scanned maps of the metro area," Sara says. "I paste a small red arrow where the property exists, and instantly, the client knows where the house is. Most of the people outside of the state don't know Flatbush from Fifth Avenue, so this is an immense help."

Best of all, though, is Presentations' output flexibility. "I can present my show however the customer prefers. With a color printer, hard copies are a snap," Sara says, although she admits that as more customers began to request electronic presentations, she was a little intimidated. "But not for long. Once I realized how quickly Presentations can send my shows into other formats, it was hard to go back to paper — too archaic," she laughs. "Now I create CD-ROMs in Kodak Photo-CD format for my customers!" Did she ever envision herself saying that? "Actually, yes," she says with pride. Don't underestimate the power of an explorer.

CREATING A NEW SLIDE SHOW

Corel Presentations 8 is powerful presentation application that gives you the tools to create slide shows. You can project your slides onto a screen using the automatic show setting, which changes the slides automatically at a given interval. Whether you want to present your department's sales strategy for the next year or provide an overview of your company for new employees, Presentations can do the job. By using eye-catching graphics, bulleted lists, animated objects, and even sound, you can keep your audience's attention while providing the information it needs. Once you create a show, you can project it from your computer using an LCD panel, convert the Presentations file to actual slides using a service bureau, or print the slides for use as handouts. In this chapter, you get your feet wet with the basics of Presentations — how it works, how it handles slides, and so on. Then you move on to creating your first slide show.

Understanding Presentation Concepts

A Presentations slide show is made up of *slides*, individual pages containing the text, graphics, and bullet points you want to use in a presentation. Even if you don't need to convert your slide show to actual photographic slides, Presentations still refers to each page of the show as a slide.

Choosing a Type of Show

Depending on the purpose of your slide show, you will use different tools and different approaches for creating the show. There are four basic types of shows you can produce:

* An *informative* show provides straightforward information to your audience.

* A *persuasive* show is like a sales tool, trying to convince the audience to either use or purchase your product or service.

* A *special occasion* show might welcome the audience to a conference, workshop, or meeting, or provide a brief introduction about a person or organization you may be honoring with an award.

* A *teaching* or *instructional* show helps explain concepts or skills to an audience that may or may not be familiar with the topic.

When you first start Presentations, you can select from any number of specific slide show types that fall under one of the general categories above. PerfectExpert can walk you through the process of creating these many types of presentations.

Reviewing Slide Layouts

The basic elements of all slide shows are the slides themselves. Presentations ships with six predefined slide layouts, sometimes referred to as slide *templates*. These templates provide slide formats that help you present information in different ways. For example, the *title slide* layout provides areas for typing the title and subtitle for your show. The *bulleted list* layout makes it easy to list several key points in a bulleted list. Each slide template contains *placeholders*, the containers that will hold your text, clipart, and other elements. Table 9-1 describes each of the predefined slide layouts in Presentations. Note that if none suits your needs, you can use the blank layout to design a slide.

TABLE 9-1   Presentation Slide Layouts

Use This Type	For
Title	The first slide in a show. It contains title and subtitle placeholders.
Bulleted List	Listing items or short points you want to make. The slide contains title, subtitle, and bulleted list placeholders.
Text	Longer, descriptive paragraphs. The slide contains title, subtitle, and text placeholders.

Use This Type	For
Organization Chart	Showing the hierarchy of a company or department. The slide contains title, subtitle, and organization chart placeholders. See the Bonus section in Chapter 10 for more information.
Data Chart	Showing relationships between data, such as quarterly sales for the past year. You can represent these relationships using bar, flow, or pie charts. The slide contains title, subtitle, and data chart placeholders.
Combination	Illuminating ideas using both a bulleted list and a data chart. The slide contains title, subtitle, bullet list, and data chart placeholders.

Creating a New Slide Show

After you've determined the type of slide show you need, you can begin creating the show, setting up your slides and entering the text and other elements you want to include. Presentations lets you create a show from scratch or offers the services of the PerfectExpert to take you by the hand as you create your first show.

Creating the Show

In Chapter 2, I mentioned that when you start Presentations, it opens a bit differently than the other applications, displaying the New dialog box that enables you to create a new show or work on an existing one. This first section assumes that you have not started Presentations, so we review the use of the New dialog box here.

To create a new slide show, follow these steps:

 1. Click the Presentations button on the Desktop Applications Director toolbar. Alternatively, you can choose Start → Corel WordPerfect Suite 8 → Corel Presentations 8 . Presentations starts and displays the New dialog box (see Figure 9-1).

Choose an existing slide show
Create a new blank slide show
Create a specific type of slide show

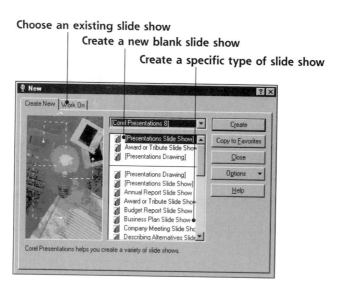

Figure 9-1 Create a new slide show.

2. Because Presentations assumes that you want to create a new blank slide show, click Create. Presentations displays the Startup Master Gallery dialog box, allowing you to select a look for your slide show (see Figure 9-2).

Select a background   Select a category

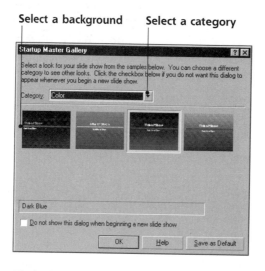

Figure 9-2 Select a background look for your slide show.

3. Click the Category down arrow button, then choose a category from the drop-down list. Choose a background look from those that display and click OK. Presentations opens, using the master background you chose with the first slide — a title slide. You're ready to go.

If you select one of the slide show types in the New dialog box, Presentations provides several standard slides of various layouts with text to help you complete the show. You'll also see the PerfectExpert panel for the type of show you selected so you can get assistance on tasks related to that particular slide show.

For more on the PerfectExpert panel, see Chapter 2. In this chapter, I use a blank slide show so that you can get familiar with the various elements that make up a show.

Understanding the Presentations Window

If you worked through the section on WordPerfect, much of the Presentations window will look familiar (see Figure 9-3). It has a toolbar, just like WordPerfect, as well as it's own special property bar that's just right for doing slide show-type stuff.

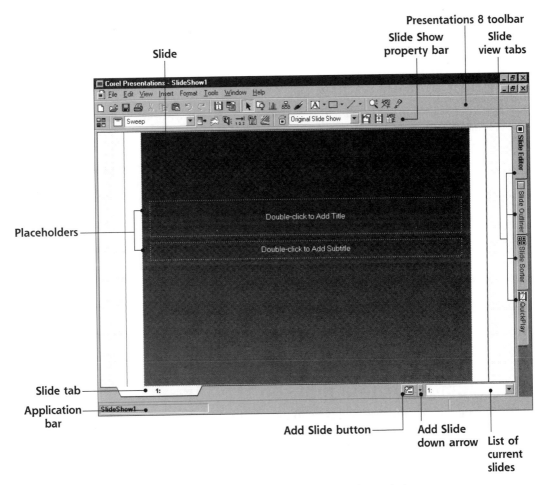

Figure 9-3 Work with your slides in the Presentations window.

Many of the Presentations toolbar buttons differ from those on the WordPerfect standard toolbar. To refresh your memory on which buttons remain the same, see Table 3-1 in Chapter 3. Most of the buttons on the Presentations toolbar unique to Presentations relate to clipart and objects, and I cover these buttons in detail in Chapter 10. The Slide Show property bar contains all the tools you need to put together your show for presentation purposes. I cover this in-depth in Chapter 11.

Setting Up Your Slide Show

As you saw, Presentations inserts the first slide — a *title slide* — for you and stands ready for you to add the text to it. Once you've added text, you may decide you don't want to use the default *slide master*, which controls the background color for all slides in your show, and that you need to begin adding and working with additional slides. In this section, you look at how to do all these things.

Adding Text to a Slide

Your slides consist of placeholders that can contain text, bulleted lists, clipart, and charts. Placeholders are boxes that you can work with independent of the text or object they contain. Notice that each new placeholder provides instructions on what to do with it — Double Click to Add Title, for example. When you select a text box, sizing handles appear, similar to those you encountered with graphics in Chapter 6. To add text to a slide, double-click the text placeholder to position the insertion point and then type the text.

TIP **You can also secondary-click the placeholder and choose Edit Text from the QuickMenu to position the insertion point inside the placeholder.**

If you make a mistake, you can use the Delete and Backspace keys to correct it, just as you do in WordPerfect.

You add text to most slides using these steps. The one exception is bullet slides, which I cover in the next section.

Adding Text to a Bulleted List Slide

Adding text to a title or text slide is pretty straightforward — you double-click the placeholder and then type the text. However, bulleted list slides work a little differently because you're dealing with bulleted items. When you double-click the Bulleted List placeholder, Presentations activates the placeholder, inserting the first bullet. Here are some things to remember about adding text to a bulleted list slide:

 ✳ Type the text for a bulleted item and press Enter.

 ✳ To enter a sublevel, press Tab or click the Next Level button on the Edit Bulleted List property bar and then type the text. To promote a level (go to previous), press Shift+Tab or click the Previous Level button on the Edit Bulleted List property bar.

 X-REF For information on inserting a bulleted list slide, see "Inserting and Selecting Slides" in this chapter. For information on working with bulleted lists, see Chapter 5.

SIDE TRIP

BULLET BONANZA

You can easily change the appearance, color, and other aspects of bullets and bulleted text. Just display the bulleted list slide you want to change and select the bulleted list placeholder. Presentations displays the Bulleted List property bar.

Click the Bulleted List Properties button or select Format→Bulleted List Properties to display the Bulleted List Properties dialog box shown here.

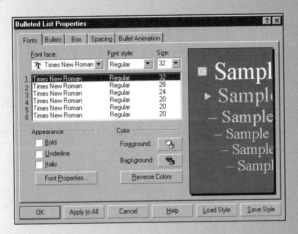

This dialog box contains five tabs for changing the elements of a bulleted list and defaults to the Fonts tab. Use the following information to customize your bulleted list:

✳ *Fonts* determines how the text will look at each level in the bulleted list.

✳ *Bullets* determines the actual shape and appearance of the bullet itself.

✳ *Box* determines the appearance and shape of the placeholder containing the bullet list.

✳ *Spacing* determines how much space appears between the bullet and the text. You can use any of the symbols you explored in Chapter 2 as a bullet.

✳ *Bullet Animation* enables you to add a little pizzazz to bullets as they appear on the slide. See "Animating Bullet Points" in Chapter 12 for more information.

CREATING A NEW SLIDE SHOW **183**

Changing the Master Background

When you create a new slide show, Presentations uses a default slide show master for your slides. However, you may want to change this to suit the show's needs. Presentations ships with a variety of backgrounds to invoke the right mood for your show. You can even create your own slide master. Check out online help for more information: On the Index tab, type **master** and double-click Create in the list box under the box labeled 2.

 To change the slide master, click the Master Gallery button or choose Format→Master Gallery. Presentations displays the Master Gallery dialog box, which is identical to the Setup Master Gallery you saw earlier. Click the Category down-arrow button and select a master category. Select the desired slide master and click OK. Presentations changes all current slides to reflect your selection.

Inserting and Selecting Slides

Once you've completed the title slide, you'll need to add more slides for the rest of your presentation. And you'll need to know how to display your different slides so that you can work with them.

INSERTING SLIDES

Earlier in Table 9-1, I listed the types of slides (slide layouts) available. You can add a single slide or several slides at once. To add a single slide, display the slide that will come before your new slide(s) and then do one of the following:

* To add the same slide layout as the last slide you inserted, click the Add Slide button.

* To add a slide with a different slide layout, click the Add Slide button down arrow and select the desired layout from the pop-up list.

SIDE TRIP

MORE MASTERS, PLEASE

The WordPerfect Suite ships with a number of additional slide show masters. You can install them using a custom install. Once you begin the installation process, make sure you use Custom Install. In the Installation Settings dialog box, select Presentations 8 (*not* the checkbox), then click Components. Setup displays the Presentations dialog box. You should not see any check marks in the check boxes. Select Slide Show Masters in the list, again making sure you don't select the check box, and then click Components. Select all masters you wish to include. Don't worry about installing duplicates; Corel will just replace them.

STAYING IN THE BACKGROUND

If you would like to have more than one look in your slide show, you can change the background for a single slide while leaving the background for the remaining slides the same. To change the background for a single slide, display the slide you want to change. Chose Format→Background Gallery to display the Appearance tab in the Slide Properties dialog box. Click the Background category down-arrow button and select a category for the background. Then select a background and click OK.

FEATURE FOCUS The Add Slide button enables you to quickly insert a new slide.

To add multiple slides with the same layout, display the slide that will come before your new slides and choose Insert→New Slide to display the New Slides dialog box. Under Layout, select the slide layout you want to use for all the slides you are inserting. In the Number of slides text box, type the number of new slides you want to add, and click OK. Presentations adds the number of slides you indicated after the current slide. All slides will use the slide template you selected.

TIP Use the blank (Slide with no layout) slide layout for slides that will contain just graphics or drawings you've made. For more on graphics and drawings, see Chapter 10.

SELECTING AND DISPLAYING SLIDES

Once you have more than one slide in your slide show, you need to know how to display different slides so that you can work on them. Presentations provides two methods for selecting slides — the slide tab and the slide list at the bottom of the screen (see Figure 9-4). To select a slide using the slide tab, simply click the tab. To select a slide using the pop-up list, click the down arrow button, then choose the desired slide.

Select a slide tab

Select a slide
from pop-up list

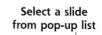

Figure 9-4 Select and display a slide.

FEATURE FOCUS The slide tab at the bottom of each slide enables you to quickly display any slide from your slide show, in Slide Editor view.

Working with Slide Text

One of the first things you do when creating a new slide show is add text to your slides. You've already learned how to add text to a title slide and bullet slide. Now look at how to edit and format slide text.

Editing Text

You edit text on your slides much as you do in WordPerfect. You can type over text, cut and copy text and objects, and delete and change them. Use the same techniques you learned in Chapter 3 to select text and replace it. Or select text, then cut or copy and paste it to a new location. Although you can move or copy text to another slide, you cannot move or copy an entire placeholder to another slide.

Formatting Slide Text

As mentioned earlier, your text will use the font, size, and color settings associated with the background you selected in the Master Gallery. However, you can easily change text on a single slide to suit your needs.

If you're comfortable formatting text in WordPerfect, you'll feel right at home formatting text in Presentations. You perform the same steps — selecting text and applying formats. Let's do a quick review of these steps and then explore some of the formatting that's different in Presentations. When you double-click a text placeholder, Presentations displays a new property bar. You will use a number of the buttons on this property bar, so check out Table 9-2 to get familiar with the most common formatting buttons in Presentations. For those buttons that are identical to WordPerfect, see Chapter 4.

 TIP An alternative to double-clicking a text box is to secondary-click the placeholder and select Edit Text from the QuickMenu.

TABLE 9-2 Edit Text Property Bar

Button	Name	Description
	INCREASE FONT SIZE	Increase the current font size in 6 point increments.
	DECREASE FONT SIZE	Decrease the current font size in 6 point increments.
	JUSTIFICATION	Align text or bulleted list.
	LINE SPACING	Change line spacing for text.
	INSERT SYMBOL	Insert a WordPerfect Character (appears when the insertion point is active in a placeholder).
	UNDELETE	Restore deleted text at the insertion point.
	FOREGROUND FILL COLOR	Change the text color.

You can change the font face and size of slide text the same way you do in WordPerfect, using the Font Select and Size drop-down lists on the Edit Text property bar. You can also choose a font and size you used previously via the

QuickFonts button. You can also add attributes such as bold, italics, and under-line, as well as change text colors. To change all text in the placeholder, select the placeholder or position the insertion point within the text. To change only specific text, select the text within the placeholder.

X-REF   For more on text formatting, see "Formatting Text" in Chapter 4.

TIP   You can undo any formatting or deletion by clicking the Undo button on the Presentations toolbar.

Working with Slides

Earlier you learned how to insert and display slides — after all, you would-n't have much of a slide show with only a title slide. But what if you decide that it makes more sense for Slide 2 to be a bulleted list instead of a Text slide? Or for Slide 3 to follow Slide 5? Using a little slide of hand (heh-heh), you can reorganize or reformat slides as well as remove them altogether.

SIDE TRIP

A PLACE FOR EVERYTHING

So far, you've worked strictly with the text inside a placeholder, editing it and format-ting it to suit the needs of your slide show. However, there may be times when you want to move, resize, or format the placeholder itself. Because placeholders are objects in their own right, you can select them and move, copy, align, resize, or delete them like other objects. Here are a few things to remember when you work with placeholders:

✱ Click the placeholder once to select it. You should see sizing handles surrounding it. Make sure that you don't see the insertion point blinking inside the placeholder.

✱ To move a placeholder, simply click and drag it to the new location.

✱ Aligning a placeholder moves the entire box to a particular place on the slide. To align a placeholder, select it, secondary-click it, and choose Align from the QuickMenu. Select the desired alignment option.

✱ To resize a text placeholder, use the click-and-drag techniques for sizing graphics covered in Chapter 6. The text within will retain its original size. Depending on the new placeholder size, you may need to change the font size.

Changing Slide Layout

Say you're working on your text slide and then realize that you really want bullet points on the slide. Not a problem. If you need to change the layout of a slide, you can do it in a snap. Simply display the slide that needs a different format, click the Slide Layout button on the Slide show property bar, and choose the desired slide layout.

If the Slide Layout button is not available on the property bar, it means you have something selected on the slide, and Presentations is displaying a context-sensitive property bar instead of the Slide Show property bar. Click in any empty area of the slide to display the Slide Show property bar.

Changing Slide Views

When you start a new slide show, Presentations defaults to the Slide Editor view, which shows one full slide at a time. However, there may be times when you just want a quick overview of your slides, or you want to quickly enter text without seeing the background and any graphics you may have on your slides. For these tasks, as well as for moving, copying, and rearranging slides, Presentations provides three other views in addition to Slide Editor view. You can access these views using the tabs along the right side of the slide (refer back to Figure 9-3). The following sentences describe all four views:

* Use *Slide Editor* view to see an entire slide, complete with all its elements.
* Use *Slide Outliner* view to see an overview of your slide content in outline format.
* Use *Slide Sorter* view to see *thumbnails* of all your slides, getting a bird's eye view of the entire show.
* Use *QuickPlay* to see what your slides will look like when you play the slide show. You learn how to use QuickPlay in Chapter 12.

Note that Presentations will use the last view you selected for all new slide shows you create or existing slide shows you open. For example, say you display your current slide show in Slide Sorter view. When you close it and open another slide show, the new show will display using Slide Sorter view.

FEATURE FOCUS The Slide View tabs along the right side of your slides enable you to switch quickly among the different views of your slide show.

Rearranging Slides

If you decide that Slide 3 makes more sense after Slide 5, or that Slide 8 really should follow Slide 2, you can quickly rearrange your slides in Slide Sorter view. Slide Sorter view displays each slide in miniature, allowing you to move, cut, copy, and paste single and multiple slides. Here's how.

USING SLIDE SORTER VIEW

Before you can move, copy, or delete slides, you need to display them in Slide Sorter view. With your slide show open, choose the Slide Sorter tab or choose View→Slide Sorter. Presentations displays each of your slides as a thumbnail in the order they appear in your show (see Figure 9-5). The slide number and slide transition appear below each slide. The current slide is selected, indicated by heavy border around it. When you begin adding different effects to your slides (as you will in Chapter 11), Presentations adds slide icons beneath each slide, indicating what effects the slide uses. By default, you see at least two icons beneath your slides — the *slide layout* icon and the *mouse* icon. The slide layout icon shows you an example of the layout the slide uses (title, bulleted list, and so on). The mouse icon tells you the slide is set to *manual timing*. This means that you must click the mouse to display the slide during a show. The *speaker notes* icon is not a default icon and is here for illustration purposes. You get a full dose of transitions, timings, and speaker notes in Chapter 11. Here you get a quick overview of Slide Sorter view.

FEATURE FOCUS

When you add slide show effects such as transitions, sound, and timing, an associated icon appears beneath the appropriate slide. You learn more about these elements in Chapter 11.

Use the Decrease and Increase buttons to change the size of the slides in Slide Sorter view, allowing more or fewer slides to display in each row.

SELECTING SLIDES

If you have worked through Chapter 4, which deals with moving and copying text, you know that before you can do anything with a slide, you must select it first. There are three ways to select slides, and they're identical to the way you select files in a file management dialog box (Chapter 2):

* To select a single slide, click it once.

Currently selected slide | Slide layout icon | Mouse icon | Speaker notes icon | Decrease | Increase

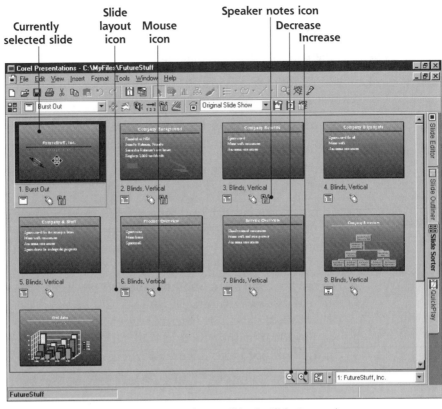

Figure 9-5 Get a thumbnail view of your slides in Slide Sorter view.

✳ To select a range of slides, click the first slide in the range and then press and hold the Shift key. Click the last slide in the range. Presentations places a distinctive border around the first through last slides inclusively.

✳ To select slides that aren't next to each other, press and hold Ctrl, then click each slide you want to include in the selection. Presentations places a thick border around each slide you select. The solid border indicates the active slide if you've selected multiple slides.

✳ To deselect any one slide from a group of selected slides, press and hold Ctrl, then click the slide.

TIP If you want to edit the contents of a slide from Slide Sorter view, simply double-click the slide. Presentations will display that slide in Slide Editor view.

MOVING, COPYING, AND DELETING SLIDES

Sometimes a slide makes more sense in a different place in your slide sequence. Or perhaps you have a slide that you want to duplicate and just want to change a few lines of text. Or, if you just don't need a slide anymore, you can delete it in Slide Sorter view.

To perform these tasks, follow these steps:

1. If you're not currently using Slide Sorter view, click the Slide Sorter tab or choose `View` → `Slide Sorter`.

2. Select the slides you want to move, copy, or delete by using one of the techniques described in the previous section.

3. Use the following techniques to perform the appropriate action on your selected slide(s):

   ✳ To move a slide, click and drag the slide to its new location. A red vertical line appears to indicate where the slide will be inserted. When the line is in the right location, release the mouse button. The slide comes in to the *right* of the red vertical line.

   ✳ To copy a slide, press and hold the Ctrl key, then click and drag the slide to its new location. The red vertical line appears to indicate where the slide will be inserted, as well as a small hand with a plus sign inside it telling you that this is a copy. When the vertical line is in the right location, release the mouse button.

   ✳ To delete a slide, select it and press Delete. Click Yes to confirm.

 TIP If you're not fond of drag and drop techniques, you can use the Cut, Copy, Paste, and Delete options on the Edit menu to move, copy, and delete slides. You can also delete the current slide in Slide Editor view by choosing Slide→Delete Slides and clicking Yes to confirm the deletion.

BONUS

Working with Slide Outliner View

If you want to get a quick overview of your slides, viewing just some of the text, use the Slide Outliner view. As I mentioned earlier, Outliner lets you work with your slides in an outline, similar to an outline you create in WordPerfect (see Chapter 5). And Outliner provides a list of your slides with their number and title.

TIP As I noted in Chapter 2, this is the best view to use when you want to spell check your slide show as all text appears here. If you spell check in Slide Editor view, you must select each placeholder containing text and spell check it individually.

Using the Slide Outliner

To work in Slide Outliner view, follow these steps:

1. Click the Slide Outliner tab or choose **View** → **Slide Outliner** .
   Presentations displays the slides in outline form (see Figure 9-6).

2. Use one of the following methods to perform the desired task:

   ✳ To move a slide, point to the slide icon and click so that all text for the slide is selected and the move box is attached to the pointer. Click and drag the slide to the new location, using the red horizontal line as your destination indicator. The slide inserts *above* the red line.

   ✳ To change slide text, position the insertion point in the location for the change and then make your changes.

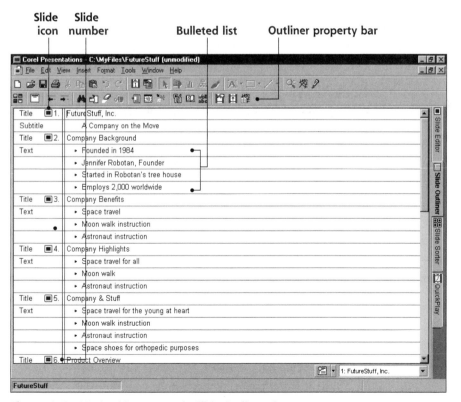

Figure 9-6 Work with your text in Slide Outliner view.

* To add a slide, position the insertion point after the last item in a slide and press Enter. If you see a new slide icon, type the title for the slide, press Enter, type a subtitle, and press Enter. If you don't see a new slide icon, press Shift+Tab or click the Previous Level button on the Outliner property bar, repeating as necessary until the new slide icon appears.

There are a number of other tasks you can perform in Slide Outliner view. Check the QuickTips for the Outliner property bar buttons to find out some of your options.

Inserting a WordPerfect Outline

If you have a WordPerfect outline that would be great for a Presentations slide show, you can easily import it. Each top level heading in the WordPerfect outline will become a title for a new slide. For example, if your outline used Roman numerals I, II, III, and so on, each of these headings would become the title on a new slide. The number of top level headings in the outline determines the number of slides in the show.

To use a WordPerfect outline to create a presentation, follow these steps:

1. Create a new slide show by choosing File → New. On the Create New tab, make sure Presentations Slide Show is selected and click Create. Choose a look in the Master Gallery dialog box; click OK.

2. Choose Insert → File to display the Insert File dialog box.

3. Locate and select the outline document and then click Insert. Presentations uses the outline text for the slide text.

When you insert a WordPerfect outline into Presentations, Presentations tries to match a slide template to the corresponding outline headings and subheadings. If you want subtitles for your slides, you'll need to add these once you've inserted the WordPerfect outline.

Summary

This chapter introduced you to some fundamentals of creating a slide show. You explored a variety of slide show and presentation concepts, looking at the elements of a slide show and what makes up an individual slide. You also learned how to add text to slides and format and edit it. Finally, you learned how to work with placeholders and slides, moving and copying slides, changing slide templates, and rearranging slides in different views. In the next chapter, you'll take a look at customizing your slides by changing slide backgrounds and adding clipart, and objects.

CUSTOMIZING YOUR SLIDES

IN THIS CHAPTER YOU LEARN THESE KEY SKILLS

In Chapter 9, you saw how easy it is to create an attractive slide show using existing bullet styles, backgrounds, and layouts. Now it's time to add more pizzazz to your shows by working with clipart and objects. Corel Presentations allows you to insert clipart images on any slide and then rearrange and format the images. You can also use the Tool palette to add shapes and free-floating text boxes to further drive home your message. In this chapter, you explore these features to improve the appeal of your slide show.

Working with Clipart

Your basic show looks pretty good with an assortment of slide types. Now you're ready to illustrate your slides with artwork. Presentations provides access to a variety of images, the most easily accessible being the images stored in the Scrapbook. As mentioned in Chapter 6, you can select from thousands of images to jazz up your slides.

Once you insert an image on your slide, you can manipulate it in all sorts of ways, using many of the techniques for inserting images into WordPerfect documents covered in Chapter 6. You can move and resize the image, change its colors, and rotate it, too.

As explained in Chapter 9, much of the right side of the Presentations tool-bar contains tools for working with clipart and objects. These tools provide just about everything you need to create and format lines, shapes, and free-floating text. Because most of the tools relate to objects, I've included a table of explanations for the buttons in the "Working with Objects" section later in this chapter.

Inserting Images

You insert images much like the way you inserted images in WordPerfect.

To insert an image on a slide, follow these steps:

 With the slide displayed, click the Clipart button on the Slide Show toolbar or choose Insert→Graphics→Clipart. Presentations displays the Scrapbook. Remember, the Clipart tab displays folders and clipart that were copied to your hard drive during installation. The CD Clipart accesses the CD-ROM where thousands of images and photos are stored. To insert an image, select the Clipart or CD Clipart tab. Double-click a folder to see its contents.

 To return to the previous folder, click the Up One Level button. When you've located the image you want to use, click and drag it directly onto the slide. When you're finished inserting images, close the Scrapbook by clicking the Close button. Depending on the image you inserted, it may appear quite large and overbearing once on your slide. Not to worry. As you know from Chapter 6, it's a breeze to move and resize images.

Moving and Sizing an Image

So,the image of gold coins you inserted in your presentation looks great on the slide that lists ways for clients to save money. But it's big, overwhelming your text. You want the image to *enhance* your text — not overtake it — so you should resize it. You can also move the image if it's too close to your text or you think it would be more effective in another location.

Moving and sizing an image is identical to moving and sizing a placeholder, and to moving and resizing images in WordPerfect. To move an image, click the image once to display the sizing handles and then click and drag the image to its new location. To size the image, click and drag the appropriate sizing handle until the image is the desired size.

Editing Images

So, you decreased the size of the coins so that they no longer overwhelm your message. But now you're not satisfied with their color — they're very *yellow*, and they're glaring against your dark background. You want to mute the color. No problem.

When you select an image or an object you created using one of the object tools on the toolbar, Presentations displays the Drawing Object property bar, providing quick-click access to a variety of formatting features for your object. Table 10-1 describes each of these buttons so you can use them effectively. You'll use many of them throughout the rest of the chapter.

TABLE 10-1 Drawing Object Property Bar

Button	Name	Description
`Graphics ▾`	GRAPHICS MENU	Display a menu of object options.
	SHADOW OPTIONS	Add a shadow to the object.
	ROTATION OPTIONS	Rotate or skew an object.
	OBJECT ANIMATION	Make the object move or transition during a slide show.
	QUICKLINK	Activate the object so that it performs an action.
	FILL PATTERN	Select a pattern for the object.
	FOREGROUND FILL COLOR	Select a foreground color for the object.
	BACKGROUND FILL COLOR	Select a background color for the object.
	REVERSE COLORS	Reverse the current foreground and background colors.
	LINE STYLE	Select a line style for the object.
	LINE WIDTH	Select a line width for the object.
	LINE COLOR	Select a line color for the object.
	GET ATTRIBUTES	Copy formatting attributes of the selected object.
	APPLY ATTRIBUTES	Apply copied attributes to selected object.
	SELECT LIKE	Select all objects similar to the selected object.
	SELECTED OBJECT VIEWER	Show object in thumbnail view.
	FILL ATTRIBUTES	Modify fill and line attributes for the selected object.

Use the various buttons on the Drawing Object property bar to format your clipart image. Note that the Foreground Fill Color button looks slightly different when you have an object, as opposed to a graphic, selected.

CREATIVE COLORING

If you really want to control your image's appearance, you can use some additional color options on the Drawing Object property bar. These options let you change the image to a silhouette, make it an outline, and apply other changes to an image's color and appearance. Play around with these options to see what works for your image. To experiment with the color options, select the image and click the Graphics menu button on the Drawing Object property bar. Select Image Settings and choose one of the options from the submenu: Silhouette, Black and White, Gray Scale, Invert, or Outline. You can use Undo if you don't like the result.

Rotating Images

If you worked through the Bonus section in Chapter 6, I mentioned that you can rotate a graphic within its box to create a different effect in WordPerfect. You can also do that with images in Presentations. Additionally, you can stretch or otherwise distort an image to further change it.

To rotate an image using a preset degree, select the image you want to rotate. Click the Rotation Options button down arrow and select the desired rotation degree. To rotate an image manually, click the Rotation Options button down arrow and select Manual Rotation, or right-click the image and select Rotate from the QuickMenu. Presentations displays rotation handles around the image. Use one of the following methods to rotate your image:

* To rotate the graphic while maintaining its proportions, click and drag a corner *rotation* handle in the direction you want to rotate the image. When you release the mouse button, the image remains in its new position.

* To distort or *skew* the image for effect, click and drag one of the top, bottom, left, or right rotation handles. These handles force only that side of the image to move, leaving the rest of the image anchored in place (see Figure 10-1).

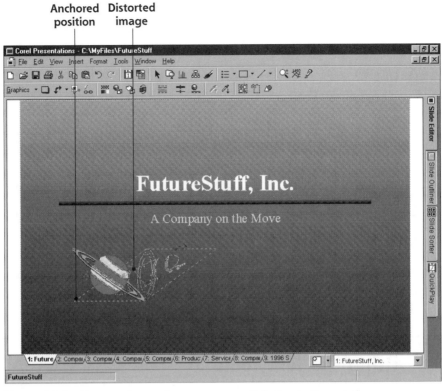

Figure 10-1 You can skew an image to your satisfaction in Presentations.

Working with Objects

E xisting graphics are a great way to enhance your slides and jazz up what might otherwise be a straightforward show. But sometimes you may want to do your own thing. Perhaps a slide just needs a few circles to enhance your point, or you want to create a basic house with a square, a triangle, and a few rectangles for windows and doors. You can do all this using the object tools on the Presentations toolbar. You can also add text boxes, as well as horizontal and vertical lines. Each of these things is called an *object,* and Presentations treats them as being independent of each other.

Understanding the Object Tools

As I mentioned, the tools on the right side of the Presentations toolbar contain tools for creating and working with objects and are sometimes referred to as the *object tools.* As with other buttons on various Presentations property bars, if you see a down arrow on the button, you can click the arrow to display additional options. Remember, if you're unsure of a tool's purpose, point to it to see its

QuickTip. Table 10-2 provides descriptions of these tools, as well as the Selection and Clipart buttons.

TABLE 10-2 Corel Presentations Drawing Object Tools

Tool	Name	Description
	SELECTION TOOL	Enables you to select objects.
	CLIPART	Insert a new image from the Scrapbook.
	CHART	Insert a data chart or Quattro Pro spreadsheet.
	ORGANIZATION CHART	Insert and works with an organization chart.
	BITMAP	Create a bitmapped image.
	TEXT OBJECT TOOLS	Create a text box or text line.
	CLOSED OBJECT TOOLS	Create a filled shape.
	LINE OBJECT TOOLS	Create different line types or draw freehand.

Using the Text Tools

Say that you have an image of a map on a slide and you want the words *You are here* to appear next to a dot on the map. You can create those words using the text tool. Because the text is an object, Presentations will let you move, rotate, and otherwise format it.

Presentations provides four types of text objects: the *Text Box* tool, the *Text Line* tool, the *Bulleted List* tool, and the *Special Effects* tool (aka TextArt). The Text Box tool lets you define a placeholder that will contain multiple lines of text. Presentations automatically wraps the text within the text area you create. Text Box is the default option for the Text Object tool. The Text Line tool lets you type a single line of text without defining the width or height of the area. The Bulleted List tool lets you add a bulleted list to the current slide, and the Special Effects tool allows you to add TextArt to your slide. Since TextArt is covered in detail in Chapter 6, I focus on the first three text tools here.

CREATING A TEXT BOX

 If you require multiple lines of text, use the Text Box tool to create the box in which your text will wrap. To create a text area, display the slide you want to use and then click the Text Box tool on the Presentations toolbar. (If the Text Box tool is not currently visible, click on the Text Object Tools down arrow and select the Text Box tool.) Click and drag in the location for the text, releasing the mouse button when you have the desired width. Type the text in the text box and then click outside the box when you're finished.

CREATING A TEXT LINE

If you have a short phrase or heading you want to add to your slide, you can do it quickly with the Text Line tool. For example, the text describing each shape in Figure 10-2 uses two text lines, one for each row of shapes.

 To create a text line, display the slide you want to use, click the Text Object Tools down arrow on the Presentations toolbar, and select the Text Line tool. Click the slide in the location for the text and type the text. Click outside the box when you're finished.

CREATING A BULLETED LIST

 The Bulleted List tool allows you to insert a bulleted list on any slide, not just a bulleted list slide. To use this tool, click the Text Object Tools down arrow on the Presentations toolbar, and select the Bulleted List tool. Click and drag in the location for the list, releasing the mouse button when you have the desired width. Type the bulleted list, indicating subpoints where necessary.

 X-REF   **For more on working with bulleted lists, see Chapter 9. For more on TextArt, see Chapter 6.**

EDITING TEXT

You can edit your text box just as you do placeholders on a slide. Use these techniques to make changes to your text box:

* *Move* the text box by clicking once to select the placeholder, then clicking and dragging it to its new location.

* *Resize* the text box by clicking once to select it, then clicking and dragging one of the sizing handles.

* *Rotate* the text by selecting a predefined angle from the Rotation drop-down list. Alternatively, you can manually rotate text by right-clicking it and choosing Rotate from the QuickMenu. Then click and drag one of the corner rotation handles to the desired angle.

 X-REF   **You can align objects the same way you align placeholders. See the Side Trip, "A Place for Everything," in Chapter 9.**

Using the Closed Object Tool

Remember the house I mentioned earlier? The one made up of a square, a triangle, and a few rectangles? You can create the entire thing using the Closed Object tool, which lets you insert a variety of shapes, from circles and ovals to triangles and large arrows, using the Closed Object tool (see Figure 10-2). And you can combine text and closed objects, in ways such as adding a circle and then placing text inside the circle. You can combine different objects for a variety of effects; the only limit is your creativity and imagination. Presentations calls these *closed* objects to differentiate them from objects that don't form a complete shape per se, such as lines.

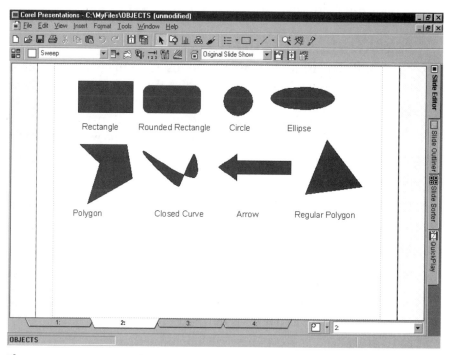

Figure 10-2 Examples of closed objects.

Table 10-3 guides you through the techniques for creating the closed object shapes. The instructions in the third column assume that you have the correct slide displayed and are ready to use the appropriate tool by clicking the Closed Object down arrow and selecting the desired object. Note that when you release the mouse button, Presentations inserts the shape, filled with a default color.

TABLE 10-3   Creating Closed Objects

Tool	Shape	How to Create the Shape
▢	RECTANGLE	Click and drag until you see the desired size and shape for the rectangle. For a square, press and hold Shift while you drag.
▢	ROUNDED RECTANGLE	Click and drag until you see the desired size and shape for a rectangle with rounded corners. For a perfect square with rounded corners, press and hold Shift while you drag.
◯	CIRCLE	Click and drag until you see the desired size for the circle.
◯	ELLIPSE	Click and drag until you see the desired size for the ellipse (a fancy word for oval). For a circle, press and hold Shift while you drag.
◹	POLYGON	Click and drag for the first segment, then click to end it. Repeat for additional segments and double-click to complete the shape.
◠	CLOSED CURVE	This can be a really fun tool. See Figure 10-3 for examples of closed curves. To create one, click and drag for the first segment, and then click to end it. Repeat for additional segments and double-click to complete the shape.
⇨	ARROW	Click once to anchor the arrowhead. Without clicking again, press and hold the Shift key and drag for the length of the arrow. When it's the desired length, click once. To create a curved arrow, point to the location for the arrowhead, then click and drag for the general length of your arrow. When you release the mouse button, you can curve and stretch the arrow. Click once to complete the arrow.
△	REGULAR POLYGON	Select the tool to display the Regular Polygon dialog box. Indicate the number of sides and then click and drag the shape on the slide. The dialog box disappears when you release the mouse button.

You can move, resize, or rotate shapes just as you do with images. To work with shape colors, see "Formatting Objects" later in this chapter.

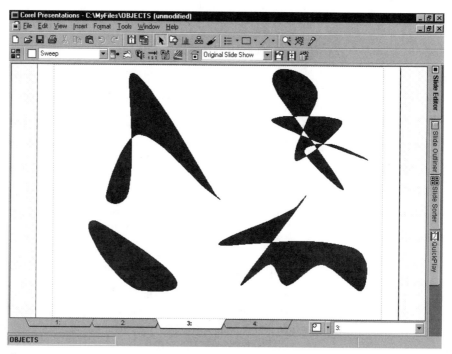

Figure 10-3 Examples of closed curve shapes.

Using the Line Tool

Remember that *You Are Here* text you may have added to a slide? You can also add a thin arrow pointing to a spot on the map using the Line Object tool. Once you add the line, you can format it with an arrowhead on either or both ends. You can also create straight and curved lines to enhance your slides. Check out Figure 10-4 for samples of common lines.

Table 10-4 guides you through the techniques for creating lines. The instructions in the third column assume that you have the correct slide displayed and are ready to use the appropriate tool by clicking the down arrow on the Line tool and selecting the desired line type. Note that when you release the mouse button, Presentations inserts the line, filled with a default line color.

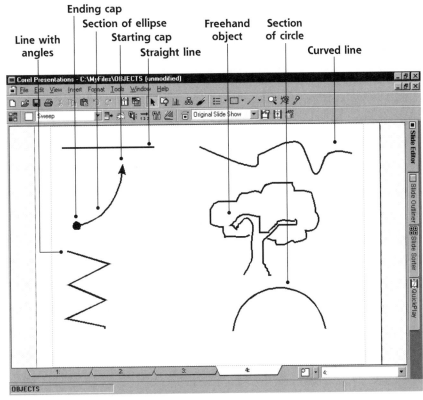

Figure 10-4 Examples of lines.

TABLE 10-4 Creating Lines

Tool	Line Type	How to Create the Line
⟋	LINE	Click and drag for the line length. Click the ending point for the line. To create a straight horizontal, vertical, or diagonal line, press and hold Shift while you drag.
⟋	CURVED LINE	Click and drag to create the first curved segment and then click for that segment. Repeat for each curve and double-click to complete the curved line.
⌒	SECTION OF ELLIPSE	Click and drag until you see the desired arc, then release the mouse button. To create a circular section, press and hold Shift while you drag.
✎	FREEHAND	Click and draw as you would with a pencil, then release the mouse button. This tool is definitely for those of you who are artists (which I am not, as you can see). Yes, that's supposed to be a tree in Figure 10-4!

(continued)

TABLE 10-4 Creating Lines (*continued*)

Tool	Line Type	How to Create the Line
	LINE WITH ANGLES	Click the point for each angle in the line and then double-click the ending point.
	BEZIER CURVE	Click the first point for the curve, then click at each point where you want the line to curve in another direction. When you reach the last point for the curve, double-click it. If you've never heard of Bezier, you probably don't need this tool! (Note that Figure 10-4 does not show an example of this curve. I couldn't do it justice.)
	SECTION OF CIRCLE	Click and drag for the diameter of the circle section and then release the mouse button. Drag to size the circle section, and click when it is correct.

Formatting Objects

I f you created any of the objects in the previous section, you probably noticed that they took on the default colors and formatting. Often, the defaults probably won't do it for you, and you'll need to make changes. You can easily change the color, pattern, and lines surrounding an object, as well as the color and width of lines themselves. Refer back to Table 10-1 for the buttons on the Drawing Object property bar.

Changing Object Colors

If you don't like the default pattern or color for an object you've created, you can quickly change it. You can change the color of a single or multiple objects. And if you know what color you want to use ahead of time, you can change it before creating the object. Once you create the object, Presentations will use the last color selected.

To change the color of objects, select the object(s) you want to change. Click the Foreground Color button on the Drawing Object property bar and select a color from the color palette. See "Changing Line Attributes" for instructions on changing the color of a line. Click the Shadow button to add a shadow to an object. Click the Rotate button to rotate the object, just as you did for images earlier in this chapter.

Changing Object Fill Patterns

If you want to do more with your rectangle or circle than merely change its colors and resize it, you can use the Fill Pattern button on the Drawing Object property bar. You can select a funky pattern, use a texture, or even add a picture as the fill for the object. Play around with the Fill Pattern and Foreground Fill Color buttons on the Drawing Object property bar to see what you like best. To change the fill pattern, click the Fill Pattern button on the Drawing Object property bar and select a pattern. If you want to do a bit more, check out the next set of steps.

To add a texture or picture, follow these steps:

1. Click the Fill Attributes button on the Drawing Object property bar to display the Fill tab in the Object Properties dialog box (see Figure 10-5).

2. Under Fill Style, choose the Texture or Picture button. Corel Presentations displays the Texture or Picture Settings button and the Browse button.

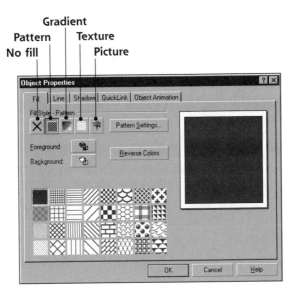

Figure 10-5 Add a texture or picture to an object.

3. Click the Category down arrow button and select a category for your texture or picture. Then select the desired texture or picture from those that display.

4. After you're finished, click OK. Presentations changes the selected object according to your choices.

And here's a handy tip: when you select an object, its fill color, pattern, texture, or picture is represented on the Fill Pattern button on the Drawing Objects property bar.

 TIP **You can also display the Fill tab in the Object Properties dialog box by clicking the Fill Pattern button on the Drawing Objects property bar and choosing More.**

Changing Line Attributes

You can change a variety of line attributes just as you did object attributes. This includes changing a line's pattern, color, style, and width. Keep in mind that lines include not only those you create with the Line tool but also lines that surround an object you create with the Closed Object tool.

To change line attributes, select the lines you want to change or the object containing the lines. To select multiple objects, press and hold Ctrl and click each line. Use the following tools to format your line:

Changes the look of the line with a line style

Changes the line width. Note that you can also click and drag sizing handles to change a line's width.

Changes the line color

Adding Arrowheads and Caps to Lines

You saw in the previous section that you can change a line's pattern and color. But earlier I mentioned that you could also add arrowheads to a line to call attention to something on your slide. Corel Presentations provides a variety of ways to display arrowheads for lines to get just the look you need. For example, you can also add a rounded end instead of an arrowhead. Note that Corel Presentations refers to these as *caps* because you're "capping off" one or both ends of a line. The *starting cap* is the point where you clicked to begin creating the line, and the *ending cap* is where you clicked to stop creating the line. The section of an ellipse shown in Figure 10-4 uses an arrowhead for its starting cap and a circle for its ending cap.

To add arrowheads and caps to lines, follow these steps:

1. Select the line(s) you want to change. To select multiple lines, press and hold the Ctrl key and then click each line.

2. Click the Fill Attributes button on the Drawing Object property bar or choose Format → Object Properties → Line Presentations displays the Line tab in the Object Properties dialog box (see Figure 10-6). You can see how your selections affect the line's appearance in the sample window on the right side of the dialog box.

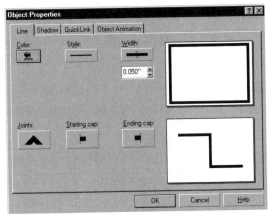

Figure 10-6 Add arrowheads or circles to lines.

3. If your line has bends or joints in it, select the way those joints will appear by clicking the Joints button and selecting a joint style.

4. To add an arrowhead or other style to your line, determine if you want it on the starting or ending cap, click either Starting cap or Ending cap, and select the desired style.

5. After you're finished, click OK. Presentations changes the selected line(s) according to your selections.

FEATURE FOCUS Presentations contains a number of new cap styles to add to lines, including the circle cap, brand new with this version.

TIP You can adjust the length, angle, or direction of a line by selecting it and then clicking and dragging a sizing handle.

Object Juggling

Once you start adding objects to a slide, you may notice that they stack on top of each other, and one might hide part or all of another object. This may cause problems when you try to work with each object. However, you can easily change which object appears in front, as well as group objects to work with them as a single entity or flip them to face a different way.

To change object order, select the object you want to reorder, click the Graphics menu button on the Drawing Object property bar, and select the desired action: To Front to make it the top object; To Back to make it the bottom object; Forward One to move it in front of the object directly in front of it; Backward One to move it behind the object directly behind it.

If you've drawn a house made of several objects and want to move the house en masse, you can group it. Then when you need to work just on the roof, or just the chimney, you can separate the objects again. To group objects and treat them as one, select all the objects you want to group. Click the Graphics menu button on the Drawing Object property bar and choose Group. To ungroup the objects, select the grouped object, click the Graphics menu button on the Drawing Object property bar, and choose Separate Objects.

To change the direction an object is facing, click the Graphics menu button on the Drawing Object property bar and then choose Flip and either Left/Right or Top/Bottom.

BONUS

Working with Organization Charts

An organization chart provides an overview of your company or organization in a hierarchical manner. In Presentations, you can quickly add an organization chart slide, then enter the people and titles for the hierarchy and format it to your taste.

Inserting an Organization Chart Slide

Your first step to adding an organization chart is to determine where you want a slide to appear in your show. If your slide show is an overview of the company and company policies for new employees, you may want to leave the organizational structure toward the end, after your audience is familiar with some of the more global aspects of the company.

Once you determine where you want the slide, display the slide that the organization chart slide will *follow*. Then click the Add Slide button and select Insert Org Chart Slide. Alternatively, choose Insert→New Slide, select the Org Chart layout, and click OK.

Creating the Organization Chart

Once you have the organization chart slide, you can begin creating the organization chart itself. This is where you choose the layout and other initial features of the chart and enter chart information.

Follow these steps to create the organization chart:

1. With the Organization Chart slide displayed, type a title and subtitle in the appropriate placeholders. If you don't need a subtitle, select and delete the subtitle placeholder.

2. Double-click the bottom placeholder, where it says *Double Click to Add Org Chart*. Presentations inserts a default organization chart layout (see Figure 10-7). Notice the thick placeholder with hashmarks surrounding the chart. This indicates that the chart is *active* and ready for editing. If you don't see the thick placeholder with hashmarks, double-click the chart.

3. Double-click the top placeholder. <Name> disappears and the insertion point blinks in its place.

4. Type the name of the top person and press Tab to position the insertion point for the top person's title. Alternatively, you can double-click <Title> to position the insertion point.

5. Type the title for the top person and press Tab to position the insertion point in the next placeholder, ready for the name. Repeat for all position placeholders.

Editing the Organization Chart

Reorganizing your organization chart is easy using the Edit Organization Chart property bar. You can add and remove positions, change the chart layout, and do a variety of other things. Table 10-5 describes the buttons on this property bar that you haven't encountered on other property bars and that are unique to creating and working with organization charts. Use Table 10-5 to help you make changes to your organization chart and check out the items following the table for more information. Refer back to Figure 10-7 for the types of positions available — Manager, Subordinate, and Coworker. Staff positions will extend from the associated branch connector. Note that, depending on your organization chart layout, the positions may be arranged differently. In the default layout in Figure 10-7, subordinates are beneath managers. However, in a vertical layout, subordinates could appear to the right or left of managers.

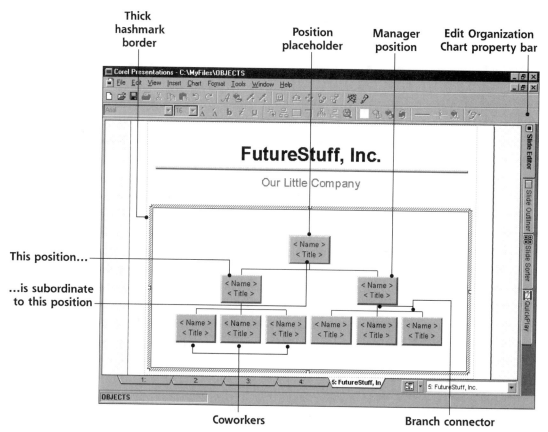

Figure 10-7 The default organization chart.

TABLE 10-5 Edit Organization Chart Property Bar

Button	Name	Description
🔲	SUBORDINATE	Insert one or more subordinates beneath the selected placeholder.
🔲	CONNECTOR STYLE	Select a style for the lines connecting the org chart boxes.
🔲	BOX STYLE	Select a style for the org chart boxes.
🔲	BORDER STYLE	Select a style for the lines surrounding the org chart boxes.
🔲	MAXIMIZE SPACING	Increase the space between placeholders.

Button	Name	Description
	COLLAPSE/EXPAND	Hide subordinates of selected branch. Click arrow to display again.
	ZOOM BRANCH	Display only the selected branches.

Use the following techniques to work with your organization chart:

* To add a subordinate to an existing person, select the box to which you want to attach the subordinate. Presentations also selects the branch connectors. Click the Subordinate button. Choose Insert → Subordinates to insert more than one at a time.

* To insert a manager, coworker, or staff position, first select the placeholder that will be adjacent to the new position. Choose Insert and then choose one of the following options:

  * Coworkers allows you to add one or more coworkers equal in rank to the selected position. You can also indicate whether the coworker will insert to the Left or Right of the selected position.

  * Manager allows you to insert a single manager above the selected position.

  * Staff allows you to insert one or more staff positions to the selected position. Staff positions extend off the branch connector line of the selected position.

* To move a position, click and drag the position you want to move so that it covers or overlaps the target position placeholder. You'll see a transparent arrow attach to the pointer. Align the dragged position so the arrow is pointing left or right to insert it as a coworker or align so the arrow is pointing down to insert it as a subordinate.

Summary

I n this chapter, you got a little fancy, customizing bulleted lists by changing the bullet type, bullet text fonts, and size, and by adjusting the spacing between bullet points. You learned how to insert a QuickArt image and format it. Finally, you learned how to use the Tool palette to insert objects, adding lines, squares, circles, and other objects to your slides. Next you'll learn how to pull your slide show together so it's ready for an audience.

CHAPTER ELEVEN

WORKING WITH SLIDE SHOWS

IN THIS CHAPTER YOU LEARN THESE KEY SKILLS

n Chapters 9 and 10, you learned how to create the content of your slides and format them with fonts, color, clipart, and objects. Now you pull it all together into a full-blown show. This is where you add bells and whistles that make your slide show run smoothly. You'll look at animating bullet points so your audience only sees one or some of the points at a time, and you'll add transitions between slides to blend them together. I begin with creating effects for individual slides, move into effects between slides, and then look at playing the slide show.

Animating Bullet Points and Objects

f you've ever attended a conference or workshop where the speaker used slides or a slide show, you may have noticed that when he or she displayed a Bulleted List slide, you saw each point appear individually. Perhaps you saw the title of the slide first and then the first bullet point slid in from the left of the slide. A few seconds later, the second bullet point slid in from the left or bounced down from the right corner. Presentations calls this *animating* the bullet points. In either case, you have the bullet points make their entrances at different intervals and in different ways while the slide is displayed. You can achieve a similar effect for objects.

Animating Bullet Points

Are the points you want to make difficult to convey? Or do you want to make sure your audience stays with you at each point and doesn't read ahead while you're elaborating on a previous point? In either case, animating the bullet points leaves you in control of what bullet point displays when. Presentations allows you to animate the bullet point *in place* or *across the screen*. When you animate the bullet point in place, the bulleted list remains in its spot on the slide but appears using one of many transition effects. These effects are for more traditional or professional presentations. If you want your slide show to be more lively, you can animate across the screen, which will allow your bullets to slide, bounce, or otherwise make themselves known in an attention-grabbing fashion. You can choose to animate bullets on the current Bulleted List slide or all Bulleted List slides in the show.

To animate bullets on a Bulleted List slide, follow these steps:

1. Display the Bulleted List slide you want to animate and select the Bulleted List placeholder on the slide.

2. Click the Object Animation button on the Edit Bulleted List property bar to display the Bullet Animation tab in the Bulleted List Properties dialog box (see Figure 11-1). Alternatively, you can choose Format → Object Properties → Object Animation .

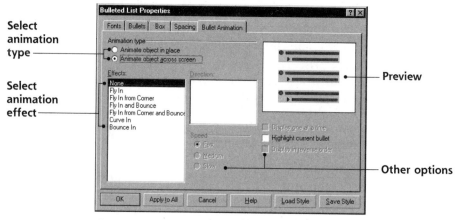

Figure 11-1 Animate your bullet points in the Bulleted list Properties dailog box.

3. Select Animate object in place or Animate object across screen. Depending on your selection the Effects list will change to display the appropriate effects.

4. In the Effects list, select the desired effect and watch an example of it in the preview area. If your effect has a direction, choose from one of the options in the Direction list.

5. Under Speed, indicate how quickly you want the bullet points to appear.

6. Choose from the following additional options on the right side of the dialog box and click OK to apply the animation to the current Bulleted List slide or Apply to All to apply it to all Bulleted List slides.

   * *Display one at a time* displays bullets points one at a ti me at predefined intervals.

   * *Display in reverse order* displays bullet points from last point to first.

   * *Highlight current bullet* highlights each point as it appears on the screen. If you haven't chosen to display bullet points one at a time, Presentations displays the entire list and then highlights each bullet point.

Animating Objects

You've added animation to a Bulleted List so your points move onto your slide in the desired way. Wouldn't it be great if that stack of gold coins on Slide 4 could bounce into view? This would make your audience sit up and take notice. You can animate images and objects on your slides, just as you did bullet points. Animating an object is similar to animating a bullet point, with just a few differences.

Animated objects call attention to the slide and bring the focus on the object itself. Make sure you want the object to be the focus. For example, if your presentation is about a new line of running shoes, you may animate a photo of the image as you describe its features.

To animate an object, follow these steps:

1. Display the slide containing the image or object you want to animate and select the image(s) or object(s) on the slide.

2. Click the Object Animation button on the Drawing Object property bar or choose `Format` → `Object Properties` → `Object Animation` to display the Object Animation tab in the Object Properties dialog box. This tab is similar to the Bullet Animation tab except that it lacks any bullet-specific options, such as displaying bullet points one at a time.

3. Select Animate object in place or Animate object across screen. Depending on your selection the Effects list will change to display the appropriate effects.

4. Set the effect, direction (if applicable), and speed, and then click OK.

ORDER ON THE SLIDE!

If you have several objects on the slide and want them to make their appearances one at a time, you can set the object *display sequence*. To do so, follow these steps:

1. Animate the first object as described in "Animating Objects."

2. Select the next object and click the Object Animation button on the Drawing Object property bar.

3. Set the animation options for the object. Notice that Presentations has already determined a default sequence number for the object in the Object display sequence text box.

4. Click the Object display sequence down-arrow button and select the number that indicates in what order this object will appear on the slide. Alternatively, you can type the number in the Object display sequence text box.

5. Click OK when finished. Repeat Steps 2 through 5 for all objects you wish to animate and sequence.

Note that you can't select the same Object display sequence number for two or more slides. If you set the same number, Presentations will automatically renumber the remaining objects so each displays sequentially.

Working with Slide Transitions

You've seen what transitions and animation can do for bullet lists and objects. Now how about creating a nice transition between *slides?* Using the Slide Transition feature, you can have slides dissolve into each other, open and close like window shutters, or slide in from the screen's corner. You can also automate the show even more by indicating how long you'd like a slide to stay up before the next slide displays. You can set your slide transitions and other options in either Slide Editor or Slide Sorter view. If you want to set them for more than one slide, Slide Sorter is the way to go.

Using the Slide Show Property Bar

The fastest way to add transitions to several slides at once is to use Slide Sorter view, where most of the tools you'll need are on the Slide Show property bar. In this chapter, I focus mainly on using this property bar but do discuss alternative methods for working with your show. Table 11-1 describes each of the buttons on the Slide Show property bar.

TABLE 11-1 Slide Show Property Bar

Button	Name	Description
	Master Gallery	Add or change the current background for all slides.
	Select Layout	Change the slide layout.
Blinds	Slide Transition	Select transitions for slides.
	Direction	Indicate a direction for the selected slide transition.
	Speed	Indicate a speed for the selected slide transition.
	Sound	Add a sound to the slide.
	Display Sequence	Set timings for slides and objects on slides.
	Speaker Notes	Create speaker notes for the current slide.
	QuickKeys	Create shortcut keys that can perform actions during a show, such as play a sound.
	Skip	Don't display this slide during the show.
Original Slide Show	Custom Audiences	Select the audience for your show.
	Play Slide Show	Set options and play a slide show.
	Show on the Go	Create a portable show.
	Internet Publisher	Convert your show for use on the Web.

FEATURE FOCUS The property bar is context-sensitive and will change depending on what you've selected on your slide, or if you haven't selected any element.

Adding Slide Transitions

No doubt you've seen a slide show with photographic slides. As the moderator clicks the next button, the screen goes dark briefly, and then the next slide appears. That's fine for a basic slide show, but Presentations lets you create transitions that take the audience smoothly from slide to slide with hardly a break in the action. You can add a transition to a few slides or all slides. However, keep in mind that too many types of transitions will disrupt the show's flow. You may want to use one type of transition for the first and last slides and one for all slides in between. If you don't choose a slide transition, Presentations uses Sweep Close as the default transition.

To add a slide transition, follow these steps:

1. With your slide show open, display the slide to which you wish to add transitions or — to add transitions to multiple slides — select the Slide Sorter tab and select the slides, using the technique explained in Chapter 10.

2. Click the Slide Transition down arrow button on the Slide Show property bar and point to a transition. Presentations shows how the transition will look on a sample slide to the right of the list (see Figure 11-2).

3. Click the transition you'd like to use. If you're in Slide Sorter view, you'll see the name of the selected transition below the slide.

4. To set the direction for your transition (if applicable), click the Direction button on the Slide Show property bar and select the desired option. If the Direction button is grayed out on the Slide Show property bar, no direction is applicable to your transition.

5. To set the speed for your transition, click the Speed button on the Slide Show property bar and select the desired option.

FEATURE FOCUS The Slide Transition drop-down list and the sample slide provide a fast and easy way to preview and add transitions to your slides.

Adding a Delay Sequence to Slides

In addition to adding a transition to each slide for a smooth visual move, you can also tell Presentations to display each slide after a certain number of seconds have passed. Presentations calls this a *delay sequence*. By default, Presentations will wait for you to click your mouse or press the space bar to display the next slide during a show. However, if your show can basically communicate everything to the audience, or you have your comments timed well, you may want Presentations to do more of the work. This is especially good if your show will run at a trade show or similar event where you want to talk with visitors while the slide show runs on a computer next to you.

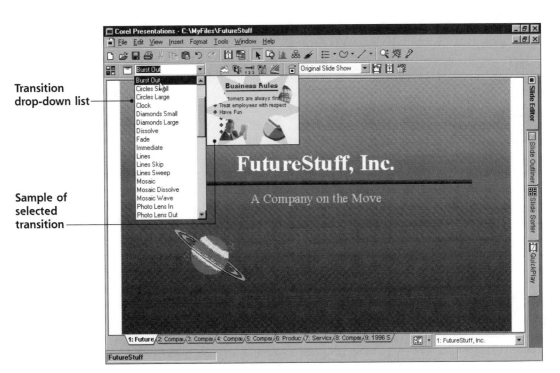

Transition drop-down list—

Sample of selected transition—

Figure 11-2 Select a slide transition.

Depending on the information contained on each slide, you may want to have different durations. You may only need to display the title slide for a few seconds, but because the first Bulleted List slide contains several points, you may want to keep it up for several seconds so the audience can read and digest the information as you speak.

To add delay sequences to slides, follow these steps:

1. With your slide show open, display the slide to which you wish to add transitions or select the Slide Sorter tab to add transitions to multiple slides and select the slides.

2. With your slide(s) displayed or selected in Slide Sorter view, click the Display Sequence button on the Slide Show property bar or choose `Format` → `Slide Properties` → `Display Sequence`. Presentations displays the Delay Sequence tab in the Slide Properties dialog box (see Figure 11-3). Note that the tabs in the Slide Properties dialog box contain a list and buttons for displaying other slides. This means you don't have to close and reopen the dialog box for each slide to which you wish to add effects.

3. If you want the delay times to apply to all slides, choose the Apply to all slides in the slide show check box near the bottom of the dialog box.

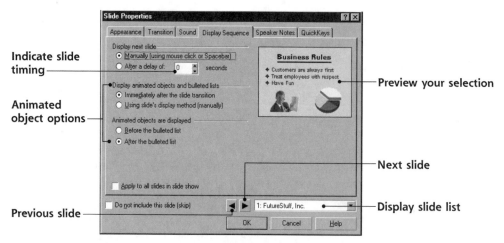

Indicate slide timing

Animated object options

Preview your selection

Next slide

Previous slide

Display slide list

Figure 11-3 Set a delay sequence.

4. Under Display next slide, choose Manually to allow you to click to display the next slide during the show, or choose After a delay of to have slides advance after a specific number of seconds. In the seconds text box, type the number of seconds you want the slide(s) to display before the next slide appears.

5. Under Display animated objects and bulleted lists, select the desired option using the following information, and then click OK:

* *Immediately after the slide transition* will display all animated objects according to your selections in the Animate Bullet or Animate Object Properties dialog boxes.

* *Using slide's display method* means that if you chose Manually, you must click once to display the first animated object; then the rest will follow. If you chose After a delay of, the animated objects will display automatically once the transition to the slide is complete.

* *Before the bulleted list* means any animated objects will display before the bulleted list displays.

* *After the bulleted list* means any animated objects will display after the bulleted list displays.

FEATURE FOCUS

You can add movie or video clips to your presentation. See online help for more details. Choose Help→Help Topics and then the Find tab. Type **about movie** in the first text box. Double-click About Movie in the third text box to display the help window.

Adding a Sound to a Slide

You've seen how you can create some pretty dazzling visuals using Presentations, from animated bullet points to fancy transitions between slides. If your computer is equipped with a sound card and you have access to sound clips or a microphone, you can make your show a walking *and talking* show. With the right sound files, you can add your own narration, music, or sound effects to specific slides. Imagine hearing the clink-click of coins when that stack of coins comes bouncing onto Slide 5!

Presentations ships with a variety of sound files in WAVE (WAV) and MIDI (MID) format. I won't get into the details of the differences between these types of sound files; there are many excellent books on this topic. Let's press on and add sound to a slide.

 Most, if not all, of the sounds may remain stored on your CD-ROM. Make sure it's in your CD-ROM drive before you select your files.

1. Open the slide show to which you want to add sound and then display the slide that will contain the sound object.

2. Click the Sound button on the Slide Show property bar or choose **Format** → **Slide Properties** → **Sound** . Presentations displays the Sound tab in the Slide Properties dialog box (see Figure 11-4).

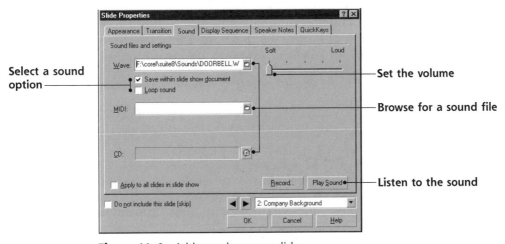

Figure 11-4 Add sounds to your slides.

3. Under Sound files and settings, insert the desired sound files in the Wave, MIDI or CD text boxes. Notice that you can add multiple sounds to the slide. If you're creative with sound, this could be quite fun, as they will play simultaneously.

4. To listen to a sound you inserted, click Play Sound. To stop the sound in the middle, click Stop.

5. Use the Soft and Loud controls to set a volume for the sound and choose Loop sound to have the sound play continuously as long as the slide is displayed. If you choose to save the sound within the slide show, this ensures that the sound will always be available and not dependent on your hard drive or CD-ROM drive. This is good if you plan to take your show on the road.

6. When you've set all sound options, click OK. Presentations adds the sound to your slide and will play it when the slide displays.

TIP **If you have a microphone, you can add your own sounds or narration to a slide using the Sound Recorder. Click Record on the Sound tab in the Slide Properties dialog box and record your sound.**

Note that you can click the Slide Appearance button on the Presentations toolbar and use the Slide Properties dialog box to set slide transitions and other settings all at once instead of using the Slide Show property bar.

FEATURE
FOCUS **When you're using Slide Sorter view, Presentations displays icons for elements such as transitions, timing, and sound. Double-click any icon to display the associated dialog box and make changes to the effect. Take a gander back at Figure 9-5 in Chapter 9 to see these icons. Note that these are for your information only; you wouldn't mix so many things in a single slide show.**

Playing a Slide Show

Once you've created your slide show and added transitions and timings, you're ready for the final output. You can either project your show from your computer using a video projection system, convert your Presentations file to photographic slides, print your show as a hard copy, or publish it to the World Wide Web.

X-REF **For information on this last option, see "Internet Slide Shows" later in this chapter.**

The most effective way to present your show is by playing it on your computer, complete with a darkened room and a large screen for the projector. In this section, you look at how to play a show as well as how to print it. For information on converting your show to photographic slides, see "A Slide is Worth a Single Photo" later in this chapter.

FEATURE FOCUS Presentations supports Intel Corporation's MMX technology. If you have a Pentium computer that uses this technology, your slide displays and transitions will be faster.

Playing a Show

Presentations lets you play a show directly from your computer or from a computer that doesn't have Presentations on it. In the second case, you create a *runtime* version of the show, which you cover in more detail next.

Remember how your teachers used to circle things on the board when they were driving a point home? The circled word or equation really stood out and you found yourself continuing to look at it during the class. If you need to emphasize something during a show, you can circle it, underline it, or draw an arrow to it using the highlighter. You'll learn about this as you play the show.

FEATURE FOCUS To see a review of your slide show with all current settings, choose the QuickPlay tab. Presentations will present your show, starting with the current slide. This is helpful to view the current slide as it will appear in your slide show. For information on advancing your slides and other techniques, see "Using Slide Show Techniques" later in this chapter.

CAUTION At this writing, Corel had not determined whether DirectDraw would ship with the software. If you see a message about DirectDraw when you try to play a slide show (whether with QuickPlay or another method), decide whether to download it from Corel's Web site now or continue with your show.

To play an open slide show beginning with the first slide and using default settings, click the Play Show button on the toolbar. Presentations starts the show, beginning with the first slide. This is nearly identical to QuickPlay except that

Play Show automatically starts with the first slide in the show. For information on advancing your slides and other techniques, see "Using Slide Show Techniques" later in this chapter.

You can also set options before playing your show, such as which slide will display first, what color you want your highlighter to use, and if you want the show to repeat when it comes to the end (as you would if the show is playing unattended at a trade show).

To play a show and set options, follow these steps:

1. With your slide show open, click the Play Slide Show button on the Slide Show property bar or choose View → Play Side Show . Presentations displays the Play Slide Show dialog box (see Figure 11-5). Presentations indicates the current or selected slide in the Beginning slide text box.

Figure 11-5 Set Slide Show options.

2. Select the slide with which you wish to begin your show, then select a Highlighter color and Highlighter width and choose the Repeat continuously until 'Esc' is pressed check box.

3. Click Play. Presentations plays the presentation, starting with the slide you indicated in the Beginning slide text box.

Using Slide Show Techniques

Once your slide show is running, you can control it in a variety of ways. Use the following techniques to help you present your slide show in the smoothest and most effective way possible.

✳ *Advancing slides.* If you selected Manual transitions when you set up your Delay Sequences, you must click the current slide or press Page Down or the spacebar to advance to the next one. If you selected Delayed transitions, sit back and let Presentations advance the slides.

✳ *Moving to the previous slide.* To return to the previous slide, press Page Up.

✳ *Moving to a specific slide.* Press Ctrl+G to display the Go To Slide dialog box, select the slide to display, and click OK.

* *Highlighting a point.* Move the mouse until you see the pointer on the screen. Click and drag to circle an item, underline a point, or draw an arrow to an important piece of information. The highlight will disappear after the slide advances. Press Ctrl+E to erase highlighting while the slide is still displayed. If you use the highlighter with delayed transitions, Presentations disables the transition to allow you to write on the slide. Once you're finished, you'll need to click the mouse button or press the space bar to continue the show.

* *Ending a show.* To stop a slide show before you've reached the last slide, press Esc.

TIP **Secondary-click the screen while a slide show is playing to display the QuickMenu and select from a variety of options. For a list of the keyboard shortcuts, see Table B-7 in Appendix B.**

Using a Runtime Version

If you go on the road with your show, you may not be able to bring along a laptop or computer that has Presentations. If this is the case, you can use the Runtime Expert to set up your show so that it plays on any computer, regardless of whether the computer has Presentations. Here's how to take your show on the road.

CREATING A SHOW ON THE GO

Before you can play your slide show on a computer that doesn't have Presentations, you'll need to create the show in a special format. Since you'll no doubt carry your show on a floppy disk, you'll need to save it to your floppy disk drive. The fastest way to create a portable show is to accept all default settings except the destination.

To create a Show on the Go with default options, follow these steps:

1. If Presentations is running, open the slide show that you want to show on other computers. If Presentations is not running, start it from either the DAD toolbar or by using the Start button on the Windows desktop and open the slide show.

2. With your slide show open, click the Show on the Go button on the Slide Show property bar or choose File → Show on the Go . If you have made changes to your slide show without saving it, Presentations will display a message telling you that you must save the show before you can create the Show on the Go version. Presentations then displays the Show on the Go dialog box (see Figure 11-6). The Summary information tells you where and how Presentations will save the show.

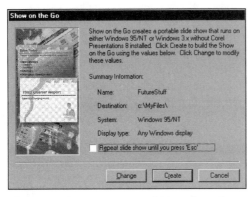

Figure 11-6 Create a portable version of your show.

3. Click Change to display the dialog box asking you where you wish to save your Show on the Go.

4. Indicate the location for your floppy drive and click Finish to accept the other default settings and continue creating the portable show.

5. Click Create. Presentations displays the *Making Intermediate File* message box. You can cancel this at any time by clicking Cancel. When finished, Presentations saves an executable file in the designated folder.

PLAYING A RUNTIME SHOW

After you create a runtime version of your show, you'll travel to your destination where you'll sit down at the computer from which you will play the show. Here's how to play a runtime show. First, pop your diskette in the disk drive. In the Windows 3.x Program Manager, open the File Manager and choose File→Run. In Windows 95, click the Start button on the desktop and choose Run. In the file-name text box, type the folder and name of the show or use the Folder button to locate and select the file, placing it in the text box. Click OK. The system loads your slide show and plays it, displaying the first slide.

If your runtime slide show contains sound files, you need to make sure the computer to play it on has a sound card capable of playing the types of sound files you included. Also, make sure your sounds were saved with your slide show; otherwise, the slide show will be unable to locate them when it comes time to play them. Refer back to "Adding a Sound to a Slide" for more information.

Printing a Slide Show

Often you may find that in addition to playing a slide show for an audience, you want a hard copy for your files or to provide as handouts. You can print all or some of your slides, using a variety of options. If you have a color printer, you can see how your slides will look in all their colorful glory. This section covers general techniques for printing your slides. For information on printing speaker and audience notes or handouts, see the Bonus at the end of this chapter.

To print the entire show using default settings, open your show and click the Print button on the Standard toolbar.

To print your slides using print options, follow these steps:

1. With your slide show open, click the Print button on the toolbar or choose **File** → **Print** to display the Print to dialog box. You'll find that this dialog box is similar to the WordPerfect and Quattro Pro Print to dialog boxes, with some unique features pertaining to slide shows.

2. Under Print, select how much of the show you wish to print and any page range necessary.

   ✳ Choose *Full document* to print the entire slide show.

   ✳ Choose *Current view* to print the current slide.

   ✳ Choose *Slides* to print multiple slides.

3. If you have additional printing needs, choose the Details tab and make any or all of the following selections:

* Clear the Adjust image to print black and white check box to print to a color printer and see the slides in color.

* Clear the Print background check box to print only the text, images, and objects without the background behind them. This gives the slides a cleaner look, which is especially helpful if you print them in black and white.

FEATURE FOCUS The Internet Publisher feature is new to Presentations and provides two options — Publish to HTML, which enables you to convert each slide to HTML code, and Publish to Show It, which enables you to convert a slide show with all its animation, sound, and other effects intact. For more on HTML and the World Wide Web, see Chapter 17.

* Choose the Print slide title and/or Print slide number check boxes if you want to include the slide title and number on the page.

4. When you've set all options, click Print.

TIP To take a look at how your slides will appear before you send them to the printer, display the Print to dialog box and set your options. Click Print Preview. To see the next slide, click once. When you click the last slide in Print Preview mode, Presentations returns to the Print to dialog box. Press Esc to return to the Print to dialog box without previewing the entire show.

SIDE TRIP

A SLIDE IS WORTH A SINGLE PHOTO

If you want to convert your slide show to 35mm slides, overhead transparencies, or prints, you can use GraphicsLand (as long as you have a modem and you installed GraphicsLand during a custom installation). GraphicsLand is a service bureau specializing in slide conversion. You can send your order and have it delivered to your doorstep. With your slide show open, choose File→Send To→GraphicsLand. You'll see the GraphicsLand welcome dialog box. To get help on using the service, choose Help and select a topic. Otherwise, click Next to display the Choose Files to Send dialog box. Locate and select the slide show file you wish to convert and click Next. Follow the instructions, indicating your selections as you go.

BONUS

Using Speaker and Audience Notes

Have you ever had to speak before a large group and ended up reading your speech because you were afraid of losing your place? Well, you may be a little fearful of presenting your first slide show but you don't need to be. With a little practice, and some handy Speaker Notes, you'll be fully prepared. And if you want to give your audience something to take away, you can either print the slide show or create audience notes.

Speaker notes are miniature representations of each slide, with room for your own notes, tips, and reminders (see Figure 11-7). Audience notes provide a miniature representation of each slide as well, with ruled lines for your audience to take their own notes (see Figure 11-8).

Creating Speaker Notes

If you want to remember to talk about your discounts for new clients when you display Slide 6, you can include this reminder on speaker notes. Keep the speaker notes in front of you as you play your show so you can refer to them easily.

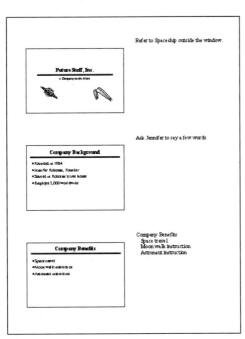

Figure 11-7 Use speaker notes to assist you during your slide show.

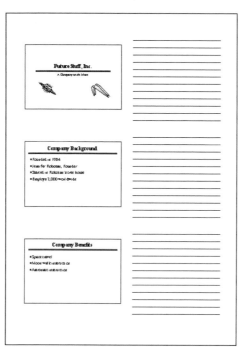

Figure 11-8 Provide your audience with a note-taking aid.

Here's how to create speaker notes that you can print later:

1. With your show open, display the first slide to which you want to add notes and click the Speaker Notes button on the Slide Show property bar. Alternatively, you can choose **Format** → **Slide Properties** → **Speaker Notes** to display the Speaker Notes tab in the Slide Properties dialog box (see Figure 11-9).

Type notes here

Insert slide text

Select another slide

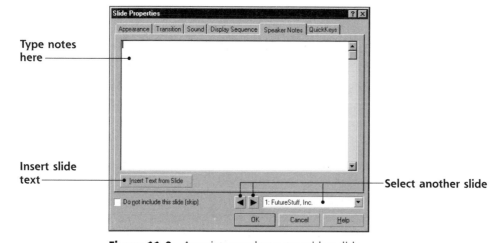

Figure 11-9 Associate speaker notes with a slide.

2. In the large text box, type the notes you want associated with the current slide and click OK. Presentations saves the notes with each slide so you can print them at your leisure.

On the Speaker Notes tab in the Slide Properties dialog box, you can click Insert Text from Slide to insert all text contained on your slide. You can then edit it to fit your speaker notes. Note that charts, images, and objects won't insert.

Printing Speaker and Audience Notes

Once you create your speaker notes, you can print them, indicating the number of slides you would like to print on each page as well as selecting the usual print options. If you want to provide your audience with a printed copy of each slide and a place for them to take notes, you can print Audience Notes or Handouts. The only difference between the two is that Audience Notes provide ruled lines for the audience to make handwritten notes; handouts provide a blank area next to or below the slide, depending on how many slides you print per page.

To print speaker notes, audience notes, or handouts, follow these steps:

1. Open the slide show containing the speaker notes you wish to print.

2. Click the Print button on the Presentations 8 toolbar or choose `File` → `Print` to display the Print dialog box.

3. Under Print, choose Speaker Notes, Audience Notes, or Handouts.

4. In the Number of slides per page text box, type the number of slides you want to print on each page, keeping in mind that the images will be small because you're printing notes or leaving room for audience notes.

5. Select any other print options and choose Print to send your speaker notes to the printer. Refer back to "Printing a Slide Show" for information on the various print options.

Summary

Thus ends your adventure in the land of slide shows. Here you learned how to add transitions and animation to bullet points and objects and to create transitions between slides for a smooth show. You also learned how to add sound to a slide and play a slide show. Finally, you checked out creating runtime slide shows and using speaker and audience notes. Bid adieu to Presentations and move on to a little number crunching with Quattro Pro.

CREATING NOTEBOOKS WITH QUATTRO PRO

THIS PART CONTAINS THE FOLLOWING CHAPTERS

Part Four gets you started working with spreadsheets, showing you how to enter, format, and calculate numbers to get the results you need. You also get to see how you can use Quattro Pro as a database, storing information such as inventory or names and addresses for use in other applications.

Even as he grew up in the sixties, Brian Leske was a pack rat. "I kept everything," he sighs, "clothes, newspapers, bicycle parts. My grandfather always told me that you never know when you might need something again. It drove my parents crazy. But at least I was organized."

Organized is an understatement. As a child, Brian filled box after box, folder after folder, and he always knew exactly what was inside. The collection that gave him the most joy, however, was his well organized set of baseball cards. "I had some older cousins and an uncle who cleaned out their attic and needed to get rid of hundreds of old cards," Brian recalls. "They knew my reputation, so they came to me before they threw the cards away. I'm glad they did."

Brian gradually lost interest in baseball cards and turned his attention to computers. Of course, he didn't throw the cards away — they were safely stored in his closet. As his interest in computers grew, Brian became especially fond of databases and spreadsheets. "They think like I do," he says, "but in the beginning, they were far too difficult to use. I'm organized, but I'm not a rocket scientist." That's when he heard about a program called Quattro Pro. "The first time I saw Quattro Pro was at a friend's house. She used it to catalog all sorts of things for her small antique business — inventory, income, payroll records. I was amazed. In about two seconds she showed me a pie chart that accounted for every penny she had spent during the previous year."

After that, Brian was sold. "I kind of went crazy. I bought Quattro Pro and installed it, and I didn't even know what I was going to use it for." It didn't take long to find a good application. "About that time, I read an article in one of my friend's antiquing magazines about the skyrocketing values of old sports cards. I immediately went to the bookstore and bought a pricing guide. I drove to my parents' house and hauled 14 shoe boxes out of my old closet. Mom was ecstatic."

Brian was ecstatic, too, when he found out that his collection was worth thousands of dollars. "I used Quattro Pro to catalog every card I own. It took over a month of spare time, but I finally got it done — over 7,400 cards. I used fields for the card manufacturer, card number, player's name, how many duplicates I have, and the quality and condition of each card. I also left plenty of room on the right of the spreadsheet so that every year, I add a column for the card's value for that year.

"With a few clicks, I can create a graph that shows the worth of my collection. In the last five years, the overall appreciation has kept pace with real estate. Not bad." Not that he would ever sell them. "I'll never get rid of them — trade a few, maybe," he says. "I just like to keep track of each one."

CHAPTER TWELVE

CREATING A NEW NOTEBOOK

IN THIS CHAPTER YOU LEARN THESE KEY SKILLS

UNDERSTANDING SPREADSHEET CONCEPTS   PAGE 238

CREATING A NEW NOTEBOOK   PAGE 239

NAVIGATING A NOTEBOOK   PAGE 242

ENTERING DATA IN CELLS   PAGE 245

USING QUICKFILL   PAGE 250

EDITING CELL DATA   PAGE 252

12

W elcome to Quattro Pro 8, the only tool you'll need for working with financial information. Using Quattro Pro, you can create and maintain something as simple as a budget or something a little more complex, like a loan amortization. Quattro Pro's layout harks back to those ledger days, where accountants hunched over rickety desks, scribbling numbers in neat columns and rows. The surroundings may not have always been pleasant, but you can't beat nice, neat columns and rows when working with numbers.

But Quattro Pro is more than just a tool for creating numbers in columns and rows. It allows you to format numbers, use colors and shading to enhance your spreadsheets, and it provides dozens of functions to help you perform complex mathematical calculations. And, if your work requires you to be a bit of a statistician, Quattro Pro has the tools for you, too.

And don't worry if you're not a mathematical genius and don't know pi from the apple pie a la mode you order at your favorite restaurant. Quattro Pro makes it easy for anyone to get the mathematical results he or she needs without a lot of effort.

Understanding Spreadsheet Concepts

I f you explored the Bonus section in Chapter 7, you may be raising an eyebrow and saying to yourself, "Can't I do this calculation business in WordPerfect? Why should I use a totally different application for my number stuff?" A good question deserves a good answer, and here it is: Numbers are Quattro Pro's specialty. That is its reason for existing, which means you'll find all the tools and features you need to make it easy. You can do a lot with numbers in WordPerfect, but you won't have the same functionality and ease of use you'll find here. Beyond the run-of-the-mill spreadsheet, where you have basic columns and rows of numbers, with totals for each, you can run the gamut of financial documents and related components, such as the following:

* *Creating business and financial forms.* Need a budget? Use Quattro Pro. Need to generate invoices for your home business? Quattro Pro can not only maintain the prices and taxes for services or goods sold, it can also print them on a professional-looking invoice form.

* *Creating charts and maps.* Though you can create a chart based on a WordPerfect table, it's much more elegant and tightly integrated in Quattro Pro. Charts allow you to present your numeric data in a visual form. You know the old pie chart? With a click of a button, your columns and rows of numbers are represented in beautifully colored pie wedges. Quattro Pro also has the ability to represent regional data on a map. See Chapter 15 for more on charts. Check out online help for more information on maps.

* *Creating and maintaining databases.* The professional version of the WordPerfect Suite ships with a database application called Paradox, which helps you maintain large amounts of information so you can use and manipulate it in a variety of ways. However, Quattro Pro has quite powerful and versatile database capabilities. For more information on using Quattro Pro to maintain a database, see Chapter 15.

TIP As you've seen in earlier chapters, the PerfectExpert and New dialog box let you select project-based tasks, including tasks where Quattro Pro does the work. Using the PerfectExpert, you can do everything from maintaining and reconciling your checkbook to tracking your fitness and exercise plan if you're a runner. Most of the templates have calculations built in, so all you need to do is fill in the blanks.

Creating a New Notebook

Now that you have a sense of what Quattro Pro can do for you, you can begin using it to create and maintain your own financial information. When you first start Quattro Pro, you see a blank *notebook* where you can begin working. A notebook is Quattro Pro's term for the file that will contain your data. You learn about it in more detail in the next section.

I start out with a clean, blank notebook so you get a feel for how a notebook works and its underlying structure.

What's a Notebook?

A notebook is the container and structure for your *data*. I use the term *data* because you may use text or numbers or both when creating a notebook. Throughout these chapters, *data* will mean anything you type into a notebook. Let's take a look at what makes up a Quattro Pro notebook.

Start Quattro Pro as described in Chapter 1. Quattro Pro displays a blank notebook (see Figure 12-1). Here you enter and work with your data. Notice that many of the window elements are the same as those in WordPerfect and Presentations — you'll see a title bar, menu bar, toolbar, property bar, and Application bar. But there are some very distinct differences that I explore next.

A notebook is made up of 256 *sheets,* each denoted by a letter or letter combination on its corresponding tab at the bottom. These are also called *worksheets,* and I'll use the terms interchangeably throughout the chapters on Quattro Pro. Sheets help you keep your data organized and allow you to interrelate data from different sheets while keeping the independent nature of the sheet intact. For example, you can have all data related to your sales in a single notebook. The individual sheets in the notebook could contain monthly, quarterly, and sales representative information.

The *cell* is the box that results from the intersection of a column and row. You enter data into cells and refer to them by their cell *address* or *reference*, which is the combination of the column letter(s) and row number. The first cell on a spreadsheet sheet is column A, row 1 — A1.

Following is a description of each of the elements that are unique to Quattro Pro. If you read Chapter 7 on WordPerfect tables, some of these concepts — such as row, column, and cell — will be familiar to you. These elements include the following:

* The *Notebook window* contains all the elements of the current Quattro Pro file.
* The *Active cell address box* indicates the cell address for the currently selected cell.
* The *Input line* allows you to enter the contents of a formula for the selected cell.

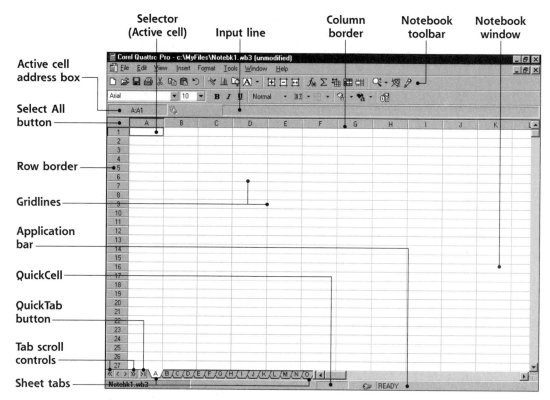

Figure 12-1 Set up your financial data in a Quattro Pro notebook.

* The *Select All* button selects all cells on the current sheet when you click it.

* The *column border* identifies a column by a letter or combination of letters. Quattro Pro allows up to 256 columns, using letters A through Z for the first 26 columns, then using AA through AZ, BA through BZ, and so on. In WordPerfect, this was called the column indicator.

* The *row border* identifies a row by a number, up to 8,192 rows. In WordPerfect, this was called the row indicator.

* The *Input line* provides another place to enter and edit data besides the cell itself. The box to the left of this line indicates the active sheet and cell(s).

* The *Selector* indicates the active cell by placing a thicker black line around it. In Figure 12-1, the selector is making cell A1 the active cell and the one into which you can enter data.

* The *gridlines* help you see the individual cells by intersecting rows and columns for you. You can turn these off if you don't need them. By default, gridlines don't print when you print a worksheet or workbook.

* The *Tab scroll controls* help you navigate between sheets in the notebook. See Table 12-2 in the next section for a detailed explanation of each control on the Tab scroll.

* The *QuickTab* button moves you directly to the *Objects sheet*, which is the last sheet in the notebook and can contain any charts, maps, and other objects you create.

* *Sheet tabs* identify the sheets in a notebook.

* The *Application bar* provides up-to-the-second information on the status of a notebook and cells, as well as allows you to move between different workbooks. The word READY on the Application bar tells you that Quattro Pro is ready and waiting for your next command.

* *QuickCell* allows you to view the status of a cell while working on other cells.

FEATURE FOCUS

As you saw in Chapter 2, the Application bar displays currently open files and allows you to move quickly between them as well as move and copy between them. For more on moving and copying between notebooks, see Chapter 3, where I describe moving and copying between WordPerfect documents in a Feature Focus just like this.

12

SIDE TRIP

TAKING SPREADSHEETS TO TASK

Earlier I mentioned that you can create business forms and other notebook types using the PerfectExpert or New dialog box. In Chapter 2, I showed you how to use the PerfectExpert or New dialog box to select a task regardless of the application you're currently using. If you're feeling comfortable with entering data and navigating a spreadsheet, you may want to explore some of the projects in the New dialog box to see if any will suit your needs now or in the future. Keep in mind that many of the spreadsheets that result from using a project may not contain cells as you've seen them in this chapter. However, you should be able to tell where you need to insert data.

As a refresher, make sure that Quattro Pro is open, and choose File → New to display the New File dialog box. Double-click a financial-related task in the list or select it and click Create. Quattro Pro builds a new notebook based on your selection, and you can enter your own data.

Using the Quattro Pro Toolbar

The default Quattro Pro toolbar is referred to as the Notebook toolbar because it provides quick access to a number of features having to do with the notebook itself. To distinguish this toolbar from other toolbars you'll use throughout the chapters, I always refer to the standard toolbar as the *Notebook toolbar*. At first glance, you'll see many familiar buttons on the Quattro Pro Notebook toolbar — New, Open, Save, Print, Cut, Copy, Paste, Undo, Bold, and Italics. However, once you get to the right side of the toolbar, things start to get a little different. Table 12-1 provides descriptions of these new buttons to help you work more efficiently with Quattro Pro.

TABLE 12-1 Quattro Pro Notebook Toolbar

Button	Name	Description
	FLOATING CHART	Create a default chart from existing data.
	CLIPART	Insert clipart or other images into the worksheet.
	DRAWING OBJECT	Create an object.
	INSERT	Insert rows, columns, sheets, and cells.
	DELETE	Delete rows, columns, sheets, and cells.
	QUICKFIT	Adjust column widths for the widest entry.
	FORMULA BUILDER	Create a complex formula.
	QUICKSUM	Total a column or row automatically.
	QUICKFILL	Fills data in cells based on a pattern.
	SPEEDFORMAT	Format selected cells using predefined line, fill, and color attributes.
	JOIN	Join and center selected cells.
	ZOOM	Magnify areas of the worksheet.

Navigating a Notebook

Before you begin the process of entering and working with data, let's take a look at the ways you move around a sheet and between sheets so that you're comfortable getting where you want to go. As you've probably guessed, before you can enter data, you must select and activate a cell. We'll start with the small stuff — moving around on a single sheet — then move onto longer journeys, such as going to a particular sheet.

Moving Around a Worksheet

One of the most common methods for selecting a cell in which you want to enter data is to click it. However, if you're a die-hard keyboard user, you can also select a cell using the keyboard. Most of these navigation keys will be familiar to you from other applications. Table 12-2 provides some common keystrokes. Check out Table B-8 in Appendix B for a complete list of the navigation keys and what they do.

TABLE 12-2   Common Navigation Keys in Quattro Pro

Press This	To Move
Right arrow or Tab	One cell right
Left arrow or Shift+Tab	One cell left
Down arrow	One cell down
Up arrow	One cell up
Ctrl+Page Down	Next sheet
Ctrl+Page Up	Previous sheet
Home	Cell A1 on the current sheet
Ctrl+Home	First cell in a notebook (Cell A1 on the first sheet)

A word about the End key. When you press End, you'll see END appear on the status line, telling you this mode is on. End mode allows you to quickly move to different cells containing data so you don't have to scroll. For example, if cell B4 is the active cell and you want to go to the grand total way down in cell J40, you can press End+Home to do so. Note that when you press these keys, Quattro Pro takes you to the *last cell containing data*. If the last cell containing data is cell J41 and you want to go to the last cell in column I, make sure a cell in column I is active, then press End+Down Arrow. However, to go to a cell that doesn't contain data, you'll have to use the method described next.

Going to a Particular Cell

If you want to go to a particular cell but you can't get to it using any of the navigation keys in Table 12-2, you can use the Go To feature to specify the cell address.

Here's how:

1. Open your notebook and display the sheet containing the destination cell, and choose | **Edit** | → | **Go To** | or press Ctrl+G to display the Go To dialog box (see Figure 12-2). You can indicate the cell on the current sheet or any sheet in your notebook.

Cell reference (address)

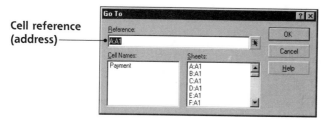

Figure 12-2   Go to a particular cell.

2. In the Reference text box, type the cell address for which you're looking. If the cell is on another sheet, include the sheet letter or name as part of the reference, separated by a colon. For example, if you want to move quickly to cell L85 on the current sheet, type **l85**. If you want to move to cell L85 on sheet F, type **F:l85**. If you've named a block of cells, select the name you're looking for in the Cell Names list.

3. Click OK. Quattro Pro moves immediately to the cell or cells you indicated.

X-REF   For more on cell names, see the Bonus Section in Chapter 13.

Moving to Different Sheets

If you have data contained on several sheets in a notebook, you'll often need to move between them to do your work. The most common way to move between sheets is to use the sheet tabs at the bottom of the notebook. However, if you need to display a sheet whose tab isn't immediately available, you can get there several other ways.

You first met the tab scroll controls when you checked out Figure 12-1. They are the four buttons in the bottom left corner of the notebook, and they help you move between sheets either a sheet at a time or by groups of sheets, as noted in Table 12-3.

TABLE 12-3 Tab Scroll Controls

This Control	Displays
≪	Previous group
‹	Previous sheet
›	Next sheet
≫	Next group

The last button after this group — the QuickTab button— takes you to and from the Objects sheet, which is the last sheet in the notebook. The Objects sheet contains icons for any objects in your notebook, such as a chart. Because working with the Objects sheet is beyond the scope of this book, you can find out more about it in online help. Note that the number of sheets Quattro Pro moves forward or backward depends on how many sheets it is displaying at one time. This depends on your monitor display size, your display settings, and if you're using the default letters on the sheet tabs to identify your sheets.

Displaying a sheet or sheets using the Tab scroll controls only *displays* the sheet(s); the sheet that was originally active stays active until you select another sheet. Once you display sheets using the Tab scroll controls, you must click the sheet tab to select the sheet with which you want to work.

Entering Data in Cells

Once you have a feel for how a notebook is laid out and how to get to cells using a variety of navigation techniques, you can begin entering data into your cells. Quattro Pro recognizes three types of entries — labels, values, and formulas:

* *Labels* are cells containing text that identify the data in a row or column. For example, if column A contains a list of your sales representatives and you've typed **Sales Reps** in cell A1, "Sales Reps" is a label. Quattro Pro automatically recognizes any text you enter into a cell as a label and will left align it in the cell.

* *Values* or *numeric values* are numbers you enter into a cell. These can be any numbers, including dollar amounts, totals, percentages, or negative numbers. Quattro Pro automatically recognizes any number you enter into a cell as a value and will right-align it in the cell.

✳ *Formulas* are those entries that instruct Quattro Pro to perform a calculation. Quattro Pro treats formula results like numbers and automatically right-aligns them in the cell.

You can change cell alignment for any data type. You learn more about this in Chapter 14.

Now that you're familiar with the types of data you can enter, you can explore three methods for activating Edit mode so you can enter data. These methods are as follows:

✳ Select the cell and then click the Input line (the gray bar above the column border).

✳ Select the cell and begin typing or double-click the cell and type the data.

✳ Select the cell and press the F2 key.

Entering Data Directly into a Cell

By entering data directly in the cell, you bypass manually activating the input line altogether and can enter and edit your data more quickly. Just click the cell into which you wish to enter data or use the arrow keys to select the cell, and then type the data. Quattro Pro displays your data in the input line as you type.

Use the following methods to work with data in your cells:

 ✳ Use the Backspace and Delete keys to correct any errors as you make your entry. To clear the entry and start over, click the Clear button on the input line.

 ✳ Press Tab to end the entry and select the next cell. Press Enter to end the entry and select the cell below. Otherwise, click the Accept button on the input line to end the entry and keep the current cell selected.

 If pressing Enter doesn't select the cell below the current cell, the option to activate this is off. To turn it on, choose Tools→Settings and choose the General tab. Under Options, choose Move Cell Selector on Enter Key and click OK.

If your entry is longer than the width of the cell, Quattro Pro spills the contents over into an adjacent cell or cells, as long as the adjacent cells are empty. Keep in mind, however, that the cell you are entering data into is the one *containing the entire contents*, even though you may see part of the contents in adjacent cells. If the adjacent cell is *not* empty, Quattro Pro will only display as much of the content as it can in the width of the cell. When you select the cell, you'll see the entire contents in the Input line. You'll learn about ways to display long entries in Chapter 14.

TIP You can also double-click the cell or select it and press the F2 key to turn on Edit mode. You'll see the insertion point in the cell, and the input line buttons become active.

If you like the look and feel of the input line, you may feel more comfortable using it to enter your data. Just select the cell and click the input line. You'll see EDIT on the status line, and the input line becomes a white box with the insertion point blinking inside it. Type your data and press Enter to end the entry.

FEATURE FOCUS When your cell is in Edit mode and you're entering data, you'll see the property bar change. See Chapter 14 for more information on the formatting buttons that appear on this property bar.

Selecting Cells

Selecting cells in Quattro Pro is similar to selecting text or elements in other WordPerfect Suite applications. However, there are a few tricks you can perform in Quattro Pro that are different, and we look at them here. You select cells if you want to enter data in multiple cells quickly or to format several cells at once.

SELECTING MULTIPLE CELLS

Quattro Pro provides three different methods for selecting the exact cells with which you want to work:

* To select a *range of cells* (cells adjacent to each other), point to the first cell you'd like to include in the block, then click and drag over all cells you want to include. You can also click the cell that will constitute one corner of the block, then press and hold Shift and click the opposite corner (see left side of Figure 12-3).

* To select *non-adjacent (or noncontiguous) cells*, press and hold Ctrl, then click each cell you wish to include (see right side of Figure 12-3). With the Ctrl key still pressed, click the first cell in which you wish to enter data.

* To select *a column or row*, click the column letter or row number in the column or row border. Click and drag to select multiple columns or rows.

* To select *all cells* on the active sheet, click the Select All button (corner button to the left of column A and above row 1) or choose Edit → Select All .

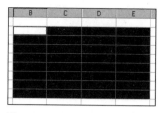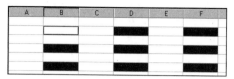

Figure 12-3 Selected range/block (left) versus selected noncontiguous cells (right).

USING POINT MODE TO SELECT CELLS

If you have a dialog box open and you need to indicate a range of cells, you can use *point mode* to select the cells and insert them into the dialog box. For an example of the point mode in the Go To dialog box, see Figure 12-2.

To use point mode in an open dialog box containing a point mode button, click the Point Mode button next to the appropriate text box. Quattro Pro shrinks the dialog box so you see only the title bar. Select the cells on the worksheet that you wish to insert and then click the Restore button on the dialog box title bar. Quattro Pro restores the dialog box and enters the selected cell range into the appropriate box.

You'll use point mode later in this chapter and in subsequent chapters.

Entering Data in Multiple Cells

If you have a lot of information you need to enter into your cells, you can select the number of cells you'll need and enter the data quickly, either across rows or down columns.

Here's how you enter data in selected cells:

1. Select the cells using one of the methods described previously. Notice that the active cell (the one ready to accept data) will be white. All other selected cells remain highlighted (black).

2. If you selected noncontiguous cells, press Ctrl and select the cell which you wish to be the first active cell.

3. In the active cell, type your data. To enter data in the cell to the right, press Tab. To enter data in the cell below, press Enter. Note that either of these keys will take you to the next selected cell in *noncontiguous* cells. If you have noncontiguous cells selected across rows as well as down columns, Quattro Pro will move across to the next noncontiguous selected cell before going down to the next row containing a noncontiguous selected cell.

After entering data in the *first noncontiguous* cell, you will need to press Tab or Enter *twice* to move to the next noncontiguous cell.

Entering Dates

Similar to numbers, Quattro Pro is programmed to recognize certain date formats. This is so you can use your dates in calculations, such as finding out the number of days between two dates. You'll learn more about formulas in Chapter 13.

To enter a date, type it in any of the formats in Table 12-4, making sure you include the slashes or dashes where indicated. Here are two things you should remember about date formats:

✴ When you accept the entry, Quattro Pro converts the entry to the numeric equivalent of the date in the Input line, displaying the actual date in the cell. For example, the numeric equivalent of 05/1/97 is 35551. Quattro Pro uses these numeric equivalents to calculate dates in formulas. If you type a single digit date using any of the formats in Table 12-4, Quattro Pro changes it to a date with a leading zero when you press Tab or Enter.

✴ You can use standard three-letter abbreviations for months: Jan, Feb, Mar, Apr, May, Jun, Jul, Aug, Sep, Oct, Nov, and Dec.

TABLE 12-4   Valid Date Formats in Corel Quattro Pro

Format	Example
MM/DD/YY	05/16/97
MM/DD	05/16
DD-MMM-YY	16-May-97
DD-MMM	16-May
MMM-YY	May-97

Notice that you can't type 5-13-97 (a date with dashes); Quattro Pro doesn't recognize this as a valid date format and treats it as a formula, subtracting each number from the previous.

Using QuickFill

Earlier you learned how to enter data in individual cells as well as in a group of selected cells, called a block or range. But guess what? If you have a familiar series of data you need to enter, such as sequential numbers, months of the year, or days of the week, Quattro Pro can help you. The easiest way is to enter the first one or two elements of the series — called *seed values* — and let Quattro Pro fill in the rest. You can use the QuickFill dialog box to select a series type and have Quattro Pro fill in the cells for you. You look at both methods in this section.

Letting QuickFill Finish Your Series

As I mentioned, you can begin a series with as little as the first cell entered, and Quattro Pro can complete the series for you. For example, you can type Mon in the first cell, then select the Mon cell and six additional cells. When you choose QuickFill, Quattro Pro fills in the remaining days of the week. Table 12-5 shows you each seed value and the series that will result from it. Note that if the series is not consecutive, you'll need to enter two or three seed values to help Quattro Pro recognize your series.

To create a series using QuickFill, follow these steps:

1. Select the cell that will contain the first value in the series, and then type the value and press Enter to accept it. Some series may require more than one seed value so that Quattro Pro will recognize it as a series. Enter additional seed values if necessary in the appropriate cells.

2. Select the cell containing the first and/or second seed value(s) and all blank cells that will contain the remaining data in the series. For example, if you've typed **Mon** in cell A3 and want the remaining days of the week to continue in the same row, select cells A3-A9.

3. Click the QuickFill button on the Notebook toolbar. Quattro Pro completes the series in the selected cells.

TABLE 12-5 Examples of QuickFill Seed Values

Seed Value	Resulting Series
1, 3	1, 3, 5, 7, 9 . . . (odd numbers)
1st	1st, 2nd, 3rd, 4th . . .
Qtr 1	Qtr 1, Qtr 2, Qtr 3, Qtr 4 . . .
1st Qtr	1st Qtr, 2nd Qtr, 3rd Qtr, 4th Qtr . . .

Seed Value	Resulting Series
Week 1	Week 1, Week 2, Week 3, Week 4 . . .
05/01	05/01, 05/02, 05/03, 05/04 . . .
02/03, 02/10	02/03, 02/10, 02/17, 02/24 . . . (date by week)
Sunday	Sunday, Monday, Tuesday, Wednesday . . .
Jan	Jan, Feb, Mar, Apr . . .

If you enter data that Quattro Pro doesn't recognize as a seed value, it will simply repeat the data in all selected cells.

Using QuickFill for Empty Cells

If you have a series of empty cells that you'd like to fill with a common sequential series, and you aren't sure what the seed value is, you can use the QuickFill dialog box to select it. QuickFill provides Month, Quarter, and Days of the Week series from which to choose.

Follow these steps to use QuickFill to fill empty cells:

1. Select the first empty cell in the series or select all cells that will contain the QuickFill data.

2. Click the QuickFill button or right-click and select QuickFill from the QuickMenu. Quattro Pro displays the QuickFill dialog box (see Figure 12-4).

Figure 12-4   Select a QuickFill series from the QuickFill dialog box.

3. Click the Series Name down arrow and select a series name from the drop-down list. The *Quarter* options provide different ways to display a series of quarters. Quattro Pro displays the data in the selected series in the Series Elements list box.

4. Under Fill As, indicate if the series will go down Columns, across Rows, or as names on sheet Tabs, and click OK. If you've selected cells before displaying this dialog box, Quattro Pro will fill your selected cells, regardless of what's selected here.

 X-REF To create your own QuickFill series, see the Bonus section at the end of this chapter.

 FEATURE FOCUS You can quickly name related sheets using the Tabs option in the QuickFill dialog box. For more on naming sheet tabs, see "Working with Worksheets" in Chapter 14.

Editing Cell Data

If you change your mind about the contents of any entry, or realize you entered the wrong number by mistake, you can edit it. In Quattro Pro, you can replace the entire entry in a cell or edit the cell contents individually. For example, if you have 25 in a cell and it should read 35, it's easier just to replace the 25 with 35 because it's only two characters. However, if you have a long phrase or complex formula in a cell, it makes sense to edit the contents and make the change without having to retype everything.

Replacing the Entire Cell Contents

To replace the entire contents of a cell, select the cell, then type the new data. You'll see the input line become active as you type. After you're finished, click the Accept button or press Enter.

Editing Cell Contents

You can edit the contents of a cell by turning Edit mode on and positioning the insertion point in the location for your changes. You can then add or delete data, using the Backspace and Delete keys to assist you. To edit cell contents, use one of the following methods:

* Double-click the cell, position the insertion point, and make your changes.
* Select the cell and press F2. Position the insertion point, and make your changes.

✳ Select the cell, then position the insertion point in the input line and make your changes.

By default, Quattro Pro is in Insert mode, which you may recall from Chapter 3 when you entered and edited text in WordPerfect. If you want to type over existing text in a cell or in the input line, press the Insert key so you see the Overtype icon on the Application bar. Type the replacement text and then press the Insert key again to return to Insert mode. Note that Overtype turns off automatically after you accept a cell entry.

Once you've created a notebook, save it using the techniques you learned in Chapter 2. Quattro Pro saves the notebook with a WB3 extension.

BONUS

Creating Your Own QuickFill Series

If you have one or more series that aren't part of the series that QuickFill recognizes, you can create your own series. For example, say you create sales reports by region and your regions are East, Northeast, Southeast, West, Northwest, Southwest, and Central. You can create a QuickFill series that fills in this series when you type **East** as a seed. When you create your own series, you can use one of two series types:

✳ *List* displays a list of values, like the region example and those in Table 12-5. You fill in the elements in the Series Elements text box.

✳ *Formula* displays a series of formulas. You enter a seed value and the actual formula for the Formula Definition options.

To create your own QuickFill list, follow these steps:

1. Select the first empty cell in the series or select all cells that will contain your new series data and click the QuickFill button on the Notebook toolbar.

2. Click Create to display the Create Series dialog box (see Figure 12-5). Notice that List is the default series type.

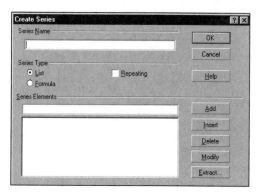

Figure 12-5 Create your own QuickFill series.

3. In the Series Name text box, type a name for your series. For example, if you're creating the regional example, type **Region** or something similar.

4. In the Series Elements text box, type the first element in your series and press Enter or click Add. For example, if you're creating the regional example, type **East**.

5. Repeat Step 4 for each entry in the series. Quattro Pro adds the entry to the Series Elements list box and selects the entry in the Series Elements text box.

TIP Add inserts your Series Elements entry *after* (below) the currently selected entry in the Series Elements list box. Insert inserts the entry *before* (above) the currently selected entry in the Series Elements list box.

6. If you want the series to repeat from the beginning if you select more cells than are in the series, click the Repeating check box.

7. When you're finished creating your series, click OK. Quattro Pro returns to the QuickFill dialog box, adding your series to the list of series names and displaying it as the selected name.

8. If you want to use your series now, click OK. If you want to use it later, click Cancel to return to the notebook sheet.

You can remove any series you don't think you'll use by clicking the QuickFill button on the Notebook toolbar. Use the Series Name down arrow button to select the series you wish to delete and click Delete. Click Yes to remove the series permanently.

Summary

Congratulate yourself on diving headfirst into Quattro Pro! You learned about many of the things you can do using Quattro Pro, including creating business forms and maintaining a database. You learned how to create a notebook and understand notebook elements. Then you learned how to enter data, both in individual cells and into selected cells, and including a series of data using QuickFill. Next, you'll learn how to sum your numeric data and work with formulas.

CHAPTER THIRTEEN

WORKING WITH FORMULAS AND FUNCTIONS

IN THIS CHAPTER YOU LEARN THESE KEY SKILLS

UNDERSTANDING AND USING FORMULAS PAGE 257

UNDERSTANDING AND USING FUNCTIONS PAGE 265

PRINTING A NOTEBOOK PAGE 268

N ow that you've had a chance to create a notebook and enter data into a worksheet, you can move into what Quattro Pro does best — perform calculations. Using a variety of features, you can total a row or column quickly and create more complex formulas for calculating such things as an amortized loan. Quattro Pro provides other features — such as cell names — to make this process easy and logical. When you use a formula or function to obtain a result, you will see the resulting value in the cell and the formula in the input line.

Understanding and Using Formulas

B efore you begin entering formulas in a worksheet, it's important to have a good sense of what formulas are and what you can do with them. A *formula* begins with a plus (+) sign and contains cell references, *operators*, and sometimes actual values to create a mathematical result.

TIP   You can type a plus or equals (=) sign. Quattro Pro will convert it to a plus sign or, if your formula begins with a negative value, will drop the plus sign altogether.

Learn how to format cells either numerically or in appearance in Chapter 14.

Understanding Relative and Absolute References

Quattro Pro can handle two types of cell references in a formula — relative and absolute. When you use cell references in a formula, Quattro Pro formats them as *relative* references by default. This means that even if you move or copy the formula, the cell references will be updated in the formula to reflect the new location.

 For information on moving and copying formulas, see "Moving and Copying Formulas" in Chapter 14.

For example, say that you have a formula in cell D2 that multiplies cell B2 by cell C2. If you copy this formula to cell F6, the formula will adjust to multiply the two cells immediately preceding F6; that is, cells F4 and F5. This means the cell references are always *relative* to their current location.

However, if you want to move a formula but want it to continue to refer to the original cells, you'll need to make the cell references *absolute*. This means that if you move or copy the formula, the cell references will remain the original references. Using this example, say that you make the formula in cell D2 absolute so that it always multiplies cell B2 by cell C2, no matter where the formula is located. If you copy this formula to cell F6, the formula will still show cell B2 multiplied by cell C2.

To format a reference as absolute, type a dollar sign ($) immediately before both the column letter and row number for the address. For example, if you want cells B2 and C2 to become absolute, you would type **B2** and **C2**. The dollar sign acts as a lock on the cell references and tells Quattro Pro not to adjust the reference if you move or copy it. Figure 13-1 shows an example of a formula containing both relative and absolute references.

	A	B	C	D	E
	Billing:C6		@ { } ✗ ✔	+B6*B3	
1			**Client Billing**		
2					
3	Rate	45			
4					
5	Client	Hours	Total Due	Discount	Total Billed
6	Henderson Cable	5	+B6*B3	0.00%	$225
7	Greens Motor	12	$540	15.00%	$459
8	Venter Inc	8	$360	5.00%	$342
9	Borders Office Supplies	5	$225	0.00%	$225
10					

Relative reference for hours of service performed

Absolute reference for hourly rate (B3)

Figure 13-1 Relative and absolute cell references in a formula.

TIP You can make either the column or row absolute but not both, if necessary. For example, if you want to force Quattro Pro to use column B but adjust the reference for the current row, you would type $B*x* where *x* is the relative row number.

Working with Operators

If you worked through the Chapter 7 Bonus on calculations in WordPerfect tables, you know that *operators* are symbols that an application uses to perform a calculation. Quattro Pro uses three types of operators, two of which are as follows:

* ✦ *Arithmetic operators* calculate mathematical calculations, those you should be familiar with from your grade school days. Arithmetic operators are listed in the first section of Table 13-1.

* ✦ *Logical operators* allow you to get a true or false result based on the formula. Remember those word problems in grade school? Some of them probably had a few logical operators stuck in to really make you think. For some examples of logical operators, see "Logically Speaking" following Table 13-1. Logical operators appear in the second section of Table 13-1.

Quattro Pro also contains *text operators*, but because they aren't as common, we don't look at them here. You can learn more about them in online help.

Quattro Pro prioritizes operators the same way you were taught in grade school — multiply first, then divide, then add, and finally subtract. Quattro Pro refers to this prioritizing as an operator's *precedence*. This means that Quattro Pro doesn't necessarily calculate your formula in the order it appears from left to right on the input line. For example, if Quattro Pro comes across a formula that reads =100+200/2, it will first divide 200 by 2 and then add the result to 100 for a final resulting value of 200.

However, if you want Quattro Pro to add 100 and 200 and then divide that result by two, you'll need to tell it specifically to do so. And just as in your school days, you can also force Quattro Pro to perform a specific calculation before another calculation by using parentheses. To use the just-described example, if you enter the formula as =(100+200)/2, Quattro Pro will add 100 and 200 for a result of 300 and then divide this result by 2 for a final resulting value of 150. Note that every open parentheses you type must have a closing parentheses paired with it.

Table 13-1 describes operators Quattro Pro recognizes in order of their precedence, from the operator with the highest precedence listed first to the operator with the lowest listed last.

Table 13-1   Quattro Pro Operators by Type and Precedence

Arithmetic Operator	Description
^	Exponentiation (power of)
+	When indicating positive as opposed to addition
-	When indicating negative as opposed to subtraction
*	Multiplication (same precedence as division)
/	Division (same precedence as multiplication)
+	Addition (same precedence as subtraction)
-	Subtraction (same precedence as addition)

Logical Operator	Description
>	Greater than
<	Less than
>=	Greater than or equal to
<=	Less than or equal to
=	Equal to
<>	Not equal to
#NOT#	All values that don't meet the #NOT# condition will come back true
#AND#	Both conditions must be met for the value to come back true.
#OR#	Either condition must be met for the value to come back true.

For more on operators, see the online help.

Using QuickSum to Total Numbers

If your calculation is merely a simple total or subtotal of a column or row, you can use the QuickSum feature to quickly add up the numbers. When you use QuickSum, Quattro Pro not only displays the result in the cell, it also inserts the corresponding formula. QuickSum works just as it did in WordPerfect tables (Chapter 7).

Logical operators help you create your own conditional statements within a formula, enabling the formula. You'll use logical operators most often with functions such as @IF. For example, say you make the following statement: "If my sales reps generated sales greater than $10,000 this month, they'll get a bonus." If you have a cell containing the sales total, you can easily create a formula that tells you whether the rep deserves the bonus or not. See "Exploring Common Functions" later in this chapter for an example that uses a logical operator.

To use QuickSum, select the cell where you want the total to appear or select multiple cells using one of the selection techniques suggested in Table 13-2. Click the QuickSum button on the Notebook toolbar. Quattro Pro totals the selected cells and places the totals in the blank cells using the @SUM function.

Note that if you select an empty cell and click the QuickSum button, Quattro Pro sums the column above the cell.

 X-REF See "Understanding and Using Functions" later in this chapter for more on the @SUM function.

You may want to check each formula to make sure that Quattro Pro totaled the correct cells.

13

TABLE 13-2 Selection Techniques for QuickSum

To Total	Do This
A SINGLE COLUMN	Select the empty cell below the column that will contain the total.
A SINGLE ROW	Select the empty cell to the right of the row that will contain the total.
MULTIPLE COLUMNS	Select all cells containing the data you wish to total, plus the empty row below the columns. For example, to total the values in cells B2 through E5, select B2 through E6. The totals for each column appear in cells B6, C6, D6, and E6.
MULTIPLE ROWS	Select all cells containing the data you wish to total, plus the empty column to the right of the rows. For example, to total the values in cells B2 through D4, select B2 through E4. The totals appear in cells E2, E3, and E4.

(continued)

TABLE 13-2 Selection Techniques for QuickSum *(continued)*

To Total	Do This
COLUMNS AND ROWS	Select all cells containing the data you wish to total, plus the empty column to the right of the rows and the empty row below the columns. For example, to total the values in cells B2 through D4, select B2 through E6. The row totals appear in cells E2, E3, E4, and E5 and the column totals appear in cells B6, C6, D6, and E6. The grand total of both columns and rows appears in cell F6.

Note that when you use one of the first two selection methods, Quattro Pro uses its best guess to determine how much of the column to include in the total. If your column or row is broken up by labels, Quattro Pro will ignore the label(s) and total all numeric values in the column or row.

Entering Formulas

As I mentioned before, each formula begins with either the plus sign (+), or if you type an equals sign (=), Quattro Pro will convert it to a plus sign. When you type either of these, you're telling Quattro Pro you are about to enter a formula. Once you've typed one of these symbols, you can enter the cell references and operators for your formula. Figure 13-2 shows an example of a simple formula that multiplies cell D6 by cell C6 and then subtracts the result from the value in cell C6.

Here's the brief step by step for entering a formula:

1. Select the cell to contain the formula and type + or = to begin the formula.

2. Type the references to be included in the formula or begin with an open parentheses if you wish to force a calculation to occur before the normal precedence of calculations.

3. Type the operators in the appropriate spots.

 4. When you're finished entering the formula, press Enter or click the Accept button on the input line. Quattro Pro performs the calculation immediately and places the result in the cell. The formula remains in the input line. Note that even though you see the result in the cell, the contents of the cell are actually the *formula* and not the resulting value.

Colored outline indicates cells included in formula

Operators (+, −, *)

Parentheses indicate priority

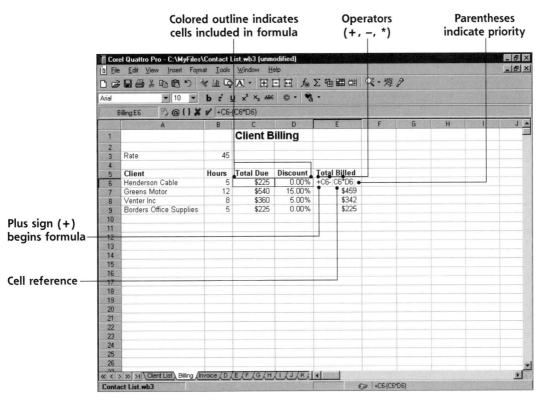

Plus sign (+) begins formula

Cell reference

Figure 13-2 A sample formula.

TIP Rather than typing the cell reference into the cell or input line, you can select the cells you wish to include in the formula to ensure accuracy. To insert a cell reference into your formula, make sure that the insertion point is in the right place for the reference in the formula, then click the cell you want to include.

You can edit formulas just as you do cells containing numeric or text data. Just double-click the cell containing the formula and make your changes.

Using the Cell Reference Checker

The new Cell Reference Checker ensures formula accuracy as you insert, move, and copy formulas in your notebook. If there is some type of discrepancy regarding absolute and relative cell references in your formula, Quattro Pro's Cell Reference Checker will let you know (see Figure 13-3). You can then ask Quattro Pro to help you fix it, or fix it yourself.

When Quattro Pro detects a potential problem, it automatically displays the arrows and dialog box you see in Figure 13-3. You can then choose from the following options:

* Click Fix It to have Quattro Pro fix the problem according to the indicator arrows.

* Click Undo Fix to return the formula to its original state.

* Click Close to close the Cell Reference Checker dialog box and make your own changes.

* Click Details to take a peek at how the formula will look after Quattro Pro fixes it.

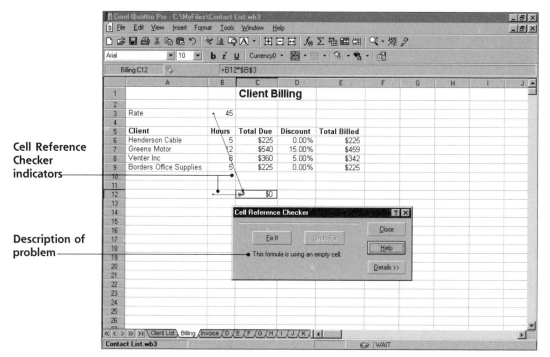

Cell Reference Checker indicators

Description of problem

Figure 13-3 Cell Reference Checker warns you of potential problems.

FEATURE FOCUS Quattro Pro automatically checks the integrity of cell references in a formula with the new Cell Reference Checker.

You can watch how one cell affects another using the QuickCell feature. Click and drag the cell you want to observe to the QuickCell on the Application bar (refer back to Figure 12-1 in Chapter 12 for the location of the QuickCell). You can also select the cell you wish to observe and then secondary-click the QuickCell on the Application bar and choose Display Current Cell in QuickCell from the QuickMenu.

Understanding and Using Functions

A *function* is a built-in mathematical formula that performs a calculation and returns a single value. Quattro Pro calls functions *@functions* because each one begins with the at (@) sign. Functions are a great invention because they do much of the calculating for you, taking the place of what once was a long, complicated, and extremely complex formula. Quattro Pro functions enable you to perform a variety of tasks with little effort. However, it's important to understand how functions are put together and how they work.

Note that this section won't be an explanation of financial terms and financial strategies; that's best left to other books on the subject. Here I focus on the types of functions available, the parts of a function, and how you can put one together so it works for you. For a detailed description and example of each function, look for the specific @function using the Find tab in the Help dialog box.

Working with Functions

Quattro Pro contains more than 450 @functions, many of which you'll never need to perform the most common calculations. In this section we look at the parts of an @function and actually use some common functions so you can see how they're put together.

The four most common @functions are financial, logical, mathematical, and statistical. Additional categories include database and engineering.

An @function is made up of four basic elements — name, arguments, commas, and parentheses. These elements and the order in which they appear is called the *syntax*. The syntax will vary depending on what function you're using. Following is a brief description of each element.

Name is the actual name of the function as it appears in the Functions dialog box. For example, @SUM, @PMT, @AVG, and so on.

Arguments are the cell references, cell names, values, or text strings that will be used in the calculation. Arguments often contain operators within them to perform calculations within calculations.

Commas are the separators between arguments within a single @function.

Parentheses indicate the beginning and end of the arguments for an @function. Every @function must begin with an open parentheses and end with a closing parentheses. The @functions may contain parentheses within them to force subcalculations.

Exploring Common Functions

Following are some common functions you may find useful in your work.

As with all things you've learned up to now, the first thing you must do when you want to use an @function is to select the cell that will contain the function. Then you can type the function and enter the arguments, separated by commas, within the parentheses. Here are a few to get you started. Refer to Figure 13-4 to understand the examples for each @function.

	A	B	C	D	E	F	G	H
1		Qtr 1	Qtr 2	Qtr 3	Qtr 4	Total	Commission	Bonus
2	Abby	$25,000	$24,000	$28,000	$26,000	$103,000	$8,240	$0
3	Burton	$26,500	$25,000	$28,000	$31,000	$110,500	$8,840	$1,500
4	Jones	$26,000	$28,000	$26,000	$29,000	$109,000	$8,720	$0
5	Smith	$27,000	$28,000	$27,500	$30,000	$112,500	$9,000	$1,500
6	Zuckerman	$28,500	$30,000	$27,500	$29,000	$115,000	$9,200	$1,500
7	Total	$133,000	$135,000	$137,000	$145,000	$550,000	$44,000	$4,500
8								
9		Qtr 1 CE	Qtr 2 CE					
10	Abby	X	X					
11	Burton	X						
12	Jones	X	X					
13	Smith	X	X					
14	Zuckerman	X	X					
15	Attendance	5	1					

Figure 13-4   Use a variety of functions to calculate your data.

TIP   When you enter a function, Quattro Pro displays the syntax on the Application bar (bottom right corner). You can use this to assist you when entering your @function.

@SUM introduced itself rather sneakily when you used QuickSum. @SUM totals all values in a range of cells. Here's how to use @SUM in cell F6 to total the numbers in Row 6 of Figure 13-4: @SUM(B6..E6). The resulting value is $115,000.

@SUMIF adds only those cells in the *Block* that meet your *criteria*. For example, say that you only want to add sales for the second quarter that equal $28,000. Your function would look like this: @SUMIF(C2..C6,28000). Quattro Pro would total only those cells containing $28,000. The resulting value is $56,000.

@PMT calculates the periodic payment (fully amortized) you need to make to repay a loan. The principal amount will be represented in present value dollars (Pv). This @function calculates the payment using the assumption that you're making interest payments *at the end* of each period.

X-REF   See "Using a Cell Name in a Formula" in the Bonus section at the end of this chapter for an example of the @PMT function.

@AVG finds the average (arithmetic mean) of the values in a selected block of cells. For example, @AVG(B2..B6) finds the average of the values in cells B2 through B6. The resulting value is $26,600.

@MAX finds the highest value of the values in a selected block of cells. For example, @MAX(B2..B6) locates the highest value in cells B2 through B6. The resulting value is $28,500.

@MIN finds the lowest value of the values in a selected block of cells. For example, @MIN(B2..B6) locates the lowest value in cells B2 through B6. The resulting value is $25,000.

@IF evaluates a condition to determine if it's true or false. You can then tell Quattro Pro what to do depending on if the condition is true or false. This is a valuable function for such things as determining if your sales force has reached their sales goal and will receive a bonus. For example, cell H2 contains the formula @IF(F2>=110000,1500,0) to determine whether or not the sales representative will receive a $1,500 bonus (pretty skimpy, I know). This formula says that if the number in cell F2 is greater than or equal to 110000, insert *$1500* as the resulting value (the rep gets the bonus). If the cell value in F2 is less than 110000, enter *0* in the formula cell. Note that you aren't limited to numeric values for your results; instead of using 0 if the rep didn't make it, you could have the formula insert "Sorry, no bonus." Simply type the text that you want to appear and surround it with quotation marks in the formula.

The example in Figure 13-4 uses the @COUNT and @COUNTBLANK functions in cells B15, and C15 to determine which reps attended Continuing Education classes. These @functions count cells with (B15) and without (C15) data, respectively.

Printing a Notebook

Once you've set up your notebook with the worksheets you want to use, you may want to print it so that you and others can use the data. Like the other applications in the WordPerfect Suite, Quattro Pro offers a variety of options for printing your notebook, from printing a single worksheet to printing only specific blocks of cells.

Previewing a Notebook

Before you actually print your worksheet or notebook, you can take a look at it in Print Preview. Print Preview gives you a bird's eye view of your notebook, enabling you to check out how your data will fill the page and what changes you may want to make before sending it the printer. You can also zoom in on different areas to get a closer look. Print Preview is an especially good idea if you're on a network and your file is going into a queue, where you may have to wait awhile to see it.

To preview a document, follow these steps:

1. With your notebook open, choose File → Print Preview. Quattro Pro displays the current worksheet in Print Preview mode, using full page as the default view (see Figure 13-5). Table 13-3 describes the buttons on the Print Preview toolbar. Note that unless you've selected the Margin button, you won't see the Margin lines as you do in Figure 13-5. Note that header and footer margins won't appear unless you've created them in Page view or the Page Setup dialog box.

2. Use the buttons as described in Table 13-3 to view your notebook in different ways.

3. If you're ready to print after viewing, click the Print button to send your notebook directly to the printer.

4. To close Print Preview and return to the notebook sheets, click the Close button.

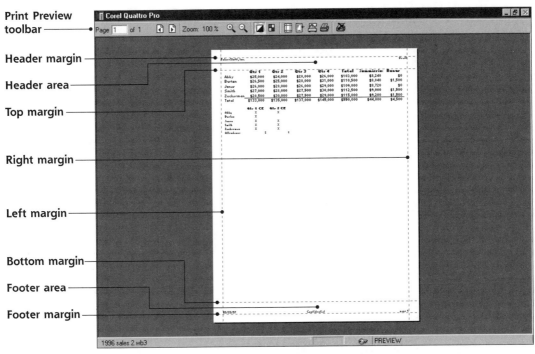

Print Preview toolbar

Header margin

Header area

Top margin

Right margin

Left margin

Bottom margin

Footer area

Footer margin

Figure 13-5 See how your notebook will look when it's printed.

TABLE 13-3 Print Preview Buttons

Button	Name	Description
	PREVIOUS SHEET	Display the previous worksheet.
	NEXT SHEET	Display the next worksheet.
	ZOOM	Select a zoom percentage.
	ZOOM IN	Zoom in to see the data better; percentage increments double each time you click.
	ZOOM OUT	Zoom out to get a bird's eye view; percentage increments double each time you click.
	BLACK-AND-WHITE	Show your data in black and white, regardless of any color you've added to data, shading, or lines.
	COLOR	Show your data with any colors you selected when formatting.
	MARGIN LINES	Display margin lines on screen (they will not be printed).

(continued)

TABLE 13-3 Print Preview Buttons (continued)

Button	Name	Description
	PAGE SETUP	Add headers, footers, and other page settings to the notebook.
	PRINT OPTIONS	Set any print options for the notebook.
	PRINT	Send the notebook to the printer, using the print options you've set.
	CLOSE	Close Print Preview.

If you display margin lines, you can click and drag them to adjust your margins (top, bottom, left, and right), as well as the header and footer areas. For more information on Page Setup options, see the Bonus section at the end of Chapter 14.

Customizing Your Print Job

If you don't like what you see in Print Preview and don't want to send your notebook to the printer as is, you can select from a variety of print options.

To set Spreadsheet Print Options, follow these steps:

1. With your notebook open, click the Print button on the Notebook toolbar or choose File → Print to display the Spreadsheet Print dialog box.

2. Make the necessary selections on the Print tab and then click Page Setup and choose the Options tab (see Figure 13-6).

TIP **If you're currently in Print Preview, click the Print Options button.**

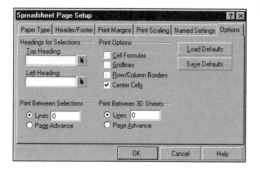

Figure 13-6 Tell Quattro Pro what to print.

3. Make the necessary selections on the Options tab, using the descriptions that follow, and then click Print. Quattro Pro sends the notebook pages to the printer.

✦ *Headings.* You can choose to print a top or left heading (or both) using the labels on your worksheet. Quattro Pro allows you to select the cells containing the headings you wish to print.

✦ Under *Print Options*, use the following information:

   ✦ *Cell Formulas* will print the formula instead of the resulting value. This is helpful if you want a backup to show how you came up with your numbers.

   ✦ *Gridlines* will print the gridlines that surround each cell since they don't print by default. This is helpful if you didn't add lines to your data cells — something you learn to do in Chapter 14 — and you'd like the separation between the cells.

   ✦ *Row/Column Borders* prints the actual Row and Column Borders from the worksheet. Yep, those lovely gray letters and numbers above and to the left of the cells. This feature could be useful in a backup which includes Cell Formulas, described previously.

   ✦ *Center Cells* prints the cells containing data so they are centered between the left and right margins. By default, the first column of your data will print against the left margin. The Center Blocks feature is great if you only have a few columns containing data and you'd like your printed page to look balanced.

✦ *Print Between Selections* allows you to have Quattro Pro insert the specified number of blank lines between different, noncontiguous cells on a worksheet (Lines) or place each section on a separate page (Page Advance).

BONUS

Using Cell Names

Earlier you saw how easy it is to point to a cell to include its reference in a formula. But what if you're down in cell J59 and need to refer to the interest rate in cell B4 — or was it C5? For example, say you're setting up a worksheet that will help you determine how much you must put down on a car you've had your eye on so that your payments remain at $450 per month. You can name all the elements of this worksheet and then refer to them by name. For example, you can call the loan amount *Loan*, the interest rate *Interest*, and the number of months the *Term*.

You can name a single cell or multiple cells. In this Bonus, I use the example of buying a car with a price of $20,000, interest at 10 percent, and a sixty-month (five-year) term to help you understand the value of cell names and see how you can use them.

Naming a Cell

Quattro Pro allows a maximum of 63 characters, including spaces, for your cell name. Keep in mind that you can't use operators as part of a name. Quattro Pro has no limit to the number of cell names a notebook can have, and you can overlap cell ranges for different names. You can also give more than one name to the same cell or block of cells.

To name a cell, follow these steps:

1. If you're going to create a separate area for your named cells, as in the car loan example, type your labels in the appropriate cells. For example, in cell A1, type **Car Price**; in cell A2, type **Interest**; and in cell A3, type **Term**. Next, enter your values in the appropriate cells. In the car loan example, you would type **20000** in cell B1, **.10** in cell B2, and **60** in cell B3.

2. Select the cell or block of cells you want to name, making sure that they contain the *value* to which you want to refer, and then choose Insert → Name → Cells . For example, select cell B1, which contains the price of the car. Quattro Pro displays the Cell Names dialog box. Quattro Pro will list any existing cell names in the larger box below the Name text box.

TIP You can also secondary-click the cell and choose Name Cells from the QuickMenu or press Ctrl+F3 to display the Cell Names dialog box.

3. In the Name text box, type a name for the cell and press Enter or click Add. For example, for the price of the car, you may want to type **Price**. Names are case-sensitive; the way you type your cell name here is how it will appear in the formula and in the Active cell address box on the input line.

4. To name additional cells, use the point mode button to select the cell or cells so you don't have to close the Cell Name dialog box. Click Close when you're finished. Quattro Pro names the cells and displays the name in the area on the input line where the cell reference usually appears (see Figure 13-7).

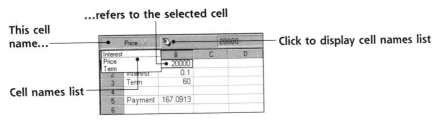

Figure 13-7 Cells with cell names.

> **TIP** You can also use existing labels for cell names. Select the cell(s) containing the values you want to name and then choose Insert→ Names→Cells to display the Cell Names dialog box. Click Labels. Indicate the direction of the labels in relation to the value cells and click OK. Then click Close.

Using a Cell Name in a Formula

Once you've named a cell, it's easy to use the name in a formula. Using cell names makes it so much easier when dealing with complicated formulas. Instead of saying "Let's multiply cell B1 by B2 and divide it by cell B3," you can say "Let's multiply the cost of the product by the markup rate and divide that by the number of products sold." Cell names allow you to use plain, descriptive English in your formulas.

To use a cell name, simply use the name in place of the cell address in your formula. You can type the name in the formula or click the Navigate button on the input line and select the name from the drop-down list. Make sure that you include the commas to separate each argument. See Figure 13-8 for an example of cell names in the car payment example. The cell name appears with a tilde (~) preceding it.

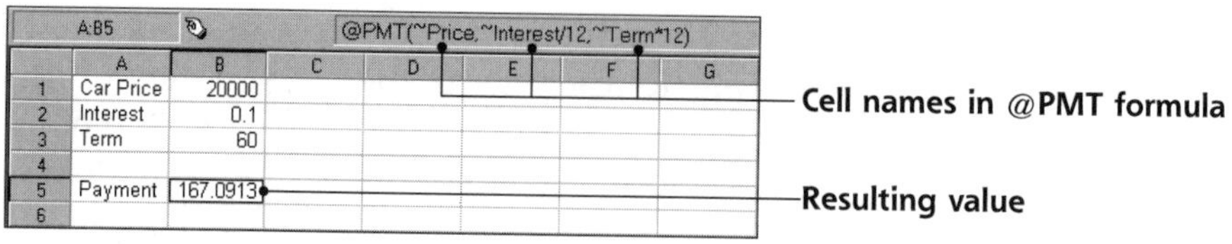

Figure 13-8 Use cell names to make a formula easier to understand.

Summary

That was some trip, wasn't it? You should feel very proud of yourself for working through a chapter that covers the heavy stuff, such as how to use formulas, functions, and cell names, and how to work with page setup and printing. You've covered a lot of good, solid ground in this chapter, learning the "meat" that will help you use Quattro Pro effectively and efficiently. Now it's time for dessert. In the next chapter, you'll get to explore the many ways you can make your data look oh-so fine.

CHAPTER FOURTEEN

FORMATTING A NOTEBOOK

IN THIS CHAPTER YOU LEARN THESE KEY SKILLS

WORKING WITH CELLS   PAGE 275

MOVING AND COPYING DATA   PAGE 277

WORKING WITH ROWS AND COLUMNS   PAGE 279

FORMATTING CELLS   PAGE 281

ALIGNING DATA   PAGE 283

WORKING WITH LINES   PAGE 286

WORKING WITH WORKSHEETS   PAGE 287

N ow that you've had a chance to create a notebook and enter data into a worksheet, you can learn some of the editing and formatting techniques that make your work more efficient and your notebook more appealing. As in WordPerfect and Presentations, you can cut and copy cell contents, and use many of the same formatting features, such as bold, italics, and changing the colors of data and cells. You can also add borders and shading to a cell or group of cells. You'll look at a variety of editing and formatting techniques in this chapter.

Working with Cells

I n Chapter 12, you learned a variety of ways to enter and edit data in cells. You also learned how to delete characters within cells using the Delete and Backspace keys. But there are other, more efficient ways of removing data from your cells. Not only that, if you need to, you can insert or delete one or more cells completely from the worksheet without having to rearrange the rows or columns containing them.

Clearing Cell Contents and Formatting

When you want to keep your layout of rows and columns the same but would like to remove the contents of one or more cells, you can *clear* the cells. This removes all cell contents, including formulas, but it doesn't affect the cells themselves. It's sort of like wiping off a white board; you don't lose the white board, only the information you had written on it:

* To clear cell *contents*, select the cell or block of cells you wish to clear and press Delete. This is the same as choosing `Edit` → `Clear` → `Values`.

* To clear cell *contents and formatting*, secondary-click the selection and choose Clear from the QuickMenu or choose `Edit` → `Clear` → `Cells`. Quattro Pro removes the contents of the cell, as well as any formatting associated with it. Formatting can include fonts, font sizes, colors, lines, and shading.

* To clear cell *formatting* only, choose `Edit` → `Clear` → `Formats`. This removes the formatting for the cells but leaves the contents of a cell, including a formula, intact.

 TIP   Remember that you can use Undo to revert back to your original setting.

Deleting Cells

If you have several columns of data representing different elements of a budget, you may find that you need to remove cells because your information has changed. But what if the data you need to remove is in the middle of a column? If you clear it, you'll have to move everything else up to fill in the gap, right? Not if you *delete* the cells instead. When you delete cells, you have the option of shifting remaining cells so there aren't any blank areas where the deleted cells were.

To delete cells and have the remaining cells fill in the empty cell(s), follow these steps:

 1. Select the cell(s) you wish to delete and click the Delete button on the Notebook toolbar or choose `Edit` → `Delete`. Quattro Pro displays the Delete dialog box (see Figure 14-1). Here you can change the range of selected cells and set other options.

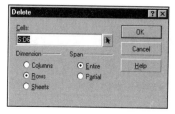

Figure 14-1   Delete selected cells from a worksheet.

2. Under Dimension, select Columns, Rows, or Sheets, depending on which cells you wish to delete.

3. Under Span, choose Entire to delete the entire dimension you indicated in Step 2, or choose Partial if you only want to delete a selected block of cells. For example, if you choose Entire, Quattro Pro will remove the *entire* column, row, or sheet regardless of the cells you may have selected.

4. Click OK. Quattro Pro removes the cells according to your selections in the Delete Block dialog box, shifting cells to take the place of deleted cells.

If you delete an entire row or column, Quattro Pro renumbers the remaining ones to accommodate the deletion(s).

Keep in mind that deleting cells may cause cells to shift in ways you don't want them to shift. For example, if you delete cells spanning two columns, the cells that shift to take their place will no longer be in the correct column, which may affect your data results.

Inserting Cells

Remember the budget I mentioned in the section on deleting cells? You can apply the inverse, too, adding a few cells to the middle of a column or row without having to rearrange everything around it to make it all work. Just as when you delete cells, when you insert new cells, existing cells shift to make room.

To insert blocks, follow these steps:

1. Select the cells that are currently in the location for the new cells. For example, if you want to insert three cells above cell F6, select cells F3 through F5. These are the cells that will shift once you insert the new cells.

2. Click the Insert button on the Notebook toolbar to display the Insert dialog box, which looks similar to the Delete dialog box.

3. Choose the Dimension and Span and click OK. Quattro Pro inserts the new cells, shifting existing cells according to the selection you made in the Insert Block dialog box.

Moving and Copying Data

I f you're familiar with moving and copying in WordPerfect, you'll have a sense of *déjà vu* as you go through this section. However, there are some important differences when moving and copying cell contents, so even if you know cut and copy techniques from WordPerfect, read through this section for things that are unique to cutting and copying in Quattro Pro.

Using Cut and Copy

Most likely, you're familiar with the Cut, Copy, and Paste features from the other applications. They work identically here in Quattro Pro, except that you're moving the contents of cells instead of text. If you find your data is in the wrong place or it just makes sense to have it somewhere else, you can move it. Or, if you find you'll need nearly identical information from one worksheet to another, you can copy it, making the minor changes in the pasted data. Just as in WordPerfect, when you use the Cut and Copy features, Quattro Pro places the data on the Clipboard from which you can paste again and again.

To cut or copy text, select the block of cells you wish to move or copy and click the Cut button or the Copy button on the Notebook toolbar. Select the sheet if the destination will be on another worksheet, and then select the destination cell. If you're going to paste multiple cells, the destination cell will be the upper-left corner cell of the pasted block so make sure you select the correct one. Click the Paste button on the Notebook toolbar.

Using Drag and Drop

You may remember drag and drop from WordPerfect. This feature allows you to move or copy information quickly by selecting it and then dragging the selection to a new location. The best thing about using drag and drop in Quattro Pro is that you have visual cues about what's selected and where it's going to end up.

To drag and drop data, select the block of cells, then point to the selection, moving the pointer until it becomes a four-headed arrow. Click and hold the mouse button until you see the pointer change to a hand and a heavy colored line surround the block (usually yellow). Drag the selection to the new location, watching the colored outline as you go. When the outline covers the destination cells, release the mouse button. Quattro Pro inserts the data in the new location, using any formatting contained with the original cells. To copy, press and hold Ctrl before releasing the mouse button.

Moving and Copying Formulas

You move and copy formulas much the way you move and copy data. Just as when you move or copy data, Quattro Pro moves or copies the cell *contents* which, in the case of a formula, are the formula itself, not the resulting value. Any relative cell references will change to reflect the new location of the formula, and any absolute references will remain static, referring to the original cells in the formula. When you're copying a formula to several cells, make sure that you select all empty cells you want to contain the formula before you use the Paste feature.

TIP If you want to move or copy the *resulting value* of a formula, select the cell that contains the formula whose value you wish to move or copy. Choose Edit→Convert to Values to display the Data Values dialog box. In the To text box, indicate the target cell and click OK. Quattro Pro will insert the *value*, not the formula, into the target cell.

Working with Rows and Columns

As you begin creating your worksheet, entering and removing data and deleting cells, you may also find a need to insert, remove, or rearrange entire columns and rows. Perhaps you realize you've left out a column for the Southeast region or you need to include a row for a new sales rep and her sales for the quarter. You can easily add or rearrange rows and columns to add cells to your worksheet.

Inserting Rows and Columns

If you find you have additional data you need to include in a spreadsheet, you can insert rows or columns to create additional cells in the middle of existing cells. Before you begin, make sure you've got the Notebook toolbar displayed. You can display this toolbar by right-clicking the current toolbar and choosing Notebook from the QuickMenu. New columns will insert to the left of the selected column(s) and new rows will insert above the selected row(s).

To insert rows or columns, use one of the following methods:

✳ Click the column letter or row number where you want the column/row inserted and click the Insert button on the Notebook toolbar.

✳ Click the column letter or row number where you want the column inserted and choose `Insert` → `Column` or `Insert` → `Row`.

✳ Select a cell in the column or row where you want the new column/row inserted and choose `Insert` → `Cells` to display the Cells dialog box. Under Dimensions, choose Columns or Rows and click OK.

TIP To insert multiple columns or rows at once, select the number of columns or rows you want to insert first and then use one of the methods just described.

Adjusting Column Width and Row Height

In addition to inserting columns and rows, you can also adjust the height of rows and the widths of columns. This is helpful if you can't see all of your data in the cell or you like the extra space around your data an increased row height provides. Here are some things to remember about adjusting column width and row height:

* Don't drag a column to the *left* or you will hide the column.
* Don't drag a row *up* or you will hide the row(s) above.
* To adjust multiple columns or rows at once, select the columns or rows to adjust, and then click and drag the sizing pointer for the first selected column or row to the desired width (column) or height (row).

ADJUSTING COLUMN WIDTH

If you find you can't see all your data in a column, you can increase the width. Conversely, if your data is short, you can decrease the width to create space for other columns.

 To adjust column width, point to the *right edge* of the column letter in the column border you want to adjust so that you see the sizing pointer. Click and drag the column to the right until you reach the desired width.

 TIP To adjust a column width so that the column is as wide as the widest data entry, select the column and then click the QuickFit button on the Notebook toolbar.

FEATURE FOCUS The Fit-As-You-Go option automatically increases column width when a number value is too wide. This prevents Quattro Pro from displaying the value as a series of asterisks, *******. To change this option, choose Tools→Settings and then choose the General tab. Clear the Fit-As-You-Go checkbox and click OK.

ADJUSTING ROW HEIGHT

Row height adjusts automatically to accommodate large fonts and other formatting you perform on cells. However, you may find you want to increase the height of row to add some white space around your data.

To adjust row height, point to the *bottom edge* of the row number in the column border so that you see the sizing pointer. Click and drag the row down until you reach the desired height.

RESETTING COLUMN WIDTH OR ROW HEIGHT

Once you start adjusting columns, you may start to go a little adjustment crazy. If you want to get back to square one — that is, return to the default column widths and row heights — follow these steps.

 Select the rows you want to adjust and click the Cell Properties button on the Quattro Pro property bar, or choose Format→Selection to display the Active Cells dialog box. Choose the Row/Column tab. To reset column width, choose Reset width under Column Options. To reset the row height, choose Reset height under Row Options. Click OK to set the column width(s) and/or row height(s) back to the default measurements. Note that you can also set specific measurements for column widths and row heights in this dialog box.

TIP To reset the entire worksheet, select it by clicking the Select All button (the blank button at the intersection of the row and column borders), and proceed as just described.

FEATURE FOCUS Locking Titles is easier than ever in Quattro Pro 8. To ensure that you can see column and row headings when you scroll far and wide, select the cell that intersects the column and row headings and choose View→Locked Titles. For example, to lock Row 1 and Column A, select Cell B2.

Formatting Cells

In Chapter 12, you learned about date formats and which ones Quattro Pro recognizes for calculation purposes. However, you can use any number of formats to get the most out of your data and display it in a way that is most meaningful. When you enter numeric values, Quattro Pro uses the Normal format, which is the default. This format inserts the number exactly as you enter it, without any zeroes after decimal points. You can format your numbers so they have zeroes after decimal points, use percentages, include commas, dollar signs and other symbols. Formatting your numbers doesn't affect the actual cell value, only the way Quattro Pro displays the values in the cells.

Using the Quattro Pro Property Bar

Just as you're able to format text in WordPerfect and format text and objects in Presentations, you can also format elements of your spreadsheets. Using the Quattro Pro property bar, you can format data in cells much the same way you did in the other applications (see Figure 14-2). You can also add borders and lines to groups of cells. You'll be familiar with many of these features if you've worked through the chapters on WordPerfect and Presentations.

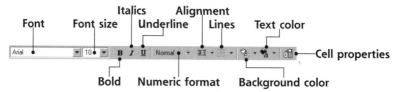

Figure 14-2 Format your cells and cell contents with the property bar.

Using Numeric Styles

Quattro Pro provides two methods for formatting numeric cells. The first allows you to use the Numeric Format button on the property bar, which, when you click it, displays a list of common numeric formats using default settings. The second allows you to display the Numeric Format tab in the Active Block dialog box and select more customized formats. Table 14-1 shows examples of each of these formats for easy reference. Note that by "significant numbers," I mean any number from 0-9 that indicates a fractional part of the number. If the number is a whole integer, Quattro Pro displays the requisite number of zeroes.

TABLE 14-1 Common Numeric Formats

Example	Name	Description
1,200.00	COMMA	Includes two significant numbers after the decimal point.
1,200	COMMA0	Does not include any numbers after the decimal point.
$1,200.00	CURRENCY	Dollar sign with two significant numbers after the decimal point.
$1,200	CURRENCY0	Dollar sign with no numbers after the decimal point.
15%	PERCENT	Converts number to a percentage.

To format numeric cells using one of the styles, select the cells containing the numbers you want to format, click the Numeric format button on the Quattro Pro property bar, and select the desired numeric format.

When you use the Percent format, Quattro Pro assumes the value in the cell is the percentage value. For example, if you want the cell to display 15%, the value should be .15.

TIP If none of these number formats suits you, you can create your own format and use it. Choose Format→Selection, choose the Numeric Format tab, and click User Defined. Select your options and click OK.

Formatting Cell Contents

You can change the font face and size of slide text the same way you do in WordPerfect, using the Font and Size drop-down lists. You can also add attributes such as bold, italics, and underline, as well as change text colors. To change all text in cells, select the cell(s). To change only specific text, select the text within the cell.

X-REF For more on text formatting, see "Formatting Text" in Chapter 4.

Select cells and use the following buttons on the Quattro Pro property bar to change cell text and background colors:

* Click the Background Color button on the Quattro Pro property bar and select a background color.
* Click the Text Color button on the Quattro Pro property bar and select a text color.

TIP If you will print your worksheet on a black and white printer, consider changing your text color to white and the shading to solid black for an eye-catching contrast in a cell or two.

FEATURE FOCUS In Quattro Pro 8, you can format individual text *within* a cell, not just the entire cell.

Aligning Data

In Chapter 12, you saw that text data aligns against the left side of the cell, whereas Quattro Pro recognizes numeric data as a value and aligns it against the right side of the cell. You can easily change how cell contents align if you want a different look. Quattro Pro provides both horizontal and vertical alignments. Horizontal alignments align the data between the left and right edges of a cell, and vertical alignments align the data between the top and bottom edges of a cell. You can also center a cell or cells over several columns. For examples of these alignments, see Figure 14-3. Notice that though Centered across block and joined and centered *look* the same, centered across block keeps the existing cells intact and joined and centered combines existing cells into one.

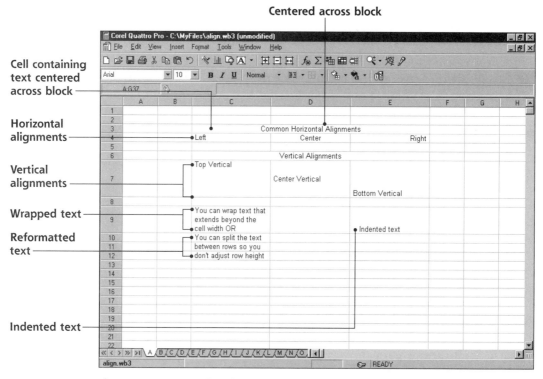

Figure 14-3   Examples of cell alignments.

Aligning Data Horizontally

To align data horizontally, so that it is either positioned left, center, or right within the cell, you use the Alignment button on the Quatto Pro property bar. You can also center a cell or cells over several other cells. This is helpful if you have a title or heading you want to span several columns, as in the example in Figure 14-3.

To align data horizontally, select the cell(s) you want to align. Click the Alignment button on the Quattro Pro property bar, then select the desired alignment. To center data across a block, select all cells that the data should span, including the cell containing the data you wish to center. For example, if you want the data in cell B2 to span columns A, B, C, and D, select cells A2 through D2, then click the Alignment button and choose Center Across Block. See Table 14-2 for a description of each alignment type.

TABLE 14-2 Horizontal Alignments

Option	Description
▣	General (right-aligned values and left-aligned labels)
▪	Left
▪	Right
▪	Center
▤	Center Across
▤	Indent

FEATURE FOCUS To join and center cells, select the cells you wish to join and click the Join and Center button on the Notebook toolbar. Remember that this *joins* all selected cells, making them a single cell.

TIP To return alignment to its original state, use Undo or select the cells, click the Alignment button on the Standard property bar, and select the General button.

Wrapping and Aligning Data Vertically

Your data aligns against the bottom of a cell by default. If you don't increase the row height, you can't determine the vertical alignment. However, if you decide to increase the row height, you'll see the data along the bottom of the cell. You can change the alignment so that it's centered between the top and bottom of the cell, or against the top of the cell (as in Figure 14-3).

Follow these steps to align and wrap your data:

1. Select the cell(s) you want to align and click the Cell Properties button on the property bar to display the Active Cells dialog box.

2. Select the Alignment tab and select Top, Center, or Bottom under Alignment. Check the sample in the bottom right corner of the dialog box.

3. Under Cell Options, choose Wrap text to ensure that text stays within the cell width and click OK when finished.

DOING THE SPLITS

An alternative to wrapping text in cells is to have the text in the cells take up multiple rows using the Reformat feature. This avoids having the row height increase, which may make the worksheet look unbalanced. To reformat cells, select the cell containing the entry you wish to reformat and the cells you wish the data to overlap. For example, if your long entry is in cell B2 and you want it to appear in cells B2, B3, and B4, type or select cells B2 through B4. Choose Format → Text Reformat and click OK.

Working with Lines

When you print a notebook, Quattro Pro doesn't include any lines around your data to delineate cells. If you want lines, you'll need to ask Quattro Pro to print gridlines. Or, if you want something a little fancier, you can add lines as you did in Chapter 8 for WordPerfect tables. Use lines in combination with background color to get just the look you want.

Adding Lines to Cells

Need to impress your boss? Want to jazz up that rather dull budget report? Add a little flair with lines. To add lines, select the cells you want to format, and then click the Lines button and select the desired line style.

To change the line color, follow these steps:

1. Select the cells, then choose Format → Selection and choose the Border/ Fill tab. Unfortunately, Quattro Pro doesn't recognize any existing line style you may have selected from the property bar so you'll need to set the style (Border type) again before you can select a border color.

2. Indicate which line segment you want to format by clicking the segment on the sample at the left. Or click the appropriate button to indicate how much of your selection you want to format: All, Outline, or Inside.

3. Click the Border Color button, select a color from the pop-up palette, and click OK.

TIP   If you want to format fonts, shading, colors, alignment, and lines all at once, use the Active Block dialog box. Simply select the cells you want to format and then choose Format→Selection. Use the appropriate tabs to format the cells and then click OK.

HIRING A SPREADSHEET DECORATOR

Don't have time to play around with lines, colors, and fonts? Quattro Pro provides you with your own personal decorator — SpeedFormat. You may remember this feature from a Side Trip in Chapter 7. It works the same way here. Just select the block of cells you wish to format or select a single cell within the block you wish to format and click the SpeedFormat button or choose | Format | → | SpeedFormat | to display the SpeedFormat dialog box. In the Formats list, select the format you wish to use. Check the Example to see if you like the format. Under Include, click each element you don't want to format to clear the check box. The example worksheet cells will reflect your selections. Most often, you'll want to include all elements. Click OK to apply the format to your cells.

Working with Worksheets

In addition to formatting cells, you can customize your worksheets to optimize your notebook. You can name sheets, add and remove sheets, and set the minimum number so you only see the sheets you need.

Setting the Minimum Number of Sheets

In Chapter 12, I told you that the default Quattro Pro notebook contains 256 sheets. If you know you'll only need four sheets, why have all that extra baggage? To tell Quattro Pro to drop Uncle Ed's golf clubs, choose Tools→Settings and select the Display tab. In the Minimum Number of Sheet Tabs text box, indicate the minimum number you want to use and click OK. You can always add additional sheets by inserting them, as described in "Inserting and Deleting Worksheets" later in this section.

FEATURE FOCUS You can now do away with worksheets you don't need by indicating the minimum number of sheets you want to use in a notebook.

Naming Your Sheets

As you learned in Chapter 12, Quattro Pro names each sheet with a letter, continuing with AA, AB, AC, and so on down the alphabet for each of the 256 sheets in a notebook. But rather than these dull little letters, you can give your sheets real, appropriate names to help identify what the sheets contain. Back in Chapter 12 you saw how to use QuickFill to fill selected cells with a range. You also may have noticed that you can use QuickFill to name worksheet *tabs*. If your tabs don't really use a series, you can name them individually.

To name a sheet, simply double-click the worksheet tab, type the name, and press Enter or click outside the tab. Quattro Pro adjusts the width of the tab to accommodate the name. You can use up to 63 characters, including spaces. Keep in mind that the longer the name, the fewer sheets Quattro Pro can display at one time.

FEATURE FOCUS You can also secondary-click the worksheet tab you want to name and select Edit Sheet Name from the QuickMenu. The new worksheet QuickMenu provides easy access to common worksheet tasks.

Selecting Worksheets

Just as you can select cells on a worksheet, you can select multiple worksheets in a notebook. Why would you want or need to do this? Well, perhaps you've decided to move one or more pages so your pages appear in a different order. Or you want to delete or insert several pages. Here's how you do it:

* To select a single worksheet, simply click the sheet tab.

* To select a range of sheets in sequence, click the first sheet tab in the sequence, and then press and hold the Shift key and display and click the last tab in the sequence. Quattro Pro displays a heavy black line beneath all selected sheets (see Figure 14-4).

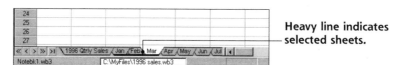

Heavy line indicates selected sheets.

Figure 14-4 Selecting multiple sheets.

TIP You can move and copy sheets by selecting them and then dragging the selected sheets to the new location. To copy a sheet, press and hold Ctrl when you drag the sheet(s). You can also select the sheet(s) and choose Edit→Move Sheets.

Inserting and Deleting Worksheets

If you find you've left March out between your February and April worksheets, you can insert a blank sheet for your data. Conversely, if you decide you no longer need a sheet, you can remove it.

Any time you need additional worksheets between other sheets, you can insert them. To insert a new sheet, select the worksheet(s) that will follow the new sheet. Quattro Pro always inserts new sheet(s) *before* the selected sheet(s). Secondary-click the sheet tab and choose Insert Sheet from the QuickMenu.

To delete a worksheet you don't need, select the worksheet(s), secondary-click the sheet tab, and choose Delete Sheet from the QuickMenu.

Just as you selected multiple columns and rows and inserted that number, you can select and insert multiple worksheets. To insert multiple worksheets, select the number of sheets you wish to insert, then choose Insert→Sheet. To delete multiple sheets, select them, click the Delete button on the Notebook toolbar, select Sheets under Dimensions, and then click OK.

BONUS

Setting Page Options

If you worked through Chapter 5, you'll probably remember the advantages of having a header or footer in a WordPerfect document. If you recall, a *header* runs across the tops of pages, and a *footer* runs along the bottoms of pages, providing such information as page numbers, titles, or other important information. You can add a header or footer to your Quattro Pro notebooks so that when you print them, they are organized and ordered. You can also set margins, which is helpful if you're trying to get all your data to fit on a portrait-sized piece of paper.

Creating Headers and Footers

Quattro Pro provides a lot of flexibility when creating headers and footers, allowing you to enter your own text and adding page numbers, the date and time, and other predefined elements, just as you can in WordPerfect.

When you want to add page numbers, the date, or the name of your notebook to a header or footer, you must insert a special code. Quattro Pro uses this code to identify the element you want to include on your printed pages. Quattro Pro also uses a code to align the contents of your header or footer. By default, everything you enter for a header or footer is left-aligned. If you want to center or right-align part or all of the contents of your header or footer, you must use the vertical line |. This character is usually found on the backslash key on your keyboard and often appears broken in the middle on the key itself. Depending on your keyboard, you may find the key next to the +/= key at the end of the number keys row above your alphabetic keys or just below the Backspace key.

The first time you put this line in front of text or codes, Quattro Pro centers the text and codes. The second time a vertical line appears, Quattro Pro right-aligns the text and codes following it. Use the following examples to help you align your header or footer contents:

* ✹ Type ||**Miscellaneous Stuff, Inc.** to right-align the company name.

* ✹ Type **#D|Miscellaneous Stuff, Inc.** to left-align the date (#D) and center the company name (because there is only one vertical line).

* ✹ Type **#D||Miscellaneous Stuff, Inc.** to left-align the date (#D) and right-align the company name.

* ✹ Type |**Miscellaneous Stuff, Inc. |#D** to center the company name and right-align the date (#D). Nothing will be left-aligned.

* ✹ Type **#D|Miscellaneous Stuff, Inc.|page #p** to left-align the date (#D), center the company name, and right-align the word *page* and the associated page number (#p) as in the example in Figure 14-5.

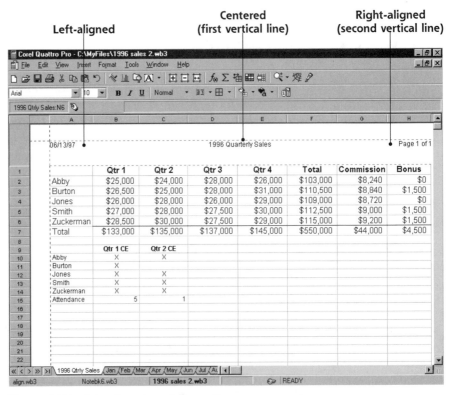

Figure 14-5 A header using all three alignments.

You are allowed up to two alignment codes in both the header and/or footer. For more on which codes do what, see Table 14-2.

To add a header or footer to your notebook, choose View→Page. This is similar to Page view in WordPerfect, allowing you to not only see your headers, footers, and other elements as you do in Print Preview, but also to *work* with these elements. The header area is the blank area above the cells, and the footer is the blank area below the cells on the sheet. To add the actual header or footer text, double-click in the header or footer area or select File→Page setup and select the Header/Footer tab. Click Create Under Header or Footer and position the insertion point in the text box. Use the examples at the beginning of this section and Table 14-3 to enter and justify your header or footer.

TABLE 14-3 Common Header/Footer Codes

Code	Description
#D	Displays the current date in the long format specified in Tools→Settings→ International (MM/DD/YY is the default for the United States). Example: 05/14/97.
#t	Enters the current time in standard Short Time format using AM and PM Example: 9:15AM. To display a leading zero in front of single digits (09:15 AM), type #ts.
#p	Displays the page number.
#P	Displays the number of total pages in the document.
#f	Displays the name of the notebook only (1996 SALES.WB3).
#F	Displays the name of the notebook with its complete path (C:\MYFILES\1996 SALES.WB3)

Table 14-3 lists the most common codes you'll use. For a complete list of the codes, use the online help and the Index tab to locate *headers and footers*. When you click Display, you'll see the About Headers and Footers help window, where the complete list of codes appears.

TIP You can combine the page number codes — #p of #P — which would give you *page x of y*, where *x* is the current page number and *y* is the total pages in the print range.

Page view is a great way to see the various parts of your worksheet, including headers and footers. And check out this handy little tip: After you add header or footer elements to a notebook, you can edit them simply by double-clicking the header or footer area in Page view. The text reverts to the codes and you can make your changes without displaying the Spreadsheet Page Setup dialog box. After you're finished, just click in the worksheet to see the header or footer text.

Setting Notebook Margins

If you're looking at your worksheet and see that you have data in several columns, you may have difficulty printing all the columns on one page. If Quattro Pro can't print all columns on a page, it prints as many as it can and continues with the remaining columns on the next page. However, you may be able to fit more columns on a page by adjusting the margins.

To adjust margins, choose View→Page. Quattro Pro displays the worksheet in Page view, indicating margins and header/footer areas with colored dotted lines. This is similar to the guidelines in WordPerfect. Click and drag a margin guideline to the appropriate location.

X-REF You can also adjust the margins using margin guides in Print Preview. See "Previewing a Notebook" in Chapter 13 for more information.

To set precise measurements, choose File→Page Setup to display the Spreadsheet Page Setup dialog box. Choose the Print margins tab and enter a measurement in the Top, Bottom, Left, and Right text boxes. Click OK.

X-REF To have Quattro Pro fit your spreadsheet to a your specifications, see "All the Data That's Fit to Print" in Chapter 13.

Summary

n this chapter, you explored some serious and fun formatting stuff. First you looked at how to insert and remove columns, rows, and blocks of cells, as well as how to lock titles so you can see them from distant cells. You explored basic text and data formatting with fonts and text enhancements, such as bold and italics, you aligned data in cells, and you added color, lines, and fill. Finally, you looked at how to apply much of this formatting at once using SpeedFormat. Next, you'll look at how you can include charts in your notebooks to give your data added visual impact and use Quattro Pro as a database.

In Chapter 14, you saw how you can make your nice, neat numbers look a little jazzier with lines, colors, and backgrounds. But you can go even further by displaying your data in charts. Charts allow viewers or readers to see at a glance the impact your numbers have, either in relation to each other or to other elements. The wonderful thing about Quattro Pro charts is that when you change your data on the worksheet, the chart updates to reflect the change.

Understanding and Using Charts

To chart your course, it's important to select the right chart type for your data. Check out the following descriptions of popular chart types to see how you might want to display your data. See Figure 15-1 for examples of some of these chart types, with each chart in the figure using the same data:

* *Area, radar,* and *line charts* are good for showing trends in the data and rates of change over a specified period of time. Use these charts for a task such as investment tracking.

* *Pie charts* show the relationship of parts to the whole. Use pie charts for such things as the percentage of employees in each department.

* *Bar charts,* one of the most common chart types, show variations between similar types of data but don't provide the relationship of the parts to the whole. Use bar charts to show such things as regional quarterly sales.

* *Scatter* and *bubble charts* show the intersection of data values, inserting a marker at the intersection of the data on the X and Y axes. The scatter chart shows the intersection of *two* different data values, and the bubble chart shows the intersection of *three* different data values. Use scatter or bubble charts to show such intersecting data as units sold to net and/or gross profits. The scatter chart could show the intersection of both the units sold and gross *or* net profits, while the bubble chart could show the intersection of all three elements, with the circle (bubble) marker radius indicating one of the elements.

FEATURE FOCUS **The bubble chart allows you to display three types of relationships with your data at once.**

In Figure 15-1, the same data is presented in four different ways. You can see how the chart type you select can affect how your data is viewed and understood.

By default, many chart types use a *legend* and *labels* to help identify the parts of the chart and to help viewers understand the data. If you've ever read a map, you know what a legend is. It's the little area that explains what the symbols scattered across the map represent. The legend for the bar chart in Figure 15-1 shows how to identify the sales for three sales reps. The labels identify the data for the chart, such as *Qtr 1, Qtr 2, Qtr 3,* and *Qtr 4.* Later you learn how to format your legend and labels, as well as other elements of your bar chart.

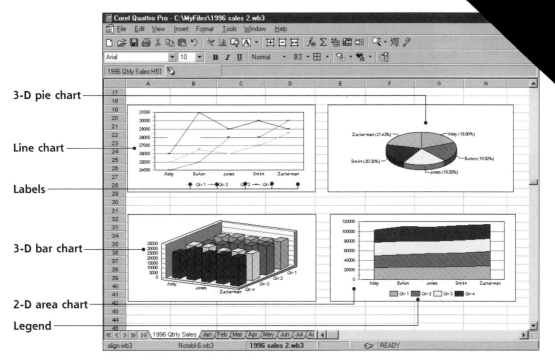

3-D pie chart

Line chart

Labels

3-D bar chart

2-D area chart

Legend

Figure 15-1 Sample charts.

Creating a Floating Chart

With Quattro Pro, you can create a chart using QuickChart or the Chart Expert and add the chart to your current sheet, a *floating chart*, or work with it in a separate window. Working in a separate chart window can get a little confusing, so I focus on working with a chart on the current worksheet. However, for those of you who like a little craziness, I'll point out where you can work with a chart in a separate window when creating a chart with the Chart Expert.

Creating a Chart with QuickChart

The fastest (and easiest) way to create a chart is to let Quattro Pro do the work. Here's how:

1. Select the cells containing the data for the chart. Make sure that you include the row and column headings so that Quattro Pro can create a legend from them. Don't include any titles you've added above the data; you'll add this to your chart later.

k the QuickChart (Floating Chart) button on the Notebook toolbar
move the pointer to an empty area on your worksheet. Quattro Pro
s your pointer into a chart pointer (see Figure 15-2), indicating that
're ready to create the chart.

ck and drag to indicate the size and shape of the chart (see Figure
-2). When you release the mouse button, Quattro Pro creates a chart
ing the chart type it deems most appropriate for your data.

see *sizing handles* surround the chart. These are similar to the sizing
handles you saw in the Presentations chapters and in Chapter 6, where you
looked at graphics in WordPerfect. You can resize the chart using these handles.
Note that when you see the sizing handles, you've selected the entire chart as a
single object and the Chart property bar displays.

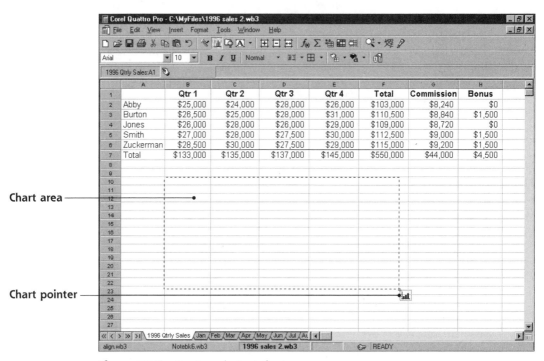

Figure 15-2 Create an instant chart.

X-REF For information on adding titles and other elements, see "Formatting a Chart" later in this chapter.

Creating a Chart with the Chart Expert

For those of you who prefer a little more hands-on activity and want to have
more input into how your chart looks before it displays, you should use the

Chart Expert. The Chart Expert leads you through a series of dialog boxes, allowing you to make choices about your chart before you actually create it on the notebook sheet.

To create a chart using the Chart Expert, follow these steps:

1. Select the data you want to use in the chart. Again, make sure that you include the row and column headings so that Quattro Pro can create a legend from them.

2. Choose ⬚**Insert** → ⬚**Chart**. Quattro Pro displays Step 1 of 5 in the Chart Expert dialog box (see Figure 15-3). Here you can make selections about how your chart will look.

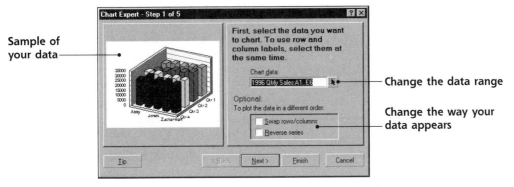

Figure 15-3 Customize your chart before you create it.

3. Change your Chart data if necessary, using point mode, and choose any optional features at the bottom of the dialog box. Click Next. The Chart Expert displays Step 2 of 5, selecting a general chart type.

4. Select a general chart type. Quattro Pro displays a number of variations on the general chart type you selected. Note that you can let the Chart Expert choose for you as well. Click Next and select a specific chart type for Step 3 of 5. Click Next.

5. For Step 4 of 5, choose a color scheme for your chart and click Next.

 TIP **If you change your mind, just click Back in Steps 3 through 5 and change your selections.**

6. You can enter text for a main title and subtitle, as well as titles that will appear next to the x and y axes if your chart type contains these axes. The X-axis runs horizontally below the chart and the Y-axis runs vertically to the left of the chart. Keep in mind that adding titles to the X and Y axes may make the chart too busy. Use these only when the information on each axis is unclear.

7. When you've made all your chart selections, click Finish. Quattro Pro turns your pointer into a chart pointer.

8. Click and drag to indicate the size and shape of the chart and then release the mouse button to see the chart in all its glory.

Working with Charts

Once you create a chart, you may find you need to move or resize it. Moving or resizing a chart works much like resizing a graphic image in WordPerfect or an object in Presentations.

X-REF See "Using Graphic Images" in Chapter 6 and "Working with Clipart" in Chapter 10 for more on moving and sizing images.

 For moving, copying, and selecting, make sure that you see the move pointer (shown at left). For resizing, make sure that you see the sizing arrows:

* To move the chart, point to any edge until you see the move pointer. Click and drag the chart to another location on the worksheet.

* To resize a chart, point to any edge until you see the move pointer and click once to display the selection handles. Point to a selection handle until you see the sizing arrow (double-headed) and then click and drag a selection handle, using the following guidelines:

  * Click and drag a left or right sizing handle to adjust the width of the chart.

  * Click and drag a top or bottom sizing handle to adjust the height of the chart.

  * Click and drag a corner sizing handle to adjust the width and height of the chart proportionally.

* To move or copy a chart, select it as a single object, and then cut, copy, and paste it to its destination. You can move and copy charts to other sheets to keep them separate from the data if you like.

* To delete a chart, select it as a single object and press Delete.

Formatting a Chart

Depending on whether you used the QuickChart tool or the Chart Expert, you may or may not have titles and other goodies on your chart. In this section, you see how to add titles and work with other elements of your chart to make it just right. You can add a chart title, change the legend, and change the colors of your bars, lines, or pie slices so that they look oh-so-swell and impress everyone who sees the chart.

TIP To work with a larger version of your chart, select the chart as a single object and click the Chart Window button on the Chart property bar. Select the chart to edit and click OK. Make your changes and then close the window to return to the notebook worksheet.

Changing the Chart Type and Arrangement

AB1
A-B2
A -B?

You picked that lovely 3-D bar chart, and your boss tells you she thinks it would make more sense as a 3-D multiple pie chart. Okay, no problem. Just select the chart as a single object, click the Chart Type button on the Chart property bar, and select the new chart type. Quattro Pro makes the changes instantly.

If you'd like to explore a variety of chart types and color schemes within a single dialog box, select your chart and click the Chart Gallery button on the Chart property bar. Quattro Pro displays the Chart Gallery dialog box. The choices you make here are similar to Steps 4 and 5 under "Creating a Chart with the Chart Expert." Click the Category down-arrow button and select a chart type from the drop-down list. Select a chart style and color scheme, watching how your selections affect your chart by watching the sample on the right side of the dialog box. After you're finished, click OK.

TIP Click Advisor in the Chart Gallery dialog box to get more help on selecting an appropriate chart type.

Swapping Your Data

When QuickChart or the Chart Expert creates a chart from your data, it makes a best guess at how to do it. However, sometimes it may not include all of your data because of assumptions it's made. Check out Figure 15-4. The chart on the left shows how the ChartExpert plotted my data when I specified a 2-D bar chart. The chart on the right shows what the chart looks like when I switch the rows and columns. Notice that the chart on the right now includes all five sales reps, whereas the left chart didn't take two of the five sales reps into account.

To swap the row and columns, select the chart as a single object and click the Chart Series button on the Chart property bar. At the bottom of the dialog box, choose Row/Column Swap and click OK. Note that swapping changes the relationships of data. If you want to maintain relationships, experiment with different chart types instead.

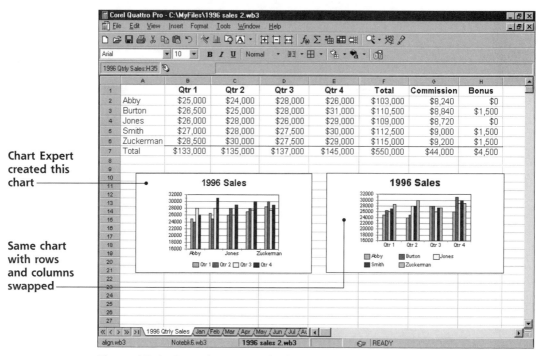

Chart Expert created this chart

Same chart with rows and columns swapped

Figure 15-4 Swap data rows and columns.

Using the Chart Property Bar

Like the other context-sensitive property bars, the Chart property bar contains tools specifically designed to make working with your data chart easier. Table 15-1 describes the buttons unique to data charts in more detail.

FEATURE FOCUS Rather than double-clicking, you need only click the chart element with which you want to work to enter edit mode and work with the element. To select the entire chart as a single object again, point to the edge of the chart until you see the move pointer and click once.

TABLE 15-1 Chart Property Bar

Button	Name	Description
📊 ▼	CHART TYPE	Change the chart type.
⬛ ▼	FILL STYLE	Change the chart fill style.

TABLE 15-1 Chart Property Bar

Button	Name	Description
	FOREGROUND FILL COLOR	Change the fill style foreground color.
	BACKGROUND FILL COLOR	Change the fill style background color (if applicable).
	BORDER STYLE	Select a line style to surround the chart.
	BORDER COLOR	Change the line color surrounding the chart.
	CHART WINDOW	Display the chart in a separate window.
	CHART SERIES	Change the data represented in the chart.
	CHART TITLES	Add or change titles in the chart.
	FULL SCREEN VIEW	Display the chart full screen.
	CHART GALLERY	Select a chart type and color scheme from a predefined list.
	FORWARD ONE	Move selected object in front of next object.
	BACK ONE	Move selected object behind previous object.
	FRONT OF ALL	Move selected object in front of all objects.
	BACK OF ALL	Move selected object behind all objects.
	OBJECT PROPERTIES	Change the properties of the selected object.

If you don't see the sizing handles or are not in chart edit mode, you won't see the Chart property bar.

Working with Chart Titles

A title can help readers understand the data they're viewing. If you used the Chart Expert, Quattro Pro allowed you to add a title, subtitle, and other titles (if applicable) to your chart. However, if you used the QuickChart tool to create your chart, you can use the Chart Titles tool to add a title or change an existing one.

ADDING A CHART TITLE

If you used the QuickChart tool and want to add a chart title to your chart, follow these steps:

1. Select the chart as a single object or click in the chart once to activate edit mode. Remember, you'll see those colored hashmarks around the chart in edit mode.

2. Click the Chart Titles button on the Chart property bar or secondary-click the chart and choose Titles from the QuickMenu to display the Chart Titles dialog box.

3. Type title names in the Main Title and Subtitle text boxes. If your chart type contains X and Y axes, enter titles for these if you want. Click OK when you're finished.

To remove a chart title, select the title text and then press Delete.

EDITING A CHART TITLE

You can easily make changes to an existing title on your chart. Just click in the chart once to activate edit mode, then click the chart title text. You'll see the blinking insertion point, which means you can edit away. Once you're finished making changes, click anywhere outside the title.

FORMATTING CHART TITLES

Don't like the default title font? Want it a bright yellow? No problem. Just click in the chart title text to let Quattro Pro know that this is the element with which you want to work. Use the property bar to change the font, font size, color, attributes (bold, italics, underline), and horizontal alignment (justification). Use Table 15-2 to help you format your chart title in other ways.

TABLE 15-2 Chart Title Formatting Tools

Button	Name	Description
ABC	STRIKEOUT	Turn strikeout on or off.
▢ ▾	BOX TYPE	Add a border around the title.
▨ ▾	BORDER COLOR	Change the border color around the title; note that you must have added a border before you can change its color.
▨ ▾	FOREGROUND FILL COLOR	Change the foreground color (color behind the text).
▨ ▾	TEXT COLOR	Change the title text color.

TIP With the insertion point inside your chart title, you can click the Object Properties button on the Quattro Pro property bar and make your formatting selections in the Chart Title Properties dialog box. Check the sample to see how your selections affect your title.

Changing the Series Properties

The bars, lines, pie slices, or other elements that represent the data on your chart are called the *series*. Each series is denoted by a different color and shape, depending on your chart type:

✴ To change the color of a particular series, click the series element (such as a single bar or pie slice), and then click the Foreground Fill Color button on the Chart property bar and select the desired color. If your chart uses a legend, the legend will change to reflect the new color for the associated series.

✴ To change other elements, double-click the series element (such as a single bar or pie slice) or select the element and click the Object Properties button on the Chart property bar. Quattro Pro displays the Series dialog box (Bar, Pie, Line, and so on). Select the desired tab to make your selections, then click OK. Keep an eye on the sample to see how your selections affect your chart.

Changing the Legend

If you selected a chart type that contains a legend, you noticed that Quattro Pro created the legend using default information and colors. You can change the location of the legend in relation to the chart and change the font attributes as well as the attributes of the box surrounding the legend. Note that if you select a legend color and change it, you'll change the series properties in the chart as well. Refer to the next section for more information.

To change aspects of your legend, select and then double-click the legend to display the Legend Properties dialog box (see Figure 15-5).

15

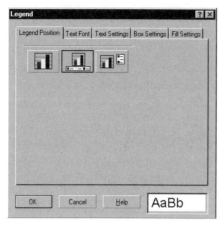

Figure 15-5 Format your chart legend.

Make your selections on each tab and then click OK. Note that on the Legend Position tab, the first option removes the legend completely, the second displays it horizontally below the chart, and the third option displays it vertically to the right of the chart.

 If you double-click a colored legend box instead of the legend area, you will display the Series dialog box instead of the Legend dialog box. Cancel the Series dialog box and double-click outside a box in the legend.

 T I P **To see a big view of your chart, click the Full Screen View on the Chart property bar. To return to the normal view, click anywhere on the chart or press any key.**

Printing a Chart

Once you create and format your chart to your liking, you'll no doubt want to print it. If you have a color printer, the bars, lines, or pie slices will come out looking just about the same as you see them on screen. However, if you'll be printing on a black and white printer, you can ask Quattro Pro to make adjustments for you. Additionally, you can print either the chart by itself or print the data and the chart if the chart shares a worksheet with the data.

To print your chart, select it and click the Print button on the Notebook toolbar or choose File→Print. Make your print selections on the Print tab. If you will print on a black and white printer, choose the Details tab and select the Adjust image to print black and white check box at the bottom of the dialog box. Click OK to send the chart to the printer.

SHADES OF GRAY

If you print your chart on a black and white printer and are lamenting the lack of pizzazz, don't despair. There's hope for the colorless. Consider selecting patterns and shades of gray for your chart elements rather than having Quattro Pro adjust the printing for black and white.

To do this, select the chart as a single object and click the Chart Gallery button on the Chart property bar. Click the Color Scheme down arrow and choose Grayscale, Black and White Patterns, or Gray Marble and click OK. Once you take a look at your chart, you can adjust individual series if necessary. To change an individual series, just double-click the series to format, then select the Fill Settings tab. Black should already be set as the Pattern color, so you'll just need to select a different pattern for the series and click OK.

Setting Up a Database

You may know that the Professional Version of the WordPerfect Suite comes with a database application called Corel Paradox. You may have purchased WordPerfect Suite 8 because you don't need a big database to maintain your data. However, if you would like something to help you keep track of information such as your inventory or even a list of clients, you can use Quattro Pro. In Quattro Pro, you could use a different worksheet for different information. For example, you could use the first worksheet for a client list, the second worksheet for your inventory list, the third worksheet for your list of services, and so on.

TIP If you're planning to use your voucher to obtain CorelCENTRAL, you can also store names and addresses in the CorelCENTRAL Address Book. Once you obtain CorelCENTRAL, check out my related chapter at http://www.idgbooks.com.

If you read Chapter 8, you already know about databases. "I do?" you ask. Yes, you do. When you set up the data file for your merge, you created a database. Remember the terms *records* and *fields*? Those are the primary elements in a database. How does it feel to be ahead of the game?

If you set up your data file in a table in WordPerfect, you can sleep through this part. In Quattro Pro, the records are the rows and the fields are the columns. Refer back to Chapter 8 for an explanation of records and fields.

Creating Your Database

Once you understand the concept of records and fields, it's easy to create your database. Just start at a blank worksheet and type the headings for each field in the first row (these were called *field names* in WordPerfect data files). Below each heading, enter the data. Check out Figure 15-6 for an example of a Quattro Pro database.

TIP **Consider formatting your headings so they stand out. Use a different font, a larger point size, color, or bolding. If you have a lot of entries, freeze your heading row by selecting the cell below the first heading (usually cell A2) and choosing View→Locked Titles.**

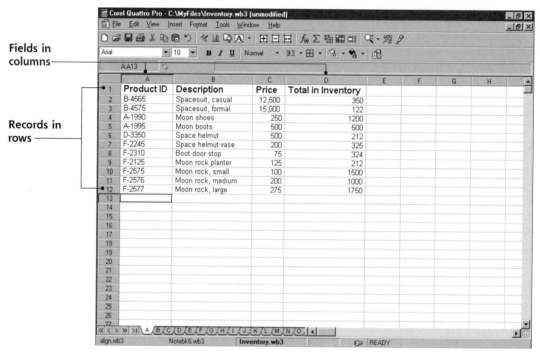

Figure 15-6 Set up a worksheet database in Quattro Pro.

Just as in WordPerfect data files, the more you break down your data, the easier it is to manipulate and use.

Editing Data

You edit data in a database just as you do in a worksheet. Keep in mind that it's important to update your data to make sure it's current. If someone has an address change or your inventory changes, make the change in your database.

Remember that you can use the Find and Replace feature to locate data you need to work with. Just choose Edit→Find and Replace to display the Find and

Replace dialog box. Enter your search and replace text, and click Find Next. Choose the applicable option for the located data.

TIP You can convert your Quattro Pro database to a merge data file for use in WordPerfect. See online help in WordPerfect for more information.

Sorting and Filtering Data

Once you have your data organized in nice, neat rows and columns, you can use a variety of features to help you pinpoint information quickly. For example, if you need to quote the price of your latest chocolate creme or locate the phone number of a distributor, you can use search. You can also display your data in different ways using Sort and QuickFilter.

Sorting by a Single Criterion

You have a wonderful database listing all your products and the amount left in inventory. You need to see if any products are below 300 in your inventory, but it would take forever to go through each product and check the inventory number to determine this. Instead of getting a headache, let Quattro Pro sort your records by inventory total in ascending order. Then you'll see immediately which products have less than 300 left in inventory.

Quattro Pro's Selection Formatting toolbar provides the sort tools you'll need to perform your sorts. To display it, secondary-click the current toolbar and choose Selection Formatting. Quattro Pro places the Selection Formatting toolbar beneath the current toolbar. The Sort button on this toolbar is actually *two* smaller buttons. To sort in ascending order, click the top button and to sort in descending order, click the bottom button.

 To sort your data, make sure you have your database worksheet displayed, and then select any cell in the column on which you wish to sort. Click the top of the Sort button (A . . . Z, ascending) or the bottom of the Sort button (Z . . . A, descending) on the Selection Formatting toolbar.

For example, if you want to sort by inventory total in ascending order (A-Z), select any cell in the inventory total column and click the top of the Sort button on the Selection Formatting toolbar.

To hide the Selection Formatting toolbar, secondary-click the current toolbar and choose Selection Formatting.

Sorting with Multiple Criteria

Quattro Pro allows up to five levels of sort criteria using the Data Sort dialog box. The first criterion you enter is the *primary key* and is what Quattro Pro sorts the data by first. If you want to perform a subsort, you can set *secondary key* criteria. For example, if your first or *primary* sort is on the last name, you might want a secondary sort on the first name in the event you have two clients with the same last name. Think of a secondary sort as breaking the tie for the sort before it. You can access the Data Sort dialog box using the Sort Records button on the Selection Formatting toolbar. If this toolbar is not displayed, secondary-click the current toolbar and choose Selection Formatting

X-REF **For more on sorting concepts, see Appendix A which describes sorting in WordPerfect.**

To set up a multiple sort, follow these steps:

1. With the database worksheet open, select any cell containing data.

2. Click the Sort Records button on the Selection Formatting toolbar or choose [**Tools**] → [**Sort**] to display the Data Sort dialog box (see Figure 15-7). Be sure the Selection contains a heading check box is checked.

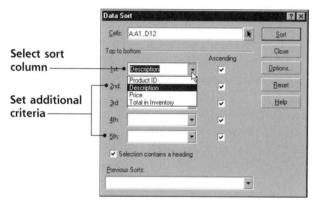

Select sort column

Set additional criteria

Figure 15-7 Indicate your sort criteria.

3. Under Top to bottom, click the 1st down arrow button and select the column heading for the column by which you wish to sort from the drop-down list.

4. Under Top to bottom, indicate any secondary sorts using the 2nd, 3rd, 4th, and 5th drop-down lists, if necessary. Indicate whether you want to sort in Ascending order using the check boxes.

5. Click Sort. Quattro Pro sorts the data according to your settings.

   To hide the Selection Formatting toolbar, secondary-click the current toolbar and choose Selection Formatting.

TIP If your sort didn't produce the results you wanted, click the Undo button on the toolbar.

Filtering Data

Sorting is good for changing the *order* of your data, but it doesn't help if you want to pick and choose what you want to see. For example, perhaps you only want to list those clients in Portland, or only your products in the chocolate creme category. You can *filter* your data so that Quattro Pro only shows you what you want to see. This is where the QuickFilter feature comes in very handy.

To filter your data, make sure that you have your database worksheet displayed. Next, select any cell containing data and choose Tools→QuickFilter to display the drop-down arrow buttons next to each field name. Click the arrow button next to the field you want to use as your filter and then select the criteria. For example, if you want to display only those clients living in Denver, click the City arrow button and choose Denver from the drop-down list. Using the Inventory example in Figure 15-6, say you only want to see those with 500 in inventory. Click the Total in Inventory down arrow button and choose 500 (see Figure 15-8). Quattro Pro displays only those from Denver (or only those products), hiding all the other data from view. The down arrow changes color to indicate a filter.

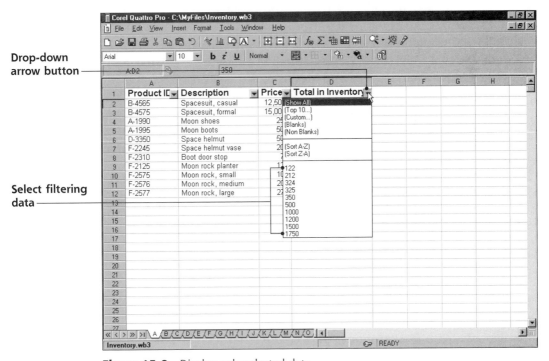

Figure 15-8 Display only selected data.

Note that you can further narrow your filter by choosing criteria from other fields. So if you display only those clients from Denver, you could filter *these* by displaying only those in Denver with a 90211 zip code.

To see all data again, click the arrow button for the *last* field you filtered and choose (Show All). Repeat for all filtered criteria. To get rid of the arrow buttons, choose Tools→QuickFilter again.

 Custom QuickFilter works identically to filtering in the Address Book. For more information, see Chapter 1.

BONUS

Using Quattro Pro Data for a Presentations Chart

I f you need further evidence that the applications in the WordPerfect Suite work tightly together, consider this: If you have a slide show about your company and would like to include a pie chart showing the breakdown of product sales, and that product sales data is already in a Quattro Pro worksheet, you can import the data to Presentations and format it as a pie chart in no time flat. Additionally, you can choose to link the data chart back to the spreadsheet or use the data as is at the time you import it. If you link it, the chart will update if you make changes to the data in your Quattro Pro notebook. If you choose not to link, the data remains fixed even if the data in the Quattro Pro notebook changes.

 TIP **To make it easier to use the data, name the range in Quattro Pro that you want to use in your Presentations chart. Refer to the Bonus section at the end of Chapter 13 for more information on naming cells or cell ranges.**

To use Quattro Pro data in a Presentations data chart, follow these steps:

1. Make sure the notebook you want to use in your Presentations data chart is not open in Quattro Pro.

2. With Presentations open, create a new Data Chart slide by clicking the Add Slide down-arrow button and choosing Insert Data Chart Slide.

3. Type the title and subtitle text for the Data Chart, and then double-click the Data Chart placeholder to display the Data Chart Gallery dialog box.

4. Select a general chart type from the Chart type list and then select a specific type from the samples on the right. Note that the types are defaulted to 3-D; if you want 2-D, you must clear the 3-D check box at the bottom of the dialog box. Click OK to display the Datasheet window and Range Highlighter. You'll also see the Edit Spreadsheet property bar behind the Datasheet window (see Figure 15-9).

5. Click the Import button on the Edit Spreadsheet property bar or choose **Data** → **Import** to display the Import Data dialog box.

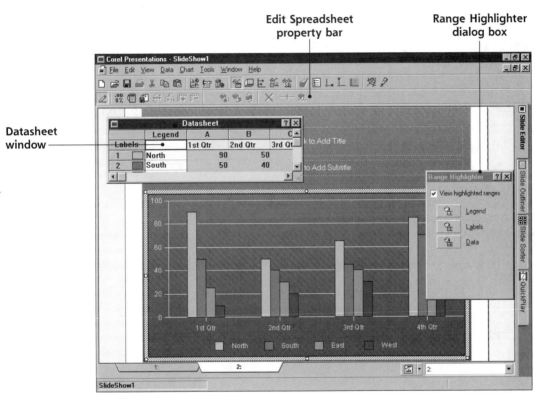

Figure 15-9 Use Quattro Pro data for a data chart in Presentations.

6. If you want to link the data chart back to the data so that your chart will update, click the Link to spreadsheet check box.

7. Make sure that the Clear current data check box is selected so Presentations will replace the sample data with your Quattro Pro data.

8. Locate and insert the Quattro Pro file in the Filename text box.

9. In the Named ranges list box, select the sheet you wish to use, and in the Range text box, indicate the range of cells if different from the default range displayed. If you gave the range a name (this is the best thing to do), select the name.

10. Click OK. Presentations inserts the Quattro Pro data into the Datasheet window.

 11. Make any necessary changes to label and legend text, and then click the View Datasheet button on the Edit Spreadsheet property bar to close the Datasheet window.

12. Format the chart as you would a chart in Quattro Pro.

FEATURE FOCUS The Range Highlighter allows you to color code the three elements you work with in the Datasheet window — Legend, Labels, and Data. If the Range Highlighter dialog box isn't showing, click the Range Highlighter button (first button on Edit spreadsheet property bar) to display it.

Summary

In this chapter you went chart wild, learning how to create, format, and print a chart from Quattro Pro data. You also learned how you can use Quattro Pro as a database to maintain your data without having to mess with a database application. Next up, some additional party favors in your WordPerfect Suite 8 party kit. Have a blast!

USING INTERNET AND CUSTOMIZATION TOOLS

THIS PART CONTAINS THE FOLLOWING CHAPTERS

Part Five gives you a peek into some of the extras that come with the WordPerfect Suite. You'll learn how to browse the Web with Netscape Navigator, design your own Web pages with Internet Publisher, and make the suite your own by customizing it to suit your needs.

Remember Sara Franklin, the relocation specialist from the beginning of Part Three? She uses Presentations to create slide shows of properties for executives relocating to the New York City area. Not too long ago, Sara had another idea, and as usual, her idea made her more efficient, more competitive, and it increased her knowledge of technology, especially of the WordPerfect Suite.

Sara's company recently completed its Web site, and while the company was briefly jubilant at its new success, the novelty soon wore off. "It was just the same old thing," she recalls. "'Welcome to our Web site. Here's what we do. Take care, and have a nice day.' That's really all it was. Of course we were happy that the site was up and running, but soon we started second-guessing ourselves. What were we doing to bring people back to the site again and again? If we couldn't answer that question, was having a Web site doing us any good?"

Sara immediately looked for the answer to that question. "I used to think that to be successful on the Web, you had to pioneer some new technology, but now, I have a better understanding." The key, she says, is finding a way to use current technology to help you do what you already do. "Look at Federal Express," she says excitedly. "The FedEx Web site doesn't have bells and whistles. It just finds your package. People like the no-frills aspect."

Using that model of simplicity, Sara went to work with a cup of coffee and Internet Publisher. "I was amazed at how quickly I could convert my Presentations slides to Web pages," she recalls. "In about 10 minutes, I had converted the presentations for six different clients. I opened the pages with Netscape, and they looked good right away. Then I went right to our Webmaster, who put them on the server. He set up a special URL for each of the clients." Sara then e-mailed the six clients and gave them their own personal, unpublished URLs. "They were amazed. They loved the personal attention. Something about typing your own name into the URL space in Netscape really makes you feel important."

Since then Sara has made some modifications to the details, but the original concept remains. For example, each client no longer has an entire set of Presentations slides under his or her URL. Instead, each client still has a personal URL, but it contains a series of property links that match up to his or her individual tastes. This requires that each slide be stored only once on the server. "When a new property becomes available, we scan our client list to see who might be interested," Sara says. "We add a new link to the client's URL, e-mail the client, and they can read about the new property instantly."

"Success has two major components," Sara reflects. "You need an equal mix of substance and the tools to convey that substance." Between her tenacity and WordPerfect Suite, Sara has both aspects covered.

N o doubt you've been exposed to the incredible hype surrounding the Internet and World Wide Web. I'm sure you know that the Internet and World Wide Web provide a crazy, sometimes labyrinthine (love that word!) means of checking out all types of information, ordering products and services, and communicating with others. In this chapter, I give you an overview of the World Wide Web and what you can find there, as well as the basics to get you started using Netscape Navigator, one of the best, easiest tools for checking out the Web.

Reviewing Internet Concepts

I f you've been online before, you know that you use a *browser*, software that allows you to locate and view Web pages on the World Wide Web. Netscape is one of the best browsers available, and it comes free with the WordPerfect Suite. You'll explore its features in more depth in a few minutes.

The Internet itself began as a network of computers related to the Department of Defense and was set up to link researchers, including those from many universities. The Internet went through several transformations, the most recent being the World Wide Web where millions of folks like you and me can access millions of pieces of information with a few mouse clicks. Because of this perceived convergence, many people use the Internet and the World Wide Web interchangeably, as I will do here.

Although I can't give you a course on the Internet here, I can try to give you a few tidbits if you're new to it. First, imagine looking at a map that not only includes criss-crossing streets, but also the buildings situated along those streets. Now imagine the streets are not always running north and south or east and west but sometimes diagonal or even circular. Next, imagine that you can get to a building using a dozen different streets. If you substitute the buildings for Web sites, you have a pretty good idea how the Web is put together.

Why is the Web so popular? For one thing, it holds a wealth of information. Second, it's a place to congregate with others. It's also a place to get stuff you can use on your computer. Following is a list of the most common tasks you'll perform on the Internet:

* **Browse for information.** If you're trying to find out how to deal with your kid's tantrums, how to invest lottery winnings, or are wondering what Joe Morgan's career RBIs were, you can find it here. But Web visitor beware: Anyone can set up a Web site and say anything. If you are doing serious research, make sure your source is valid.

* **Use message boards**. You know those bulletin boards at the grocery store and other locations where people can post an offering of their services or request help? You can read and post messages in a similar fashion using *newsgroups*. Newsgroups are divided based on any topic you can imagine, from Rolling Stone fans to attorneys to teens.

* **Subscribe to mailing lists.** Similar to that catalog you receive in the mail every month, or the newsletter you get from your favorite professional organization, mailing lists provide information to you on a regular basis. Using your e-mail address, you can receive anything from a full-blown newsletter to a brief announcement about a new product. It's easy to subscribe and unsubscribe to mailing lists, and many Web sites indicate how to subscribe to their own lists.

* **Download and upload files**. Need a graphic for your newsletter? Or the latest printer driver? What about an upgrade to your software? Files like these are available for download on numerous sites. I mention several places from which you can get more information or download files in the Web Paths throughout this book. And if you want your colleagues across town to look at the final version of your newsletter, you can upload it for them — or attach it to an e-mail.

* **Send and receive e-mail**. You can send messages to anyone who has e-mail capability and an e-mail address. You can also receive mail from others and read it in Netscape's Mail window. I cover e-mail at the end of this chapter.

* **Have live conversations.** Using *Internet Relay Chat* (IRC), you can have real-time "conversations" with others. Text you type appears in a screen that everyone in the *chat room* can read and respond to immediately. The conversation is inhibited only by your typing ability. Netscape is set up to access such chat locations as TalkCity, and you can access a number of chat lists from the excellent The Ultimate Chat List. For more on chatting, see the Web sites mentioned in this chapter. They contain information for new chatters, as do many other Web sites.

WEB PATH You can find TalkCity at `http://www.talkcity.com` and The Ultimate Chat List at `http://www.chatlist.com`.

Understanding Web Lingo

Before you get started using Netscape to navigate the Web, take a look at some terms you'll encounter. Table 16-1 lists and describes several common acronyms and terms. And no, I won't be giving a test later!

TABLE 16-1 Web Terminology

Term	Description
HTML	HyperText Markup Language is the underlying language for Web documents.
ISP	An Internet Service Provider gives you access to the Internet via its own network.
HTTP	The HyperText Transport Protocol is the transfer method for Web documents over the Web. This is what brings you to the home page of Maine Lobster Direct (`http://www.maine.com/lobsters`) or information on Corel's new products (`http://www.corel.com`).
JAVA	Though not found in a steaming mug, Java is still very hot. It's a computer language that isn't dependent on a particular application. Java programs enhance Web pages beyond the restrictions of HTML, and much of the animation and interactive elements of a Web page is Java at work.

(continued)

TABLE 16-1   Web Terminology (*continued*)

Term	Description
FTP	File Transfer Protocol is the means by which files are transferred on the Internet. When you use FTP, you are going to a place where you can download files for your own use. Often you will simply click on a Web page hyperlink for a file you wish to download, and the Web site will use FTP to get you to the download area.
URL	A Uniform Resource Locator is an address, usually beginning with *www* and ending in one of the many identifiers such as *com* (company), *org* (organization), or *net* (network). The URL for FTP sites begins with *ftp://*.
IRC	Internet Relay Chat allows you to "talk" in real time with other online folks. Think of it as the Internet's version of the CB radio. Others can "listen in" (called *lurking*) without contributing or making conversation.
TELNET	Telnet allows you to log on to another computer remotely, usually with a username and password, and have access to the system as if you were there. Telnet is most often required for getting on to library computers and other restricted systems.
USENET	Usenet combines with newsgroups to form what many people call electronic bulletin boards where people can share ideas, ask questions, and get answers.
BOOKMARK	Similar to marking your spot in a book you're reading, you can add a URL to a list so you can return to it later without having to remember the URL.
HYPERTEXT LINKS	Also called *hyperlinks* and *hot spots*, these are the areas on a Web page that allow you to jump to another page or site. When you point to either a text or graphic link, your pointer turns into a hand pointer. Text links will appear underlined, colored, or both.
HOME PAGE	The first page on a Web site; usually it welcomes the visitor and offers a table of contents in text or graphic form.
SEARCH ENGINE	A program that helps you locate sites related to a particular topic. Though not as precise as the Find and Replace Text feature in the WordPerfect Suite applications, search engines are invaluable for locating Web sites.

Getting Connected

To access these wonderful things, you must have a few basic pieces of equipment and tools. First, you'll need a modem, which comes preinstalled on most systems these days. Next, you need to make sure your modem is connected to a phone line and that you have an ISP. For a list of reliable service providers, ask colleagues, friends, or family for recommendations or check out the large commercial providers, such as the Microsoft Network, AT&T WorldNet, IBM Global Network, and SprintLink. You will also find a list in your Yellow Pages. Costs vary.

 Find out about the Microsoft Network at http://www.msn.com, **AT&T WorldNet at** http://www.worldnet.att.net, **IBM Global Network at** http://www.ibm.com/globalnetwork, **and SprintLink at** http://www.sprint.net. **Netscape provides information about selecting an ISP. Check out** http://home.netscape.com **and search for** *ISP*.

If you select the Microsoft Network as your provider, use Windows' online help to step through the process of getting connected. If you select another ISP, that company should provide you with instructions on setting up your connections using Windows Dial-Up Networking. To get information in Help, click Start on the Windows taskbar and select Help. On the Index tab, type **connecting** and double-click either to the Internet or to the Microsoft Network.

Installing and Using Netscape Navigator

Netscape Navigator doesn't install automatically when you install the WordPerfect Suite. Nor does Windows 95 set up connections for you. You must do both of these before you can use Netscape.

Installing Netscape

To use Netscape as your Web browser, you must install it from the WordPerfect Suite CD. First, use My Computer or the Windows Explorer to locate your CD-ROM drive. Next, right-click the CD-ROM drive and select AutoPlay from the QuickMenu. You'll see the WordPerfect Suite 8 Applications Disc dialog box. Click the Netscape Setup button to display the Netscape Setup dialog box (see Figure 16-1). If prompted, click Yes to continue and follow the on screen instructions. When Netscape has completed installation, you should see its icon on the Windows Desktop.

16

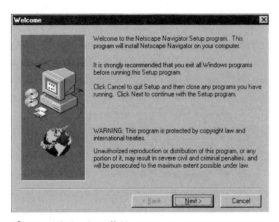

Figure 16-1 Install Netscape on your computer.

Starting Netscape

Once you've installed Netscape and set up your connection for Dial-Up Networking, double-click the Netscape icon. When you see the Connect To dialog box, fill in your username and password so you don't have to enter it the next time. Make sure you choose the Save password check box and then click Connect. Netscape will connect to the Internet, displaying the Netscape home page if no other home page is specified in Options (see Figure 16-2). Note that Web pages change constantly so the pages you see represented in this chapter will no doubt look different when you visit the site.

Directory buttons   Netscape icon

Toolbar   URL for current page   menubar   Scroll bar

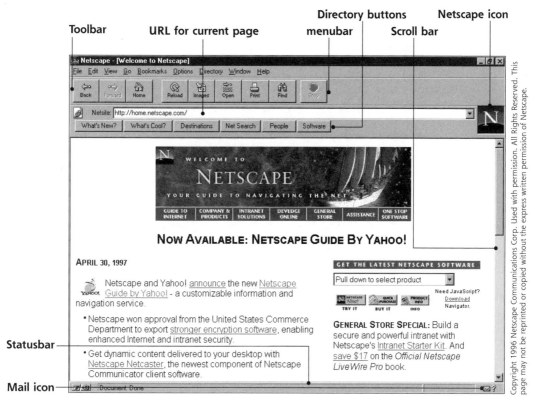

Statusbar

Mail icon

Figure 16-2   Learn more about Netscape on its home page.

Understanding the Netscape Window

The Netscape Navigator window has familiar elements — menu bar, toolbar, vertical scroll bar, and status bar. Because the toolbar is defaulted to display text and icons, it's easy to figure out the purpose of each button. However, if you're new to Netscape and browsing the Web, check out Table 16-2 for an explanation of the toolbar buttons.

TABLE 16-2   Toolbar Buttons

Button	Description
Back	Previous Web page
Forward	Next Web page
Home	Return to the default home page set in General Preferences.
Reload	Reload the current page.
Images	Load all images on the current page.

(continued)

TABLE 16-2 Toolbar Buttons (continued)

Button	Description
Open	Open a Web page by entering a URL.
Print	Print all or part of the current Web page.
Find	Locate text on the current Web page.
Stop	Stop loading the current document.

Following are some things you should know about the Netscape window:

* The *Netsite* box will display the URL of the current page. You can also type a URL directly into this box.

* The *QuickLink* button lets you drag the current URL to your bookmark list (explained later in this chapter) or copy it to the Clipboard so you can paste it into a document.

* The *Directory buttons* provide quick access to services and features.

* The *Netscape icon* will animate when the system is loading a document or performing some task. You'll see comets hurling across the *N* until the task is complete. You can also click this icon to go directly to Netscape's home page.

* The *status bar* will also provide information on what is happening at any given time.

* The *mail icon* gives you quick access to your Mail window and any waiting messages you may have.

Getting Where You Want to Go

So you're staring at either Netscape's or possibly your service provider's home page. Now what? You want to know how to get to all those wonderful places you keep hearing about, right? Well, you have two options. If you know the address you can type it in and press Enter. If you don't, you can do a search.

Typing the URL

If you know your best friend's phone number or have her number in front of you, you can punch in the numbers on your phone. It's the same way with the Internet. If you flip this book over you'll see a red bar near the bottom of the cover. That's the URL for IDG Books Worldwide. Go ahead, try it.

TIP Netscape assumes that the URL begins with http:// so you don't need to type this. If you're going to an FTP location, you'll need to type **ftp://** before the site's address.

Click in the Netsite box. Notice Netscape selects the entire address in the box. Type **www.idgbooks.com** and press Enter. You can also click again so you see the insertion point in the Netsite box and then select and replace existing text. If you check the status bar, you see that Netscape is trying a connection and when it connects, you'll see a message to that effect. Netscape will display the IDG Books home page (Figure 16-3).

If Netscape displays a message box telling you the URL doesn't exist, make sure you've entered it correctly, with the correct spelling and punctuation.

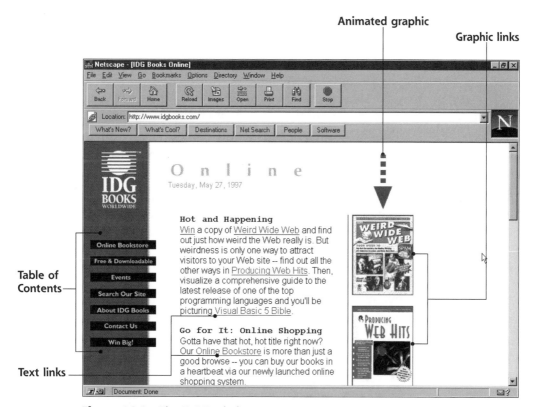

Figure 16-3 The IDG Books home page.

WHERE HAVE ALL THE PICTURES GONE?

Netscape is defaulted *not* to display all graphics on the page, so pages will load faster. However, many sites now use graphic images to list their contents and other important information. If you want the option to load graphics on different pages, leave the default as is and click the Images button on the toolbar. Alternatively, choose | View | → | Loaded Images | or press Ctrl+I. If you want images to load all the time, choose | Options | → | Loaded Images |. Keep in mind that it will take longer for Netscape to load pages when you select this option.

Navigating a Web Page

Once Netscape has loaded a page, you can do all kinds of things. If you see a hyperlink, point to it so the pointer turns into a hand. When you click on it, Netscape will jump to the associated page or site. If text isn't underlined but appears in a series of boxes as it does on the left side of the IDG home page, you can be pretty sure these are hyperlinks. But you can always point to text or graphics to make sure. Remember, the hand pointer is your indication that text or a graphic is linked to another page or Web site, and, when the hand pointer is displayed, the URL of the linked page will display on the status bar.

Use the Back and Forward buttons on the toolbar to go between pages. Refer back to Table 16-2 for more on these and other buttons.

TIP   **Want to return to a place you visited several pages ago? Rather than use the Back button, choose Window→History or press Ctrl+H to display a list of your last several pages. Double-click the site you want to visit and click Close to close the History window.**

If you'd rather not read the document now, you can save it for later viewing. When you save it as an HTML document, open it in Netscape later to read it without connecting to the Web. Or, if you prefer the printed page to staring at your monitor, print the document.

Searching for Sites

If you're a sports fanatic and want to get stats on your favorite athlete, there are hundreds of sites available. But what are their addresses? This is where search engines come in. Remember, a search engine is a software program that helps you locate Web pages and sites containing certain topics. Search engines are not an exact science, and some seem to come up with matches better than others. For example, searching for the word *sports* could yield thousands and thousands of pages. Looking for *football* will narrow it somewhat, as would any other particulars you can think of.

Many search engines have categories on their home pages to get you started with your search. These categories may include such topics as Arts, Business, Entertainment, Health, News, and Sports. You can then access these topics to further narrow your search.

Also, many require that the sites register with them so your search will only locate what's on that search engine's site. This can be quite helpful if you're looking for commercial bungee jumping outfitters and don't want to be bothered with listings for someone's personal home page detailing his or her best bungee-jumping experience. However, if you don't want to leave any page unturned, consider Lycos, Infoseek, Hotbot, or WebCrawler, all of which wander the Web indexing URLs. There are a number of good books explaining the different search engines, including Dave Taylor's *Creating Cool HTML 3.2 Web Pages, 3rd Edition* (IDG Books). You may want to take a look at these to help you determine which search engines will work best for you. I say *engines* because they often give different results. It's a good idea to search for the same thing using different engines to see what you come up with.

To search for a site, follow these steps:

1. Click the Net Search button. Netscape will connect to its Internet search page (see Figure 16-4).

2. Select a search engine from the list if you don't want to use the current one.

3. In the Search box, type the topic for which you want to search and press Enter or click the Search or Seek button.

TIP Some search engines are better than others at locating your topic. To make sure you get as close as possible to your target topic, include it in quotes or connect it with plus signs so the engine won't pull up everything with either of the words on the page. For example, if you want to locate sites on bungee jumping, type **"bungee jumping"** to locate pages that contain that phrase, or type **"bungee+jumping"** to locate pages containing either *bungee* or *jumping*, but not necessarily together as a phrase.

Enter search criteria   Current search engine

Select a different
search engine

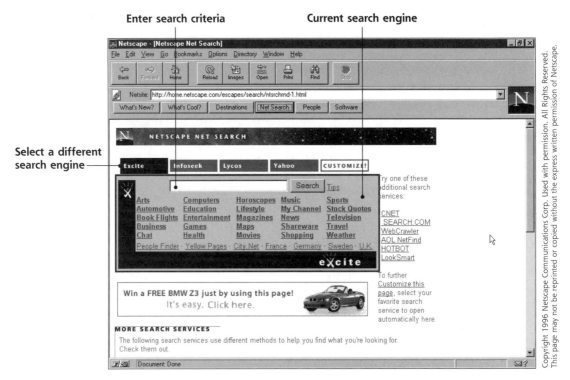

Figure 16-4   Choose a search engine to locate related Web sites.

Using Bookmarks to Keep Your Place

As I mentioned, bookmarks allow you to "mark your spot on the Internet," giving you a quick, easy way to return to a site that's helpful. Netscape comes with
a few folders and bookmarks installed. You can use these or get rid of them.
For information on keeping your bookmarks organized, see "Organizing Your
Bookmarks" later in this section.

ADDING A BOOKMARK

The most frequent task you'll perform when it comes to bookmarks is adding
them to your Bookmark list. You can add a bookmark using any of the following
methods:

* With the address you want to add in the Netsite box, choose
  Bookmarks → Add Bookmarks or press Ctrl+D. This adds the bookmark to
  the bottom of the bookmark list.

* With the address you want to add in the Netsite box, click the Restore
  button in the Netscape window to decrease the window size — you must
  do this so that you can see both the Netscape window and Bookmark
  window at the same time or this method won't work. Choose Window →
  Bookmarks or press Ctrl+B to display the Bookmark window. Click the

QuickLink button in the Netscape window and drag to the destination folder in the Bookmark window.

✳ Choose `Window` → `Bookmarks` or press Ctrl+B to display the Bookmark window. Select the folder that will contain the bookmark and choose `Item` → `Insert Bookmarks` on the Bookmark menu. Type a name, URL, and description and click OK.

TIP   **If you added the wrong bookmark or have a bookmark you no longer need, you can delete it. Choose Window→Bookmarks or press Ctrl+B to display the Bookmark window, select the bookmark, and press Delete.**

USING A BOOKMARK

Once you've added a bookmark to your list, you can access it anytime. Make sure you're connected to the Web, choose Bookmarks, and select a bookmark from the menu. If you don't see your bookmark on the Bookmark menu, choose More Bookmarks at the bottom of the menu to display the Bookmark window. Double-click the bookmark.

ORGANIZING YOUR BOOKMARKS

Earlier I mentioned that the Bookmark window contains folders in which you can store various bookmarks. But what if none of the existing folders fits the bookmark you want to store? Or you want to move a bookmark to another, more appropriate folder? You can do all of this easily. Choose Window → Bookmarks or press Ctrl+B to display the Bookmark window. Note that a plus sign (+) on a folder indicates that the folder is *collapsed* and contains items and/or subfolders. A minus sign (-) indicates that the folder is *expanded* and displaying its entire contents.

Use any of the following techniques to organize bookmarks:

✳ To move a folder or bookmark, simply click and drag it to its new location. You'll see a box attach to the pointer. When you release the mouse button, the item will drop in *after* the selected item. When you move a folder, its entire content goes along for the ride.

✳ To insert a new folder, select the folder which the new folder will *follow* (the *target* folder). Be sure that this folder is collapsed (you see the plus sign). Choose `Item` → `Insert Folder`, type a name for the folder and click OK. To display the contents of the collapsed target folder, click on its plus sign to change it to a minus sign. Note that if you insert a folder while the target folder is expanded, the new folder becomes a subfolder of the target folder.

You can do lots of other things with bookmarks, including adding separator lines, creating separate lists (for example, personal bookmarks and professional bookmarks), and more. While you are connected to the Internet, choose Help→Handbook on the Netscape main window to get more information.

TIP You select bookmarks just as you select many items in the WordPerfect 8 Suite. To select several bookmarks in succession, select the first bookmark, then press and hold Shift and select the last bookmark. To select non-consecutive bookmarks, press and hold Ctrl and select each bookmark.

Using E-Mail

N ow that you've checked out some cool Web sites, you'll want to start communicating with your online pals. Netscape's Mail feature allows you to send and receive messages, as well as store them on your hard drive.

Your Internet Service Provider maintains one or more *servers*, computers that control the flow of Internet traffic for its subscribers as well as storing e-mail messages delivered to them but not retrieved. Once you retrieve messages from the server into your Inbox, they are transferred to your hard drive and no longer reside on the server. It's like going to your mailbox and picking up your mail. Once you pick it up, your mailbox is empty, as is your electronic mailbox on your ISP's server. If you don't pick up your mail, it sits in your box until you pick it up. If you get more mail, it's added to what's already there.

Before you continue, take a second to review the status of the mail icon on your status bar. A question mark (?) next to this icon indicates Netscape hasn't checked for messages recently. An exclamation point (!) alerts you to new messages on the server. If there isn't anything next to the icon, you have no new messages.

Displaying the Mail Window

To access your mail, click the Mail icon on the status bar in the main Netscape window, or choose Window→Mail to display the Mail window (see Figure 16-5). Depending on how your system is set up, you may need to enter your e-mail password (which your ISP should have assigned to you). Notice that you can adjust the size of the different panes; I've increased the size of the message content pane in Figure 16-5 so I can read more of the message at once.

TIP To make sure you don't have to enter your password every time you open the Mail window, choose Options→Mail and News Preferences. Select the Organization tab and choose the Remember Mail Password check box. If you want Netscape to check for mail while you're logged on, choose the Servers tab and choose Every, next to Check for Mail. Indicate the number of minutes between checks and click OK.

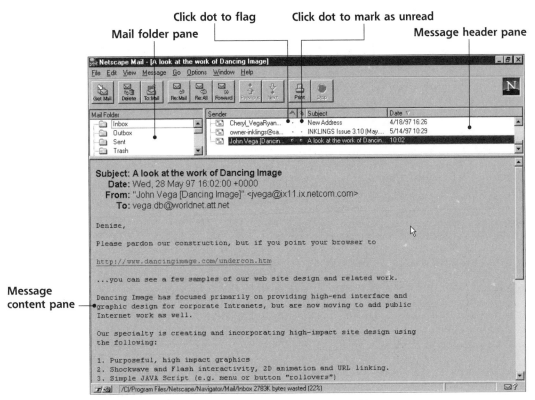

Figure 16-5 Work with incoming and outgoing mail.

Note that whenever you open the Mail window, Netscape will check the server for new messages. If you have new messages, you'll see a message on the status bar indicating Netcape is loading them. If you have no new messages, Netscape will display a message to that effect. Just click OK to continue.

TIP **If you can't see all the headings in a pane, adjust the various pane widths and the headings within panes by clicking and dragging the separators between them.**

The Mail window has is own menu and toolbar. Table 16-3 gives a description of Mail toolbar buttons. Notice that the Mail window contains three *panes*, which are as follows:

＊ The *mail folder pane* contains the folders you use to store messages. The Inbox contains incoming messages; the Outbox contains all messages that need to be sent (if you have the Deferred Delivery option selected); the Sent folder contains all messages you've sent; and the Trash contains messages you delete. Note that you can also add folders to this pane. See "Managing Your Messages" later in this chapter.

* The *message header pane* lists the messages for the selected folder, showing you the sender's name, the subject, and the date and time the message was sent.

* The *message content pane* contains the actual text of the message you select in the message header pane.

TABLE 16-3 Mail Window Toolbar

Button	Description
Get Mail	Check the ISP server for new mail.
Delete	Delete the selected message(s).
To: Mail	Send a new message.
Re: Mail	Reply to the primary sender of the selected message.
Re: All	Reply to the primary sender of the selected message and any other recipients.
Forward	Forward the selected message to another user or users.
Previous	Display the previous *unread* message in the message content pane.
Next	Display the next *unread* message in the message content pane.
Print	Print the current message.
Stop	Stops any current transfer of a message, either sending or receiving.

Sending a Message

Once you're familiar with the Mail window, you can begin sending messages to friends, family, and colleagues. The only thing you need is the person's e-mail address.

Once you have that, follow these steps to send a message:

1. Click the To: Mail button on the toolbar or choose File →
   New Mail Message to display the Message Composition window (see Figure 16-6). This is where you indicate the recipient of your message, it's subject, and the body of the message.

2. In the Mail To text box, type the *e-mail address* of the recipient.

3. Press Tab two times or click in the Subject text box. Type a subject for the message. Keep it brief and to the point; the subject should give the recipient an indication of what the body of the message contains.

Click to select an
address

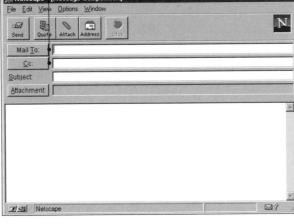

Figure 16-6   Create a new message.

4. Press Tab or click in the Message area and type the text for your
message.

5. Click the Send button to send the message immediately. To defer sending
to a later time — perhaps you'd like to compose several messages and send
them all at once — choose Options → Deferred Delivery and click the Send
button. Netscape places the message in the Out Box folder. When you're
ready to send deferred messages, choose File → Send Messages in Out Box
or press Ctrl+H.

Netscape saves a copy of every message you send in the Sent folder. Consider
setting up folders that help organize your messages and group them together.
See "Managing Your Messages" later in this section.

SIDE TRIP

Some Useful E-Mail Stuff

If you have several messages to send, consider composing them offline and deferring
delivery to save connect time. Also, rather than typing e-mail addresses each time you
create a new message, you can copy e-mail addresses for recipients into Netscape's
Address Book. See "Using the Address Book" later in the chapter.

You can attach a file to your message using the Attachment button in the Message
Composition window. Just locate and select the file you wish to attach and select any
options. Depending on the capabilities of the recipient, you may have to send it as a
text file so that he or she will be able to read the attachment.

16

Receiving a Message

No doubt your service provider has sent you a welcome message or someone you gave your address to has sent you a message. Messages you haven't read are indicated as **boldface** in the Message header pane for your Inbox. To read a message, click the message header in the message header pane. The text of the message will appear in the message content pane, and you can scroll down to read it. Once you've read a message you have three options — you can reply to it, delete it, or move it to another folder.

Replying to Messages

If you want to reply to a message you've received, make sure it's selected in the message header pane and then click the Re: Mail button on the toolbar. You'll see the Reply window, which is identical to the Message Composition window except that the recipient is already filled in. Netscape knows who sent you the message and automatically inserts the person's address in the Mail To text box and also places the body of the sender's message into the Message area, positioning the insertion point after the end of it. Complete the message with a subject and content. Then click the Send button.

Managing Your Messages

After you begin sending and receiving messages, you'll find your folders getting full. It may be difficult to find a message to which you need to refer. By default, Netscape stores all incoming messages in your Inbox folder and a copy of all outgoing messages in the Sent folder. Messages you delete appear in the Trash folder. You can create your own folders in which to store messages so you can group related messages together. This is especially helpful if you want to follow the thread of a conversation between yourself and another individual. Say you're corresponding with several people at Acme, Inc., regarding potential work. You can create a folder called *Acme* and move messages you sent to Acme people from the Sent folder to the Acme folder. You can also move messages from Acme people in the Inbox folder to the Acme folder.

To add a new folder to your mail folders pane, choose File→New Folder. In the Netscape User Prompt box, type a name for the folder and click OK. Netscape automatically inserts it alphabetically in the mail folders pane.

You can move or copy messages to folders by selecting them first and dragging them to the destination folder. Alternatively, you can select them and choose Message→Move or Message→Copy. Then select the destination folder.

If you no longer need a message or folder, you can delete it. To delete either one, select it, and press Delete. Netscape places the deleted item in the Trash folder. This works like the Recycle Bin in Windows, allowing you to retrieve a deleted message from the Trash if necessary. However, if you don't need messages in the trash, you should empty the Trash folder periodically to keep it from overflowing. To delete messages in the Trash, choose File→Empty Trash Folder or display the Trash folder contents, select the messages you wish to delete, and press Delete. Note that if you want to delete a *folder*, you must empty the entire contents of the folder first.

Working with Addresses

If you're becoming annoyed at having to type your correspondent's e-mail address every time you want to send a message, fear not. Just as you maintain a list of favorite sites in your Bookmark window, you can maintain a list of e-mail addresses in Netscape's Address window.

ADDING A NEW ADDRESS

If you have addresses scribbled on scraps of paper, get them into your Address Book before you lose them. Choose Window→Address Book to display the Address window.

Here you can work with existing names or add new ones:

1. If you have existing names, select the name you wish the new name to follow.

2. Choose Item → Add User to display the Properties tab in the Address Book dialog box (see Figure 16-7).

3. In the Nick Name text box, type a nick name (for example, Jenny or Joe), then press Tab. Handy tip: When you want to send mail to this person, type the nick name in the Mail To text box in the Message Composition window. When you press Tab, Netscape will expand it to include the full name and e-mail address.

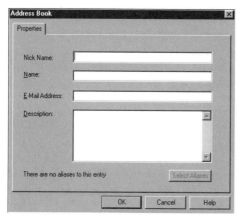

Figure 16-7   Maintain a list of e-mail addresses.

4. Type the person's full name in the Name box. This is the name that will appear in the Address Book list as well as in the Mail To text box along with the e-mail address.

5. Press Tab and type the person's address in the E-Mail Address text box. If you need a reminder of who the person is, enter a description and click OK.

COPYING AN ADDRESS FROM AN EXISTING MESSAGE

If you received a message from someone and you'd like to add her name to your Address list, select the message in the message header pane and choose Message→Add to Address Book.

USING THE ADDRESS BOOK

When you want to use an address from the Address Book, click the Send button on the Mail toolbar and use one of the following methods:

* Type the nick name you assigned to the person and press Tab.
* Click the Mail To or Cc button and then double-click the person's name in the Address Book window.

You can send a message to multiple recipients, putting all the addresses in the Mail To text box, or having one or two primary recipients and placing the remaining recipients in the Cc text box.

As I mentioned in the preface, your WordPerfect Suite 8 shipped with a voucher or coupon that allows you to obtain CorelCENTRAL and Netscape Communicator when they become available. If you send for CorelCENTRAL and Netscape Communicator, you'll have one Address Book for everything, including e-mail addresses. Remember that you can download a chapter on these applications from the IDG Books Worldwide Web site. Once you've received CorelCENTRAL and Netscape Communicator, go to http://www.idgbooks.com

and search for *Discover WordPerfect Suite 8* for information on downloading the chapter. Since this chapter covers Netscape Navigator 3.0, the online chapter will cover only those parts of Netscape Navigator 4.0 that differ substantially from Version 3.0. The rest of the online chapter will cover the other Netscape Communicator tools and CorelCENTRAL.

BONUS

Getting the News

Earlier I described a newsgroup as an electronic bulletin board of sorts, where you can read and post messages for particular topics. You can check out newsgroups and decide if they're something you want to be a part of by exploring a few right now.

Choose Window→Netscape News to display the Netscape News window. It looks similar to the Mail window with a newsgroups folder pane on the left, a message header pane on the right, and a message content pane at the bottom. Netscape will display a couple of default News Server folders. To display their contents, simply click the folder. A list of messages will appear in the message header pane.

To display a more comprehensive list of newsgroups, choose Options→Show All Newsgroups. Then clean up your desk, take a walk, or go get a drink because this could take awhile. When Netscape is finished loading the Newsgroups, their folders will appear in the Net Server folders pane (see Figure 16-8).

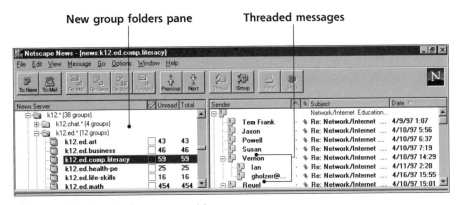

Figure 16-8 Get the latest news with newsgroups.

You'll quickly discover that messages in a newsgroup are *threaded*, which means that they connect because of a common theme. You'll see this displayed graphically in the message header pane because related, or threaded, messages appear next to the original message. To read a message, just click it in the message header pane; the text will display in the message content pane.

Most newsgroups provide some hints as to the nature of the topic. For example, *rec* relates to recreational activities and *comp* deals with computer-related topics. Keep in mind that newsgroups beginning with *alt* can run the gamut of topics, from innocent Elvis fan clubs to the truly strange and bizarre. Proceed with care! Read several messages before deciding if you really want to *subscribe* to a newsgroup. That's the best way to determine if it's worth your while.

If you decide to subscribe, click the check box next to the newsgroup in the newsgroup folder pane. When you subscribe to a newsgroup, you're asking Netscape to display the newsgroup's folder name and load it every time you display the Netscape News window. When you've ready to post your own message in a newsgroup, click the To: News button on the toolbar and continue as for creating a mail message.

Once you start subscribing to newsgroups, make sure you've changed your options back to showing only subscribed newsgroups. Choose Options→Show Subscribed Newsgroups. That way, Netscape isn't loading everything when you only want to see the newsgroups to which you've subscribed.

Summary

After this quick tour of Internet concepts and Netscape Navigator, you're pretty Internet savvy. You learned about crazy acronyms and abbreviations like URL and FTP, as well as the ins and outs of opening Web pages and navigating around in them. You learned how to save your favorite Web sites in the Bookmarks window and check out the wonders of e-mail. Next up: creating your own Web documents with Internet Publisher.

CHAPTER SEVENTEEN

DESIGNING WEB PAGES WITH INTERNET PUBLISHER

IN THIS CHAPTER YOU LEARN THESE KEY SKILLS

This chapter assumes you have read Chapter 16 and are comfortable with a browser and know how to use it to go online. Here you focus on designing a page that you or someone else would use on a Web site. You create a Web page in WordPerfect using Internet Publisher. To convert files from other applications such as Presentations or Quattro Pro, see "Getting Your Documents on the Web" at the end of the chapter.

Understanding Web Page Concepts

In Chapter 16 you learned a number of Internet terms. Here's a review of those that pertain to Web pages and their design. Remember, home is where the start is; that is, a *home page* is where you will usually begin when you visit a site for the first time. This is your welcome desk, and usually it provides an index or table of contents to help the visitor navigate the site. You can use text, graphics, lines, and tables on a Web site, as well as animation, to get your message across. Web pages can contain *hyperlinks*, sometimes called "hot spots," which allow the visitor to bounce to other areas of the page or to another page on the site with a single click. Hyperlinks for text are indicated by colored text with an underline; hyperlinks for graphics will be indistinguishable until you point and see the mouse pointer change to a pointing finger.

Although Web pages are built in a language called HTML — *HyperText Markup Language* — you don't have to have anything to do with it using the Internet Publisher. You work in Internet Publisher just as you would a WordPerfect document, and Internet Publisher automatically converts everything you create into HTML.

Because of the unique nature of HTML, there are certain things you cannot do when designing your Web page. Most of these have to do with fonts and font sizes, graphic types, and certain font attributes. Internet Publisher takes out most of the guesswork because it provides only those tools and options that will convert to HTML.

Before you begin creating your page, consider looking at some of the many books (and Web sites!) on designing an effective Web page and site. There are many things to consider, including what you want to accomplish with your site, what your image is, and how you should combine text, lines, and graphics for the most effective presentation.

FEATURE FOCUS To avoid any restrictions, you can create your document in WordPerfect or use the Internet Publisher, then publish it using Barista technology. Barista retains all formatting in the document and allows you to explode HTML barriers. For information, see "Getting Your Documents on the Web" later in this chapter.

Creating a Web Page with Internet Publisher

I t's time to turn into an eight-legged creature and start spinning away. Keep in mind that Web pages usually have some common elements to help visitors figure out what's what. These elements include a page title, a brief description of the page or, if you're creating the home page, a description of the site as well. You'll also want to include some kind of table of contents or other map so visitors can get around easily.

Using the Web Editor

As I mentioned, WordPerfect's Internet Publisher lets you create a document using familiar WordPerfect features and then converts the document to a Web document. Let's get started.

To create a Web document in WordPerfect, start at a blank new document and follow these steps:

1. Choose File → New to display the New dialog box.

2. On the Create New tab, click the down arrow button and choose Web or Web Publishing.

3. In the list, double-click WordPerfect Web Document or select WordPerfect Web Document and click Create. WordPerfect displays a barren gray page, the Internet Publisher toolbar, the Internet Publisher property bar, and the Internet Publisher Perfect Expert (see Figure 17-1). This is called the Web Editor. See Table 17-1 for a description of the buttons that are unique to both the toolbar and property bar.

Internet Publisher PerfectExpert

Document window

Internet Publisher toolbar

Internet Publisher property bar

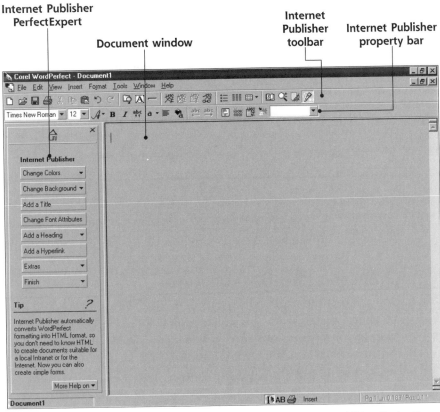

Figure 17-1 Create your Web page with help from the Internet Publisher PerfectExpert.

TABLE 17-1 Internet Publisher Tools

Toolbar Buttons

Button	Name	Description
	HORIZONTAL LINE	Insert a standard horizontal divider line.
	BROWSE THE WEB	Connect to the WWW.
	VIEW IN WEB BROWSER	Display your page as it will appear in your browser.
	PUBLISH TO HTML	Convert your document to a "Web ready" document.
	HYPERLINK	Add a link or insert a bookmark.
	INSERT BULLET	Create a bulleted list.

Property Bar Buttons

Button	Name	Description
	FONT/SIZE	Select a font and size.
	MONOSPACED	Turn the monospaced feature on and off.
	FONT ATTRIBUTES	Select an attribute such as bold or italics.
	NEW FORM	Create a Web page form.
	CREATE APPLET	Create a Java applet.
	HTML DOCUMENT PROPERTIES	Set Web properties for the selected item.
	INSERT SYMBOL	Insert a symbol or character.

Once you're in the Web Editor, you can change the page background, enter text, add graphics and horizontal lines, and create or edit links to the document.

Changing the Background

Don't like that drab background in the Web Editor? You can change it to another color or even a texture, which WordPerfect refers to as the *wallpaper*. Keep in mind that you want your text to show up on top of it, so select a nice contrast color that's muted and doesn't hurt visitors' eyes. You can change either the color or the texture, but not both.

To change the background, use one of the following methods:

* To change the background color, click the Change Colors button on the Internet Publisher PerfectExpert panel and select a color.

* To change the background texture, click the Change Background button on the Internet Publisher PerfectExpert panel to display a palette of textures. Select a background texture.

If you don't see the color or background you like, use the Custom option for either Change Colors or Change Background and select an option on the Text/Background Colors tab in the HTML Document Properties dialog box.

WEB
PATH   **Check out some additional textures at Texture Land,** `http://www.meat.com/textures`.

Working with Web Page Text

As I mentioned before, you do have some formatting restrictions when it comes to text, including font size and attributes. Note that some fonts may not display as you planned because the visitor's browser may not support them.

Adding and Formatting Text

The first thing you'll want to do is add a heading, or title, to your page. The title is often the first thing a visitor sees when he or she displays your Web site and should convey immediately who you are and what you do. It could be something as simple as the name of your company or a "Welcome to . . ." type heading. Make it short and to the point. Headings on Web pages often work like outlines, with each subsequent heading getting smaller in size. You can use the Heading button on the Internet Publisher PerfectExpert panel or use the Heading styles in the Font/Size list to format your headings.

To add a heading, click Add a Heading on the Internet Publisher PerfectExpert panel or click the Font/Size button on the Internet Publisher property bar and select the desired heading style. Remember, use Heading 1 for the first heading (usually the title) and subsequent heading styles for subtopics. Next, type the text for your heading. To change the alignment, make sure the insertion point is inside the heading. Then click the Justification button on the Internet Publisher property bar and choose the desired justification. If you plan to have a graphic with your title, consider using left or right justification for the title and placing the graphic on the opposite side.

Next, type any introductory paragraphs below the title. These could be a brief overview of yourself or your company, the purpose of your site, and other explanatory information you want visitors to know.

TITLE TRIVIA

By default, the title bar in the browser will display the text you've typed as your first heading. However, if you want the browser title bar to display something different than your first heading, you can enter a specific title for the title bar. To do this, click Add a Title on the Internet Publisher PerfectExpert panel to display the Title tab in the HTML Document Properties dialog box. Choose Custom title and type the title you want to appear on the browser title bar. Click OK. You'll see the title you typed on WordPerfect's title bar. When you preview your page, you'll see it on your browser title bar, as will visitors.

Working with Bulleted Lists

You saw in WordPerfect and on Presentations slides how a bulleted list can provide a snapshot of information. Many Web sites use bulleted lists to introduce various sections or pages for the site, doubling as a table of contents.

To add a bulleted list to your Web page, position the insertion point in the location for the list, then click the Bullet button on the Internet Publisher toolbar. WordPerfect inserts the first bullet for your list. Type the text for the first bulleted item and press Enter. Continue adding bulleted items to your list in this way. You can also add bullets to an existing list.

 WEB PATH WordPerfect uses a standard bullet for its bulleted lists. To get fancier bullets, you can use tiny graphics. Check out `http://www.cbil.vco.edu:8080/gifs/bullet.html` or `http://www.dewa.com/FREEICON`.

Adding Lines and Graphics

You may have a lot to say about yourself, but if you have too much text on your pages, visitors may jump to another site (you certainly don't want that). Break up your text with horizontal lines and add graphics to reinforce your message. Remember that your graphics can double as links to other parts of your page or site.

Adding a Line

Horizontal lines help separate different sections of your document to make them more readable. To insert a horizontal line, position the insertion point in the location for the line and click the Horizontal Line button on the Internet Publisher toolbar. You can click and drag the line to a new location, resize it, or change its length and thickness. Note that if you increase its thickness, the line will appear as a recessed bar. Play around with it to get the effect you want.

 X-REF   For more on formatting lines, see Chapter 6.

 WEB PATH   In addition to bullets, you can find a wonderful array of bars that you can use instead of horizontal lines at `http://www2.firstsaga.com/chris/clipart/clipart.html` or `http://www.vmedia.com/commodity/clipart/bb`.

Working with Graphics

If you read Chapter 16 and browsed the Web, you saw how many sites contain graphics. Graphics add life to a document, providing color and excitement to what otherwise would be a dull page. It's important to remember that graphics should *enhance* your text, not replace or overshadow it. Some graphics may stand alone as information tools (such as a picture of a product) but many are decorative. Make sure the graphics you select are appropriate for your site. If your tone is fairly serious, don't use cartoonish images. A good rule of thumb — less is more. Too many graphics can clutter your site and make it hard to navigate. Not only that, graphics slow down the display and if your visitors are impatient, they may go elsewhere before they've seen your wonderful pages.

Web documents can only use two types of graphics — GIF (CompuServe's Graphics Interchange Format) or JPEG (Joint Photographic Expert Group) format. Oh, no! you say. But I wanted to use one of the images on the Corel CD-ROM, and it's in WPG format. Not a problem. You can insert any graphic into your Web document, and WordPerfect will automatically convert it to one of the correct formats so visitors can see it.

INSERTING A GRAPHIC

Take a look at your text to determine how many graphics you think you want and where you'll place them. Don't worry too much if you don't like the first place you put them; you can always drag them to another location. When you're ready to insert a graphic, here's what to do next.

With your Web document open, click the Clipart button on the Internet Publisher toolbar or choose Insert→Graphics→Clipart. WordPerfect displays the Scrapbook, which you saw in Chapter 6. Next, locate and select the image you wish to use, then secondary-click and drag it into your Web document.

MOVING AND SIZING A GRAPHIC

As I mentioned, if you don't like where you've put a graphic, you can move it. Or if it's too big or too small, you can resize it. To move a graphic, click and drag it to the new location. To resize your graphic, select it to display the sizing handles and use these handles to adjust the size. Refer to Chapter 6 to refresh your memory.

ADDING A PICTURE PLACEHOLDER

Earlier I mentioned that depending on a visitor's browser, he or she may not be able to see the exact font you chose for your title or other headings. In the same way, if visitors aren't using a state-of-the-art browser or are using a slower modem, they may not be able to see your graphics or may opt to turn them off, viewing your page in a "text only" format. When they do this, they will see a graphic placeholder, not the graphic itself. To make sure these visitors don't miss anything, add text to a graphic that visitors will see if the graphic isn't displayed in their browser. This text will appear inside the placeholder when the page loads into their browser (see Figure 17-2).

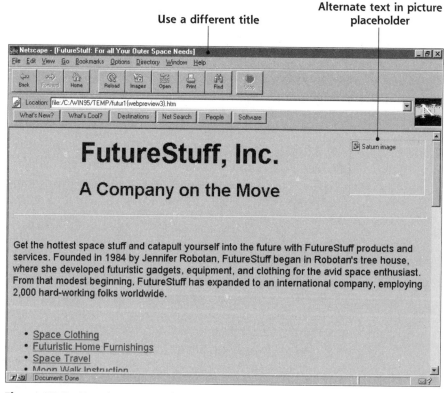

Figure 17-2 Use alternate text for graphics.

To add alternate text for a graphic, follow these steps:

1. Select the graphic in your document and click the Box HTML Properties button on the Internet Publisher Graphic Box property bar. You can also secondary-click the graphic and choose HTML Properties from the QuickMenu. WordPerfect displays the HTML Properties dialog box.

2. On the Image tab, position the insertion point in the Alternate text box and type the text you wish to use.

3. Click OK. The browser will display this text if the graphic is not displayed.

TIP **The alternate text is restricted by the size of the graphic placeholder. If your graphic isn't very big, try to limit your alternate text to make sure it displays in its entirety.**

SIDE TRIP

STRAIGHT ROWS, PLEASE

If you want your text and graphics to show up side by side, you can use columns or tables. To add a column or table to your Web page, position the insertion point and click the Column or Table button on the Internet Publisher toolbar and make your selections. Columns and tables work roughly the same here as they do in a normal WordPerfect document (see Chapters 6 and 7), although there are a number of restrictions when they're in Web documents. Note that not all browsers support columns and tables, so view your columns and tables in different browsers to see what they look like before you decide to use them. If tables seem to work better but you want a column look, remove the lines (borders) from the table.

WEB PATH Another great place to hunt for bullets, bars, and graphics for your Web page is http://www.yahoo.com. Once you're there, click Computers & Internet. Click Graphics and then Web Graphics.

Inserting Hyperlinks

If you've spent time browsing the Web, you know how vital hyperlinks are to getting around. Hyperlinks help you access the information you need quickly and are the backbone of a good Web site. Your hyperlinks allow visitors to jump to those places in your document or on your Web site that interest them most. Remember, you can have either text or graphic links, and you'll look at both of these here.

However, before you can create a link, you must have something to link to. You can link to something in the same document, another document, or another Web site. We'll focus on linking to a section in the same document here, using *bookmarks*. Ah, there's that word again. In Chapter 16, a bookmark allowed you to store a Web page address for future reference. In a Web document, a bookmark will mark a spot or section in the document so you can link to it. Your TV clicker is the perfect hyperlink example. The channel you start on is the link; the channel you go to has a bookmark. You don't have to go through all the channels consecutively to get to channel 24; just press the buttons and you're there.

Creating a Bookmark

The first step in creating a link is to mark those spots in your document that you want visitors to be able to get to quickly. Browse through your document and identify specific locations. For example, you may have a description of products or services, a company or personal biography, or a list of related Web sites. Try to think like a visitor and identify the information you would most like to see. Once you've done that, you can create bookmarks for these locations.

To create a bookmark, follow these steps:

1. Locate and display the text or section that visitors may jump to. For example, if you have a section in the document called "Company History" scroll down until you see it.

2. Select the text you want to use as the bookmark name or position the insertion point in the location for the jump. In other words, the location will appear at the top of the window when they jump to this section.

3. Click the Hyperlink button on the Internet Publisher toolbar and choose Insert Bookmark to display the Create Bookmark dialog box.

4. If you selected text prior to displaying this dialog box, the text will appear in the Bookmark name text box. If you didn't select text, type a name in the box and click OK. WordPerfect adds the bookmark to a list of bookmarks.

5. Create a bookmark for each location you want visitors to be able to jump to, using Steps 1 through 4.

Creating Links

After you've created a bookmark for each location you want visitors to jump to, you're ready to link phrases and graphics to those bookmarks. If you have several separate documents that will make up your Web site, you can link one document to another. Just make sure all your documents contain the necessary bookmarks. When you create the link, indicate the document name and bookmark.

To create a text link, follow these steps:

1. Select the text you wish to use as your link. For example, if you've created a bulleted list on your home page that you wish to use as your table of contents, select the first text item in the list.

2. Click the Hyperlink button on the Internet Publisher toolbar; choose Create Link to display the HyperLink Properties dialog box (Figure 17-3).

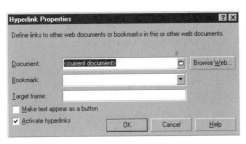

Figure 17-3   Link your text.

3. If you want to jump to another document, use the folder button next to the Document text box to select it. If you want to jump to a Web site, click Browse Web to select the Web site URL.

4. In the Bookmark text box, type the name of the bookmark you want to link to or click the arrow button and select the bookmark name from the drop-down list. Note that WordPerfect will display the bookmarks for the document indicated in the Document text box.

5. If you want your text to appear as a button, choose Make text appear as a button.

6. When you're finished setting link options, click OK. WordPerfect uses the default hyperlink settings to format your text as a link. If you chose to display it as a button, WordPerfect places your text in a button-shaped text box.

TIP   Keep in mind that the more text you select, the easier it is for visitors to jump because they have a wide area on which to click. Also, remember that you can select text within a paragraph, not just text appearing in a bulleted list or by itself on the page.

Viewing Your Page

After you're Web page is looking good, you may want to take a peek to see how it looks from a visitor's perspective. This is helpful to see how your colors look and if things are placed properly. You must have a browser installed before you can continue. If you didn't install Netscape, refer to Chapter 16 and do so before continuing.

To view your document in your Web browser, click the View in Web Browser button on the Internet Publisher toolbar or choose View→View in Web Browser. WordPerfect makes a temporary copy of your document, launches Netscape, and opens your Web document in the Netscape window. Scroll through the document and check for problems in layout and design, then close Netscape when you're finished. You'll return to your document in WordPerfect.

 TIP **If you think you'll want to be previewing your document often, leave Netscape open and return to WordPerfect. When you click the View in Web Browser button, Netscape will reload the document. This is much faster since Netscape itself doesn't have to launch.**

Getting Your Documents on the Web

The WordPerfect Suite provides two ways of getting your documents Web-ready: converting them to HTML or publishing them as is with Barista technology. You'll look at both of these methods here.

Publishing the Document to Web Format

Once your page is just right, you can publish it to Web document format. This means WordPerfect converts it to that HTML language you don't need to know anything about. To publish your document to HTML, click the Publish to HTML button on the Internet Publisher toolbar. Alternatively, you can choose File→Internet Publisher and click Publish to HTML. In the Publish to HTML dialog box, indicate the folders in which you want documents and graphics stored and click OK. WordPerfect displays a message box telling you the conversion is in progress, then returns you to the document. Note that WordPerfect automatically saves your file with an HTM extension.

Note that you don't see the HTML document in the title bar; WordPerfect saves it separately in the folder you specified. Whenever you make changes to the document, you must save it as an HTML document again.

Converting Existing Files to HTML

If you have a WordPerfect document or Presentations slide show you want to use on your Web site, you can publish them as is to HTML. The application will make the necessary changes to make sure it complies with HTML. Because of the nature of a Quattro Pro spreadsheet, you can't convert it to HTML.

To convert a WordPerfect document or a Presentations slide show, simply open the document or slide show in the associated application and choose File→Internet Publisher and click Publish to HTML. In the Publish to HTML dialog box, indicate the folders in which you want the documents and graphics stored and click OK. WordPerfect displays a message box telling you the conversion is in progress, then returns you to the document.

FEATURE FOCUS **Show It! is a new feature in Presentations, enabling you to display your slide show on the Web with all animation and other effects. For information on the Show It! feature, see Presentations online help.**

Converting Files to Barista

Earlier I mentioned that you can publish existing documents to the Web or use Barista technology to transfer a document *en masse*, with no loss of formatting or design. Using Barista frees you from the constraints of HTML because Barista converts the document to the Java language so it isn't tied to your browser, which understands HTML. Java is like a universal language; it doesn't need an interpreter as long as the browser can accept Java documents. You can publish a WordPerfect document, Presentations slide show, or Quattro Pro spreadsheet to Barista.

So if Barista is so great, why publish to HTML? For a couple of reasons, mainly to do with the type of document you want to convert. If you have a lot of graphics on your page or a fancy background, Barista may not convert the nuances of the graphic or the gradients in the background. The more graphical elements you have, the slower your Barista document will load in a browser. This is especially true with Presentations, where gradient or textured backgrounds may look quite a bit different. And Barista also includes any slide transitions, which contribute to slowing the display. Test out a few documents and slide shows in both formats (HTML and Barista) and view them in your browser to determine which works best for you. On the plus side, Barista allows visitors to run your slide show using a special toolbar that displays.

Open the file you wish to publish to Barista, then choose File→Send To→Corel Barista. Next, follow these steps:

1. Make sure the file location is \Corel\Suite8\Shared\Barista. If this isn't the default file, this means Barista isn't installed. Perform a custom install to install it before continuing.

2. If you want to see the converted Barista document in Netscape, make sure the Launch browser check box is selected, and click Send in Corel WordPerfect and Presentations or click Publish in Corel Quattro Pro.

3. If you choose to launch Netscape, it will open and then load the Barista document. Depending on your system and the size and complexity of the file, this may take some time.

SIDE TRIP

GETTING WEB EXPOSURE

Once your Web pages are finished, you need to get them out on the Web. You have a couple of choices here. You can set up your own Web server or you can rent space on an existing server. Check with your ISP to find out if it rents space or can recommend another ISP that does. Once your documents are out there, you'll need to do some networking to get the word out. Check with the top search engines for information on getting your site listed with them. Also, there are a number of great books on setting up shop on the Internet; check these out before making any decisions so you can ask the right questions.

BONUS

Creating a Web Page Form

Nearly every site you visit has some kind of form. Some may be feedback forms associated with a guest book. Others may be for ordering information or products or searching the site itself. These forms provide a way for you to interact with the site. You can use a form to find out what your customers or visitors are looking for, to have them request or order something, or to get on a mailing list. Figure 17-4 provides an example of a form I created using WordPerfect's Internet Publisher Forms feature.

FEATURE FOCUS The new Internet Publisher Forms feature lets you design and create Web forms with a few clicks.

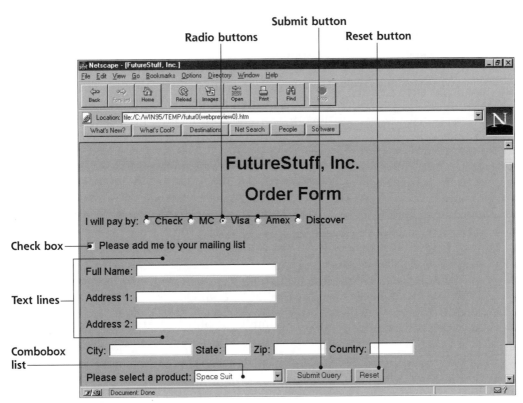

Figure 17-4 A sample order form for FutureStuff, Inc., in Netscape.

Creating a Form

Internet Publisher Forms allows you to add a number of *fields* to make your form easy to use and interactive. Figure 17-4 shows several fields — radio buttons, submit and reset buttons, a checkbox, a text line, and a combobox list.

To create a form, choose File→New to display the New dialog box. On the Create New tab, click the down arrow button and choose Web or Web Publishing. In the list, double-click WordPerfect Web Document or select WordPerfect Web Document and click Create.

Once you're in the Web Editor and see the Internet Publisher PerfectExpert pane, click Extras on the Internet Publisher PerfectExpert pane and choose Add a Form or click the New Form button on the Internet Publisher property bar. WordPerfect inserts two yellow form links and displays the Internet Publisher Forms property bar. Table 17-2 lists the buttons on the Internet Publisher Forms property bar and a description of each. Use this table to help you set up your own form.

TABLE 17-2 Internet Publisher Forms Property Bar

Button	Name	Description
	RADIO BUTTON	Insert a radio button field. Note that radio buttons are exclusive, which means that selecting one negates all the others in the group. Only the selected radio button applies. A black dot appears in a selected radio button.
	CHECKBOX	Insert a check box field. Check boxes are inclusive, which means visitors can select multiple check boxes and all selections apply. An X appears in a selected checkbox.
	HIDDEN	Create a hidden field. This can help control how the form works behind the scenes. Visitors to your site won't know this field exists.
	RESET	Insert a Reset button which clears all entries so the visitor can begin again.
	SUBMIT	Insert a Submit button which sends the information visitors fill out to the server for processing.
	SUBMIT IMAGE	Similar to the Submit button only you click an image to submit the information.
	SELECT LIST	Insert a selection list box where you can add items. Visitors can select a single item from the list. You see a good portion of the list in a selection list box.
	COMBOBOX LIST	Similar to a selection list box except you must click a down arrow button to display a drop-down list of options.
	TEXT AREA	Insert a large text box that visitors can type directly into. This is good for feedback forms where you may want visitors to write several sentences.
	TEXT LINE	Insert a text box for a single line of text. This is good for short entries such as name, address, and similar information.
	PASSWORD	Insert a password field that allows the visitor to enter a password. The actual password does not display in the password text box, just a series of asterisks.
	FORM PROPERTIES	Display the Properties dialog box so you can change properties for the form or the fields.

TIP You can use the HTML Forms PerfectExpert pane to insert many elements in Table 17-2.

Designing the Form

Your first step in creating your form is to create a title and any subheading and introductory information. When you've completed this, you're ready to begin designing your form. Consider sketching it on paper first to get a sense of what fields you'll need and where you'll place them. Once you have a rough layout, you can begin.

Most of the controls require some sort of reference text. For example, in Figure 17-4, examples of reference text are the payment options, the text next to the check box, and the text next to the text line fields, such as *Full Name*. Determine if you want the text reference on the left or the right of the field, then proceed accordingly. To add reference text, simply position the insertion point in the location for the text and type it. For example, if you want to create a text line for *Full Name*, type **Full Name:** and press the space bar two times. Click the Text Line button on the Internet Publisher Forms property bar to insert the text line directly after the text reference.

Note that your text and text lines may not line up evenly. However, view the form in Netscape before making any changes. When the browser translates the form, the text and text lines tend to line up pretty well without much help from you. If you want to do some fine tuning, remember that you can't press Tab to position your insertion point. If you are trying to line up the reference text, try using the space bar.

To add other fields to your form, simply position the insertion point in the location for the field and click the field button on the Internet Publisher Forms property bar.

Customizing Fields

Once you add fields to your form, you may need to make some adjustments. For example, if you added a select list or combobox list, you'll need to indicate what items will appear in the list. If you have a group of radio buttons, you'll need to give them unique values so the server can process them separately.

To add items to a select or combobox list, follow these steps:

1. Double-click the list field to display the List Box/Combobox Properties dialog box.

2. Click Add to display the Add Option dialog box and type your first list item. If you want this item to be the default selection, choose Initially selected, and then click OK. WordPerfect adds the item to the Options list.

3. Continue adding items for your list. WordPerfect will automatically place the Initially selected item at the top of the list and sort the rest alphabetically. If you make a mistake, select the item you wish to fix and click Modify.

4. When you're finished adding items, click OK.

Here are other tasks you may perform:

* To delete a field you don't need, position the insertion point directly before it and press Delete.

* To change the size of a text field, double-click the field to display its associated Properties dialog box. Indicate a Width and a Max Char to limit the number of characters a visitor can enter into the box.

* To work with radio buttons, double-click the radio button or secondary-click the radio button and choose Properties from the QuickMenu to display the Radio Button Properties dialog box. Indicate a unique value for the button and indicate whether or not you want this button to be initially selected — that is, the button that is selected by default when visitors use the form.

Make sure you view your form in Netscape to see how it all shapes up! To do so, click the View in Web Browser button on the Internet Publisher toolbar or choose View→View in Web Browser.

Getting Your Form to Work

No matter how beautiful your form is, it won't do anything unless you are using an application that can receive and process the information your visitors enter. The Internet Publisher can only help you design the form and add fields. Check with your ISP for information on getting your form to work on your Web site.

Summary

In this chapter, you got an eyeful about Web publishing. You learned how to create a Web page with the Internet Publisher and format it with lines, graphics, and hyperlinks. It you're not tired of publishing yet, check out the last chapter, which tells you how to tame the suite and make it your own by customizing it for your needs.

CHAPTER EIGHTEEN

CUSTOMIZING THE SUITE

IN THIS CHAPTER YOU LEARN THESE KEY SKILLS

CHANGING DEFAULT SETTINGS   PAGE 355

CUSTOMIZING YOUR TOOLBARS   PAGE 364

CHANGING TOOLBAR OPTIONS   PAGE 370

O ne of the best things about the WordPerfect Suite is that you can make it your own. You can add and remove buttons to and from toolbars and property bars or create your very own toolbar. And in WordPerfect and Presentations, you can set up shortcut keys to perform different actions. In this chapter you explore the ways you can customize your applications to work more efficiently.

Changing Default Settings

I f you've ever bought a new car, you know that you can buy the standard model or that you can ask for options, such as a sunroof, CD player, and automatic door locks. You're customizing the car to suit your needs and desires. The same is true for the applications in the WordPerfect Suite. They come with standard settings, such as the font you see when you use WordPerfect and Quattro Pro, or the toolbars that display automatically on startup. However, for example, you can decide that you want to use Times Roman as your default font in Quattro Pro or ask an application to beep at you if you goof.

Changing Default Settings in WordPerfect

Not surprisingly, WordPerfect has the most options for customization. You'll look at changing many default settings, such as the font and font size, automatically backing up documents as you work, and a variety of display options.

SETTING DEFAULT FORMATTING

WordPerfect uses a number of default settings for document formatting, some of which are listed in Table 18-1.

TABLE 18-1 Default Format Settings

Format	Default Setting
FONT/FONT SIZE	Times New Roman 12 point
MARGINS	1 inch all the way around
LINE SPACING	Single
JUSTIFICATION	Left
MEASUREMENT	Inches
TAB SET	Every half inch
PAGE ORIENTATION	Portrait

If you only want to change the default font and font size for all WordPerfect documents, you can use the Default Font feature. Choose Format→Font and then click Default Font. Choose a Font face, Font size, and Font style, and make sure the Use as default check box is marked. Click OK and OK again. This changes the font for the current document and all documents you create *using the current printer.*

If you want to set other formatting options such as line spacing, justification, or margins, you'll need to change the default document style.

To set default formatting, follow these steps:

1. Choose `File` → `Document` → `Current Document Style` to display the Styles Editor dialog box. This looks nearly identical to the Styles Editor you encountered in Chapter 4.

2. Insert the formats you wish to use as default in the Contents box, using the Styles Editor menu and toolbar to assist you.

3. Choose Use as default at the bottom of the dialog box and click OK. WordPerfect asks you if you want to use this style for all new documents.

4. Click Yes. These settings will now be the default settings for the current document and all new documents you create.

SETTING DISPLAY OPTIONS

When you start WordPerfect for the first time, you'll have a few things already in place. The shadow cursor is on, you're using Page view, and the File menu will automatically list the last nine files you've used, in order of most recently used. However, if you want to make some changes to these settings, you can do so. To change Display options, choose Tools→Settings and double-click the Display icon to show the Display Settings dialog box (see Figure 18-1).

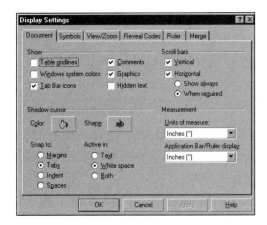

Figure 18-1 Customize your display with Display Settings.

Use Table 18-2 to help you make changes to your display settings. Each option corresponds to a tab in the Display Settings dialog box. When you're finished, click OK and then click Close to return to the document window.

TABLE 18-2 Display Settings Options

Option	Description
DOCUMENT	Indicate what elements you want to show, set your unit of measure, change shadow cursor options, and indicate when vertical and horizontal scroll bars will display.
SYMBOLS	Ask WordPerfect to show you the corresponding symbol for things that are usually hidden unless you display the Reveal Codes window. For example, if you turn this option on, you'll see ¶ for a hard return, → for a tab, and . for a space.

(continued)

TABLE 18-2 Display Settings Options (*continued*)

Option	Description
VIEW/ZOOM	Change the default view and the magnification of documents when you use WordPerfect. You can easily override these settings for an individual document using the View menu option and the Zoom button on the WordPerfect toolbar.
REVEAL CODES	Ask WordPerfect to keep the Reveal Codes window open, change the font, font size, and colors of the text and background in the Reveal Codes window, and indicate any Reveal Code options.
RULER	Indicate whether your tabs follow an invisible grid on the Ruler and whether you want the guidelines to show when you move tabs on the Ruler.
MERGE	Indicate whether you want to display merge codes as codes — FIELD (FIRST NAME); as markers — small red triangles; or to hide them altogether.

SIDE TRIP

INSTANT DISPLAY

You can secondary-click different elements to display many of the different tabs in the Display Settings dialog box. Use the following techniques to display the tabs in context:

* Secondary-click either the vertical or horizontal scroll bar and choose Settings to display the Document tab in the Display Settings dialog box.

* Secondary-click in the Reveal Codes window and choose Settings to display the Reveal Codes tab in the Display Settings dialog box.

* Secondary-click the Ruler and choose Settings to display the Ruler tab in the Display Settings dialog box.

SETTING ENVIRONMENT OPTIONS

WordPerfect also lets you change more global items using the Environment feature. This includes such things as the name WordPerfect uses for comments and document summaries, selection options, and showing or hiding the QuickTips you see when you point to a button on the toolbar or property bar. To change Environment options, choose Tools→Settings and double-click the Environment icon to display the Environment Settings dialog box (see Figure 18-2).

Use Table 18-3 to help you make changes to your environment settings. Each option corresponds to a tab in the Environment Settings dialog box. When you're finished, click OK and then click Close to return to the document window.

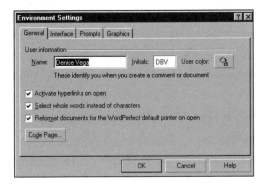

Figure 18-2 Customize your display with Environment Settings.

TABLE 18-3 Environment Settings Options

Option	Description
GENERAL	Change your user name, initials, and color, which are used in Document Summaries, Comments, and the Reviewer feature. For more on these features, check online help. Also, indicate whether you want hyperlinks active when you open a document containing them, and whether you want WordPerfect to select entire words at a time as you drag across text. By default WordPerfect will reformat your documents based on the printer selected. You can change this if you want.
INTERFACE	Indicate what you want on your menus. Currently, WordPerfect displays the Shortcut key in the QuickTip when you point to a menu item. If you want it also to show up next to the item on the menu itself, choose Display shortcut keys. You can also choose to save your workspace. If you do so, WordPerfect will remember the last document you worked on and open it when you start WordPerfect.

(continued)

TABLE 18-3 Environment Settings Options (*continued*)

Option	Description
PROMPTS	Set hyphenation, delete options, and beep options for documents. You can ask WordPerfect to confirm code deletion to make sure you don't accidentally remove a code and change your formatting. You can set your computer to beep on certain errors and when WordPerfect can't locate a search string you've indicated in the Find and Replace Text dialog box.
GRAPHICS	Drag to create new graphics boxes; lets you indicate the box size every time you want to insert a graphic. You can also set options for the Equation Editor. Check online help for more information on the Equation Editor.

Changing Default Settings in Presentations

Presentations has many default settings that you can customize. Here you can change the default slide master as well as the Display and Environment settings.

SETTING A DEFAULT SLIDE MASTER

If you plan to create several different slide shows with the same look, you can set Presentations to use the same master for each one. But if you need to change the master for any one slide show, you can do so. To set a default slide master, make sure Presentations is open and choose Format→Master Gallery. Use the Category drop-down list to select a category and then click the desired master background. Click Save as Default and then click OK. Presentations will now use the selected master for all new slide shows you create.

SETTING DISPLAY OPTIONS

To change Display options, choose Tools→Settings and double-click the Display icon to show the Screen Elements tab in the Display dialog box (see Figure 18-3). The Items to display on menus options are nearly identical to those in WordPerfect, except that Presentations provides a sample menu that shows the results of your selections:

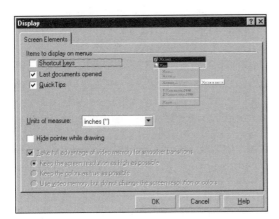

Figure 18-3 Customize your Presentations display.

* Choose Shortcut keys to display the shortcut key combinations on the menu itself. Choose Last documents opened to display the last four documents at the bottom of the File menu, and choose QuickTips if you want to see the description when you point to a button or menu item.

* Select a unit of measure that Presentations will use for any options that require a measurement.

* Indicate whether you want to hide the pointer when you're drawing objects and if you want Presentations to take full advantage of MMX technology if your system uses it.

When you're finished, click OK and then click Close.

SETTING ENVIRONMENT OPTIONS

You can change how Presentations acts when you first start it, set file conversion options, and select a language for your work. You do this using the Environment feature. To change Environment options, choose Tools→Settings and double-click the Environment icon to display the Environment dialog box (see Figure 18-4).

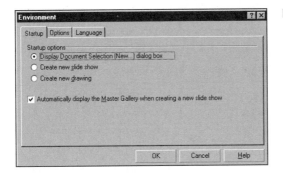

Figure 18-4 Customize Presentations Environment settings.

Use Table 18-4 to help you make changes to your environment. Each option corresponds to a tab in the Environment dialog box. When you're finished, click OK and then click Close to return to the document window.

TABLE 18-4	Presentations Environment Settings
Option	**Description**
STARTUP	Indicate how you want Presentations to behave when you first start it. You can ask to select a document in the New dialog box, have it automatically create a new slide show, or automatically open so you can create a new drawing. You can also indicate whether you want to select a slide master when you create a new slide show.
OPTIONS	Choose whether you want to use enhanced file management dialog boxes. If you deselect this option, you won't see such things as the toolbar and other elements that match the Windows Explorer dialog box. Indicate if you want WMF files to be converted to WPG files and in what WPG format you wish to save your drawings. You can also set beep options here for errors or when you perform a search and come up empty.
LANGUAGE	Use this tab to indicate any language options. Note that depending on the language version you originally purchased, you may not be able to make changes without an add-on module.

Changing Default Settings in Quattro Pro

Unlike WordPerfect and Presentations, Quattro Pro has all the settings in a single dialog box. To change default settings, choose Tools→Settings to display the Application dialog box (Figure 18-5).

Figure 18-5 Set Quattro Pro options.

Table 18-5 describes the options, with each option corresponding to a tab in the Application dialog box. Use the table to help you make changes to your settings. When you're finished, click OK.

TABLE 18-5 Quattro Pro Application Settings

Option	Description
DISPLAY	Indicate which bars you want to display (toolbar, property bar, or application bar), and whether you want to see the input line, QuickTips, and the scroll indicators, which display the current row number on the vertical scroll bar and the column letter on the horizontal scroll bar. You can also set other options including 3-D options, the default view, and how sheets are labeled if you don't name them yourself. Finally, here you can indicate the minimum number of tabs you wish to have in your notebook to keep it to a manageable number.
INTERNATIONAL	Indicate the country formats Quattro Pro should use for such things as currency, numerical separators, dates, and times. Use the Change button to change the currency symbol. You can also indicate whether you want negative values displayed with minus signs or in parentheses.
MACRO	Indicate a variety of macro options. I recommend changing these only if you're an advanced user who is comfortable with macros.
FILE OPTIONS	See the next section, "Setting File Options."
GENERAL	Set a variety of formatting options and other options, including which cell you want Quattro Pro to select when you press Enter.

Setting File Options

WordPerfect, Presentations, and Quattro Pro automatically save all your documents, slide shows, and notebooks in the MyFiles folder. If you would prefer that the application not save them in this folder, you can change the default folder. You can also change the default folder for other file types, as you'll see.

To change the default files in WordPerfect and Presentations, choose Tools→Settings and then double-click the File icon. Figure 18-6 shows the WordPerfect File Settings dialog box. To change the default files in Quattro Pro, choose Tools→Settings and choose the File Options tab.

Indicate the folders for each item. Notice that in WordPerfect you have several tabs you can choose. Once you've displayed the desired tab, set the default folders for the appropriate items and click OK. In WordPerfect and Presentations, click Close to close the Settings dialog box.

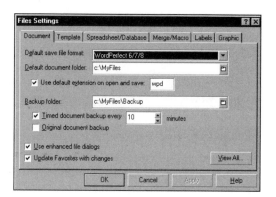

Figure 18-6 Set file options for WordPerfect.

TIP WordPerfect is defaulted to automatically back up your documents every ten minutes in case of power or system failure. Use the Backup options on the Document tab in the File Settings dialog box to change the minutes before each backup. Choose Original document backup if you want to make a copy of each document when it's backed up.

Customizing Your Toolbars

Ever tossed something you no longer needed? What about rearranging the items on top of your desk? Just as you can organize your desk, throwing away things you no longer need or rearranging things in a different way, so too can you organize your toolbars and property bars. I'll focus on toolbars here but the same concepts hold for property bars.

Each toolbar and property bar is fully customizable, which means you can add and remove buttons and rearrange the order in which buttons appear. If you rarely work with Web documents in WordPerfect, you may want to remove the Switch View button that switches between Page and Web views. Or if you would prefer the formula-related buttons to the end of the Notebook toolbar in Quattro Pro, you can move them. In any case, you have a great deal of flexibility. Remember that if you remove a button from a toolbar, you're only deleting the button, not the underlying *function*, which you can still access from the Menu bar.

Note that although Corel has made tremendous strides in making the applications work in a similar fashion, there are still some differences when it comes to working with toolbars. Because of these differences, I will address WordPerfect and Presentations in one section and Quattro Pro in another.

TIP WordPerfect ships with several custom toolbars and property bars. It makes sense to check these out to see if one suits your needs before designing one of your own. To do so, just secondary-click the current toolbar or property bar and choose Settings. Check the list of those available.

Adding Features to Toolbars in WordPerfect and Presentations

The easiest way to create your own toolbar is to copy an existing toolbar and make the appropriate changes. If none of the toolbars contains any buttons you wish to use on your new toolbar, you can create one from scratch. Once you've copied or created a new toolbar, you can add, delete, and rearrange buttons the same way.

Note that though you can work with toolbars by choosing Tools→Settings and then double-clicking the Customize icon, the methods that follow are faster and more efficient.

- ✳ To copy a toolbar in WordPerfect, secondary-click the current toolbar and choose Settings to display the Customize Settings dialog box. Click Copy, and then select the default toolbar in the Select Toolbars to copy list — WordPerfect 8. Click Copy and type a name for the toolbar in the Object text box and click OK. WordPerfect returns to the Customize Settings dialog box. To have WordPerfect add the new toolbar to the list, click Close and then secondary-click the toolbar and choose Settings to display the Customize Settings dialog box.

- ✳ To copy a toolbar in Presentations, secondary-click the toolbar and choose Settings to display the Customize dialog box. Click Copy and then type a new name in the To text box and click OK. Presentations lists your toolbar in the Available Toolbars list box.

Once you have your toolbar displayed in the list, you can edit it. Simply select the toolbar and click Edit. WordPerfect and Presentations both display the Toolbar Editor dialog box (see Figure 18-7). Notice the toolbar name displays in the Toolbar Editor title bar. Also look at the white areas between buttons on the toolbar you are editing. These are *separators* and appear as gray vertical lines when you're at the document window. Separators help group similar buttons together. For more on working with separators, see "Inserting Separators Between Buttons" later in this chapter.

Note that you can edit only one toolbar at a time.

The object of the game is to remove, add, and rearrange buttons. More than likely, you'll delete unnecessary buttons before adding buttons. But because deleting buttons is the same for all three applications, I've included it under "Organizing Your Buttons" later in this chapter. If you want to do some cleanup first, check out that section.

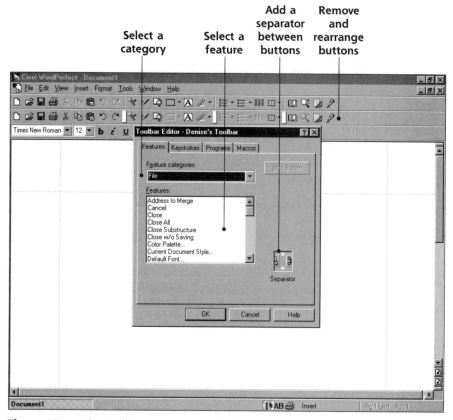

Figure 18-7 The Toolbar Editor in WordPerfect.

ADDING BUTTONS TO THE TOOLBAR

There are two ways to add a button to the toolbar in WordPerfect and Presentations. You can actually select the feature through the main menu behind the Toolbar Editor dialog box, or you can use the Feature categories and Features lists to select the features you wish to add.

* To add a feature using the application's menu, select the feature using the menu. The application adds the button as the last button on the toolbar.

* To add a feature using the lists in the Toolbar Editor, click the Feature categories down arrow button and select a feature from the drop-down list (these match the menu options). Next, select the feature you wish to add from the Features list. To place it on the toolbar, you have three options. Double-click the feature or click Add Button to add it as the last button on the toolbar. Or, click and drag the feature from the Features list to the desired location on the toolbar (ooh-ahh).

ADDING MACROS TO THE TOOLBAR

You worked through Chapter 8 in this book and recorded this really cool macro in WordPerfect. Now you want to play it with a single click. No problem. Just add the macro to your toolbar. To do so, follow these steps:

1. In WordPerfect or Presentations, make sure the Toolbar Editor is displayed. If you're at the document window, secondary-click the toolbar and choose Settings. Select the toolbar to edit and click Edit. If you're displaying the Customize Settings (WordPerfect) or Customize (Presentations) dialog box, select your toolbar and click Edit.

2. Choose the Macros tab and click Add Macro. Select the macro you wish to add and click Select or press Enter. The application will ask if you want to save the macro with its full path. If you don't plan on moving the macro to another location and will keep this folder as your default macro folder, click Yes. Otherwise, click No.

WordPerfect or Presentations adds a cassette icon as the last button on the toolbar and uses the macro's name as the QuickTip.

 X-REF For information on using a different icon for macros and changing the QuickTip text, see the Bonus section at the end of this chapter.

SAVING AND USING YOUR TOOLBAR

Once you've added all the buttons you want to your toolbar, you'll need to make sure those buttons stay where they belong. Just click OK in the Toolbar Editor to save your changes. To use your toolbar, use one of the following options, depending on which application you are using.

* To use the toolbar in WordPerfect, you should be back at the Customize Settings dialog box. Select your new toolbar to place a check mark in the check box and deselect any other toolbars you don't want to use. Click Close to return to the document window.

* To use the toolbar in Presentations, you should be back at the Customize dialog box. Select your new toolbar and click OK. Your toolbar appears at the top of the window.

 TIP WordPerfect allows you to edit any existing toolbar. However, if later you decide you want to use the original toolbar, you can use the Reset button in the Customize Settings dialog box. Presentations won't let you edit the <Slide Show> toolbar, forcing you to make a copy before proceeding.

Creating a Toolbar in Quattro Pro

Unlike WordPerfect and Presentations, Quattro Pro doesn't allow you to make a copy of a toolbar and edit it. You can edit existing toolbars or, if you don't want to change those, you can create your own from scratch.

 If you edit an existing toolbar, you can't easily restore it to its original state. Play it safe and create a toolbar from scratch.

To create a toolbar in Quattro Pro, follow these steps:

1. With Quattro Pro open, secondary-click the current toolbar and choose Settings to display the Toolbar Settings dialog box. Alternatively, you can choose View → Toolbars.

2. Click Create and type a name for your toolbar in the Toolbar Name text box. Click OK to add the toolbar to the list. Notice there is now a blank toolbar below the Notebook toolbar, which also remains selected.

3. With your toolbar selected, click Edit to display the Edit Toolbar dialog box (see Figure 18-8). Unlike WordPerfect and Presentations, you can't select directly from the menu behind this dialog box. You must use the Categories list on the Command tab.

4. To add a feature, select an option from the Categories list, then drag the desired button to the toolbar. If you're not sure what action a button performs, simply point to it to see a QuickTip display at the bottom of the Edit Toolbar dialog box.

5. When you're finished adding commands, click Close. Select and deselect the toolbars you wish to display and then click Close.

Organizing Your Buttons

In addition to adding buttons to the toolbar, you can delete and move buttons, as well as add separators. This works the same whether you're working with a toolbar in WordPerfect, Presentations, or Quattro Pro.

DELETING BUTTONS FROM THE TOOLBAR

In any clean-up chore, it makes sense to first get rid of the stuff you don't want. And look how easy it is to lose those unwanted buttons on the toolbar. Just click and drag the button off the toolbar. You'll see the pointer turn into a trash can with a button hovering above it. When you release the mouse button, the button disappears from the toolbar.

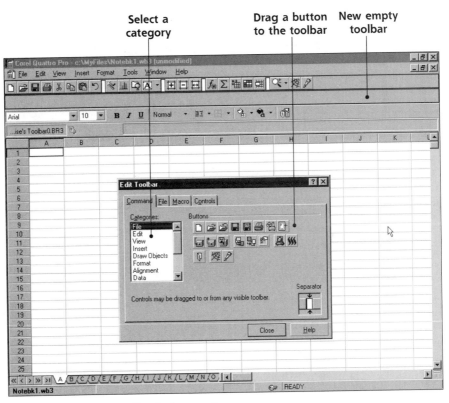

Figure 18-8 Edit a toolbar in Quattro Pro.

MOVING BUTTONS ON THE TOOLBAR

Are you one of those people who moves the lamp 16 times before deciding you'd like it best in the first place you put it? If so, you'll like how easy it is to rearrange the buttons on your toolbar. While the Toolbar Editor is displayed, click and drag the button to its new location. When you release the mouse button, the button remains in that location.

INSERTING SEPARATORS BETWEEN BUTTONS

As I mentioned earlier, you can use separators to group similar buttons and keep them organized. For example, the WordPerfect toolbar separates tools such as bullets and numbering, tables, and columns from the writing tools with a separator. To add a separator, click and drag the Separator icon between the buttons you want to separate. You can move or delete a separator the same way you move or delete a button.

 TIP You can also create custom keyboards in both WordPerfect and Presentations. This involves assigning features, macros, and text to shortcut keystrokes. Check online help for details.

Changing Toolbar Options

If you want your tools a little closer to where you work, you can move the toolbar so that it appears on the left, right, or bottom of the screen, or floats around on the screen. You can also change how the buttons look, choosing to have icons (pictures) only, text only, or pictures and text.

Moving a Toolbar

To move a toolbar, simply point to a separator between buttons or to a blank area of the toolbar until you see the move pointer (four-headed arrow). Next, click and drag it to the desired location. The shape and size of the toolbar will indicate where it will appear on your screen. For example, if you want the toolbar on one of the four edges of the screen, click and drag it until the small rectangular box "snaps" into a long, narrow bar; at that point, release the mouse button. You can also indicate the location in the Options dialog box, as follows:

* In WordPerfect and Presentations, secondary-click the toolbar and choose Settings. Next, click the Options button and select the desired location. The application will show you how the toolbar will look. When you're satisfied, click OK and then OK again to return to the document window.

* In Quattro Pro, secondary-click the toolbar and choose Settings. Next, click the Options button and select the desired location under Docking Position. Click OK and then click Close.

 TIP If you want to use several toolbars at once, place them in different locations around your screen for maximum access.

Changing Toolbar Appearance

This option is only available in WordPerfect and Presentations and allows you to display the toolbar buttons as pictures only (the default), text only, or pictures and text. Secondary-click the toolbar and choose Settings. Next, click the Options button to display the Toolbar Options dialog box (see Figure 18-9).

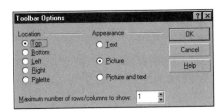

Figure 18-9 Set toolbar options in Presentations.

Select the desired option under Appearance. Click OK and OK again to return to the document window.

If your toolbar has more buttons than the application can show at once, you have a few options for each application, which are as follows:

* WordPerfect automatically places a tiny vertical scroll bar on the right side of the toolbar. You can do the following:
  * Use this scroll bar to view and use buttons.
  * Display the toolbar as a floating palette to see all buttons at once.
  * Choose to display multiple rows. See "Displaying Multiple Toolbar Rows" next.
* Presentations does not automatically display a vertical scroll bar. To see all buttons on a toolbar, you can display the toolbar as a floating palette or choose to display multiple rows. See "Displaying Multiple Toolbar Rows" next.
* Quattro Pro doesn't display the vertical scroll bar, and you can't choose to display more than one row at a time. Your only choice is to use the floating palette.

Displaying Multiple Toolbar Rows

If you prefer to have your toolbar docked against one side of the screen rather than using the palette, you can display all of your buttons by requesting that the application display multiple rows.

In WordPerfect and Presentations, secondary-click the toolbar and choose Settings. Next, click the Options button and indicate the number of rows (from one to three) you wish to display in the Maximum number of rows/columns to show. Click OK and then OK again to return to the document window.

TIP You can also make changes to the Application bar in WordPerfect. Secondary-click the Application bar and choose Settings. Select or deselect options you wish to display on the bar. To return to the default settings, click Reset. Personally, I like to add the Date icon to the Application bar so I can click the icon to insert the current date in my document.

BONUS

Customizing Toolbar Buttons

You've added three macros to your toolbar, and they each use that little cassette icon. Or you've added text to several buttons in Presentations using the Keystrokes tab, and all you have is that bland gray ball icon. Problem is, you can't always remember which macro does what so you'll always have to check the QuickTip before clicking the button. It sure would be nice to have a related icon on that button, wouldn't it? Well, here's how you can do that and change the QuickTip text tool.

 This is only available for WordPerfect and Presentations.

Changing a Button QuickTip

You like to display your buttons as text only, but whoa. Some of the text is really long. To change this text or the text you see when you display a QuickTip, use the Customize options. First, make sure you have WordPerfect or Presentations open. Then follow these steps:

1. Secondary-click the toolbar and choose Settings and select the toolbar containing the button(s) you wish to change.

2. Click Edit to display the Toolbar Editor dialog box.

3. Double-click the button you wish to change, or secondary-click the button and choose Customize to display the Customize Button dialog box (see Figure 18-10).

4. Enter text in the Button Text and QuickTip text boxes and click OK. Note that the button text and QuickTip can and should be different. Make the button text short and use the QuickTip to provide a brief description of the button's function.

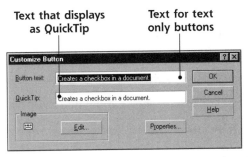

Text that displays as QuickTip

Text for text only buttons

Figure 18-10 Change the QuickTip text for a button.

Changing a Button Icon

Okay, so that cassette icon has got to go. You could erase the icon and create your own, but that can get a little tricky. A better way is to use a two-step process. The first step is copying an icon that you like from another toolbar. The second step is pasting it in to replace the cassette icon and changing it so that it looks different from the original. This can include changing the colors or removing parts of the icon. Make sure you have WordPerfect or Presentations open and then follow the steps in the next two sections.

COPYING AN ICON

Before you can replace that cassette icon with something else, you need to copy an existing icon:

1. Secondary-click the toolbar and choose Settings, and select the toolbar containing the button you wish to copy.

2. Click Edit to display the Toolbar Editor dialog box.

3. Double-click the button you wish to change, or secondary-click the button and choose Customize to display the Customize button dialog box.

4. Click Edit under Image to display the Image Editor dialog box. Make sure the icon you see is the one you want to use for your own button.

5. Click Copy at the bottom of the Image Editor dialog box and click Cancel two times to return to the Toolbar Editor dialog box.

USING THE COPIED ICON

After you copy an icon, you can paste it in to replace the cassette or generic ball icon, and then touch it up any way you want.

1. If the Toolbar Editor isn't currently displayed, secondary-click the toolbar and choose Settings. If it is, go on to Step 2.

2. Select the toolbar containing the button you wish to change and click Edit to display the Toolbar Editor dialog box.

3. Double-click the button you wish to change, or secondary-click the button and choose Customize to display the Customize Button dialog box.

4. Click Edit under Image to display the Image Editor dialog box.

5. Click Paste at the bottom of the dialog box to insert the icon you copied from the other button.

6. Under Drawing Mode, select Single pixel to work one square at a time or choose Fill whole area to work with entire areas with the same color.

7. Under Colors, your primary mouse button (left) controls one color and your secondary mouse button (right) controls another. Change these colors by selecting another color with the primary or secondary mouse button.

8. Click the primary or secondary mouse button on the icon, depending on which color you wish to use. This will change the color.

9. To erase parts of the image, use white as one of your colors.

10. When you're finished with your image, click OK two times to return to the Toolbar Editor dialog box.

If you wish to change other buttons on this toolbar, repeat the copying and pasting steps in these sections. Otherwise, click OK again to return to the document window.

Summary

In this chapter, you placed the WordPerfect Suite under your spell, customizing a variety of default settings and toolbars. Here you are at the end of the book. So why are so many pages left? Well, you have two great tools for doing what you need to do. The Discovery Center gives you an overview of tasks with quick step-by-steps without the fluff — that is, without many figures or fancy stuff getting in your way. Use the second tool — the Visual Index — to answer the question "How did she do that?" when you look at a particular document type, slide show, or spreadsheet. Finally, if you haven't had enough of the suite, check out the appendixes. Thanks for discovering the WordPerfect Suite with me. Good luck, and enjoy!

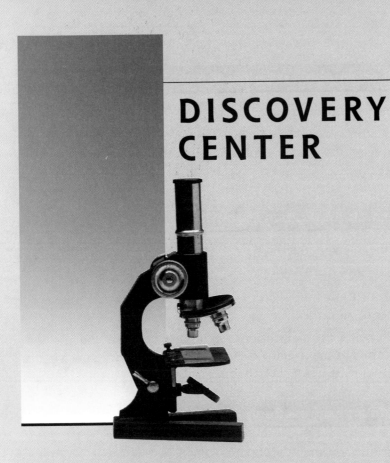

DISCOVERY CENTER

The Discovery Center serves as a quick reference to some of the most important tasks covered in this book. Use it to work quickly through the steps of a task with little or no interruption. For more information, refer back to the page indicated.

CHAPTER 1

How to Start an Application (page 10)

Do either of the following:

* Click Start → Corel WordPerfect Suite 8 on the Windows taskbar and then select the desired application from the menu.

* On the Windows desktop, click the associated application button on DAD.

How to Exit an Application (page 15)

Use one of the following methods:

* Choose File → Exit .

* Click the Close button on the right side of the title bar (upper right corner of the screen).

* Double-click the application icon on the left side of the title bar (upper left corner of the screen) or click the application icon once to display the control menu. Then click Close.

How to Add an Address Book Entry (page 19)

1. Click Start → Corel WordPerfect Suite 8 → Accessories → Corel Address Book 8.

2. Click Add to display the New Entry dialog box.

3. Select Person or Organization, and then choose OK to display the Properties for New Entry dialog box.

4. Fill in each piece of information, pressing Tab to get to the next field box, or Shift+Tab to return to the previous field box.

5. To add another entry, click New. Then click Yes to save the changes before continuing.

6. Click OK when you're finished.

CHAPTER 2

How to Open an Existing Document (page 30)

1. With the application open, click the Open button on the Standard toolbar or choose File → Open .

2. In the Filename text box, double-click the folder containing the file you wish to open and then double-click the filename you wish to open.

How to Save a File (page 34)

1. Click the Save button or choose `File` → `Save` to display the Save As dialog box.

2. In the Name text box, type a name for the file.

3. Select a folder in which to store the file and click Save.

How to Close a File (page 34)

To close a file in any application, use one of the following methods. If you haven't saved the file, click Yes to save or No to close without saving.

* Click the Close button on the menu bar.

* Double-click the Document Control button on the menu bar or click the Document Control button once and choose Close.

* Choose `File` → `Close`.

How to Use the Spell Checker (page 38)

1. Open the file you wish to check in the associated application. In Presentations, display the show in Outliner view.

2. Click the Spell Check button or choose `Tools` → `Spell Check`.

3. If the word is spelled correctly, choose to skip it or add it to the supplemental dictionary or document word list. If the word is spelled incorrectly, select the correct spelling from the Replacements list and click Replace. If the correct spelling is not in the Replacements list, click in the Replace with text box and correct the text.

4. When Spell Checker is finished, click Yes to close the dialog box or No to close the message box and still use the features in the dialog box.

How to Use Help (page 44)

1. With your application of choice open and running, choose `Help` → `Help Topics` to display the Help Topics dialog box.

2. Use the following information to work with Help:

* Use the *Contents* tab to select from a list of topics and subtopics.

* Use the *Index* tab to enter the first few characters of a topic to locate the associated help topic.

* Use the *Find* tab to search for words in the Help database.

* Use the *Ask the PerfectExpert* tab to type a word, short phrase, or entire question to get a list of topics.

CHAPTER 3

How to Insert the Current Date (page 61)

Position the insertion point for the location of the date and press Ctrl+D.

How to Convert Text Case (page 65)

Select the text you wish to convert, choose | Edit | → | Convert Case |, and then select lowercase, UPPERCASE, or Initial Capitals.

How to Move or Copy Using the Clipboard (page 65)

1. Select the text to move or copy.

2. On the Standard toolbar, click the Cut button or choose | Edit | → | Cut | to move. Click the Copy button or choose | Edit | → | Copy | to copy the text.

3. Position the insertion point in the location for the moved or copied text and click the Paste button or choose | Edit | → | Paste |.

How to Move or Copy Using Drag and Drop (page 66)

1. Select the text you wish to move or copy.

2. Point to the selection and click and drag to the new location. To copy, press and hold Ctrl before releasing the mouse button.

How to Delete Text (page 67)

Select the text you want to delete and press Delete.

How to Undelete Text (page 68)

1. Position the insertion point in the location you want to restore the

deleted text.

2. Press Ctrl+Shift+Z to display the Undelete box and click Restore.

How to Use Undo or Redo (page 68)

* To use Undo, click the Undo button on the Standard toolbar or choose Edit → Undo.

* To use Redo, click the Redo button on the Standard toolbar or choose Edit → Redo.

How to Print a Document (page 69)

1. Click the Print button on the WordPerfect toolbar or choose File → Print.

2. On the Print tab, select your print options and click Print.

CHAPTER 4

How to Justify Text (page 77)

1. Type the text you wish to justify, and select the text.

2. Click the Justification button on the property bar to display the pop-down menu and select the desired option.

How to Change Fonts (page 78)

Select the text you wish to format or position the insertion point for the new font. Use the Font and Font Size buttons on the property bar to select the desired font and size.

How to Apply Text Enhancements (page 79)

Select the text and choose one or more of the following text enhancements:

* To **bold** text, click the Bold button on the Standard property bar or press Ctrl+B.

* To *italicize* text, click the Italics button on the Standard property bar or

press Ctrl+I.

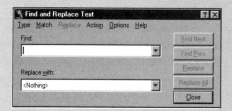

✱ To <u>underline</u> text, click the Underline button on the Standard property bar or press Ctrl+U.

How to Indent Paragraphs (page 81)

To Insert	Do This
Left indent	Press F7 or choose Format → Paragraph → Indent .
Hanging indent	Press Ctrl+F7 or choose Format → Paragraph → Hanging Indent .
Double indent	Press Ctrl+Shift+F7 or choose Format → Paragraph → Double Indent .

How to Find Text (page 83)

1. With the document open, position the insertion point at the top of the document and choose Edit → Find and Replace or press Ctrl+F. You see the following dialog box.

2. In the Find text box, type the text you wish to locate and set any options using Match on the Find and Replace Text menu bar.

3. To locate text, click Find Next and repeat as necessary to reach your location. To replace text, type the replacement text in the Replace with text box and set any Replace options. Click Find Next.

4. Choose a Find or Replace option for the next occurrence and continue.

How to Create a Style Using QuickStyle (page 88)

1. Format the text using the formatting you'd like in the style, if you haven't already done so.

2. Position the insertion point in the formatted text, click the Styles down arrow, and choose QuickStyle from the bottom of the list.

3. Give the style a name and description.

4. Under Style type, indicate whether this will be a Paragraph with automatic update or Character with automatic update and click OK.

How to Use a Style (page 89)

1. To format an existing *paragraph*, position the insertion point anywhere within the paragraph. To format existing *text* using a character style, select the text.

2. Click the Styles down arrow button on the property bar and select the style from the list.

CHAPTER 5

How to Change Line Spacing (page 98)

1. Position the insertion point in the location where you wish to begin the new line spacing and choose | Format | → | Line | → | Spacing |.

2. Type the line spacing in the Spacing text box and click OK.

How to Create New Numbered Paragraphs (page 99)

1. Position the insertion point in the location for the numbered list or paragraphs.

2. Type 1. and press Tab.

3. Type the text for the line or paragraph and press Enter.

4. Type the text and press Enter for the next numbered paragraph.

To add numbers to existing paragraphs, select all the paragraphs, click the Numbering down arrow button on the WordPerfect toolbar, and select the desired numbering style.

How to Add Page Numbers (page 104)

1. Position the insertion point on the page to begin numbering and choose Format → Page → Numbering .

2. Click the Position down arrow button and select the desired position from the drop-down list.

3. In the Page numbering format list, select the way you'd like your page number to appear on the page.

4. Click Set Value and type the starting number for the page in the Set page number text box. Click OK.

5. Click OK to close the Select Page Numbering Format dialog box.

How to Add Headers and Footers (page 106)

1. Position the insertion point on the page where you want the header or footer to begin appearing and choose Format → Header/Footer .

2. Under Select, choose the header or footer you wish to create and click Create.

3. Type any text for your header or footer and add a page number, horizontal line, and other options using the appropriate buttons on the Header or Footer property bar.

4. Click Close on the Header or Footer property bar or click in the document to return to the document window.

CHAPTER 6

How to Change Margins Using Guidelines (page 113)

1. Choose View → Page to make sure you can see the guidelines.

2. Point to the guideline you wish to adjust (left, right, top, or bottom) until you see the pointer change to a sizing arrow (black, double-headed). Click and drag the guideline to the new setting.

How to Use TextArt (page 115)

1. Position the insertion point in the location for the TextArt and choose Insert → Graphics → TextArt for the following dialog box.

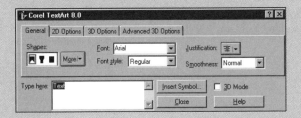

2. On the General tab, type the text for your heading in the Type here text box.

3. Use the Font and Font style options to select a font and select one of the shapes for your text in the Shapes box.

4. Click the Justification button and select a justification.

5. Select any additional options and click Close.

How to Create Newspaper Columns (page 117)

1. With your document open, position the insertion point where you want columns to begin, click the Columns button on the WordPerfect toolbar, and select the desired number of columns.

2. Type the text for your columns, letting it wrap to the next column naturally.

How to Set Tabs on the Ruler (page 121)

1. With the Ruler displayed, position the insertion point in the location for the tabular columns and secondary-click one of the tab markers on the Ruler; then select Clear All Tabs from the QuickMenu.

2. Secondary-click the Tab Line and select the desired tab type from the QuickMenu.

3. Click on the Tab Line, below the measurement on the Ruler, to insert a tab marker.

How to Return to the Default Tab Setting (page 123)

1. Position the insertion point in the location for the default tab setting.

2. With the Ruler displayed, secondary-click the Tab Line on the Ruler and choose Default Tab Settings from the QuickMenu. '

How to Insert an Image (page 127)

1. Position the insertion point in the location for the graphic image and click the Clipart button on the WordPerfect 8 toolbar or choose `Insert` → `Graphics` → `Clipart`.

2. Display the desired image in the Scrapbook and then click and drag the image to your document.

How to Move and Resize a Graphic Box (page 130)

1. Click the image once to select it to display the sizing handles.

2. To move the image, point to it until you see the move pointer, and then click and drag it to the new location.

3. To resize the image, make sure you see the sizing handles and use one of the following techniques.

   * Click and drag a corner sizing handle to adjust the height and width proportionally at the same time.

   * Click and drag a height sizing handle to increase or decrease image height.

   * Click and drag a width sizing handle to increase or decrease image width.

CHAPTER 7

How to Create a Table (page 135)

Position the insertion point in the location for the table. Next, click and hold the Tables button on the WordPerfect 8 toolbar and select the number of columns and rows from the grid that displays, as shown.

How to Select Cells (page 139)

To Select	Do This

A single cell		Point to the *left* edge of the cell to display the selection arrow and click once.
Multiple cells		Point to the *left* edge of the first cell to display the selection arrow. Then click and drag over all cells you wish to select.
⊞	Entire row	With the insertion point in the row, click the Select Table Row button on the Table property bar, or point to the *left* edge of any cell in the row to display the selection arrow, and double-click.
⊟	Entire column	With the insertion point in the column, click the Select Table Column button on the Table property bar, or point to the *top* edge of any cell in the column to display the selection arrow, and double-click.
⊡	Entire table	With the insertion point in the table, click the Select Table button on the Table property bar, or point to the *left* or *top* edge of any cell in the table to display the selection arrow, and triple-click.

How to Adjust a Table Column (page 141)

Point to the left or right line of the column you wish to adjust until you see the sizing pointer; then click and drag in the appropriate direction to increase or decrease the width.

How to Change Table Lines and Fill (page 147)

Select the cells you want to change and then use the border and line buttons on the property bar to add lines and fill. Or, click the Table menu button on the property bar and choose `Border/Fill`. Make your selections in the dialog box. Click OK.

CHAPTER 8

How to Create a Data File (page 156)

1. At a new document window in WordPerfect, choose `Tools` → `Merge` or press Shift+F9 to display the Merge dialog box.

2. Click Create Data to display the Create Data File dialog box, shown here.

3. If you want to see your records displayed in a table, choose Format records in a table at the bottom of the dialog box.

4. In the Name a field text box, type the first field name and press Enter or click Add. Repeat for all field names you wish to create.

5. When you're finished creating your field names, click OK to display the Quick Data Entry dialog box.

6. Enter your information in the field boxes for the current record, pressing Tab to move to the next field box and Shift+Tab to move to the previous field box.

7. Click New Record and repeat Step 7 for each new record. Click Close when you're finished entering records.

8. Click Yes to display the Save Data File dialog box; then type a name for the data file, locate and display the folder you wish to store it in, and click Save.

How to Associate a Data File and Create a New Form File (page 162)

1. With the data file open, click Go to Form on the Merge toolbar.

2. In the Associate dialog box, click Create.

3. Format the document and type any standard text that will remain the same for all documents.

How to Insert Field Codes (page 162)

1. With the form file open, position the insertion point in the location for the first field.

2. Click Insert Field on the Merge toolbar to display the Insert Field Name or Number dialog box.

3. In the Field Names list in the Insert Field Name or Number dialog box,

double-click the field in the Field Names list.

4. Include any spaces or punctuation around the fields.

5. When you've inserted the last field in your form file, click Close to close the Insert Field Name or Number dialog box and save your file.

How to Merge Documents (page 165)

1. Open the form file in WordPerfect.

2. Click Merge on the Merge toolbar, verify that the Data and Form files are correct, and click Merge.

How to Record a Macro (page 168)

1. Open a document that will be affected by the steps you will record, or start at a new document window.

2. Choose Tools → Macro → Record or press Ctrl+F10.

3. In the Filename text box, type a name for your macro and then press Enter or click Record.

4. Perform the actions you wish to record.

5. When you're finished typing, pressing keys, and choosing commands, click the Stop button on the Macro toolbar or choose Tools → Macro → Record to stop recording.

How to Play a Macro (page 169)

1. If you want to use the macro with an existing document, open the document. Otherwise, start at a new document window.

2. Choose Tools → Macro → Play or press Alt+F10.

3. Select the macro you wish to play in the list and click Play.

CHAPTER 9

How to Create a New Slide Show (page 179)

1. Click the Presentations button on the DAD toolbar or click Start→Corel WordPerfect Suite 8→Corel Presentations 8.

2. Select the Create New tab in the New dialog box.

3. Make sure <Presentation Slide Show> is selected and click Create.

4. In the Master Gallery dialog box, click the Category down arrow button. Select a category. Then select the background and click OK.

How to Change the Slide Master (page 184)

1. With any slide showing, click the Master Gallery button on the Slide Show property bar or choose `Format` → `Master Gallery`.

2. Click the Category down arrow button and select a master category.

3. Choose the desired master and click OK.

How to Add a Slide (page 184)

* To add the same slide layout as the current slide, click the Add Slide button below the slide.

* To add a slide with a different slide layout, click the Add Slide down arrow button and select the desired layout from the pop-up list.

How to Select and Display Slides (page 185)

Use the slide tabs or select a slide from the drop-down list at the bottom of the window.

Select a slide from the drop-down list

Click a slide tab

How to Change Slide Layout (page 189)

1. Display the slide that needs a different template.

2. Click the Slide Layout button and choose the desired slide layout.

How to Select Slides (page 190)

In Slide Sorter view, do one of the following:

✳ To select a single slide, click it once.

✳ To select a range of slides, click the first slide in the range, and then press and hold Shift. Click the last slide in the range.

✳ To select slides that aren't next to each other, press and hold Ctrl, and then click each slide you want to include in the selection.

CHAPTER 10

CHAPTER 11

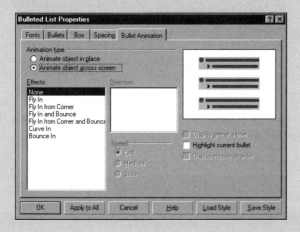

3. Select Animate object in place or Animate object across screen.

4. In the Effects list, select the desired effect and, if appropriate, choose a direction in the Direction list.

5. Indicate a Speed and any additional options and click OK.

How to Animate Objects (page 217)

1. Display the slide containing the image or object you want to animate and select the image(s) or object(s) on the slide.

2. Click the Object Animation button on the Drawing Object property bar or choose **Format** → **Object Properties** → **Object Animation**.

3. Select Animate object in place or Animate object across screen. Depending on your selection the Effects list will change to display the appropriate effects.

4. Set the effect, direction (if appropriate), and speed, and then click OK.

How to Add Transitions and Effects (page 218)

Button	Name	Description
Blinds	Slide Transition	Select transitions for slides.
	Direction	Indicate a direction for the selected slide transition.
	Speed	Indicate a speed for the selected slide transition.
	Sound	Add a sound to the slide.
	Display Sequence	Set timings for slides and objects on slides.

How to Play a Slide Show (page 225)

To play an open slide show beginning with the first slide and using default settings, click the Play Show button on the toolbar.

To set options and play a show:

1. With your slide show open, click the Play Slide Show button on the Slide Show property bar. Or choose View → Play Slide Show.

2. Select the slide with which you wish to begin your show, then select a Highlighter color and Highlighter width and choose the Repeat continuously until 'Esc' check box.

3. Click Play.

How to Run Your Show (page 226)

Use the following techniques to work with your show as you play it:

* *Advancing slides.* If you selected Manual transitions when you set up your Delay Sequences, you must click the current slide or press Page Down to advance to the next one. If you selected delayed transitions, sit back and let Presentations advance the slides for you.

* *Moving to the previous slide.* Press Page Up.

* *Moving to a specific slide.* Press Ctrl+G to display the Go To Slide dialog box, select the slide to display, and click OK.

* *Highlighting a point.* Move the mouse until you see the pointer on the screen. Click and drag to circle an item, underline a point, or draw an arrow to important information. The highlight will disappear after the slide advances. Press Ctrl+E to erase highlighting while the slide is displayed.

* *Working with sounds.* To increase a sound, press Ctrl+up arrow; to decrease, press Ctrl+down arrow. To stop a sound, press End, and to restart it, press Home.

* *Ending a show.* To stop a slide show before you've reached the last slide, press Esc.

CHAPTER 12

How to Go to a Specific Cell (page 243)

1. Choose `Edit` → `Go To` or press Ctrl+G.

2. In the Reference text box, type the cell address you're seeking, or if you've named a block of cells, select the name in the Cell Names list and click OK.

How to Use QuickFill (page 250)

1. Select the cell that will contain the first value in the series, type the value, and press Enter to accept it. Enter additional seed values, if necessary, in the appropriate cells.

2. Select the cell containing the first and/or second seed value(s), and then select all blank cells that will contain the remaining data in the series.

 3. Click the QuickFill button on the Notebook toolbar or right-click the selection, and choose QuickFill from the QuickMenu.

CHAPTER 13

How to Total Cells Using QuickSum (page 260)

1. Select all cells to total, including an empty cell below (for columns) or to the right (for rows) that will contain the total.

 2. Click the QuickSum button on the Notebook toolbar.

How to Enter a Formula (page 262)

1. Select the cell to contain the formula.

2. Type + or = to begin the formula.

3. Type the references to be included in the formula and the operators in the appropriate spots.

 4. When you have finished entering the formula, press Enter or click the Check Mark button on the input line.

How to Insert a Function (page 265)

Do one of the following:

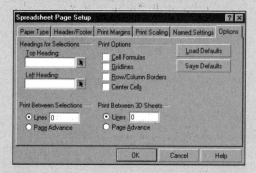

* Double-click the cell to contain the function and type the function.

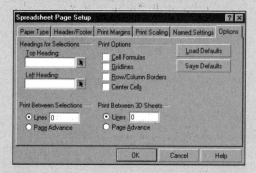

* Click on the Input line and use the Function button to display and select a function.

How to Print a Notebook (page 268)

1. With your notebook open, click the Print button on the Notebook toolbar or choose `File` → `Print`.
2. Make the necessary selections on the Print tab and click Page Setup.
3. Make the necessary selections in the Spreadsheet Page Setup dialog box (shown here), click OK, and then click Print.

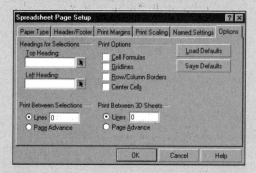

CHAPTER 14

How to Clear Cell Contents (page 276)

* To clear cell *contents*, select the cell or block of cells you wish to clear and press Delete. This is the same as choosing `Edit` → `Clear Values`.

* To clear cell *contents and formatting*, secondary-click the selection and choose Clear from the QuickMenu or choose `Edit` → `Clear` → `Cells`. Quattro Pro removes the contents of the cell, as well as any formatting associated with it. Formatting can include fonts, font sizes, colors, lines, and shading.

* To clear cell *formatting* only, choose `Edit` → `Clear` → `Formats`. This removes the formatting for the cells but leaves the contents of a cell, including a formula, intact.

How to Delete Cells (page 276)

1. Select the cell(s) you wish to delete and click the Delete button on the Notebook toolbar; or choose `Edit` → `Delete`.

2. Under Dimension, select Columns, Rows, or Sheets, depending on which cells you wish to delete.

3. Under Span, choose Entire or Partial and click OK.

How to Insert Blocks of Cells (page 277)

1. Select the cells that are currently in the location for the new cells.

2. Click the Insert button on the Notebook toolbar to display the Insert Cells dialog box, which looks similar to the Delete dialog box.

3. Choose the Dimension and Span and click OK.

How to Insert Rows or Columns (page 279)

Do one of the following:

* Click the column letter or row number to select the location for the new column/row and click the Insert button on the Notebook toolbar.

* Click the column letter or row number to select the location for the new column/row and choose `Insert` → `Colunms` or `Insert` → `Row`.

* Select a cell in the column or row to indicate the location for the new column/row and choose `Insert` → `Cells` to display the Cells dialog box. Under Dimensions, choose Columns or Rows; click OK.

How to Adjust Column Width (page 280)

Use one of the following methods, depending on the desired result:

    Point to the *right edge* of the column letter in the column border you wish to adjust so that you see the sizing pointer. Click and drag the column to the right or left until you reach the desired width.

    To adjust a column width so that the column is as wide as the widest data entry, select the column and then click the QuickFit button on the Notebook toolbar.

How to Adjust Row Height (page 280)

Point to the bottom edge of the row number in the column border so that you see the sizing pointer. Click and drag the row down until you reach the desired height.

How to Format Numeric Cells (page 282)

Select the cells containing the numbers you wish to format, click the Style down arrow button on the Standard property bar, and select the desired numeric format.

How to Align Cell Data Horizontally (page 284)

Select the cells containing the data you wish to format, click the Align down arrow button on the Standard property bar, and choose the desired alignment.

How to Align Cell Data Vertically (page 285)

1. Select the cell(s) you wish to align and click the Cell Properties button on the Quattro Pro property bar.

2. Choose the Alignment tab and select Top, Center, or Bottom under Vertical Alignment.

3. Under Cell Options, choose Wrap Text to ensure that text stays within the cell width, and click OK when finished.

How to Add Lines to Cells (page 286)

To add lines, select the cells you want to format, click the Lines button, and select the desired line style.

How to Name Worksheets (page 287)

To name a sheet, double-click the worksheet tab, type the name, and press Enter or click outside the tab.

CHAPTER 15

How to Create a Chart with QuickChart (page 295)

1. Select the cells containing the data for the chart and click the Chart button on the Notebook toolbar.

2. Move the pointer to an empty area on your worksheet. Quattro Pro turns your pointer into a chart pointer, indicating that you're ready to create the chart.

3. Click and drag to indicate the size and shape of the chart. When you release the mouse button, Quattro Pro creates a chart using the chart type it deems most appropriate for your data.

4. Use the Chart property bar to format and customize the chart.

How to Format Series Properties (page 303)

✳ To change the color of a particular series, click the series element (such as a single bar or pie slice), click the Foreground Color button on the Chart property bar, and select the desired color.

✳ To change other elements, double-click the series element (such as a single bar or pie slice) or select the element and click the Object Properties button on the Chart property bar. Select the desired tab and make your selections; then click OK.

How to Print a Chart (page 304)

✳ To print only your chart exactly as it is, select it as a single object by pointing to an edge until you see the move pointer and clicking once. Click the Print button on the Notebook toolbar.

✳ To print your chart on a black-and-white printer, select the chart and click the Print button on the toolbar or choose `File` → `Print`. Make sure Selected Chart is chosen under Print and choose your print selections on the Print tab. To print black and white, choose the Details tab and select the Adjust image to print black and white check box at the bottom of the dialog box. Click OK to send the chart to the printer.

How to Create a Database (page 306)

Start at a blank worksheet and type the headings for each field in the first row (these were called *field names* in WordPerfect data files). Below each heading, enter the data.

How to Sort by a Single Criterion (page 307)

 Display the Selection Formatting toolbar by secondary-clicking the current toolbar and choosing Selection Formatting. To sort in ascending order, click the top Sort button (A . . . Z) and to sort in descending order, click the bottom Sort button (Z . . . A).

How to Sort with Multiple Criteria (page 307)

1. With the database worksheet open and the Select Formatting toolbar displayed, select any cell containing data.

2. Click the Sort Records button on the Selection Formatting toolbar or choose [Tools] → [Sorts] to display the Data Sort dialog box, shown here.

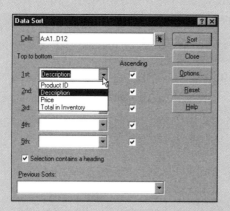

4. Under Top to bottom, click the 1st down arrow button and select the column heading for the column by which you wish to sort from the drop-down list.

5. Under Top to bottom, indicate any secondary sorts using the 2nd, 3rd, 4th, and 5th drop-down lists, if necessary.

6. Click Sort.

CHAPTER 16

How to Add a Bookmark (page 326)

To add a bookmark, use one of the following methods:

* With the address you want to add in the Netsite box, choose `Bookmarks` → `Add Bookmarks` or press Ctrl+D. This adds the bookmark to the bottom of the bookmark list.

* Choose `Window` → `Bookmarks` or press Ctrl+B to display the Bookmark window. Select the folder that will contain the bookmark and choose `Item` → `Insert Bookmarks` on the Bookmark menu. Type a name, URL, and description, and click OK.

How to Open the Mail Window (page 328)

Click the Mail icon on the status bar in the main Netscape window, or choose `Window` → `Mail`. If necessary, enter your e-mail password and click OK.

How to Work with Mail (page 330)

Use the Mail toolbar buttons to get new mail, and send, reply to, and forward mail.

How to Use the Address Book (page 334)

To add an item to the Address Book:

1. Choose `Window` → `Address Book` to display the Address window.

2. Choose `Item` → `Add User` to display the Properties tab in the Address Book dialog box.

3. In the Nick Name text box, type a nick name and then press Tab and type the person's full name in the Name box.

4. Press Tab, type the person's address in the E-Mail Address text box, and click OK.

You can also select any message in the message header pane, and choose `Message` → `Add to Address Book`.

To use an item from the Address Book, click the Send button on the Mail toolbar and use one of the following methods:

* Type the nick name you assigned to the person and press Tab.

* Click the Mail To or Cc button and then double-click the person's name in the Address Book window.

CHAPTER 17

How to Create a Web Document (page 338)

1. Choose File → New and choose the Create New tab.

2. Click the down arrow button and choose Web or Web Publishing.

3. In the list, double-click <WordPerfect Web Document> or select <WordPerfect Web Document> and click Create.

4. Use the Internet Publisher toolbar, property bar, and PerfectExpert panel to add headings and tables, and insert graphics and horizontal lines.

How to Change the Background (page 340)

Use one of the following methods to change the background of your Web document:

✳ If the Internet Publisher PerfectExpert is displayed, click Change Background and select the desired background.

✳ Choose Format → Text/Background Colors . Click the Background color button and select a color. Or click the Background wallpaper folder button and select a texture. When you have finished in the HTML Document Properties dialog box, click OK.

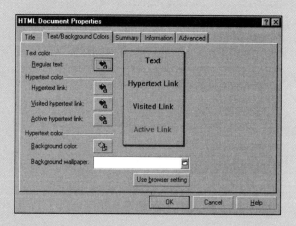

CHAPTER 18

How to Customize Settings in WordPerfect and Presentations (page 356)

✳ To change Display options, choose `Tools` → `Settings` and double-click the Display icon. Make your changes, click OK, and click Close to return to the document window.

✳ To change Environment options, choose `Tools` → `Settings` and double-click the Environment icon. Make your changes, click OK, and click Close to return to the document window.

How to Set a Default Slide Show Master in Presentations (page 360)

1. With Presentations open, choose `Format` → `Master Gallery`.

2. Use the Category drop-down list to select a category, and then click the desired master background.

3. Click Save as Default and click OK.

How to Change Quattro Pro Settings (page 362)

Choose `Tools` → `Settings`. Make your selections on the different tabs. Click OK.

How to Set File Options (page 363)

✳ To change the default files in WordPerfect and Presentations, choose `Tools` → `Settings` and then double-click the File icon. Indicate the folders for each item, click OK, and click Close.

✳ To change the default files in Quattro Pro, choose `Tools` → `Settings`, and choose the File Options tab. Set the default folders and click OK.

How to Move a Toolbar (page 370)

Use one of the following techniques:

✳ Point to a separator between buttons or to a blank area of the toolbar until you see the move pointer. Next, click and drag the toolbar to the desired location until it "snaps" into place.

* In WordPerfect and Presentations, secondary-click the toolbar and choose Settings. Next, click the Options button and select the desired location. The application will show you how the toolbar will look. When you're satisfied, click OK and then click OK again to return to the document window.

* In Quattro Pro, secondary-click the toolbar and choose Settings. Next, click the Options button and select the desired location under Docking Position. Click OK; click Close.

VISUAL INDEX

WordPerfect Documents

Memorandum

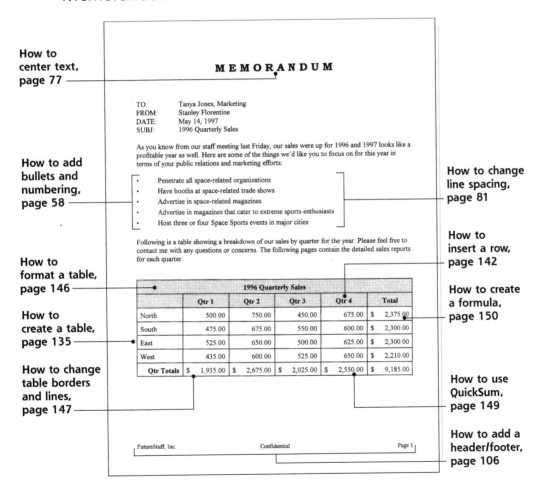

How to center text, page 77

How to add bullets and numbering, page 58

How to format a table, page 146

How to create a table, page 135

How to change table borders and lines, page 147

How to change line spacing, page 81

How to insert a row, page 142

How to create a formula, page 150

How to use QuickSum, page 149

How to add a header/footer, page 106

Résumé

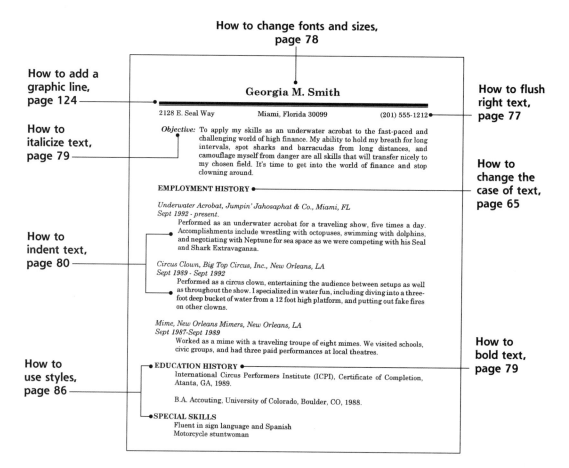

How to change fonts and sizes, page 78

How to add a graphic line, page 124

How to italicize text, page 79

How to indent text, page 80

How to use styles, page 86

How to flush right text, page 77

How to change the case of text, page 65

How to bold text, page 79

Georgia M. Smith

2128 E. Seal Way   Miami, Florida 30099   (201) 555-1212

Objective: To apply my skills as an underwater acrobat to the fast-paced and challenging world of high finance. My ability to hold my breath for long intervals, spot sharks and barracudas from long distances, and camouflage myself from danger are all skills that will transfer nicely to my chosen field. It's time to get into the world of finance and stop clowning around.

EMPLOYMENT HISTORY

Underwater Acrobat, Jumpin' Jahosaphat & Co., Miami, FL
Sept 1992 - present.
Performed as an underwater acrobat for a traveling show, five times a day. Accomplishments include wrestling with octopuses, swimming with dolphins, and negotiating with Neptune for sea space as we were competing with his Seal and Shark Extravaganza.

Circus Clown, Big Top Circus, Inc., New Orleans, LA
Sept 1989 - Sept 1992
Performed as a circus clown, entertaining the audience between setups as well as throughout the show. I specialized in water fun, including diving into a three-foot deep bucket of water from a 12 foot high platform, and putting out fake fires on other clowns.

Mime, New Orleans Mimers, New Orleans, LA
Sept 1987-Sept 1989
Worked as a mime with a traveling troupe of eight mimes. We visited schools, civic groups, and had three paid performances at local theatres.

EDUCATION HISTORY
International Circus Performers Institute (ICPI), Certificate of Completion, Atanta, GA, 1989.

B.A. Accouting, University of Colorado, Boulder, CO, 1988.

SPECIAL SKILLS
Fluent in sign language and Spanish
Motorcycle stuntwoman

Flyer

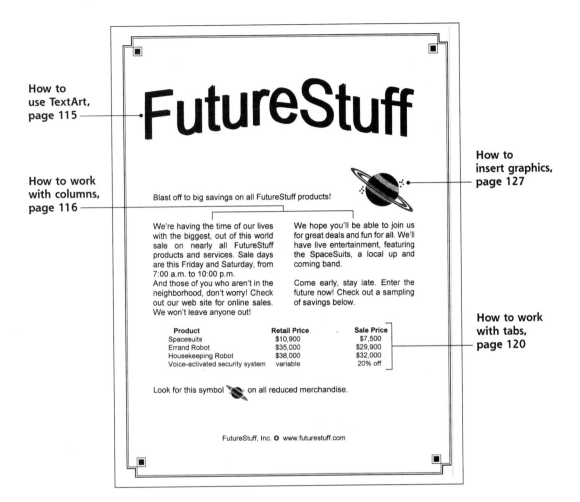

How to
use TextArt,
page 115

How to work
with columns,
page 116

How to
insert graphics,
page 127

How to work
with tabs,
page 120

FutureStuff

Blast off to big savings on all FutureStuff products!

We're having the time of our lives with the biggest, out of this world sale on nearly all FutureStuff products and services. Sale days are this Friday and Saturday, from 7:00 a.m. to 10:00 p.m.
And those of you who aren't in the neighborhood, don't worry! Check out our web site for online sales. We won't leave anyone out!

We hope you'll be able to join us for great deals and fun for all. We'll have live entertainment, featuring the SpaceSuits, a local up and coming band.

Come early, stay late. Enter the future now! Check out a sampling of savings below.

Product	Retail Price	Sale Price
Spacesuits	$10,900	$7,500
Errand Robot	$35,000	$29,900
Housekeeping Robot	$38,000	$32,000
Voice-activated security system	variable	20% off

Look for this symbol on all reduced merchandise.

FutureStuff, Inc. ☉ www.futurestuff.com

Presentations Slide Shows

Title Slide

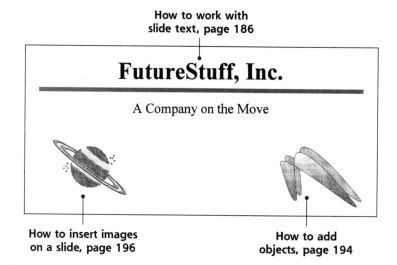

How to work with
slide text, page 186

FutureStuff, Inc.

A Company on the Move

How to insert images
on a slide, page 196

How to add
objects, page 194

Slide Sorter

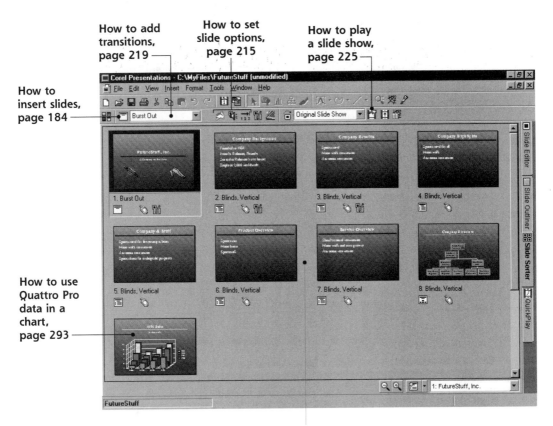

How to add transitions, page 219

How to set slide options, page 215

How to play a slide show, page 225

How to insert slides, page 184

How to use Quattro Pro data in a chart, page 293

How to move or copy slides, page 191

Quattro Pro Documents

Sales Rep Report

How to set horizontal alignment, page 283

How to add lines, page 286

How to create a formula, page 262

How to bold text, page 281

How to use functions, page 265

How to format numbers, page 282

How to use QuickSum, page 260

How to create a floating chart, page 295

How to format a legend, page 303

How to create a header/footer, page 289

How to format a data series, page 303

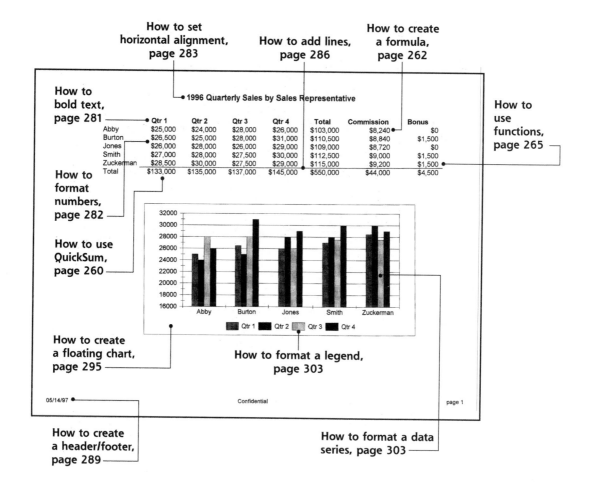

1996 Quarterly Sales by Sales Representative

	Qtr 1	Qtr 2	Qtr 3	Qtr 4	Total	Commission	Bonus
Abby	$25,000	$24,000	$28,000	$26,000	$103,000	$8,240	$0
Burton	$26,500	$25,000	$28,000	$31,000	$110,500	$8,840	$1,500
Jones	$26,000	$28,000	$26,000	$29,000	$109,000	$8,720	$0
Smith	$27,000	$28,000	$27,500	$30,000	$112,500	$9,000	$1,500
Zuckerman	$28,500	$30,000	$27,500	$29,000	$115,000	$9,200	$1,500
Total	$133,000	$135,000	$137,000	$145,000	$550,000	$44,000	$4,500

05/14/97

Confidential

page 1

Client List

How to sort data, page 307

How to create a database, page 305

First Name	Last Name	Company Name	Street	City	ST	ZIP	Phone
Frank	Angelo	Borders Office Supplies	566 E. Norton St.	Denver	CO	80231	303-555-4537
Sam	Applehans	Green Eggs Catering	3421 N. Saturn Ave.	Parker	CO	80304	303-555-7863
George	Asten	Asten Electronics	34 E. 59th St.	Littleton	CO	80121	303-555-6754
Sandra	Boyle	Venter Inc	445 S. Long Ave	San Diego	CA	92022	619-555-4431
Robert	Johansen	Nolan Robotics	213 E. 45th St.	Littleton	CO	80122	303-555-9098
Barbara	Jones	Henderson Cable	123 E. Main St.	Los Angeles	CA	92021	213-555-3434
Jose	Martinez	Greens Motor	34 E 5th Ave	Los Angeles	CA	92012	310-555-7876
Margaret	Nester	Walters Systems	2314 E. Nautical Rd.	San Diego	CA	90221	619-555-6732
Marsha	Poston	Poston Medical Supplies	4545 E. Elm Ave	San Diego	CA	90234	619-555-2317
Catherine	Simms	Elementary Fabrics	342 W. 54th St.	Denver	CO	80203	303-555-6789

Web Documents

Web Page

How to
add a title,
page 341

How to
change fonts,
page 341

How to insert
a graphic,
page 343

How to
justify text,
page 341

How to add
a bulleted list,
page 340

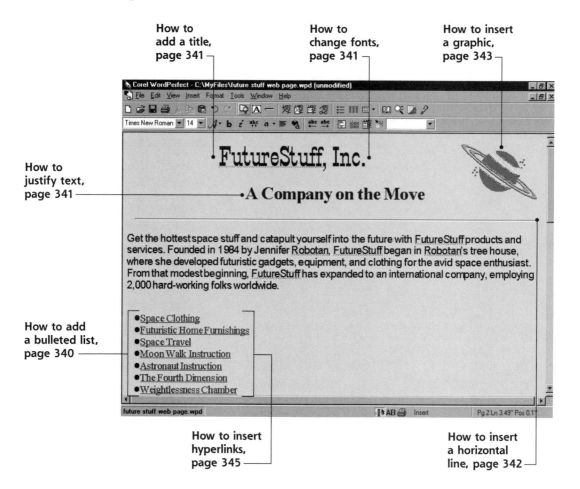

How to insert
hyperlinks,
page 345

How to insert
a horizontal
line, page 342

COOL TOOLS

This appendix is where I share information on several more advanced goodies. Here you learn how to use some additional cool tools that will take you beyond WordPerfect Suite basics. You will see how sorting works and use a few more desktop publishing features in WordPerfect. In Presentations, you'll look at how to add an action key that will perform a specific action when you click it during a slide show. Last but not least, you explore how Quattro Pro can help you fine- tune your financial information with what-if analysis.

Sorting Information in WordPerfect

In Part Two, you learned how to create all kinds of documents and set up your information in different ways. Now's your chance to give information a little order. If you have a distribution list at the bottom of your memo, you can sort it alphabetically. Or, you can sort a merge data file alphabetically so the merged documents come out in alphabetical order. And what if you want to sort the employees listed in that beautiful table according to hire date? Not a problem with WordPerfect's powerful Sort feature.

The great thing about the Sort feature is that it has several predefined sorts and usually recognizes the type of sort you want to do based on the text you've selected. For example, if you've selected several rows in a table, WordPerfect assumes you will perform a table sort. If you open a merge data file, WordPerfect selects the merge sort for you.

Understanding Sort Concepts

In Chapter 15 you learned a bit about sorting using the Filtering feature in Quattro Pro and explored the concept of primary and secondary keys. WordPerfect sorting works the same way. The primary sort is the first sort, and if you want to break the tie for the first sort, you can set a secondary sort using another key.

X-REF See "Sorting with Multiple Criteria" in Chapter 15 for additional information on sorting in Quattro Pro.

In WordPerfect, the Sort feature uses *fields* and *words* to identify the location for criteria. Figure A-1 shows how WordPerfect interprets tabular columns for sorting (see Chapter 6 for a refresher on tabular columns). Note that field 1 is empty. In tabular columns, field 1 is against the left margin and in this example, the first column starts at the first tab stop. In a merge data file, the fields are noted more obviously — by END FIELD codes. If you have your data in a table, you'll use a table sort, where information is separated into cells.

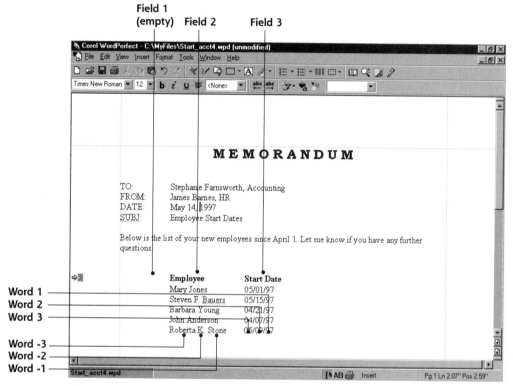

Figure A-1 Sorting tabular columns.

Are you wondering why anyone would want to count from right to left instead of left to right? Look carefully at the information in the first column. Notice that some names have a middle initial and some do not. What if you want to sort on the last name? If you count from left to right, sometimes the last name is the second word, and sometimes it's the third word, depending on whether the person uses a middle initial or not. However, if you count from right to left, the last name is always the *first* word. Pretty sneaky, eh? This little tidbit is one of many things that makes the Sort feature so powerful.

If you have numeric information — such as dates — to sort, WordPerfect denotes each "word" by the slash, space, or dash separating it. For example, if the date is 5/16/97 or 5-16-97, word 1 is 5, word 2 is 16, and word 3 is 97.

WHO'S ON THIRD?

Knowing what you do about counting right to left, what if you have a name with a title or degree after it, such as Mary P. Stanton, Ph.D., or Charles Duncan, III. You don't want WordPerfect sorting by *Ph.D.* or *III.* To ensure that WordPerfect looks at the last name and title or degree as one word, insert a hard space between them. To insert a hard space, press Ctrl+spacebar instead of the spacebar alone. In Reveal Codes, you'll see the Hspace code, for Hard Space.

Sorting Your Information

If you have a list of names, paragraphs, a table, or a merge data file, you can sort the information easily. Use Table A-1 to prepare your information for sorting. Note that if you've placed your merge data in a table, you will sort it using the Table techniques.

TABLE A-1 Preparing to Sort Information

To Sort	Do This
List or paragraphs	Select the list or paragraphs.
Tabular columns	Select all information you want to sort. Do *not* select any headings in your tabular columns unless you want to include them in the sort.
Table	Select all rows with information you want to sort. Do *not* select any heading rows unless you want to include them in the sort.
Merge data file	Open the merge data file.

Once you perform one of the actions in Table A-1, follow these steps to sort the information:

1. Choose Tools → Sort to display the Sort dialog box (see Figure A-2).

2. Click Options and select Allow Undo after sorting to make sure you can use the Undo feature if the sort doesn't do what you expected.

Figure A-2 Select or create your sort definition.

3. As long as you've performed one of the actions in Table A-1, you can click Sort to sort by the first word in your line, paragraph, merge data file, or table cell. WordPerfect performs the sort for you, reordering the information by the first word.

Creating a Custom Sort Definition

The default sort definitions that you saw in the previous section — first word in a line, first word in a paragraph, and so on — are fine for some things, but what if you want to sort your merge data file by last name, which is in field 2? Or by date in a table where the date is in column D? If you know you'll be repeating your sort often, you can create your own definition and use it. Otherwise, you can edit one of the existing definitions. Here we focus on creating your own.

WordPerfect lets you sort in ascending (A-Z or lowest number to highest) or descending (Z-A or highest number to lowest) order, just as you saw in Quattro Pro. You can also choose from two types of sorts. An *alphanumeric* sort will sort your information by letters and then by any numbers it may contain. A *numeric* sort will sort only the numbers in your information. For example, say you have a list of part numbers, two of which are S45 and D980. In an ascending alphanumeric sort, WordPerfect will list these as D980 and then S45. In an ascending numeric sort, WordPerfect will only look at the numbers, putting S45 before D980 because 45 is smaller than 980.

To create your own sort definition, follow these steps:

1. Choose **Tools** → **Sort**, and then click New to display the New Sort dialog box (see Figure A-3).

2. In the Sort description text box, type a description for the sort, indicating what it will do.

Add keys and define your criteria

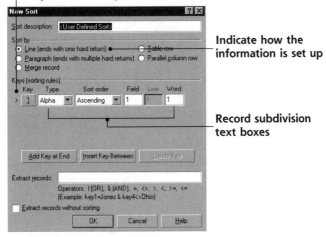

Indicate how the information is set up

Record subdivision text boxes

Figure A-3 Create your own sort.

3. Under Sort by, indicate how WordPerfect should sort the information. If you've selected text prior to displaying this dialog box, WordPerfect will select what it thinks is the appropriate method.

4. Next to Key 1, indicate the Type of sort — Alpha or Numeric — and the Sort order — Ascending or Descending.

5. Type your criteria in the Key 1 record subdivision text boxes. These may be Field, Line, Word, or Column, depending on the type of sort you selected in Step 3. For example, if you selected Table row, you'll see Column, Line, and Word as the headers for the record subdivision text boxes. If you select Line, you'll see Field and Word, with Line dimmed. Use both Figure A-4 and Table A-2 to guide you through setting up criteria.

6. If you need to perform a subsort on Key 1, click Add Key to End and define this key to break any ties WordPerfect encounters when sorting by Key 1.

7. Click OK. WordPerfect adds your definition to the list. You can use it any time you like; it's now a permanent part of the Sort list until you delete it.

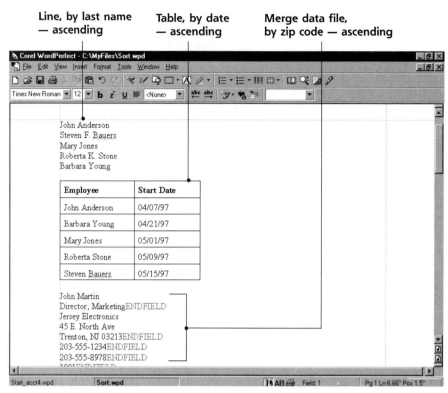

Figure A-4 How to sort information.

TABLE A-2 Sort Criteria Examples

Reference in Figure A-4	Type this
Line, by last name	Field 1, Word -1
Table, by date	Key 1: Column 2, Line 1, Word 3 (year)
	Key 2: Column 2, Line 1, Word 1 (month)
	Key 3: Column 2, Line 1, Word 2 (day)
Merge data file, by zip code	Field 2, Line -1, Word -1

In the Table example, I need three keys. Key 1 sorts by the year. Key 2 sorts any duplicate years by the month, and Key 3 sorts any duplicate months by the day.

In the Merge data file example, I counted from bottom to top for the line with -1 because some records contain two lines in field 2 and some contain 3. I used -1 for the word because some cities may have multiple names and the user may not have joined them with a hard space.

Using Drop Caps in WordPerfect

L ook at the letter beginning this paragraph. It's a big letter that drops down into the paragraph. That's right, it's called a *drop cap*. Want to create one in your own document? Here's how.

Position the insertion point in the paragraph that will contain the drop cap as the first letter of the paragraph. Choose Format→Paragraph→Drop Cap or press Ctrl+Shift+C. The first letter of the paragraph becomes a drop cap. Click in front of the drop cap at the beginning of the paragraph to display the Drop Cap property bar. You can change a number of settings for the drop cap, including how it appears (type), how big it is, its position, and other options. You can hide the Drop Cap property bar by clicking anywhere away from the drop cap letter.

 TIP To create a drop cap for a paragraph you haven't typed yet, turn on the drop cap feature and begin typing. WordPerfect will automatically change the first letter into a drop cap.

Creating QuickLinks in Presentations

I n Chapter 11 you learned how to add a sound to a slide so that it will play when you display the slide. But what if you want the sound to play after all the bullet points are displayed on Slide 4? That's when it makes sense to start the theme from "Rocky" and not when the slide first displays. Or, what if you want to go to Slide 8 from Slide 2, then return to Slide 2 again? You can do these things using a *QuickLink*. A QuickLink allows you to play a sound or perform an action by clicking an object during the show.

Adding a QuickLink

The first step to adding a sound object that you can control is to create the QuickLink itself. Once you create it, you can play the sound associated with the slide at any time. You can add a QuickLink to an object, image, bullet list, or org or data chart. If you don't have one of these elements on the slide, you can add an object using the techniques in Chapter 11. If you don't want the object to show up in the slide show, make it invisible when you create the QuickLink.

1. Open the slide show to which you want to add a QuickLink and then display the slide that will contain the QuickLink.

2. Select the object (such as a graphic or drawing object you created) that you will associate with the QuickLink, or create the object and then select it.

3. Click the QuickLink button on the Drawing Object property bar or choose **Format** → **Object Properties** → **QuickLink** to display the QuickLink tab in the Object Properties dialog box (see Figure A-5).

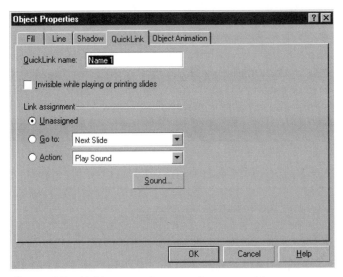

Figure A-5   Linking an action to an image or object.

4. In the QuickLink name text box, type a name for your link.

5. If you don't want the image or object to show up on the slide, choose Invisible while playing or printing slides. You'll still be able to activate the QuickLink, it just won't take up visible space on the slide.

6. Under Event/Action, select what you want Presentations to do using either the Go To or Action drop-down list.

7. Set any additional options necessary based on your selection in Step 6.

8. When you've selected all options and settings, click OK. If you added a sound, Presentations adds it to the object and will play it when the slide displays during your show. If you added another action, this action will occur when you click the QuickLink during the show.

Using a QuickLink

Once you've added a QuickLink to a slide, you can activate it while you're playing the slide show. Here's how:

1. Play the slide show containing the QuickLink as you would any other slide show. For a refresher, see "Playing a Slide Show" in Chapter 11.

2. When the slide containing the action link displays, point to the object you associated with the slide until you see the pointer change to a hand pointer. If you made the QuickLink invisible, point to the area where you know the object is located until you see the pointer change to a hand pointer.

3. With the hand pointer visible, click once. Presentations plays the sound or performs the event or action you indicated in the QuickLink Properties dialog box.

Asking What If? in Quattro Pro

If you've ever tried to figure out what sort of interest rate you need to have a certain house payment or tried to estimate the effect on your budget if your expenses increase a certain amount, you know how frustrating it can be to change the numbers and recalculate. Luckily, Quattro Pro makes the process pretty easy for you, using what-if tables.

You can create a what-if table that uses new data, or you can use data that already exists in one of your notebooks. Quattro Pro allows you to have either one or two *variables* in a what-if. A variable is the value that will change (your income, for example). For simplicity's sake, this section focuses on single-variable what-if tables. To make it easier to understand the process, I'll walk you through the steps of creating the what-if table in Figure A-6.

To create a what-if table using only one variable, follow these steps:

1. On a blank worksheet, set up the values you'll use and the formula that calculates those values. In Figure A-6, you would type the following information: In cell A1, **House Payment**; in cell B1, **160000**; in cell A2, **Interest rate**; in cell B2, **.10**. In cell A4, type **Payment**, and in cell B4, type **@PMT(B1,B2/12,30*12)**.

2. Choose Tools → Numeric Tools → What If to display the What If dialog box. Here you can enter your own info or use the Expert. You'll use the Expert.

3. Click Expert to display Step 1 of 7 in the What-If Expert dialog box. Notice the default option is Vary one cell against one or more formulas. This is what you want so click Next to move on.

4. For Step 2 of 7, type the cell reference containing the formula in the Formula Cell text box, or click the cell in the worksheet to insert the reference in the text box. In our example, this is cell B4. Click Next to continue.

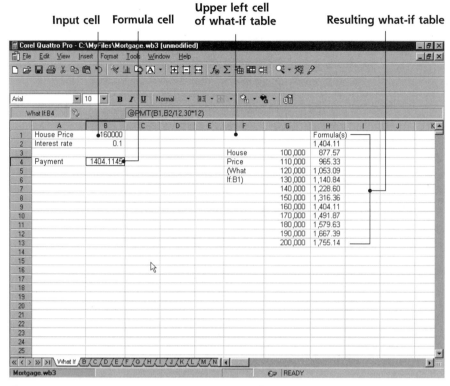

Figure A-6   Figure your house payments with different home prices.

5. For Step 3 of 7, you don't want to refer to any other formulas so click Next.

6. For Step 4 of 7, type the cell reference containing the value you want to check in the Input Cell text box, or click the cell in the worksheet to insert the reference in the text box. In our example, this is cell B1.

7. If you want to, you can type a name for the what-if table. Type **House Price**. Click Next to display Step 5 of 7. Depending on your scenario, Quattro Pro may provide a list of suggested values it can use to calculate different payment amounts, ranging from $80,000 to $320,000. Or it may just give you a label — Home - actual. Since your price range is probably quite different, you'll make a few changes here.

8. In Step 5 of 7, click Calculate Different Values to display increment boxes to the right of the suggested values list.

9. In the Start text box, type the value you wish to start with. This would be the minimum you will pay for a house. For our example, type **100000**. In the Step text box, type the value Quattro Pro should increase each

time. Type **10000**. In the Stop text box, type the highest amount you're willing to pay for the house: **200000**. When you're finished, click Rebuild List and then click Next.

10. In the last step, type or select the cell that will be the upper left cell of the what-if table. In the example, I use cell F1. Click Make Table to let Quattro Pro do the calculations for you.

Format your numbers any way you want. The numbers in columns G and H used the Comma numerical format.

TIP If you change your formula, you can update the what-if table by choosing Tools→Numeric Tools→What-If to display the What If dialog box. Click Generate to recalculate the what-if table.

Working with Photo House

One of the bonus applications that ships with WordPerfect Suite is Photo House. This amazing little program lets you touch up existing photos on your system or those you've scanned in and saved on disk. In addition to adding text and special effects to an existing image, you can also create your own bitmap images.

Installing Photo House

Since Photo House is a bonus application, WordPerfect Setup doesn't install it during a Typical installation unless you select it. If you didn't select Photo House during installation, you can do so now using the Custom Install option.

1. Close all WordPerfect Suite applications that are running — this includes DAD and PerfectPrint.

2. On the Windows desktop, choose Start → Corel WordPerfect Suite 8 → Setup & Notes → Corel WordPerfect Suite Setup and make sure the Corel WordPerfect Suite 8 CD is in your CD-ROM drive. Setup displays the Welcome dialog box.

3. Choose Next to display the License Agreement dialog box and click Yes to accept the agreement. Setup displays the Registration Information dialog box. Click Next to display the Installation Type dialog box.

4. Choose Custom and then click Next. Setup displays the Destination dialog box. Select a destination, if necessary, and click Next. Setup displays the Custom Installation dialog box.

5. Click Reset to display the Custom Installation Settings dialog box, choose Deselect All in the list, and click OK.

6. In the list, select Corel Photo House and click Next. Follow the on-screen instructions. WordPerfect Setup will add the Photo House button to DAD and to the menu as a main application.

When you install Photo House, it "takes over" the Windows file associations with .PCX, .GIF, and .JPG file extensions and renames them with Photo House extensions. You can still use them as you normally would, but they will have these other extensions.

Starting Photo House

To start Photo House and begin using it, choose Start→Corel WordPerfect Suite 8→Corel Photo House. You'll see the main Photo House window, as in Figure A-7.

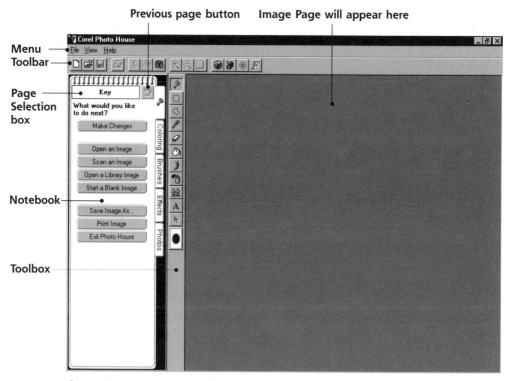

Figure A-7 Edit photos and images in Photo House.

The Notebook is probably the most unfamiliar Photo House element, but once you begin to use it, you'll see that it's actually a lot like the PerfectExpert feature you find in the main applications. The Notebook offers five main pages, each marked with a tab on the right side. Once you select a page, you can select other options that may take you to additional pages.

- The *Key* page lists general tasks you can perform in Photo House to work with images. You can also click the Key tool on the Toolbox to display this page.
- The *Coloring* page lets you select a paint color or a color you want to use as the page color.
- The *Brushes* page lets you select a brush size and style with which to paint using the Brush tool (see Table A-3).
- The *Effects* page lets you change the overall appearance of your image using a variety of options.
- The *Photos* page lets you select an image from the CD library of images.

To return to a previous page, click the Previous Page button next to the Page Selection box.

X-REF For more information on the PerfectExpert, see Chapter 2.

Using the Photo House Toolbar and Toolbox

You'll notice that Photo House has two toolbars, one across the top that contains many familiar buttons, and one that runs vertically down the screen called the *Toolbox*. Figure A-8 describes those buttons with which you may not be familiar. Table A-3 describes each button in the Toolbox.

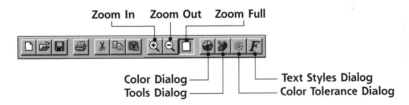

Figure A-8 The Photo House toolbar.

TABLE A-3 Photo House Toolbox

Tool	Name	Description
	KEY	Provide a list of general tasks.
	RECTANGULAR SELECTION	Select an area of your image in the shape of a rectangle.

TABLE A-3 Photo House Toolbox

Tool	Name	Description (continued)
	FREEHAND SELECTION	Select a specific area of your image without the restraints of a specific shape.
	EYEDROPPER	Capture a color from your image to use as a painting color.
	ERASER	Erase parts of your image using white or another color.
	FLOOD FILL	Fill in areas that share the same color with the selected color.
	BRUSH	Paint freely with the selected brush type and color.
	SPRAY	Paint freely using a spray can look.
	CLONE	Copy parts of the image to other areas.
	TEXT	Add words such as titles and captions to your images.
	PICK	Select and then move or resize your text.
	CHANGE COLORS	Show you your existing colors and let you select new ones.

Enhancing an Existing Photo or Image

WordPerfect Suite ships with thousands of images, including hundreds of photographs. You can edit these or any other graphic, including a photograph or other image you've scanned. You can also scan an image directly into Photo House and work with it. If you're not an artist, or even if you are, you can do a ton of fun and creative things with an existing image. Put the head of a tiger on the body of an elephant or combine parts of three different images to create your new logo. The possibilities are endless.

OPENING AN IMAGE

Photo House lets you either open an image or a library image. The only difference is that when you select the Open an Image option, Photo House looks for it on your hard drive, whereas if you select the Open a Library Image option, Photo House checks your CD-ROM drive for either the WordPerfect Suite CD or another Photo House CD. This is the same as selecting the Photos tab in the Notebook.

 WEB PATH To obtain information on purchasing additional photos and images, check out http://www.corel.com/products/clipartandphotos.

To open an image, select the Key tool on the toolbox or click the Key page in the Notebook to display the Key page. Click either Open an Image or Open a Library Image and select your image. Depending on the speed of your system, it may take some time for the image to load.

CREATING A NEW IMAGE

Though Photo House is designed primarily for working with existing images, you can create a masterpiece from scratch if you're a closet Monet or Degas. Simply click the New button on the toolbar or choose File→New. You can also click Start a Blank Image on the Key page in the Notebook. Photo House displays the Create New Image dialog box. Make your selections for the following options and click OK.

* *Color mode* controls the color quality of your image, including choosing black and white or gray scale if you plan to print to a black and white printer.

* *Image size* controls the type of document you're creating. If it's a greeting card, select one of the many card options. You can also choose to create a full-page image or a postcard.

* *Resolution* controls the clarity and sharpness of an image. Note that though you can select a dpi (dots per inch) setting that is greater than your printer can print, your printer will only print using its highest resolution capability.

TIP If you want to create an image using shapes and lines, use the Drawing tools in either Presentations or WordPerfect, rather than trying to use Photo House.

WORKING WITH YOUR IMAGE

Once your image is open, you can use all the tools on the Toolbox, as well as the Coloring, Brushes, and Effects pages to change it. For example, say you've opened the image of a rose and want to change it from red to yellow. Simply choose the Coloring page and select yellow as your color. Next, select the Flood Fill tool on the Toolbox and click the areas of the rose you wish to color yellow.

If you've created a new image, you can use the Brush tool to paint your picture, selecting a brush shape and style on the Brushes page as well as a color on the Coloring page. Use the Effects page to change the overall look of your images with a variety of photo-related techniques. The best way to see how they work is to choose them and experiment!

TIP You can flip and rotate your images in Photo House just as you did in Presentations and WordPerfect. Choose Image→Rotate or Image→Flip

APPENDIX B

KEYBOARD SHORTCUTS

This appendix lists shortcut keys to many of the most common actions in the WordPerfect Suite.

Keyboard Shortcuts for All Applications

Table B-1 shows the most common actions and their keyboard shortcut equivalents. Table B-2 provides shortcuts for common formatting and editing features. You can use these keyboard shortcuts in any application in the WordPerfect Suite.

TABLE B-1 General Shortcuts for All Applications

Action	Shortcut
Open	Ctrl+O
Close	Ctrl+F4
Save	Ctrl+S
Save As	F3
Print	Ctrl+P
Help Topics	F1
Help What's This	Shift+F1

TABLE B-2 Editing and Formatting Shortcuts for All Applications

Action	Shortcut
Go To	Ctrl+G
Next window	Ctrl+F6

TABLE B-2 Editing and Formatting Shortcuts for All Applications (*Continued*)

Action	Press
Beginning of a document	Ctrl+Home
Ctrl+End	End of document
Find	Ctrl+F
Cut	Ctrl+X
Copy	Ctrl+C
Paste	Ctrl+V
Bold	Ctrl+B
Italics	Ctrl+I
Underline	Ctrl+U
Undo	Ctrl+Z
Redo	Ctrl+Shift+R
QuickCorrect	Ctrl+Shift+F1
Spell Check	Ctrl+F1

WordPerfect Keyboard Shortcuts

You can use a variety of keystrokes in WordPerfect to move around a document as well as perform other actions. Tables B-3, B-4, B-5, and B-6 show the different shortcuts you can use in WordPerfect.

TIP For a graphic example of how to use your keyboard template, choose Help→Help Topics and choose the Index tab. Type **cua keyboard** and click Display.

TABLE B-3 Document Navigation Keys

To Move to	Press
Previous page	Alt+Page Up
Next page	Alt+Page Down

To Move to	Press
Beginning of current line	Home
End of current line	End
Word to the right	Ctrl+right arrow
Word to the left	Ctrl+left arrow

TABLE B-4 Justifying Text

Action	Shortcut
Center, single line	Shift+F7
Flush right	Alt+F7
Indent	F7
Double indent	Ctrl+Shift+F7
Left justify	Ctrl+L
Right justify	Ctrl+R
Center justify	Ctrl+E
Fully justify	Ctrl+J

TABLE B-5 Moving the Insertion Point in Columns

Action	Shortcut
Insert a new column	Ctrl+Enter
Next column	Alt+right arrow
Previous column	Alt+left arrow
Top of current column	Alt+Home
Bottom of current column	Alt+End

TABLE B-6 Moving Around in Tables

To Move to	Press
Next cell	Tab
Previous cell	Shift+Tab
Up one cell	Alt+up arrow
Down one cell	Alt+down arrow
First cell in current row	Home, Home
Last cell in current row	End, End

Presentations Keyboard Shortcuts

There are a number of shortcuts you can use while running a slide show in Presentations. Table B-7 gives you the lowdown.

TABLE B-7 Playing Slide Shows

Action	Shortcut
Erase highlighting	Ctrl+E
Go to a particular slide	Ctrl+G
First slide	Ctrl+Home
Last slide	Ctrl+End
Previous slide	Left arrow, up arrow, or Page Up
Next slide	Right arrow, down arrow, or Page Down
Next transition	Space bar
Backtrack	Backspace
Increase sound volume	+ or Ctrl+up arrow
Decrease sound volume	- or Ctrl+down arrow
Stop sound	End
Restart sound	Home

Quattro Pro Keyboard Shortcuts

Y ou can easily find your way around your worksheet or notebook using the shortcut keys in Table B-8.

TABLE B-8 Worksheet Navigation Keys

To Move to	Press
One cell right	Right arrow or Tab
One cell left	Left arrow or Shift+Tab
One cell down	Down arrow
One cell up	Up arrow
One screen right	Ctrl+right arrow
One screen left	Ctrl+left arrow
One screen down	Page Down
One screen up	Page Up
Next sheet	Ctrl+Page Down
Previous sheet	Ctrl+Page Up
Cell A1 on the current sheet	Home
Last cell containing data on a sheet	End, Home
Last cell containing data in the notebook	End, Ctrl+Home
Last cell containing data in the direction of the arrow	End, any arrow key

TROUBLESHOOTING GUIDE

This appendix provides answers to some common questions regarding the WordPerfect Suite. The sections break out here like they do in the book, with the first section covering Part One — the suite itself — and other problems that are common to all the applications. After that, I cover questions involving WordPerfect, Presentations, and Quattro Pro. Finally, I address issues in Netscape Navigator, Internet Publisher, and customization.

General Suite and Printing Problems

DAD has disappeared from the Windows taskbar. To display DAD, click Start on the Windows desktop and then choose Corel WordPerfect Suite 8→Accessories→Corel Desktop Applications Director.

Some of my screens look different than those in the book. You can customize your system and the way your applications work in a variety of ways. This book tries to use the default settings wherever possible, and any discrepancies you see are a result of customization. For more on this, see Chapter 18.

I accidentally added a word to my supplemental dictionary and need to remove it. At a blank document window, choose Tools→Spell Check to display the Spell Checker tab. Click No when asked to close the Spell Checker. Click Options and choose User Word Lists to display the User Word Lists dialog box. The word you added will be in the box at the bottom of the dialog box with the word *<skip>* next to it.

Locate the word you added (the words are in alphabetical order) and select it. Click Delete Entry and then click Yes to confirm the deletion. Click close to close the User Word Lists dialog box and Close again to close the Spell Checker.

I'd like to print several files in a folder without opening them in the application. Open any file management dialog box and make sure the menu is displayed. If it isn't, click the Menu button on the right side of the dialog box. Select all files you wish to print and choose File→Print. To print a *list* of files in a folder, display the folder and choose File→Print File List. Choose any options and click OK.

I made a mistake and want to stop printing my document. You can stop a print job through the application (WordPerfect, Presentations, or Quattro Pro) or the Windows Print queue. For information on the Windows Print queue, see your Windows documentation. To stop printing a document using the WordPerfect Print dialog box, follow these steps:

1. Click the Print button on the toolbar or choose File → Print .

2. Click Status at the bottom of the dialog box to display the Print Status and History dialog box.

3. Select the document or file you want to cancel and choose Document → Cancel Printing .

Note that this only stops pages that haven't been sent to your printer already. Your printer may continue printing after you choose to cancel because it has pages in its own memory. If you don't want to see jobs that have already been printed, choose Display→Hide Completed Jobs in the Print Status and History dialog box.

I want my WordPerfect or Presentations document to print on both sides. If you have *duplex* capabilities on your printer, you can print on both sides of the page. Otherwise, you'll need to print even pages, then refeed them into your printer and print odd pages. For either method, first click the Print button on the toolbar or choose File→Print. Next, choose the Two-Sided Printing tab. If you have a duplex printer, select Flip on long edge or Flip on short edge under Automatic by printer. If you don't have a duplex printer, choose Step 1: print odd pages, or Step 2: print even pages. Note that depending on how your printer prints out pages, you'll do one before the other to make sure pages come out in order. Select any options under Shift image for binding, and then click OK.

If you're printing manually, insert pages into the printer to print on the other side when prompted.

WordPerfect Problems

The shadow cursor disappears when I position my pointer over text. The shadow cursor is defaulted to display only in blank document areas. To have it show up in both areas, choose Tools→Settings and double-click the Display icon. Choose the Document tab, and under Shadow Cursor, choose Both under Active and click OK. Click Close to return to the document window.

I deleted some text and then decided I needed it in another location. When I used Undo, it put it back in the original spot. When you want to undelete text in another location, you must use the Undelete feature. Position the insertion point in the new location for the deleted text, press Ctrl+Shift+Z, and click Restore.

I used full justification to format my paragraph but now the last line is stretched between the left and right margins. You used All justification instead of Full justification. Position the insertion point in your paragraph, click the Justification button on the Standard property bar, and choose Full.

I want to copy a format to two other headings but don't need to create a style. Use QuickFormat. Select the text containing the formatting and click the QuickFormat button on the WordPerfect toolbar (it looks like a paint roller with a lightening bolt on one tip). Choose Characters to format individual characters or choose Headings to format an entire paragraph and click OK. Your pointer changes and has a paintbrush attached. To format characters, click and drag over the text you wish to format. To format a paragraph, click once in the paragraph. Repeat for all text you wish to format. When you're finished, click the QuickFormat button on the WordPerfect toolbar to turn it off.

I want to replace text but when I fill in the boxes in the Find and Replace dialog box, the Replace button is dimmed. To replace text, WordPerfect must *select* the located text so it knows what to replace. In the Find and Replace Text dialog box, choose Action→Select Match. The Replace button is now active, and you can proceed.

I turned on my paragraph style and typed my paragraph. When I pressed Enter, WordPerfect continued using the style but I don't want to use it. The style is chained to itself which means pressing Enter will turn on the style for the next paragraph. To have the Enter key chain to no style, edit the style and select <None> for the Enter key will chain to option.

I set line spacing to double but only part of my document has double line spacing. When you set line spacing, WordPerfect starts the line spacing at the beginning of the line containing the insertion point. Any text before the insertion point won't be affected by your change. Make sure you position the insertion point where you want double spacing to begin before setting it.

I want my separator line for my footnotes to be longer and thicker. You can customize the separator line in a variety of ways. Position the insertion point at the top of the document and choose Insert→Footnote/Endnote. Make sure Footnote Number is selected, and then click Options and choose Separator from the pop-down menu. Indicate a measurement for the Length of line and select a Line style. Click OK, and then click Close to return to the document window.

My footnote or endnote font is different than the font for the rest of my document. Your footnotes and endnotes use the Document Initial Font for their font settings. If you change the font using the Standard property bar, your fonts won't match. To set your footnote and endnote fonts to match your document font, choose Format→Font and click Default Font. Select the font you want and click OK and then OK again. To make sure the fonts always match, remove any font codes that affect the entire document and set all fonts in the Document Default Font dialog box.

I need to switch my endnotes to footnotes. You can use a macro that ships with WordPerfect to convert your endnotes to footnotes or footnotes to endnotes. Choose Tools→Macro→Play and make sure the default macro folder displays. In the file list, double-click `endfoot.wcm` to convert endnotes to footnotes or `footend.wcm` to convert footnotes to endnotes.

I have a large table in a document that I want to print landscape, but I want the rest of the document to print portrait. You can mix landscape and portrait paper types in a single document to help display your information. Position the insertion point on the page you want as landscape and choose Format→Page→Page Setup. On the Size tab, choose Landscape and then choose the Following pages different from current page check box. Under Following pages, choose Portrait, and click OK.

I want to add captions to my graphics. You can quickly add captions to your graphics, letting WordPerfect automatically number them for you. Secondary-click the graphic and choose Create Caption from the QuickMenu. WordPerfect inserts the word *Figure* followed by an automatic number. You can delete this if you don't want it. Type the text for your caption and click outside the graphic. To edit the caption, secondary-click the graphic and choose Edit Caption from the QuickMenu.

I can't get my graphic to stay where I've positioned it. When WordPerfect inserts a graphic, it attaches it to the current page by default. This means the graphic maintains specific measurements from the top and left edges or margins of the page to get its location. These are like coordinates on a map, telling you the "latitude" (horizontal distance) and "longitude" (vertical distance) of your image in relation to the top and left edges/margins of the page.

However, there may be times when you don't want the graphic to be in a specific location on a page. Perhaps you want it to stay with a paragraph that it illustrates, which means attaching it to a *paragraph*. Or, perhaps you want it to be *inline*, which means attaching it to a *character*. These inline graphics act as actual characters on the line, moving with the line just as the characters do. To anchor your graphic to a paragraph, character, or page, follow these steps:

1. Secondary-click the image and choose Position from the QuickMenu to display the Box Position dialog box.

2. Click the Attach box to button, select Page, Paragraph, or Character from the pop-up menu, and set the appropriate options.

3. When you're finished, click OK.

I have a short announcement in my document to which I'd like to draw attention with a border. If it's a standard paragraph, you can add a paragraph border to it. Just position the insertion point in the paragraph and choose Format→Paragraph→Border/Fill. On the Border tab, select the border under Available border styles and click OK.

If you want to be able to position the announcement in different places like a graphic, place it in a text box. Select the text and click the Cut button on the WordPerfect toolbar. Position the insertion point in the location for the text box and click the Text Box button on the WordPerfect toolbar (there's a capital letter A in it). With the insertion point inside the text box, click the Paste button on the WordPerfect toolbar. Move and format the box as you would any graphic box. To change the border, select the text box and use the Border Style button on the Graphics property bar.

I'm using calculations in my table and the total isn't correct. Make sure you aren't using numbers in any headings, such as *Qtr 1* or *1996*. If you are, WordPerfect will include these in the calculation unless you instruct otherwise. You have two methods for resolving this. You can either format the cells as text so WordPerfect no longer sees them as numbers or tell WordPerfect to ignore the cells during calculation.

To make sure WordPerfect doesn't include certain cells in calculations, select the cells *not* to include in the calculations. Then use one of the following methods:

- Click the Numeric down arrow on the Table property bar and choose Text.
- Click the Table menu button on the Table property bar, and choose Format. Choose the Cell tab and then choose Ignore cell when calculating under Cell attributes. Click OK.

I merged two documents and came up with a blank new document. First, make sure you've associated your form file with a data file or Address list. If you have, then make sure the fields you inserted in your form file match those in the associated data file. If they don't, WordPerfect has nothing to merge.

On the Contents tab in online help, I double-clicked Macros and then double-clicked Macro Programming. I got a message telling me Windows can't find the wpwp8ens.hlp **file.** Because the macro help file takes up approximately 1.6MB of disk space and many users don't use advanced macro commands, this help file is not installed during a typical installation. To install it, you must perform a custom installation. First, close all WordPerfect Suite applications that are running — this includes DAD and PerfectPrint. Next, click Start on the Windows taskbar→Corel WordPerfect Suite 8→Setup & Notes→Corel WordPerfect Suite Setup and make sure the Corel WordPerfect Suite CD is in your CD-ROM drive. Choose Next to display the License Agreement dialog box and click Yes to accept the agreement. Setup displays the Registration Information dialog box. Click Next to display the Installation Type dialog box. Choose Custom→Next. Setup displays the Destination dialog box. Select a destination, if necessary, and click Next. Setup displays the Custom Installation dialog box. Click Selection Options, choose Deselect All in the list, and click OK. In the list, select Corel WordPerfect (not the check box) and click Components. Click the WordPerfect Macro Help check box and click OK. Finally, at the

Custom Installation dialog box, click Next and then click Install at the Ready to Install dialog box.

Presentations Problems

I want to change the text color of the title for every slide in my slide show. Presentations ships with a macro that allows you to change the fonts for your slide show. With your slide show open, choose Tools→Macro→Play. Double-click the Additional macros folder to display its contents, then double-click `Chngfnt.wcm` and make your selections.

I'm presenting my show to an audience that doesn't need the information on slides 5, 6, and 7. You can skip slides in a presentation to tailor it to a particular audience. With your slide show open, choose the Slide Sorter tab and select all slides you wish to skip. Click the Skip button on the Slide Show property bar. If you plan to show this tailored show to several groups, you can save it. Once you've selected and skipped slides in Slide Sorter view, click the Custom audiences down arrow button and choose Audience Manager. Click New to insert a copy of the existing name in the list. Type a new name for your tailored show and press Enter. Click OK. When you want to run the tailored show, just select it from the Custom audiences drop-down menu.

I used the Text tool to add text to a slide, and it isn't wrapping. You used the Text Line tool instead of the Text Box tool. Select the tool with the letter A surrounded by a box and then click and drag for the text box size. When you release the mouse button, you can type your text, and it will wrap within the text box.

I want to indicate the order of animated objects, but the Object display sequence option is dimmed on the Object Animation tab. You have more than one object selected on the slide. Cancel the Object Properties dialog box and make sure you select only the object you wish to format.

I need to speed up my slide show. Even with speedy transitions between slides, there's still a delay when your slides display because the computer must rewrite the screen as it presents each slide. To speed up the display of each slide, you can create a QuickShow, which saves each of your slides as a *bitmap image*, which is a type of graphic image. It's sort of like taking a picture of each slide on screen, then being able to quickly flip through the pictures. Once a slide is an *image*, Presentations can display it quickly, as a single element, rather than having to display all the elements on the slide one after the other.

To create a QuickShow file for an existing slide show, click the Play Slide Show button on the Slide Show property bar or choose View→Play Slide Show. Click Create QuickShow. When Presentations is finished, it selects the Use QuickShow file check box. You can proceed with playing your slide show as usual, using the QuickShow version, or clear the check box to use the

Presentations file for your show. Keep in mind that because you're saving a static image of the slides, you'll have to re-create a QuickShow file every time you make a change to a slide. Also, Presentations saves your QuickShow in the same folder as the original slide show file, using a PQF extension.

Quattro Pro Problems

When I press Enter, Quattro Pro remains on the current cell; it doesn't move to another cell. The Enter Key option is turned off in your settings. Choose Tools→Settings and choose the General tab. Choose Move Cell Selector on Enter Key and click OK.

The text in my cell is cut off. If your text is too long to fit in a cell and there is data in the adjacent cell, it will appear to be cut off. To display it, you can do one of the following:

* Increase the column width.

* Decrease the font size.

* Wrap the text within the cell. Choose Format→Selection and choose the Alignment tab. Choose Wrap Text under Cell Options and click OK.

* Reformat the text so it spans multiple cells. Select all cells that will contain the text (including the cell currently containing the text) and then choose Format→Text Reformat and click OK.

I want to force part of my data to print on a separate page. You can easily add a page break to your spreadsheet. Just select the cell for the row that will begin on the new page and choose Insert→Page Break→Create. If you're using Draft view, you'll see a heavy dark line above the row. If you're using Page view, Quattro Pro displays the new page.

Quattro Pro performed a calculation and now I see ***** in the cell. Several asterisks in a row indicate that the number is too wide to display completely in the cell and that the Fit-As-You-Go option is not on. To turn this option on, choose Tools→Settings and then select the General tab. Choose Fit-As-You-Go and click OK. You can also increase the column width or choose to set the column to its widest entry.

Quattro Pro is cutting text off when I print. Make sure you've selected all cells you wish to include in the print range. If a label is longer than its cell and you haven't selected the cell adjacent to it, Quattro Pro only prints the first cell, thereby cutting off some text.

Quattro Pro printed a lot of blank pages with my report. Before you print, select only the data you want to appear in your report. Make sure you don't select entire rows or columns, or you'll print any blank cells in them.

I created a formula, but it isn't calculating what it's supposed to calculate. Make sure Quattro Pro isn't interpreting your formula as a label. If you didn't include a plus sign (+) or equals sign (=) before your formula, Quattro Pro treats the entry as a label, inserting it as text.

When I entered a formula, Quattro Pro inserted ERR in the cell. ERR tells you that your formula contains something that Quattro Pro can't interpret and therefore can't calculate. It may be trying to multiply by a value that doesn't exist, you used the wrong cell address or name or you are trying to divide a value by zero. Check each part of your formula for accuracy.

When I select a cell containing a formula, Quattro Pro is displaying CIRC on the Application bar. CIRC tells you that your formula contains what's called a *circular-cell reference*. This means the formula contains a cell reference for itself. For example, if your formula is in cell G5 and your formula refers to cell G5, you have a circular-cell reference. Since the formula depends on itself to calculate, your results can be inaccurate.

I want to refer to a cell on another sheet in my formula. You can refer to a cell on another sheet by typing it or selecting it. To type the reference, include the sheet name and a colon before the block reference. For example, to refer to cell A4 on sheet C, type **C:A4**. To select the cells, make sure you're creating the formula on the input line. Then select the sheet and select the cell. When you return to the sheet containing the formula, Quattro Pro inserts the sheet name and cell reference on the input line.

My pie chart doesn't have a legend. By default, pie charts don't have legends because the labeling for each pie slice provides the necessary information. This is also true of doughnut and column charts. To change how this labeling displays, double-click a pie slice to display the Pie Chart dialog box and make your selections.

Netscape Navigator Problems

I typed the URL for a Web site and received an error. Make sure the address is correct, including all punctuation. If you still get an error after repeated tries, it's possible the site no longer exists or that you have been precluded from accessing it for some reason.

I tried to print a Web document while I was browsing, but Netscape told me there was nothing to print. Make sure you've clicked somewhere in the document before selecting Print. If that still doesn't work, select the text and click the Print button again.

I want to work on an e-mail message later and then send it. Once you place a message in the Out Box to be sent later (Deferred Delivery), you can't edit it anymore. To avoid this, minimize the Message Composition window until you're ready to work on it again.

Internet Publisher Problems

I **want to edit a hyperlink, but whenever I click it I jump to the link location.** To edit an active hyperlink, secondary-click the link and choose Edit Hyperlink from the QuickMenu.

When I try to preview my Web page in my browser, I get an error. Your browser software may not be installed correctly. If you aren't using Netscape, refer to your browser documentation and check the installation procedure.

The Web page I created in WordPerfect doesn't look the same in my browser. The browser may not support the fonts you've selected or may place a graphic differently because it can't support your option. You'll need to tweak your page to make sure it views the way you want it to in the browser.

When I view my graphics in my browser, they have white boxes around them. When you insert a graphic that isn't native JPEG or GIF format or transparent, WordPerfect does its best to convert it when you view it in the browser. However, many graphics — such as WPG graphics — are actually within a box so you'll see the white background of the box in the browser. The best way to avoid this is to use graphics that are transparent and are already in JPEG or GIF format.

 WEB PATH For sites that provide Web graphics, check out `http://www.yahoo.com` and click Computers & Internet→Graphics→Web Graphics.

Customization Problems

I **am working with a header, and I don't see the shadow cursor, even though I have it set to display in text in Display Settings.** Elements such as headers, footers, and footnotes are not part of the main document area, and the shadow cursor can display only in the main area.

I prefer to use an LTR extension for most of my documents, but WordPerfect uses WPD. You can change the default file extension by choosing Tools→Settings and double-clicking the Files icon. In the Use default extension on open and save text box, type the extension you wish to use and click OK.

I added a macro to my toolbar in Presentations, but when I try to run it, I get an error telling me the file is not found. It sounds as if you've moved the macro file. When you add a macro to a toolbar and save its path, Presentations checks for it in the macro folder you've specified in File Settings. Choose Tools→Settings and double-click the Files icon. Make sure the Macros folder is pointing to the folder containing your macros, click OK, and click Close. If the macro folder was correct, make sure the macro is in that folder.

INDEX

SPECIAL CHARACTERS

A

B

F

field codes, inserting in form files, 162–164
field names, data file
    defined, 156
    rearranging, 157
fields, data file
    adding, 161
    defined, 156
file management, default settings, 362
file options, default settings, 363–364
File Transfer Protocol (FTP), 318
files
    closing, 34–35
    displaying, 29
    file management dialog boxes, 27–29
    File Management toolbar, 28–29
    finding with QuickFinder, 18, 50–52
    maximum number, 30
    moving between, 31
    opening, 30–31
    saving, 34–35
    selecting multiple, 30
fill patterns, slides, 207–208
filtering databases, 309–310
filtering operators, 23
Find and Replace, 83–86
Find tab, 45–46
finding files and folders, 18
Fit-As-You-Go, 280
flyers, creating, 113–133
folders
    displaying, 29
    Favorites, 29
    finding, 18
font family, defined, 78
font size, defined, 78
fonts
    adding, 78–79
    default settings, 356–357
    defined, 78
    notebook cells, 283
    previewing, 79
    slides, 187–188
footers
    adding, 106–108
    editing, 108
    hiding, 109
    notebooks, 289–292

footnotes
    creating, 102–103
    defined, 101–102
    deleting, 104
    editing, 103
    searching for, 104
form files
    associating with data files, 162
    inserting field codes, 162–164
formatting
    with QuickMenus, 35
    WordPerfect, default settings, 356–357
formulas, in notebooks
    See also @functions
    $ (dollar sign), in absolute references, 258
    = (equal sign), starting formulas, 262
    + (plus sign), starting formulas, 262
    absolute addresses, 258–259
    arithmetic operators, 259–260
    cell names in, 273–274
    Cell Reference Checker, 263–264
    checking cell references, 263–264
    copying, 278–279
    defined, 246
    entering, 262–263
    logical operators, 259–261
    moving, 278–279
    in notebooks, 246
    operators, 259–260
    order of operations, 259
    QuickSum, 260–262
    relative addresses, 258–259
    summing numbers, 260–262
    summing ranges, 260–262
    text operators, 259
formulas, in WordPerfect tables, 150–152
FTP (File Transfer Protocol), 318
@functions
    See also formulas
    averaging a range of cells, 267
    @AVG, 267
    calculating loan payments, 266
    defined, 265
    finding maximum/minimum values, 267
    help for, 267
    @IF, 267
    @MAX, 267
    @MIN, 267
    @PMT, 266

@SUM, 266
@SUMIF, 266
summing a range of cells, 266
true/false evaluations, 267

G

grammar check
  with Grammatik, 41–42
  on-the-fly, 76
Grammatik, 41–42
graphic images
  See also slides, clipart
  drawing, 131
  flipping, 131–132
  inserting, 127–130
  mirroring, 131–132
  moving, 130–131
  rotating, 133
  sizing, 130–131
  URL for, 345
  wrapping text around, 127, 132–133
graphic images, Web page
  inserting, 343
  moving, 344
  placeholders, 344–345
  sizing, 344
  types supported, 343
  URL for, 345
graphic lines
  See also horizontal rules
  See also vertical rules
  inserting with QuickLine, 36
Graphic property bar, 129–130
graphics boxes, default settings, 360
GraphicsLand service bureau, 230
gridlines, Quattro Pro window, 240

H

hanging indent, 81–82
headers
  adding, 106–108
  editing, 108
  hiding, 109
  notebooks, 289–292
headings
  TextArt, 115–116

Web page, 341
help
  annotating help text, 44
  for application elements, 45
  Approved Partners Help, 17
  Contents tab, 45
  context-sensitive, 46
  Corel Web site, 47–48
  Find tab, 45–46
  for @functions, 267
  Help windows, 44
  index, 45
  Index tab, 45
  online manuals, 18, 48–50
  PerfectExpert, 46–47
  Question Mark button, 46
  QuickTips
    changing, 372–373
    defined, 14
  Reference Center, 18, 48–50
  Release Notes, 18
  searching for topics, 45–46
  service bureaus, 17
  table of contents, 45
  Technical Support Help, 18
  training, 17
Help windows, 44
highlighting slides, 225
home pages, 318
horizontal rules
  See also graphic lines
  inserting, 124–126
  in newspaper columns, 117
  URL for, 343
  on Web pages, 342–343
hot spots, 338
HTML (HyperText Markup Language), 317
  converting files to, 348–349
  Internet Publisher restrictions, 338
HTTP (HyperText Transfer Protocol), 317
hyperlinks
  creating, 346–347
  defined, 338, 345–346
hypertext links, 318
HyperText Markup Language (HTML). *See*
  HTML (HyperText Markup Language)
HyperText Transfer Protocol (HTTP), 317

I

IBM Global Network, URL for, 319
icon size, 29
IDG Books Worldwide, URL for, 322
@IF function, 267
indenting paragraphs, 80–82
index, help, 45
Index tab, 45
Input line, 239
insert mode *versus* type over mode, 253
insertion point
    defined, 57
    placing in empty document, 62
international formats, default settings, 363
Internet. *See* WWW (World Wide Web)
Internet Publisher
    backgrounds, 340–341
    Barista, converting files to, 349–350
    bookmarks, 346
    bulleted lists, 342
    columns, 345
    graphics
        inserting, 343
        moving, 344
        placeholders, 344–345
        sizing, 344
        types supported, 343
    headings, 341
    horizontal rules, 342–343
    hot spots, 338
    HTML, converting files to, 348–349
    HTML, restrictions, 338
    hyperlinks
        creating, 346–347
        defined, 338, 345–346
    paragraphs, 341
    property bar, 340
    publishing documents to the Web, 348
    tables, 345
    text, 341–342
    titles, 342
    toolbar, 340
    viewing your Web page, 348
    wallpaper, 340–341
    Web Editor, 339–340
Internet Relay Chat (IRC), 318
Internet Service Providers (ISPs)
    defined, 317
    selecting, URL for, 319
IRC (Internet Relay Chat), 318
ISPs (Internet Service Providers)
    defined, 317
    selecting, URL for, 319

J

JAVA, 317

L

labels
    charts, 294
    notebooks, 245
language, default settings, 362
letters, writing, 55–74
line charts
    defined, 294
    illustration, 295
Line Object tool, 204–206
line spacing
    changing, 98
    default settings, 356–357
lines, graphic
    See graphic lines
list boxes, defined, 15
loan payments, calculating, 266
locking titles, 281
logical operators, 259–261
logical statements, 22
logos, 115–116

M

macros, Quattro Pro
    default settings, 363
macros, recording, 18
macros, WordPerfect
    editing, 170
    playing, 169–170
    recording, 168–169
Mail Window toolbar, 330
Make It Fit, 82–83
margin guidelines, 57
margins
    default settings, 356–357

(continued)

question mark (?), on mail icon, 328
Question Mark button, 46
QuickBullets, 99
QuickFill, 250–255
QuickFinder Manager 8, 18
QuickFinder Search Results window
    toolbar button for, 29
QuickFinder Searcher, 18
QuickLines, 36, 124
QuickMenus, 35
QuickOrdinals, 36
QuickPlay, 189
QuickStart, 295–296
QuickStyle, 88–89
QuickSum, 260–262
QuickTab button, 241
QuickTips
    changing, 372–373
    defined, 14
QuickWord, 72–74
quotes, straight
    converting to curly, 36

R

Range Highlighter, 312
records, data file
    adding, 161
    defined, 156
    editing, 159–160
red squiggly underscore, 40
Redo, 69
Reference Center, 18, 48–50
Reformat, 286
Registry, editing, 18
relative addresses, 258–259
Release Notes, 18
Remove Program, 17
résumés, writing, 75–94
Reveal Codes
    default settings, 357–358
    displaying, 93–94
Reveal Codes toolbars, 57
Reveal Codes window, 93–94
Rolodex. *See* Address Book
rotating
    graphic images, 133
    slide clipart, 198–199

row borders, Quattro Pro window, 240
rows, notebook
    inserting, 279
    row height, 279–281
ruler, default settings, 358
rules (lines)
    See graphic lines
    See horizontal rules
    See vertical rules
runtime versions of slide shows, 227–228

S

scatter charts, defined, 294
Scrapbook, 128–129
scroll bars, WordPerfect, 57
search engines, 318, 324–326
secondary keys, 307–308
seed values, 250
Select All button, 240
Selector, 240
servers, Netscape, 328
Settings Editor, 18
shadow cursor
    defined, 57
    placing insertion point in empty
    document, 62
sharing information, 32
sheets
    defined, 239
    moving between, 244–245
Sheets tab, 241
Show It!, 349
sizing handles, 126
skewing slide clipart, 198–199
Slide Editor view, 189
slide layouts
    Bulleted List layout
        adding text to, 182–183
        defined, 178
    changing, 189
    Combination layout, 179
    Data Chart layout, 179
    Organization Chart layout, 179
    Text layout, 178
    Title layout, 178
slide masters, default settings, 360

(continued)

Z

The Fun & Easy Way™ to learn about computers and more!

10/31/95

Windows® 3.11 For Dummies,® 3rd Edition
by Andy Rathbone

ISBN: 1-56884-370-4
$16.95 USA/
$22.95 Canada

SUPER STAR

Mutual Funds For Dummies™
by Eric Tyson

ISBN: 1-56884-226-0
$16.99 USA/
$22.99 Canada

SUPER STAR

DOS For Dummies,® 2nd Edition
by Dan Gookin

ISBN: 1-878058-75-4
$16.95 USA/
$22.95 Canada

SUPER STAR

The Internet For Dummies,® 2nd Edition
by John Levine & Carol Baroudi

ISBN: 1-56884-222-8
$19.99 USA/
$26.99 Canada

Personal Finance For Dummies™
by Eric Tyson

ISBN: 1-56884-150-7
$16.95 USA/
$22.95 Canada

SUPER STAR

PCs For Dummies,® 3rd Edition
by Dan Gookin & Andy Rathbone

ISBN: 1-56884-904-4
$16.99 USA/
$22.99 Canada

Macs® For Dummies,® 3rd Edition
by David Pogue

ISBN: 1-56884-239-2
$19.99 USA/
$26.99 Canada

SUPER STAR

The SAT® I For Dummies™
by Suzee Vlk

ISBN: 1-56884-213-9
$14.99 USA/
$20.99 Canada

SUPER STAR

Here's a complete listing of IDG Books' ...For Dummies® titles

Title	Author	ISBN	Price
DATABASE			
Access 2 For Dummies®	by Scott Palmer	ISBN: 1-56884-090-X	$19.95 USA/$26.95 Canada
Access Programming For Dummies®	by Rob Krumm	ISBN: 1-56884-091-8	$19.95 USA/$26.95 Canada
Approach 3 For Windows® For Dummies®	by Doug Lowe	ISBN: 1-56884-233-3	$19.99 USA/$26.99 Canada
dBASE For DOS For Dummies®	by Scott Palmer & Michael Stabler	ISBN: 1-56884-188-4	$19.95 USA/$26.95 Canada
dBASE For Windows® For Dummies®	by Scott Palmer	ISBN: 1-56884-179-5	$19.95 USA/$26.95 Canada
dBASE 5 For Windows® Programming For Dummies®	by Ted Coombs & Jason Coombs	ISBN: 1-56884-215-5	$19.99 USA/$26.99 Canada
FoxPro 2.6 For Windows® For Dummies®	by John Kaufeld	ISBN: 1-56884-187-6	$19.95 USA/$26.95 Canada
Paradox 5 For Windows® For Dummies®	by John Kaufeld	ISBN: 1-56884-185-X	$19.95 USA/$26.95 Canada
DESKTOP PUBLISHING/ILLUSTRATION/GRAPHICS			
CorelDRAW! 5 For Dummies®	by Deke McClelland	ISBN: 1-56884-157-4	$19.95 USA/$26.95 Canada
CorelDRAW! For Dummies®	by Deke McClelland	ISBN: 1-56884-042-X	$19.95 USA/$26.95 Canada
Desktop Publishing & Design For Dummies®	by Roger C. Parker	ISBN: 1-56884-234-1	$19.99 USA/$26.99 Canada
Harvard Graphics 2 For Windows® For Dummies®	by Roger C. Parker	ISBN: 1-56884-092-6	$19.95 USA/$26.95 Canada
PageMaker 5 For Macs® For Dummies®	by Galen Gruman & Deke McClelland	ISBN: 1-56884-178-7	$19.95 USA/$26.95 Canada
PageMaker 5 For Windows® For Dummies®	by Deke McClelland & Galen Gruman	ISBN: 1-56884-160-4	$19.95 USA/$26.95 Canada
Photoshop 3 For Macs® For Dummies®	by Deke McClelland	ISBN: 1-56884-208-2	$19.99 USA/$26.99 Canada
QuarkXPress 3.3 For Dummies®	by Galen Gruman & Barbara Assadi	ISBN: 1-56884-217-1	$19.99 USA/$26.99 Canada
FINANCE/PERSONAL FINANCE/TEST TAKING REFERENCE			
Everyday Math For Dummies™	by Charles Seiter	ISBN: 1-56884-248-1	$14.99 USA/$22.99 Canada
Personal Finance For Dummies™ For Canadians	by Eric Tyson & Tony Martin	ISBN: 1-56884-378-X	$18.99 USA/$24.99 Canada
QuickBooks 3 For Dummies®	by Stephen L. Nelson	ISBN: 1-56884-227-9	$19.99 USA/$26.99 Canada
Quicken 8 For DOS For Dummies,® 2nd Edition	by Stephen L. Nelson	ISBN: 1-56884-210-4	$19.95 USA/$26.95 Canada
Quicken 5 For Macs® For Dummies®	by Stephen L. Nelson	ISBN: 1-56884-211-2	$19.95 USA/$26.95 Canada
Quicken 4 For Windows® For Dummies,® 2nd Edition	by Stephen L. Nelson	ISBN: 1-56884-209-0	$19.95 USA/$26.95 Canada
Taxes For Dummies,™ 1995 Edition	by Eric Tyson & David J. Silverman	ISBN: 1-56884-220-1	$14.99 USA/$20.99 Canada
The GMAT® For Dummies™	by Suzee Vlk, Series Editor	ISBN: 1-56884-376-3	$14.99 USA/$20.99 Canada
The GRE® For Dummies™	by Suzee Vlk, Series Editor	ISBN: 1-56884-375-5	$14.99 USA/$20.99 Canada
Time Management For Dummies™	by Jeffrey J. Mayer	ISBN: 1-56884-360-7	$16.99 USA/$22.99 Canada
TurboTax For Windows® For Dummies®	by Gail A. Helsel, CPA	ISBN: 1-56884-228-7	$19.99 USA/$26.99 Canada
GROUPWARE/INTEGRATED			
ClarisWorks For Macs® For Dummies®	by Frank Higgins	ISBN: 1-56884-363-1	$19.99 USA/$26.99 Canada
Lotus Notes For Dummies®	by Pat Freeland & Stephen Londergan	ISBN: 1-56884-212-0	$19.95 USA/$26.95 Canada
Microsoft® Office 4 For Windows® For Dummies®	by Roger C. Parker	ISBN: 1-56884-183-3	$19.95 USA/$26.95 Canada
Microsoft® Works 3 For Windows® For Dummies®	by David C. Kay	ISBN: 1-56884-214-7	$19.99 USA/$26.99 Canada
SmartSuite 3 For Dummies®	by Jan Weingarten & John Weingarten	ISBN: 1-56884-367-4	$19.99 USA/$26.99 Canada
INTERNET/COMMUNICATIONS/NETWORKING			
America Online® For Dummies,® 2nd Edition	by John Kaufeld	ISBN: 1-56884-933-8	$19.99 USA/$26.99 Canada
CompuServe For Dummies,® 2nd Edition	by Wallace Wang	ISBN: 1-56884-937-0	$19.99 USA/$26.99 Canada
Modems For Dummies,® 2nd Edition	by Tina Rathbone	ISBN: 1-56884-223-6	$19.99 USA/$26.99 Canada
MORE Internet For Dummies®	by John R. Levine & Margaret Levine Young	ISBN: 1-56884-164-7	$19.95 USA/$26.95 Canada
MORE Modems & On-line Services For Dummies®	by Tina Rathbone	ISBN: 1-56884-365-8	$19.99 USA/$26.99 Canada
Mosaic For Dummies,® Windows Edition	by David Angell & Brent Heslop	ISBN: 1-56884-242-2	$19.99 USA/$26.99 Canada
NetWare For Dummies,® 2nd Edition	by Ed Tittel, Deni Connor & Earl Follis	ISBN: 1-56884-369-0	$19.99 USA/$26.99 Canada
Networking For Dummies®	by Doug Lowe	ISBN: 1-56884-079-9	$19.95 USA/$26.95 Canada
PROCOMM PLUS 2 For Windows® For Dummies®	by Wallace Wang	ISBN: 1-56884-219-8	$19.99 USA/$26.99 Canada
TCP/IP For Dummies®	by Marshall Wilensky & Candace Leiden	ISBN: 1-56884-241-4	$19.99 USA/$26.99 Canada

For scholastic requests & educational orders please call Educational Sales at 1. 800. 434. 2086

FOR MORE INFO OR TO ORDER, PLEASE CALL ▶ 800 762 2974

For volume discounts & special orders please call Tony Real, Special Sales, at 415. 655. 3048

The Internet For Macs® For Dummies® 2nd Edition	by Charles Seiter	ISBN: 1-56884-371-2	$19.99 USA/$26.99 Canada
The Internet For Macs® For Dummies® Starter Kit	by Charles Seiter	ISBN: 1-56884-244-9	$29.99 USA/$39.99 Canada
The Internet For Macs® For Dummies® Starter Kit Bestseller Edition	by Charles Seiter	ISBN: 1-56884-245-7	$39.99 USA/$54.99 Canada
The Internet For Windows® For Dummies® Starter Kit	by John R. Levine & Margaret Levine Young	ISBN: 1-56884-237-6	$34.99 USA/$44.99 Canada
The Internet For Windows® For Dummies® Starter Kit, Bestseller Edition	by John R. Levine & Margaret Levine Young	ISBN: 1-56884-246-5	$39.99 USA/$54.99 Canada

MACINTOSH

Mac® Programming For Dummies®	by Dan Parks Sydow	ISBN: 1-56884-173-6	$19.95 USA/$26.95 Canada
Macintosh® System 7.5 For Dummies®	by Bob LeVitus	ISBN: 1-56884-197-3	$19.95 USA/$26.95 Canada
MORE Macs® For Dummies®	by David Pogue	ISBN: 1-56884-087-X	$19.95 USA/$26.95 Canada
PageMaker 5 For Macs® For Dummies®	by Galen Gruman & Deke McClelland	ISBN: 1-56884-178-7	$19.95 USA/$26.95 Canada
QuarkXPress 3.3 For Dummies®	by Galen Gruman & Barbara Assadi	ISBN: 1-56884-217-1	$19.95 USA/$26.99 Canada
Upgrading and Fixing Macs® For Dummies®	by Kearney Rietmann & Frank Higgins	ISBN: 1-56884-189-2	$19.95 USA/$26.95 Canada

MULTIMEDIA

Multimedia & CD-ROMs For Dummies® 2nd Edition	by Andy Rathbone	ISBN: 1-56884-907-9	$19.99 USA/$26.99 Canada
Multimedia & CD-ROMs For Dummies® Interactive Multimedia Value Pack, 2nd Edition	by Andy Rathbone	ISBN: 1-56884-909-5	$29.99 USA/$39.99 Canada

OPERATING SYSTEMS:

DOS

MORE DOS For Dummies®	by Dan Gookin	ISBN: 1-56884-046-2	$19.95 USA/$26.95 Canada
OS/2® Warp For Dummies® 2nd Edition	by Andy Rathbone	ISBN: 1-56884-205-8	$19.99 USA/$26.99 Canada

UNIX

MORE UNIX® For Dummies®	by John R. Levine & Margaret Levine Young	ISBN: 1-56884-361-5	$19.99 USA/$26.99 Canada
UNIX® For Dummies®	by John R. Levine & Margaret Levine Young	ISBN: 1-878058-58-4	$19.95 USA/$26.95 Canada

WINDOWS

MORE Windows® For Dummies® 2nd Edition	by Andy Rathbone	ISBN: 1-56884-048-9	$19.95 USA/$26.95 Canada
Windows® 95 For Dummies®	by Andy Rathbone	ISBN: 1-56884-240-6	$19.99 USA/$26.99 Canada

PCS/HARDWARE

Illustrated Computer Dictionary For Dummies® 2nd Edition	by Dan Gookin & Wallace Wang	ISBN: 1-56884-218-X	$12.95 USA/$16.95 Canada
Upgrading and Fixing PCs For Dummies® 2nd Edition	by Andy Rathbone	ISBN: 1-56884-903-6	$19.99 USA/$26.99 Canada

PRESENTATION/AUTOCAD

AutoCAD For Dummies®	by Bud Smith	ISBN: 1-56884-191-4	$19.95 USA/$26.95 Canada
PowerPoint 4 For Windows® For Dummies®	by Doug Lowe	ISBN: 1-56884-161-2	$16.99 USA/$22.99 Canada

PROGRAMMING

Borland C++ For Dummies®	by Michael Hyman	ISBN: 1-56884-162-0	$19.95 USA/$26.95 Canada
C For Dummies® Volume 1	by Dan Gookin	ISBN: 1-878058-78-9	$19.95 USA/$26.95 Canada
C++ For Dummies®	by Stephen R. Davis	ISBN: 1-56884-163-9	$19.95 USA/$26.95 Canada
Delphi Programming For Dummies®	by Neil Rubenking	ISBN: 1-56884-200-7	$19.99 USA/$26.99 Canada
Mac® Programming For Dummies®	by Dan Parks Sydow	ISBN: 1-56884-173-6	$19.95 USA/$26.95 Canada
PowerBuilder 4 Programming For Dummies®	by Ted Coombs & Jason Coombs	ISBN: 1-56884-325-9	$19.99 USA/$26.99 Canada
QBasic Programming For Dummies®	by Douglas Hergert	ISBN: 1-56884-093-4	$19.95 USA/$26.95 Canada
Visual Basic 3 For Dummies®	by Wallace Wang	ISBN: 1-56884-076-4	$19.95 USA/$26.95 Canada
Visual Basic "X" For Dummies®	by Wallace Wang	ISBN: 1-56884-230-9	$19.99 USA/$26.99 Canada
Visual C++ 2 For Dummies®	by Michael Hyman & Bob Arnson	ISBN: 1-56884-328-3	$19.99 USA/$26.99 Canada
Windows® 95 Programming For Dummies®	by S. Randy Davis	ISBN: 1-56884-327-5	$19.99 USA/$26.99 Canada

SPREADSHEET

1-2-3 For Dummies®	by Greg Harvey	ISBN: 1-878058-60-6	$16.95 USA/$22.95 Canada
1-2-3 For Windows® 5 For Dummies® 2nd Edition	by John Walkenbach	ISBN: 1-56884-216-3	$16.95 USA/$22.95 Canada
Excel 5 For Macs® For Dummies®	by Greg Harvey	ISBN: 1-56884-186-8	$19.95 USA/$26.95 Canada
Excel For Dummies® 2nd Edition	by Greg Harvey	ISBN: 1-56884-050-0	$16.95 USA/$22.95 Canada
MORE 1-2-3 For DOS For Dummies®	by John Weingarten	ISBN: 1-56884-224-4	$19.99 USA/$26.99 Canada
MORE Excel 5 For Windows® For Dummies®	by Greg Harvey	ISBN: 1-56884-207-4	$19.95 USA/$26.95 Canada
Quattro Pro 6 For Windows® For Dummies®	by John Walkenbach	ISBN: 1-56884-174-4	$19.95 USA/$26.95 Canada
Quattro Pro For DOS For Dummies®	by John Walkenbach	ISBN: 1-56884-023-3	$16.95 USA/$22.95 Canada

UTILITIES

Norton Utilities 8 For Dummies®	by Beth Slick	ISBN: 1-56884-166-3	$19.95 USA/$26.95 Canada

VCRS/CAMCORDERS

VCRs & Camcorders For Dummies™	by Gordon McComb & Andy Rathbone	ISBN: 1-56884-229-5	$14.99 USA/$20.99 Canada

WORD PROCESSING

Ami Pro For Dummies®	by Jim Meade	ISBN: 1-56884-049-7	$19.95 USA/$26.95 Canada
MORE Word For Windows® 6 For Dummies®	by Doug Lowe	ISBN: 1-56884-165-5	$19.95 USA/$26.95 Canada
MORE WordPerfect® 6 For Windows® For Dummies®	by Margaret Levine Young & David C. Kay	ISBN: 1-56884-206-6	$19.95 USA/$26.95 Canada
MORE WordPerfect® 6 For DOS For Dummies®	by Wallace Wang, edited by Dan Gookin	ISBN: 1-56884-047-0	$19.95 USA/$26.95 Canada
Word 6 For Macs® For Dummies®	by Dan Gookin	ISBN: 1-56884-190-6	$19.95 USA/$26.95 Canada
Word For Windows® 6 For Dummies®	by Dan Gookin	ISBN: 1-56884-075-6	$16.95 USA/$22.95 Canada
Word For Windows® For Dummies®	by Dan Gookin & Ray Werner	ISBN: 1-878058-86-X	$16.95 USA/$22.95 Canada
WordPerfect® 6 For DOS For Dummies®	by Dan Gookin	ISBN: 1-878058-77-0	$16.95 USA/$22.95 Canada
WordPerfect® 6.1 For Windows® For Dummies® 2nd Edition	by Margaret Levine Young & David Kay	ISBN: 1-56884-243-0	$16.95 USA/$22.95 Canada
WordPerfect® For Dummies®	by Dan Gookin	ISBN: 1-878058-52-5	$16.95 USA/$22.95 Canada

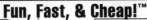

Fun, Fast, & Cheap!™

NEW!

The Internet For Macs® For Dummies® Quick Reference

by Charles Seiter

ISBN:1-56884-967-2
$9.99 USA/$12.99 Canada

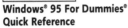

NEW!

Windows® 95 For Dummies® Quick Reference

by Greg Harvey

ISBN: 1-56884-964-8
$9.99 USA/$12.99 Canada

SUPER STAR

Photoshop 3 For Macs® For Dummies® Quick Reference

by Deke McClelland

ISBN: 1-56884-968-0
$9.99 USA/$12.99 Canada

SUPER STAR

WordPerfect® For DOS For Dummies® Quick Reference

by Greg Harvey

ISBN: 1-56884-009-8
$8.95 USA/$12.95 Canada

Title	Author	ISBN	Price
DATABASE			
Access 2 For Dummies® Quick Reference	by Stuart J. Stuple	ISBN: 1-56884-167-1	$8.95 USA/$11.95 Canada
dBASE 5 For DOS For Dummies® Quick Reference	by Barrie Sosinsky	ISBN: 1-56884-954-0	$9.99 USA/$12.99 Canada
dBASE 5 For Windows® For Dummies® Quick Reference	by Stuart J. Stuple	ISBN: 1-56884-953-2	$9.99 USA/$12.99 Canada
Paradox 5 For Windows® For Dummies® Quick Reference	by Scott Palmer	ISBN: 1-56884-960-5	$9.99 USA/$12.99 Canada
DESKTOP PUBLISHING/ILLUSTRATION/GRAPHICS			
CorelDRAW! 5 For Dummies® Quick Reference	by Raymond E. Werner	ISBN: 1-56884-952-4	$9.99 USA/$12.99 Canada
Harvard Graphics For Windows® For Dummies® Quick Reference	by Raymond E. Werner	ISBN: 1-56884-962-1	$9.99 USA/$12.99 Canada
Photoshop 3 For Macs® For Dummies® Quick Reference	by Deke McClelland	ISBN: 1-56884-968-0	$9.99 USA/$12.99 Canada
FINANCE/PERSONAL FINANCE			
Quicken 4 For Windows® For Dummies® Quick Reference	by Stephen L. Nelson	ISBN: 1-56884-950-8	$9.95 USA/$12.95 Canada
GROUPWARE/INTEGRATED			
Microsoft® Office 4 For Windows® For Dummies® Quick Reference	by Doug Lowe	ISBN: 1-56884-958-3	$9.99 USA/$12.99 Canada
Microsoft® Works 3 For Windows® For Dummies® Quick Reference	by Michael Partington	ISBN: 1-56884-959-1	$9.99 USA/$12.99 Canada
INTERNET/COMMUNICATIONS/NETWORKING			
The Internet For Dummies® Quick Reference	by John R. Levine & Margaret Levine Young	ISBN: 1-56884-168-X	$8.95 USA/$11.95 Canada
MACINTOSH			
Macintosh® System 7.5 For Dummies® Quick Reference	by Stuart J. Stuple	ISBN: 1-56884-956-7	$9.99 USA/$12.99 Canada
OPERATING SYSTEMS:			
DOS			
DOS For Dummies® Quick Reference	by Greg Harvey	ISBN: 1-56884-007-1	$8.95 USA/$11.95 Canada
UNIX			
UNIX® For Dummies® Quick Reference	by John R. Levine & Margaret Levine Young	ISBN: 1-56884-094-2	$8.95 USA/$11.95 Canada
WINDOWS			
Windows® 3.1 For Dummies® Quick Reference, 2nd Edition	by Greg Harvey	ISBN: 1-56884-951-6	$8.95 USA/$11.95 Canada
PCs/HARDWARE			
Memory Management For Dummies® Quick Reference	by Doug Lowe	ISBN: 1-56884-362-3	$9.99 USA/$12.99 Canada
PRESENTATION/AUTOCAD			
AutoCAD For Dummies® Quick Reference	by Ellen Finkelstein	ISBN: 1-56884-198-1	$9.95 USA/$12.95 Canada
SPREADSHEET			
1-2-3 For Dummies® Quick Reference	by John Walkenbach	ISBN: 1-56884-027-6	$8.95 USA/$11.95 Canada
1-2-3 For Windows® 5 For Dummies® Quick Reference	by John Walkenbach	ISBN: 1-56884-957-5	$9.95 USA/$12.95 Canada
Excel For Windows® For Dummies® Quick Reference, 2nd Edition	by John Walkenbach	ISBN: 1-56884-096-9	$8.95 USA/$11.95 Canada
Quattro Pro 6 For Windows® For Dummies® Quick Reference	by Stuart J. Stuple	ISBN: 1-56884-172-8	$9.95 USA/$12.95 Canada
WORD PROCESSING			
Word For Windows® 6 For Dummies® Quick Reference	by George Lynch	ISBN: 1-56884-095-0	$8.95 USA/$11.95 Canada
Word For Windows® For Dummies® Quick Reference	by George Lynch	ISBN: 1-56884-029-2	$8.95 USA/$11.95 Canada
WordPerfect® 6.1 For Windows® For Dummies® Quick Reference, 2nd Edition	by Greg Harvey	ISBN: 1-56884-966-4	$9.99 USA/$12.99/Canada

or scholastic requests & educational orders please
all Educational Sales at 1. 800. 434. 2086

FOR MORE INFO OR TO ORDER, PLEASE CALL ▶ 800. 762. 2974

For volume discounts & special orders please call
Tony Real, Special Sales, at 415. 655. 3048

9/19/95

Order Center: **(800) 762-2974** *(8 a.m.–6 p.m., EST, weekdays)*

Quantity	ISBN	Title	Price	Total

Shipping & Handling Charges

	Description	First book	Each additional book	Total
Domestic	Normal	$4.50	$1.50	$
	Two Day Air	$8.50	$2.50	$
	Overnight	$18.00	$3.00	$
International	Surface	$8.00	$8.00	$
	Airmail	$16.00	$16.00	$
	DHL Air	$17.00	$17.00	$

*For large quantities call for shipping & handling charges.
**Prices are subject to change without notice.

Ship to:

Name _____

Company _____

Address _____

City/State/Zip _____

Daytime Phone _____

Payment: ☐ Check to IDG Books Worldwide (US Funds Only)

☐ VISA   ☐ MasterCard   ☐ American Express

Card # _____ Expires _____

Signature _____

Subtotal _____

CA residents add
applicable sales tax _____

IN, MA, and MD
residents add
5% sales tax _____

IL residents add
6.25% sales tax _____

RI residents add
7% sales tax _____

TX residents add
8.25% sales tax _____

Shipping _____

Total _____

Please send this order form to:

IDG Books Worldwide, Inc.
7260 Shadeland Station, Suite 100
Indianapolis, IN 46256

Allow up to 3 weeks for delivery.
Thank you!

IDG BOOKS WORLDWIDE REGISTRATION CARD

Visit our Web site at http://www.idgbooks.com

ISBN Number: ISBN: 30860

Title of this book: Discover WordPerfect® Suite 8

My overall rating of this book: ❏ Very good [1] ❏ Good [2] ❏ Satisfactory [3] ❏ Fair [4] ❏ Poor [5]

How I first heard about this book:

❏ Found in bookstore; name: [6] ＿＿＿＿＿ ❏ Book review: [7] ＿＿＿＿

❏ Advertisement: [8] ❏ Catalog: [9]

❏ Word of mouth; heard about book from friend, co-worker, etc.: [10] ❏ Other: [11]

What I liked most about this book:
＿＿＿＿＿＿＿＿＿＿＿＿＿＿＿＿＿＿＿＿＿＿＿＿＿
＿＿＿＿＿＿＿＿＿＿＿＿＿＿＿＿＿＿＿＿＿＿＿＿＿

What I would change, add, delete, etc., in future editions of this book:
＿＿＿＿＿＿＿＿＿＿＿＿＿＿＿＿＿＿＿＿＿＿＿＿＿
＿＿＿＿＿＿＿＿＿＿＿＿＿＿＿＿＿＿＿＿＿＿＿＿＿

Other comments:
＿＿＿＿＿＿＿＿＿＿＿＿＿＿＿＿＿＿＿＿＿＿＿＿＿

Number of computer books I purchase in a year: ❏ 1 [12] ❏ 2-5 [13] ❏ 6-10 [14] ❏ More than 10 [15]

I would characterize my computer skills as: ❏ Beginner [16] ❏ Intermediate [17] ❏ Advanced [18] ❏ Professional [19]

I use ❏ DOS [20] ❏ Windows [21] ❏ OS/2 [22] ❏ Unix [23] ❏ Macintosh [24] ❏ Other: [25]＿＿＿＿＿
(please specify)

I would be interested in new books on the following subjects:

(please check all that apply, and use the spaces provided to identify specific software)

❏ Word processing: [26] ＿＿＿＿ ❏ Spreadsheets: [27] ＿＿＿＿

❏ Data bases: [28] ＿＿＿＿ ❏ Desktop publishing: [29] ＿＿＿

❏ File Utilities: [30] ＿＿＿＿ ❏ Money management: [31] ＿＿＿

❏ Networking: [32] ＿＿＿＿ ❏ Programming languages: [33] ＿＿

❏ Other: [34] ＿＿＿＿＿＿＿＿＿＿＿＿＿＿＿＿＿＿＿

I use a PC at (please check all that apply): ❏ home [35] ❏ work [36] ❏ school [37] ❏ other: [38] ＿＿＿

The disks I prefer to use are ❏ 5.25 [39] ❏ 3.5 [40] ❏ other: [41]＿＿＿＿＿＿＿

I have a CD ROM: ❏ yes [42] ❏ no [43]

I plan to buy or upgrade computer hardware this year: ❏ yes [44] ❏ no [45]

I plan to buy or upgrade computer software this year: ❏ yes [46] ❏ no [47]

Name: ＿＿＿＿ Business title: [48] ＿＿＿ Type of Business: [49] ＿＿＿

Address (❏ home [50] ❏ work [51]/Company name: ＿＿＿＿＿)

Street/Suite# ＿＿＿＿＿＿＿＿＿＿＿＿＿＿＿＿＿＿＿

City [52]/State [53]/Zip code [54]: ＿＿＿＿＿ Country [55] ＿＿＿

❏ **I liked this book!** You may quote me by name in future
IDG Books Worldwide promotional materials.

My daytime phone number is ＿＿＿＿＿＿＿＿＿＿＿

IDG BOOKS
WORLDWIDE

THE WORLD OF
COMPUTER
KNOWLEDGE®

☐ YES!

Please keep me informed about IDG Books Worldwide's World of Computer Knowledge. Send me your latest catalog.